Hudson Taylor Armerding is president of Wheaton College, Illinois. An alumnus of the college, he earned an M.A. at Clark University and a Ph.D. in history at the University of Chicago and did further study at Harvard. After serving as professor and dean at Gordon College, he returned to Wheaton as professor of history in 1961. He was appointed provost of Wheaton College in 1963 and became president in January of 1965. Dr. Armerding is a director of the North Conway Institute, an interdenominational organization established for research in problems related to the use of alcohol, and serves on the executive committee of the World Relief Commission of the National Association of Evangelicals.

CHRISTIANITY
AND THE
WORLD OF THOUGHT

CHRISTIANITY
AND THE
WORLD OF THOUGHT

Edited by
HUDSON T. ARMERDING

Contributors

BEATRICE BATSON

DOUGLAS A. BLOCK

EARLE E. CAIRNS

ARTHUR F. HOLMES

KAREL HUJER

CORNELIUS JAARSMA

S. RICHEY KAMM

R. ALLAN KILLEN

JOHN W. KLOTZ

DAVID O. MOBERG

JAMES M. MURK

LEE OLSON

E. MANSELL PATTISON

WILLIAM W. PAUL

JOHN M. VAYHINGER

HOWARD F. VOS

MOODY PRESS
CHICAGO

Library of Congress Catalog Card Number: 68-18884

A MOODY PRESS BOOK

FIRST PRINTING

Manufactured in the United States of America

CONTENTS

INTRODUCTION

In today's culture, to speak of Christianity is to use an imprecise term. Its definitions are almost as numerous as those for religion. To some, these two terms—Christianity and religion—have essentially the same meaning. The phrase "Christian Atheism" provides a contemporary illustration.

Despite this handicap, the publishers have selected an assumption about Christianity which is distinct from the popular and amorphous one as the basis for the discussions in this volume. The writers were chosen because of their commitment to a historic, biblical faith. They believe in a personal, self-existent, self-revealing God who has disclosed Himself uniquely in the person of Jesus Christ and propositionally in biblical truth. Each one writes from the perspective of an individual who has committed himself to Jesus Christ as Saviour and Lord. In short, the presuppositions of the authors are explicit. This should be borne in mind by the reader.

Yet the circumference of commitment is not so narrowly sectarian as to preclude a provocative diversity of viewpoint. Important and complex issues are discussed upon which, within evangelicalism, there is not now full agreement nor yet the prospect of such. Here is one reason for the publication of this work. It should provoke discussion, investigation and evaluation. The evangelical world will not only be better informed but also challenged to a deeper, more thoroughgoing analysis of Scripture and its relationship to the world of thought.

Furthermore, these essays, while not exhaustive, do reveal the kind of concern and speculation increasingly characteristic of in-

7

formed evangelicals. The writers' presentations represent significant arguments and conclusions. These should be stimulating and helpful to the biblically oriented Christian. They should also be informative to the theologically liberal who too often assess biblical orthodoxy from an ivory tower of almost incredible provincialism.

In a work of this kind, diversity may be more a feature than a fault. Changes in style and method are evident from one chapter to another. The synthesizing which a single author can provide is not present. Yet each essay is sufficiently self-contained to be an entity in itself. Hence, the volume with profit can be read selectively, based upon the reader's interests and needs, or taken collectively as a many-faceted approach to the world of the intellect.

Without question, much more can and should be said about Christianity and the world of thought. This volume, however, is calculated to make a significant contribution to this vital discussion. Even more, it is published in the hope that those who read will not become overly preoccupied with the structure of argument or the semantics of expression but rather will be strengthened in their most holy faith and encouraged the more to live to the honor and praise of our Lord Jesus Christ.

HUDSON T. ARMERDING

President, Wheaton College

THE SOCIAL SCIENCES:

A

CHRISTIAN PERSPECTIVE

S. Richey Kamm

S. Richey Kamm is professor of history and social science and chairman of the division of social science at Wheaton College. A graduate of Greenville College, he holds the M. A. from the University of Michigan and the Ph. D. from the University of Pennsylvania. He previously taught at Wessington Springs College, Seattle Pacific College and Monmouth Junior College, New Jersey. He has authored *The Civil War Career of Thomas A. Scott* and is a frequent contributor of articles to scientific journals and religious periodicals.

1

THE SOCIAL SCIENCES: A CHRISTIAN PERSPECTIVE

S. Richey Kamm

THERE IS NO MORE frightening experience than to be alone in a group of people. This is the plight of the child as he leaves his home or family group to begin his preschool training, and then advance through his elementary school education, his high school preparation, and his college or university experience. If he moves later from one community to another or has the opportunity to travel abroad, he finds that he must make continual adjustments to new people and to different ways of life.

He may be too frightened at such times to do any reflective thinking about this kind of life experience. It is quite likely that somewhere in his attempt to adjust to new groups he will begin to realize that life is not lived by individuals who are separated from other individuals. Rather, life is lived by individuals who are members of one or more groups. And with the realization of this fundamental condition in human life, the groundwork of the person's understanding of social science will be laid. Social science is based upon the fundamental proposition that people do live together in groups and that their life experience cannot be studied apart from their association with others. It is in these realizations that the concept of society is born. Without this concept there can be little or no curiosity concerning the situations that lead men to develop some explanation for these relationships. And as these explanations are organized and refined, those bodies of knowledge concerning man which are identified as the social sciences come into being.

The earliest answers to these questions concerning the nature of man and his society were laid within a theological context. The man-god relationship expressed in the terms "creature" and "Creator" was held to be fundamental to all explanation of human existence and human association. The earliest society was looked upon as growing out of the man-god relationship; communication was possible only in a vertical pattern between the original pair and their Creator and between themselves.

It was out of these communicating relationships that society was born. This was true whether the culture of the particular people studied was monotheistic or polytheistic. All human relationships were viewed through a "given" pattern of life, a pattern laid down by a deity. Such a pattern acted as a social cement as well as a basis of law. Social participation was accepted or rejected on the basis of its conformity to the principles of living conveyed in the revealed law. Communication and interaction within the group was on the issue of conformity and nonconformity to the divinely imposed pattern of conduct. Rational understanding was grounded in a revelational vision. The natural was intimately related to the supernatural.

Social science as it is usually conceived is said to have had its origins with the philosophical speculation of the Greeks in the sixth century B.C. In this period of recorded history men began to reject the theologically based ideas of law or norms of action and to posit the belief that all governing principles of life are to be discovered through an analytical study of the forces of nature. Following the basic assumptions of some of the older polytheistic cosmologies that natural objects such as sea, sky and air are the originators of life and basic patterns of living, a strong tendency emerged to build up a body of laws for human living based upon analogies with the forces of nature.

Plato, a leading Greek philosopher of the fourth century B.C., assumed that a community was like a man. The local group would respond to laws formulated by the "brains" of the community, the philosopher kings, just as men in themselves responded to the orders of the mind. Ideas, then, were very important, and men were governed by them as they endeavored to master them. Plato's pupil, Aristotle (384-322 B.C.), contended that ideas which had developed in the course of history through trial and error experience would be the most convincing influences in directing the acts of men. In both instances the mind of man would be of utmost importance in determining the course of human living.

Others, such as the Epicureans, found this explanation too abstract on the one hand and too much like the older theistic systems on the other. For what were ideas, after all, but messages from the gods that placed responsibility upon man? Why not conceive of man, his mind, and his social institutions as the natural outgrowth of the atomically viewed order of nature? Social institutions, conceived in this manner, were not the creation of man's intelligence but the result of the "fortuitous concourse" of the atoms. Man was not responsible for life in society, he simply tried to use the natural atomic forces then at work in society to bring about helpful social ends.

Each of these views played its part in the formulation of the cultural systems of the Middle Ages. Eventually under Thomas Aquinas (1225-74) the church endeavored to effect a harmony of the conflicting systems by accepting the idea that nature revealed certain truths concerning man and his life with other men but that the theological view held by the church must be accepted also as giving the final explanation.

With the rise of experimental science in the sixteenth and seventeenth centuries, more stress was placed upon the truths of life to be discovered in the study of nature. The increased emphasis upon the experimental approach to the study of the natural universe in the nineteenth century gave rise to new efforts to explain man and his social relationships. This trend not only tended to ignore completely the theological backgrounds of man's understanding of himself but tended also to divorce social science from its basic philosophic underpinnings. This situation led to the development of new so-called scientific approaches to the study of man in his societal relationships and to the further differentiation of this knowledge into the various disciplines which are recognized today.

WHAT IS THE OBJECT OF SOCIAL SCIENCE?

It is the object of social science to develop understandings concerning the social behavior of men that will be useful in helping man to achieve the life worthwhile. In fulfilling this purpose the social scientist develops an imaginative construct or image of the life of man as he sees it. The sociologist is guided in this creative work by his own observations concerning the life of man and the observations of laymen and other social scientists. Having then set up his imaginative view of the life of man in society, he proceeds to ask questions of it. What is man? What is his origin? How did man come to behave as he does? Is life a conscious or an unconscious process? Is man guided by imaginative or intuitive concepts generated in the mind, or is he guided by sense data which is received and interpreted by the brain and transformed into patterns of action? Is man influenced by past experience or is he the product of inner drives? And, finally, what do the answers to these questions contribute to our knowledge of the institutions which formulate and direct the life of man into acceptable patterns of living?

Consider each of the disciplines which are now in use among social scientists. Basically it is to be noted that each one is a mental discipline. Each of these disciplines endeavors to isolate certain features of man's social life for its intensive study, strives to apply some form of scientific method to this field of study, and attempts to formulate a body of organized knowledge concerning this phase of human relations that will be helpful to other social scientists and to men in general in accomplishing worthwhile social goals. It is to be noted that not one of these disciplines attempts to present a total picture of man in his social relationships. It is to be noted further that each discipline will employ at times data derived by one or more of the other disciplines in elaborating its findings.

Anthropology

Anthropology is the scientific study of the physical, social and cultural life of human beings viewed as a universal object of study in its natural environment. It is an effort to discover whether *genus homo* the world over exhibits common characteristics of physical structure, social organization and cultural patterns of thought and action. It embraces the historical study of man as a physical object and a cultural being through such evidence as may be found in fossil remains and the artifacts of preliterate populations; the classification of modern physical types and their geographic distribution throughout the world; and the various forms of cultural life now extant with special reference to linguistics, the scientific study of language as a universal mode of communication among men.

Anthropologists have applied their inductive approach most successfully in those societies where the population is limited in size and the cultural patterns are relatively uniform. Highly industrialized societies such as the United States and some of the states of Europe have not responded to the inquiries of anthropologists with the same degree of clarity because of the mixing of cultures which often prevails in these areas.

Economics

Economics is the scientific study of those processes whereby men distribute goods and services within a given society. It involves a detailed description of the manner in which goods and services are produced, the process by which they are distributed to various mem-

bers of the community, and the manner in which the various pro-
ducers and distributors are compensated for the part they play in
the economic process. Such a study often involves a consideration
of the purposes or values which govern the economic process and
the means whereby these purposes or values are to be realized.

Are economic goods produced and distributed more equitably when
the emphasis is placed upon the responsibility of the individual en-
trepreneur for these processes, or is equitableness best achieved
when that responsibility rests in the hands of the politically organized community, namely, the state? Is the price of a commodity
or service to be the sole determinant in the movement of goods
from producer to consumer in the market, or shall community interests, such as defense or national welfare, enter into the market
through government action to regulate this movement? Is the privilege of entering the field of business to be a matter of individual
choice, or is it to be regulated by the state in the interests of the
consuming public and the other competitors in the field? These and
other questions are some of the matters which concern economists.
In each instance the focus is upon man in his effort to acquire
wealth. Other questions are marginal to the main concern, man's
effort to sustain the good life through the accumulation of economic
goods.

Geography

Geography is one of the earliest of the social sciences. It is concerned with the spatial distribution of man and his relation to the
physical environment. It is that field of social study which seeks
to relate man in a meaningful fashion to his physical habitat. It
differs from anthropology in that the latter discipline endeavors to
relate man largely to his physical environment of the past, while
geography seeks to relate him to his physical environment in the
present. It is when the geographer and the anthropologist begin to
deal with the characteristics of human culture that it is most difficult to distinguish between the two disciplines.

Perhaps the most convenient method of differentiation is to be
found in the fields of physical science from which geography draws
its concepts, namely, astronomy, geology, meteorology and biology.
Anthropology, while also concerned with geology, receives its supporting knowledge from such physical sciences as geology, archaeology and anatomy. Geography would tend to stress man's distribution over the earth's surface in response to certain physical features
such as land and water divisions; valley and mountain differenti-

ations; arctic, temperate or tropical climatic conditions; or non-mineral-bearing and mineral-yielding regions. Data derived by the geographer through such concentrations of study often help other social scientists to explain certain anthropological phenomena or economic, political or sociological practices.

History

History is that discipline in the social sciences which endeavors to reconstruct the past for the avowed purpose of giving meaning to both the past and the present. This is to distinguish history from mere chronology and to make plain the fact that the historian as a social scientist is involved in the scientific process of determining what happened as well as in the creative or artistic process of explaining why it happened. As a social scientist the historian is limited in his inquiry by the principles which govern the proper use of historical evidence (documents); and as an artist he is guided in his creative work by the evidence of historical trends which he discovers in the process of his scientific inquiry. If he writes history primarily for the purpose of telling a good story, he will stress the unique and what appear to him to be significant developments in his range of inquiry. If he is concerned with establishing the historical context of a given belief or institution, he will stress the frequency with which this particular idea or institutional practice appears in the evidence available.

Historical data forms the basis of each of the social sciences. This means that every social scientist will be obliged to know something of the manner in which historical data is recorded, identified and organized for purposes of scientific study. It implies also that each social scientist will be familiar with those trends of historical development in each phase of man's life that give order and continuity to the story of man's experience in society. Beyond that the various social scientists select data which is appropriate to their own field of study. The historian, on the other hand, is obliged to consider the total body of historical evidence on the life of man even though he may be interested in only one phase such as intellectual, political, religious or diplomatic history.

History is influenced in both its findings and interpretations by the scholarly work of the other social scientists. Anthropologists in their research may unearth artifacts which throw light upon the cultural life of a given people and thereby enable the historian to understand earlier or contemporary historical movements. Geographers may be able to demonstrate the presence or absence of physical environmental factors that have influenced the decisions of men in the past concerning residence, trade, or movements of population from one part of the earth to another. Economists may be able by a thorough analysis of a given nation's economy to show why that particular nation experienced economic strength or weakness at a given historical period. An analysis of different developments in a nation's system of production and distribution of economic goods may point up the reason why that country experiences political revolution. Political scientists have often been helpful to the historian in describing with greater clarity the operation of a particular political system. This has enabled the historian to discover the reason why a government acted or failed to act at a critical moment in its history. The sociologist, by his analysis of social structure in a given society, can assist the historian to understand the leadership of a given country at a particular time in history.

Political Science

The political scientist is concerned with a study of power relationships within given societies and the manner in which these relationships are formalized into governmental institutions. He is broadly interested in the nature of government, the sanctions for its existence, its variety of institutions and practices, and the values which states hope to perpetuate through the political process. This leads him into a consideration of political theory, political institutions, law, constitutions, sovereignty, practical politics, public administration and international relations.

The political scientist must be alert to all of the factors which tend to influence men in their quest for certain formal goals in political life. This may lead such a scientist into a study of political ideologies which embrace some conception of the nature of the world, the nature of man, and the goals which are to be achieved by the use of force, either cultural or punitive, in the life of the community. Such questions as the relation between politics and ethics will inevitably arise because he soon discovers that the state as well as the church is involved in presenting standards of life for men. Legislatures, administrative offices and courts all become objects of study as institutional arrangements for the realization of politically defined goals.

The problem of law—its origin, nature and function—becomes a basic consideration for the student of government. Here he finds himself delving into questions of theology, philosophy, economics, history, anthropology and sociology. The question of geography may arise as he observes differences in ideologies and political institutions which appear to follow spacial patterns. Psychology, the nature of man's thought processes, will inevitably enter into the political scientist's inquiry. Before he has finished, he will have exhausted the information which is made available by all of his fellow social scientists.

Sociology

Sociology is a newcomer to the social sciences. It is a discipline which owes its origin to the effort of Auguste Comte (1798-1857) and others to study human society on the basis of an analogy with the natural order. Social physics was its original name because Comte hoped to establish laws of human behavior that could be demonstrated on the basis of experimentally discerned uniformities of conduct on the part of human beings. Even though most sociologists have largely abandoned this initial emphasis, the assumption still remains that man can be studied within the orbit of a purely imaginative idea known as "society." The sociologist is now much more concerned with the structure of a given society in terms of leadership functions, the identification of all functions performed by the entire social group, and the processes of life which go on within a given group. Some of these processes are conscious to the participants, others not so conscious. This suggests that the sociologist may be similar to the anthropologist in his basic methodology. Even though both social scientists deal with man in society, the sociologist is more interested in what he terms "social change," that is, changes affecting the structure and functioning of society, rather than in "cultural change," the modifications in social behavior which are due primarily to a change in the value system of the group.

LIMITATIONS OF THE SOCIAL SCIENCES

Nineteenth century proponents of the social sciences expected much of these new approaches to the study of human behavior. Many looked forward to the day when men would have at their disposal sufficient scientifically established knowledge of human affairs that leaders in society and government could direct the course of human life into patterns of useful behavior in much the same manner that scientists were directing natural forces in the service of humanity. Education would become the indoctrination of human beings with those scientific principles of living which would enable people to make steady progress toward socially beneficial goals. Government would be the process of bringing a whole society into conformity with those scientifically discovered laws which govern the life of a society. Men would no longer be concerned with the historical study of values or the realities of religious experience. Inspiration for living would come from the scientific knowledge of life as it is lived.

This dream has been rudely shattered by a number of twentieth century developments. Two world wars have conveyed to many the truth that there is no easy answer to the problems of human relationships. Further, the increasing enslavement of vast populations under Communism, a totalitarian system which professes to be based upon a scientific knowledge of man and society, has given pause to those who once accepted unqualifiedly the idea that social science could serve as the only basis of social organization. Developments of this type have effected a reevaluation of the basic assumptions adopted by social scientists in general.

It is helpful to realize that social scientists early committed themselves to follow the assumptions and the methodology of the natural scientists. This meant that they would employ physically demonstrable models to bring the society of man within the realm of human comprehension. Classical and Christian writers had frequently employed the human body or the human personality as a working model for the understanding of society. Social scientists then turned to models drawn from the field of natural science: the bee, the primate, or the Newtonian concept of an ordered mechanical universe. These in turn were replaced by models conceived in the light of Darwin's evolutionary concept of the universe. Ultimately, society was viewed as an existential field patterned after the physicist's concept of the atomic universe. Each of these models distorted man into an object identified with the world of nature. Each lost sight of him as a man, a person made in the image of God.

Social scientists committed to following the natural science approach have found it difficult also to establish an adequate system for conserving the knowledge they develop. Generalizations they had based upon natural science analogies were termed laws. It was soon discovered, however, that the demonstration of these so-called laws as universal principles was impossible. Differing cultural influences made universal generalizations untenable. The best that could be said was that these general rules were a statement of probability. Their claim to universality depended in large part upon the size and structure of the sample employed and the accuracy of the computation.

Semantics, the development of a vocabulary adequate to convey an accurate picture of the scientific phenomenon under observation, proved to be a companion problem in the work of the conservation of knowledge in the field of social science. Each discipline has found it necessary to establish its own vocabulary. The meanings of the words in these special vocabularies will differ from the common sense definitions of the terms. Words may have differences of meaning when used by students in varied disciplines. It has been very difficult for social scientists to come to any common agreement on the term "social science" as well as on key terms such as "culture." Recent developments in the behavioral sciences—political science, economics, sociology, social psychology, social biology—have helped to eliminate these disciplinary differences of meaning. Handbooks of scientific terminology and encyclopedias of social science concepts have helped to bridge the gap in vocabulary differences.

Prediction has been an outstanding goal for all scientists. The early social scientists, such as Auguste Comte, looked to the day when the scientific analyses of human behavior would be so well understood that the trained social scientist would predict successfully the course of human action.

The increased application of mathematical procedures in the measurement of social phenomena has enlarged greatly the accuracy of predictive procedures in social investigations. Social scientists, in fact, are now claiming that they can predict successfully the future decisions of public officials, such as a president or a member of the Supreme Court, if they possess an adequate understanding of the official's past experience and a mathematically determined demonstration of his previous decisions. Mathematicians, however, continue to warn social scientists against relying completely upon this method of prediction. It is probably safe to say that social scientists will never be able to predict the future course of individuals as well as they can determine the future course of action for a well-defined group. Prediction in social science then partakes of the nature of an actuarial science.

These observations suggest that social science is limited largely in its findings to the realm of human behavior. It can provide insights into the life of man as part of the world of sense. It can describe quite well the role of ideas in human existence. But it meets with difficulties when it endeavors to explore the realm of the spirit. Sociologists and cultural anthropologists have come to recognize that this area of human experience is not open to scientific inquiry. Both groups of scientists are often able to develop a systematic description of certain religious practices or institutions. However, to describe adequately the inner meaning of these phenomena is beyond the scope of the methodology of scientific inquiry. These matters lie within the realm of theology and the studies known as the humanities. It has been argued, for instance, that one may secure a more comprehensive understanding of a people through the study of their religion and their literature. Here one has an opportunity to view the whole man in his personal and societal relationships.

IS A CHRISTIAN PERSPECTIVE TENABLE?

This concern for meaning in the study of man opens the door again to a Christian interpretation of the social sciences. An objective evalution of every attempt to present an answer to the question of the meaning of man's life in society apart from the Christian revelation reveals that it provides no satisfactory answer. For social science in its observations is limited to time and space. It is of the temporal and can say nothing concerning the eternal. It can describe with increasing clearness the practices of men and can provide insights into the ideas and myths which have guided their minds. Of ultimate goals it can say little. What contribution, then, may a Christian perspective offer the social scientist in his study of man in society?

1. The concept of a three-dimensional universe as a basis for scientific comprehension

The Christian perspective proceeds from a revelational basis of thought and observation. It has its roots in the Hebrew-Christian tradition which holds that faith in an eternal, omnipotent, omniscient, personal, self-revealing God is the foundation of all knowledge. To the Protestant this means that the approach to all truth must be through the revelation of God as found in the Bible and in the world of nature. Both are looked upon as the work of God; both reveal His mind and character at different levels; and both testify that the ultimate truth concerning man and the universe is to be discovered only by understanding first of all that man and the universe are the handiwork of God. Therefore, neither man nor society nor the world of nature in which they exist can ever be viewed as of natural origin.

The universe of the Christian social scientist is three-dimensional and pyramidal in form. He agrees with the naturalist that the world of nature is important but denies that the truths of social science are to be found alone in man's society viewed as part of the natural universe. He agrees with the qualitative or idealist social scientist that man must be considered as more than an object of sense (i.e., that he is different from the world of nature by virtue of his ability to exercise will or decision). He holds that the social universe is not complete without a recognition of the eternal God, the Creator of the world of nature and the world of man, as an active agent in both worlds.

Modern social science, in contrast, proceeds with a horizontally conceived universal in which man is believed to be identical with nature or as an object within a dual universal of mind and nature. In either case all of the answers concerning man's identity and his relationships with the world of nature and the world of men as part of that world of nature are to be found in a systematic study of man's society in the natural universe. There are no active agents admitted to the universal which cannot be discovered through the senses or at best the mind.

The Christian social scientist would hold this premise to be faulty because it ignores the revelation of God concerning the agents at work in human society. The faith of science, that by discovering all of the active natural agents (i.e., variables) in a given situation man could thereby bring all natural phenomena in the realm of human society within his control, is thereby held to be untenable. This does not deny the validity of scientific findings within the prescribed universal, provided sound methods of scientific procedure be followed. Thus, Huntington's tested observation that climatic factors such as seasonal change and atmospheric fluctuation may provide the conditions favorable to certain changes in human behavior is valid for the universe of cases tested. However, one could not reason from it that all fluctuations or changes in human behavior were due to climatic conditions.

2. The concept of man as ambivalent in phenomenal performance and unique in his quality of personality

To approach man from the perspective of his total identification with a model drawn from the world of nature or the world of ideas is to suggest that man's identity is to be traced to either a natural or an ideational universe which existed antecedent to the life of man. This tends to confuse either nature or ideas with their Author, God, and to relate men to abstract concepts such as a material universe of eternal standing or the world of eternal ideas. Such presuppositions lead scholars to make assumptions concerning the alleged uniformities of human action. "Every man," affirmed Aristotle, "is continually striving to do that which he considers good." Paul Tillich suggested that every man is continually following his inner sense of "ultimate concern." Such assumptions run aground on the Christian understanding of the biblical revelation which affirms that man is continually falling short of the goals which he has set. He possesses no omniscience concerning the nature of these goals, nor does he have that motivated understanding which enables him to reach them.

Similarly, every system of scientific thought, whether materialistic or idealistic, ultimately ends in a denial of the unique personality of man. The materialist in emphasizing the factors of natural environment reduces personality to the end product of all associational interaction. The individual is therefore never responsible or accountable for his behavior. He is the product of his "natural" community; therefore he is an animal.

The qualitative scientist comes closer to the truth in insisting that culture—the ideas, tools, and established practices of men in association with each other—and the environment of physical nature produce human personality.

But the hypothesis breaks down when one observes that those who are best adjusted to the culture do not always live up to its highest standards or value judgments. It is only the insight of the Christian social scientist that gives the answer to the problem. He holds, on the basis of God's revelation, that man is the product of God's handiwork and that human personality is the result of the fatal contradiction in man between man as created in the image of God and yet in rebellion against God. This view does not deny the influence of the natural environment or of the cultural elements in that environment. All of these are important. However, these factors can never give the final or conclusive answer concerning the nature and meaning of human personality.

The character of man's unique personality is to be found in his differentiation from the world of nature of which he is a part. This differentiation is distinguished by two features: (1) man's ability to make decisions within the limits imposed by a divine Creator, and (2) man's inability to realize those ends which his reason and judgment hold good—the Christian doctrine of sin. Because of this first quality—that which has recently been spoken of as the power to make the "dynamic assessment"—it is impossible to predict with the same degree of accuracy the future behavior of man as is possible in dealing with the behavior of many natural elements.

The second conditioning factor points to the fact that all of man's attempts to improve his life in association with others will continually fall short of his desired goal. This is true both because of the moral imperfection of man which renders his reason and action imperfect and because of the active opposition of that spiritual personality who is described in Scripture as the enemy of both God and man. Man's social aspirations are realized, therefore, only through the common grace of God which is given to all men and the special grace of God which is mediated to those who have committed themselves to Christ through faith in His atoning work.

3. The concept of history as divine revelation

Modern social scientists have sought to correlate human history with the movement of identifiable elements in the natural world. Such an approach to history presumably opens the way for the student to recognize patterns of motion. These become identified as laws. To such generalizations are ascribed the role of regulative authority in society as well as a basis of understanding of social phenomena. Man becomes identified with the natural universe. He loses his unique character, his humanity.

The scientific approach to history reduces it to the idea of process (i.e., those elements of change which man can observe from the outside). The life of man tends, as a consequence, to lose both its creative and its tragic character. Man can neither succeed or fail in his effort to achieve. He loses his freedom and his sense of responsibility. He is carried along by processes which are discernible to him but are beyond his control.

The Christian social scientist sees more than process in the idea of history. His revelational perspective enables him to apply the understanding of religious faith. This premits him to posit the assumption that history is more than man's experience of events. History is the continuing demonstration of a divine will, a divine plan. Man may not be able to bring the Author within the limits of his mode of observation. He may, however, on the basis of his faith in the divine revelation, postulate the qualifying understanding that the objects of his observation are somehow related to a plan or design for man. This plan or pattern far exceeds the law or pattern derived on the basis of man's experience with history. It gives meaning to life and provides a basis for the concept of human freedom. Without this perspective man becomes a slave to the very force of history itself.

4. The concept of the redemptive role in human society

Society has always been held to have meaning in its functions. In the thought life of the ancient Near East, society was considered as the private domain of the local deity. For the Greeks it was conceived as coincident with community. As such it served as a means of exchange for goods and services of all kinds, including those of personal and collective security against other communities. The Romans, operating under Stoic influences, looked upon society as that universal community of rational beings who were associated together for the care of things public. Modern views have consisted largely of elaborations of these fundamental hypotheses.

For the Christian social scientist, society is meaningful for both God and man. The origin of society is held to reside in that original relationship between God the Creator and man the created. In this original "face to face" relationship, the will of God was the will of man. The basis of all associational life was the community of affection and interest between God and His creature. There was no consciousness of divergence between the individual actions of man and the normative will of God. The term "conscience" had no meaning under these circumstances. Likewise, there was no formal, positive law such as is now known to man. Such institutional forms suggest a continuing state of alienation between God and man. And man, thus alienated, moves toward self-destruction.

Viewed from this perspective the place of institutions in society becomes manifest. The family, the government, the law, the mode of making a living, all become part of God's provision for the care of man, who through the fall lost his first love. The family becomes necessary to the orientation of each succeeding generation to its relationship with God and with other men. The government receives sanction as that institution which extends the benefits of personal security both in life and in property to the members of the community as against those other members of the community who would destroy both life and property. The law becomes the norm of action by which the community endeavors to establish those principles of justice which shall govern the members of the community.

These institutions do not arise because of mutual advantage, because they are "natural" to man, because they are rationally conceived by man, or because of "fears" or "needs." They are part of God's beneficent provision for man in revolt against His will as law. They were conceived and established in the mind of God in anticipation of man's individual and collective experience. They form a conserving influence in the program of redemption by which men are brought again into fellowship with God.

Some students of the social sciences have argued that this concept gives to social institutions a static character which admits of no change. A careful study of the biblical texts points to the fact that the original revelation concerning the nature and function of these institutions does not change. There have been changes, however, in the form of these institutions. The institution of the family has undergone considerable alteration both in the form which it has assumed and in the totality of the discharge of its functions. These changes may be said to be in part the resistance of man's will to God's law or revelation, as in the case of polygyny, or the lack of clear vision concerning the nature of that revelation. This does not infer that God refuses to deal with men who have thus forgotten or ignored His original sanction of monogamous marriage. It does mean that He endeavors to bring men through experience to a consciousness of their divergence from His original plan.

The institution of the state has been governed by many different types of constitutions. The former never changes in its divine sanction, whereas the latter has undergone frequent alteration in form and function. In each instance as the distribution and exercise of power in the name of the state tends to usurp the authority over men which is reserved to God, the constitutional arrangement becomes subject to change. Change may be said to occur as institutional arrangements depart from or return to the authoritative principles of divine revelation.

5. The concept of moral conflict as the basis of social problems

Much has been written in recent years on the theme of social problems. There is inherent in these discussions the assumption that social problems are a deviation from an assumed norm. As a general rule it has been assumed that the law of nature in society is one of harmony. It follows, therefore, that areas of conflict in society are in violation of this universally assumed law of relationships.

It is immediately manifest that such an assumption is based upon a postulated analogy between the character of the world of nature and that of the world of man. Careful study of this analogy will reveal the fact that the scientific student is here dealing with two distinct types of phenomena. The one is physical and without purpose in its own being; the other is moral, being endowed with reason and spirit which enable it to transcend many natural forces and to appropriate those spiritual forces which have their residence outside the natural world. The latter, therefore, is able to exercise purpose within those limits imposed by its original endowment. It possesses personality with all that that implies in its association with God.

What then are social problems? They are areas of conflict between purposive beings. Recent students of social science such as Gunnar Myrdal, R. M. McIver and Robert S. Lynd have reminded scientists in general that the social scientist is dealing with a moral being in the study of social problems. This position does not deny that many forces of nature such as temperature, climate, diet, physical heredity and geographical location, as well as cultural factors revealed in a study of the customs, habits, traditions and tools of a society, have contributed greatly to the development of this moral person. It is to say, however, that these external factors do not make the whole man. Myrdal would say that it is the decisions which one makes in relation to all of these factors which make the man. The Christian social scientist would add that these decisions would also include an assessment of the individual's relationship to God as the most important decision in the life history of that personality.

Social problems are to be considered, then, in the light of the decisions which people have been making concerning the "whole" of life. In analyzing the labor problem, it is necessary to evaluate the external factors of wages, working conditions, employment systems, retirement systems, production systems and living conditions in the area affected by the conflict. But it is also important to know something of the cultural and spiritual factors involved. If the decisions of the persons involved are based entirely upon a view of life which holds that man is merely an animal and that wage increases are the most important consideration because they will permit him to secure more power to satisfy his "animal" demands, then it is to be presumed that one solution of the problem is sufficient. If it is assumed that man is both animal and reason, then it is evident that other factors such as social and cultural benefits may enter into the solution of such a problem. If it is further assumed that all persons involved possess spiritual qualities of time-transcending importance, it is likely that the question of wages will be looked at in a very different light. David L. Lawrence, a former governor of Pennsylvania, in his World War II appeal to labor and management in the coal industry to recognize the spiritual issues of their dispute, is an example of the point of view which is assumed when the Christian view of the world and man becomes the basic approach to social problems.

Is this Christian view predicated upon the assumption of a utopia? The writer thinks not. It is true that the Christian view does advocate the application of Christian love to every problem involving man in association with other men. In so doing it emphasizes the fact that each man's view of the problem is probably limited; that is, no man possesses omniscience. It further contends that because of man's sinful nature, divine grace will not be fully operative in overcoming the blinding effect of sin in the decisions of persons called upon to solve the problem. What the Christian position does hold is this: that as men in conflict submit themselves to the grace of God, the principle of divine love has a greater opportunity to be manifested in the solution of a problem. This permits distortions of vision to be corrected and the consequent emotional conflicts to be eased. For in seeking the grace of God and in desiring to apply the principle of Christian love, the individuals concerned find that they must recognize their own individual and collective inability to solve such conflicts by and of their own volition and knowledge.

The sense of personal justification in such conflict is therefore dissolved in the firm belief that God has undertaken to apply His grace and love to those concerned, and that the resulting solution will rest in the hands of God and not in the hands of any particular individual or group of individuals involved. In the end no utopia can be realized until God Himself reigns in person through His Son and His church in the world of time and space.

A Christian perspective in the study of human affairs is essential to the progress of social science in this day. The modern tendency to distort the nature of man by divorcing his associational life from its Author and Sustainer continually provides opportunity for the development of half-truths and false hypotheses. God must be recognized as the Creator of man, his society, and the natural world in which he lives. Without this basic premise of a theistic monism there can be no adequate answer to the great social issues of our time. It is the very foundation of a Christian liberal arts education in the social sciences.

FOR FURTHER READING

ELIOT, T. S. *The Idea of a Christian Society*. New York: Harcourt Brace & Co., 1940. An exposition of the value system of a Christian society written by a British-American man of letters.

HALLOWELL, JOHN. "Political Science," in HOXIE N. FAIRCHILD (ed.), *Religious Perspectives in College Teaching*. New York: Ronald

Press, 1952, pp. 384-422. A Christian orientation for the study of government by a university teacher of political science.

HARBISON, E. HARRIS. "History," in HOXIE N. FAIRCHILD (ed.), *Religious Perspectives in College Teaching*. New York: Ronald Press, 1952, pp. 67-97. Guidelines to a Christian perspective in the teaching of history by a university professor.

HEIMAN, EDUARD. "Christian Foundations of the Social Sciences," *Social Research*, 26:325-46 (Autumn, 1959). A critical essay on the secularism of the social sciences. The author pleads for the reinstitution of Christian doctrine as a basis for all studies dealing with man in society.

HOSELITZ, BERT F. (ed.). *A Reader's Guide to the Social Sciences*. Glencoe, Ill.: Free Press, 1959. An excellent summary of the literature in the social sciences. Includes a discussion of the various subdivisions in the respective fields and the major trends in social theory in each.

JONES, G. V. "Some Presuppositions of a Christian Sociology," *The Expository Times*, LXII:163-66 (March, 1951). A statement of principles governing the development of a Christian approach to sociology.

KAMM, S. R. "A New Orientation in Social Science," *Social Science*, 25, No. 3, 190-96 (June, 1950). The impact of natural science methodology upon the social sciences. Evidences of a return to a religious orientation in the work of ARNOLD TOYNBEE, REINHOLD NIEBUHR and PITIRIM SOROKIN.

LATOURETTE, KENNETH SCOTT. "The Christian Understanding of History," *American Historical Review*, LIV:259-76. The presidential address for the American Historical Association in 1948.

MORGENTHAU, HANS J. "The Scientific Solution of Social Conflicts," in LYMAN BRONSON, *et al.*, editors, *Approaches to National Unity*. New York: Conference on Science, Philosophy and Religion in their relation to the Democratic Way of Life, 1940; distributed by Harper. Pp. 419-37. The author argues that the modern scientific approach to such social problems as marriage, education, poverty, freedom, authority and peace is inadequate because these problems do not grow out of the "temporary insufficiencies of intellectual capacity, but from the wickedness which is the very essence of man." Such an approach retards rather than furthers man's mastery over the social world.

NICHOLS, ROY F. "History and the Social Science Research Council," *American Historical Review*, L:491-99. History provides a fourth dimension for the social sciences, namely, a reliable concept of long-term institutional trends. Controlled experimentation provides an analogous function in natural science.

REDFIELD, ROBERT. "Prospects for the Scientific Study of Human Relations," *Round Table*, No. 510, p. 9 (December 28, 1947). The nature of objectivity in the social sciences.

Social Science Research Council: Committee on Historiography. *The Social Sciences in Historical Study*. New York: Social Science Research Council, 1954. A recent exposition of governing principles in the fields of social science.

THE CHRISTIAN

AND

MODERN LITERATURE

Beatrice Batson

Beatrice Batson is professor of English literature at Wheaton College. A graduate of Bryan College (where she has also taught), she received the M. A. at Wheaton and the Ph. D. at George Peabody College and also has studied at Middlebury College, Northwestern University and Oxford. She is author of *A Reader's Guide to Religious Literature.*

2

THE CHRISTIAN
AND
MODERN LITERATURE

Beatrice Batson

LITERATURE is an integral part of the world of thought. This premise must be accepted before this chapter has any vital significance. In the minds of many people, including some on college campuses, literature is subject matter to read when one is too tired to think. If one does not read to escape thinking, then it is probably not too gross an exaggeration to say that he reads to escape boredom, or to pass away the time, or to escape into a world that fulfills what he wants to be and is not, or to escape the trivial details or the terrifying realities of his twentieth century world.

WHAT CONSTITUTES LITERATURE?

Perhaps part of the rather indifferent, passive attitude toward the reading of literature comes from a distorted impression of what constitutes literature. All books, even of imaginative or fictional nature, cannot be classified as literature. Sentimental romances, mystery thrillers, detective whodunits, and religious pollyanna are hardly entitled to the name *belles lettres*. But what about the scores of popular books that are on best seller lists for weeks until they are replaced by another popular work that has its run for several other weeks until replaced by still another? Are these books literature? Without question they often demonstrate a craft that commands respect. And they contain some lofty and provocative thoughts. Yet there is still a difference between these widely read books and the kind of literature that is the subject of this chapter. Can the difference be accurately stated? Henry Zylstra definitely reveals something of the distinctiveness of literature worthy of the name in a few cogent statements regarding great authors and their works:

> The big ones are more than makers, that is fabricators, of stories: they are also seers and prophets. Such are the Hugos and Balzacs and Flauberts, the Prousts and Mauriacs and Gides. Such are the Goethes, . . . the Kafkas and the Manns. . . . Such are the Tolstoys and the Dostoevskis and the Turgenievs. Such in England are the Fieldings and Jane Austens and Scotts, the George Eliots and Thackerays. . . . And such in America are the Melvilles . . . the Henry James and the William Faulkners. . . . To come from the *Moby Dick* of Melville. . . , the *War and Peace* of Tolstoy, the *Brothers Karamazov* of Dostoevski . . . or yet again from *The Plague* of Camus . . . ; to come from one of those is to know that one has touched powerfully on life at many points. It is to have seen the chaos of life transmuted into the order of significant form. . . . To read such a novel is to have entered a universe comprehensive in scope and intensive in quality. It is to have confronted the moral issues of men, not in the skeleton of theory or the bones of principle, but in the flesh and body of concrete experience. Such authentic literature is the rewarding literature. It is a vision of life profoundly seen, greatly embodied and valid.[1]

To be sure, the reading of such literature may be and should be a pleasurable, satisfying experience, but it calls for an alert, thinking reader in confrontation with the mind and art of a writer whose created world releases a pregnant expression of truth.

It should be clear too that literature is a work of art. It is "truth in vital form," but if one is to see the work as a totality, he must guard against the two extremes of studying the mechanics and hunting the "message." Works of literature are not just the mechanical aggregation of assorted parts or an exercise in mental gymnastics, but they consist of a dynamic and vital interrelationship of all the component parts such as character, tone, action and thought. On the other hand, discovering the "message" or finding the moral to the exclusion of everything else is not a serious and genuine study of literature. Readers of Chaucer's *The Pardoner's Tale*, for example, could immediately state without thinking at all that the "message" of the tale is that the love of money is the root of all evil. After all, this is explicitly mentioned several times throughout the work by the preacher, the pardoner himself. Is not there more to this tale than the obvious, surface moral or "message"? Notice should be taken of the one who preaches this sermon. His actions, his vocabu-

---

[1]Henry Zylstra, *Testament of Vision* (Grand Rapids: Wm. B. Eerdmans Publishing Co., 1958), pp. 66-67.

lary and the tone of his words should all be studied. The pardoner, who preaches the sermon on the sin of avarice, himself lies, cheats, and stops short of nothing in order to get money. Simply by letting the pardoner's words, actions and character speak for themselves, Chaucer goes beyond the obvious moral to satirize in an implicit manner, among other vices, the sins of hypocrisy and ruthlessness. Even a brief look at *The Pardoner's Tale* suggests that the whole "meaning" of a work is far greater than a summarizing statement of a moral principle. It is also more than the formal analysis of technique as though it were only a demonstration of craftsmanship. "Literature is truth in vital form," and it demands of the reader caliber of mind and power of thought.

Great literature does grapple with the important questions and implications of who man is, why he is on this earth, and where he is going from here. Large universal principles and great moral concepts within a given piece of writing, however, do not necessarily mean that the work is good literature. Literature is "full of all kinds of import—religious, philosophical, social, practical, and other,"[2] but unless these universal themes are creatively patterned, reshaped and transformed, treatises or discourses rather than literature are written. William York Tindall gives clear insight on the issue in these statements:

> That moral substance fails to insure greatness, however, is proved by the work of Horatio Alger; and that it fails to guarantee moral effect is proved by those of Mickey Spillane. Not moral ideas but its embodiment in what Eliot called objective correlatives, suitably arranged, determines value. Far from inciting action as moralizing does, embodied morality invites contemplation, and to become an object of contemplation, substance must be distanced by form. The question is not how much morality is there but how much is under control.[3]

Literature then is the dynamic interrelationship of "substance . . . distanced by form." The interrelationships of all the parts of a specific work must be rigorously studied and the meaning gathered from the synthesis of the various parts, such as tone, character, action, point of view and thought. It is most essential to keep this clearly in view as various manifestations from the world of thought are considered in this chapter.

---

[2]*Ibid.*, p. 32.
[3]William York Tindall, "The Ceremony of Innocence," *Great Moral Dilemmas*, ed. R. M. MacIver (New York: Harper & Bros. Publishers, 1956), pp. 75-76.

CHRISTIAN APPRAISAL OF LITERATURE

Students of literature should remember that just because an author wrestles with major moral issues, this does not mean that he automatically and necessarily writes Christian literature. He may simply be writing an unrealistic, morally evasive work that is covered over with good-sounding, religious phraseology. All books must be read responsibly. Each requires Christian appraisal; but not one of the books, even those with which one violently disagrees, should be read, appraised or judged in the spirit of intellectual pride. Some works may demand a Coleridgean "suspension of disbelief," but everything a person encounters in these works can become "grist for the mill of his Christian education."[4] Just because a writer is positivistic or deterministic in his view of life and the world, Christians cannot afford simply to label him as erroneous and ignore his thinking. That there are also many positive values for the Christian reader must be readily admitted. Perhaps one of the clearest assertions of such values is presented by Henry Zylstra. Recognizing that the English writer Thomas Hardy is fatalistic in his vision of life, Zylstra still says:

> There is more of you, after reading Hardy, to be Christian with than there was before you read him. . . . In Hardy there is a comprehensive view of life, sensitively perceived, greatly embodied, by a man of considerable mind and imagination, and he can by the quality of insight illuminate whole areas of life, which, had we depended upon ourself, we would never have seen. Since Hardy's vision of life blossoms up out of the bud of fatalism instead of flowering up out of the seed of Christianity, and since the light falls on it from the wrong angle, we must in the knowledge of faith cause it to fall from the right one. But when we do this we have in his novels a legacy to inherit which it would be impoverishing to refuse.[5]

Literature commits itself to seeing life as a whole, and it adds another dimension to individuals' lives as they appropriate its liberalizing powers. With this significant principle in mind, the remainder of this chapter will concern itself with an examination of various patterns of thought in literature together with a few suggestions for a Christian appraisal. The study will not include a rigorous analysis of each individual work used for illustrative purposes. Because the scope of this examination must necessarily be limited, it seems wise to refer only to representative movements from the modern era.

---

[4]Zylstra, *op. cit.,* pp. 67-68.
[5]*Ibid.,* pp. 67-68.

IMPACT OF MODERN LITERATURE

Rationalism

The actual beginning of the modern period may be debatable, but many good scholars date the starting point in the eighteenth century, with the foundation for the Age of Reason being laid by such thinkers as Descartes, Spinoza and Locke of the previous century. Perhaps few periods, if any, contributed more to the world of ideas than the Age of Reason. The literature of the day was bristling with thought, and the rational approach to life was the prominent one among the educated. With this emphasis on the intellect, there developed the prevailing belief that reason—man's unaided reason—was the unerring avenue to truth. This rational temper did not exclude a belief in God, but "god" too had to be brought up to date. Discarding a belief in the God of revelation and miracles, the rationalists—those who were concerned about God at all—reasoned that their god created the mechanistic universe and set it in motion by mathematical laws. Having created the world and the universe as a completely rational machine, he left the scene, allowing the universe to pursue its predetermined course. He would not think of interfering with the regular, rational operation of the universe. The aloofness of this god, removed from a concern for man and his life in the world, was a far cry from the transcendent yet immanent God of revelation who is interested in the most minute detail in the lives of His children.

The rule of reason transformed all types of literature, and poetry was most affected. Because the long poem was the best poetic medium for presenting sustained thought, it assumed preeminence during this Age of Reason. Long lines, rhymed in closed couplets to carry ideas in epigrammatic fashion, suited the facts and knowledge that the poets attempted to convey. Characteristic of this intellectual period, poetic ideas were taken from a rationalized picture of man, human nature and the world and presented in a generalized, highly abstract diction. However, the Age of Reason was not primarily an age of poetry but an age of prose. Essays, polemics, histories, biographies, novels, letters, memoirs, periodicals and newspapers also served as media through which men discussed and expressed the rationalistic attitude toward religion, politics, society and life.

This new emphasis on reason found expression in literary works across the Western world. One could speak of Voltaire whose prodigious productions popularized the aims and methods so widely that much of the literate public of France and the rest of Europe was fired with passion for the concepts and ideals of the rationalists. Nothing escaped his fearless, caustic pen as he used the weapon of reason against political, social and religious ideas and institutions of his day.

Perhaps one of the classic statements of the ideology of rationalism is found in Thomas Paine's *Age of Reason*. The underlying thesis of the book is that Christian theological doctrines are irreconcilable not only with man's reason but also with the knowledge that he gains through a scientific study of the laws of the universe. Holding the Genesis account of creation to be mythological, Paine insists that it is possible to know through reason that the universe was created by a First Cause working through the laws of nature. To him the only identifying term man can give to "god" is that of First Cause, and it is only through the exercise of reason that man can discover this First Cause.

Denying special revelation in a distinctive sense, Paine calls creation God's revelation. "Some perhaps will say," asserts Paine, " 'Are we to have no word of God—no revelation?' I answer, 'Yes; there is a word of God; there is a revelation. *The word of God is the creation we behold.* And it is this word, which no human convention can counterfeit or alter, that God speaketh universally to man.' "[6] Paine's god then is the First Cause. His "word of God" is creation, and his avenue to knowledge and truth is by way of man's unaided reason.

A master of persuasion, Paine had the ability to express his views simply and clearly. That he had the capacity to sway man's mind through his power with words is unquestionable, and he seemed always to have a well-defined purpose in mind when he wrote. To be sure, many of his ideas were and are anathema to many people.

What should be the position of the Christian reader? However erroneous Paine is from the Christian viewpoint, the Christian must be willing to admit that Paine knew how to organize his work into a coherent whole that made a powerful impact upon readers. That his view of reason took the wrong angle is regrettable, but among other accomplishments, Paine has brought into focus a significant issue that every Christian thinker must face—the relation between faith and reason. When reading *The Age of Reason*, the Christian should attempt to deduce that Paine's thinking may have come from an honest search for truth and that somehow his search went awry; but the Christian should also discover why and at what point the

⁶Thomas Paine, *Age of Reason* (New York: Wiley Book Co., 1942), p. 38.

search went wrong. This takes a considerable amount of doing, but it is an essential in careful appraisal. Unfortunately, Paine believed that reason was a sufficient means of understanding the "truth" of God. He denied special revelation, and this must not be overlooked. Yet Christians must be very careful that they do not minimize the place of reason in clarifying the truth of God to the world. Clichés and shallow thinking did not cope with the Tom Paines of the eighteenth century nor will they challenge his counterparts of the twentieth. While the Christian insists on revelation on the one hand, on the other he must also insist on the need for solid, hard, logical thinking to explicate and communicate the great truths of the Christian revelation.

Romanticism

Reason was de-emphasized during the decades that followed Paine, and a "return to nature" was stressed in a distinctive sense. However, the kind of nature that appealed to Romantic writers of the early nineteenth century was not that of the geometric, natural laws that interested writers such as Paine, but nature which could be perceived by the senses. Students of literature know that an appreciation for nature was not something on which the early nineteenth century writers had a monopoly. One finds an interest in the created world throughout various periods of literature. Some will recall the attitude of several religious writers of the seventeenth century who thought of nature as a living library or as a repository of instructions on man's relation and responsibility to God. Centuries before, the psalmist voiced a universal thought when he said, "The heavens declare the glory of God, and the firmament sheweth his handiwork." But there is a new note in the Romanticists' view of nature which Randall Stewart clearly identifies:

> . . . one begins to capitalize *Nature,* for Nature becomes an emana-
> tion of God. In romantic poets like Wordsworth, Emerson, Whit-
> man, God is identified with Nature, and Nature is part and parcel
> of God. One worships Nature, or God-in-Nature, one is not quite
> sure which, for in much romantic nature poetry, Nature-worship
> and God-worship seem a bit confused, one with the other.[7]

That the contemplation of nature drew the poets' souls toward God is understandable. As previously stated, others have marveled at the handiwork of God in His creation. But there was this differ-

---

[7]Randall Stewart, *American Literature and Christian Doctrine* (Baton Rouge, La.: Louisiana State University Press, 1958), p. 44.

ence. To the psalmist and to the seventeenth century writers, God was a supernatural, transcendent, yet immanent Creator distinct from the works of nature which He had created; but to the Romantics, God appeared to be fused with nature, and consequently He was often lost in nature as the supernatural and natural were intertwined.

From the goodness and marvel of nature in general, it is not far to the goodness and marvel of man. An important aspect of the romantic attitude is an implicit faith in the inalienable worth of man. Denying the existence of any conflict between good and evil in man's nature, the Romanticists conceived of man as sinless and capable of knowing the truth intuitively.

Ralph Waldo Emerson speaks of man's innate powers in his "Divinity School Address." To Emerson this innate power

> is the beatitude of man. It makes him illimitable. Through it the soul first knows itself. It corrects the capital mistake of the infant man, who seeks to be great by following the great, and hopes to derive advantages *from another,* by showing the fountain of all good to be in himself, and that he, equally with every man, is an inlet into the deeps of Reason.[8]

Later in the same address, Emerson speaks even more clearly of man's ability to know because of innate powers when he says, "Whilst the doors of the temple stand open, night and day, before every man, and the oracles of this truth cease never, it is guarded by one stern condition; this, namely; it is an intuition. It cannot be received at second hand."[9]

Emerson makes his point. Man himself knows the truth by his own private, authoritative intuition. He does not need revelation. But Emerson makes his view of the deification of man even more pointed. Continuing in the same address, he affirms, "One man was true to what is in you and me. He saw that God incarnates himself in man, and evermore goes forth anew to take possession of his World. He said in this jubilee of sublime emotion, 'I am divine. . . . Would you see God, see me; or see thee, when thou also thinkest as I now think.' "[10] Discerning readers are immediately aware that in the scriptural sense Emerson robs Christ of His divine essence and gives to man a divinity which is not his.

[8]Ralph Waldo Emerson, "An Address Delivered Before the Senior Class in Divinity College," *The Harvard Classics,* ed. Charles W. Eliot (New York: P. F. Collier & Son Co., 1909), p. 28.

[9]*Ibid.,* p. 29.

[10]*Ibid.,* p. 30.

There is no question regarding the vast influence and wide acclaim of the opinion that asserted the divinity of man. Yet "its most important result in literature was to stimulate a reaction in the opposite direction. The most important literature of the period must be regarded as a countermovement to the romanticism of . . . Emerson."[11] It is interesting to note in passing that American writers of the countermovement, like Melville and Hawthorne, pictured the presence of sin in man and the world; they described the conflict between good and evil, and they demonstrated man as capable of redemption but not of redeeming himself. This is a truer and more accurate picture of man and his predicament.

Yet one must not be misled into believing that only negative qualities characterized the Romantics. They did remind men anew of the beauty and wonder of life. "The loss of wonder, of awe, of the sense of the sublime, is a condition leading to the death of the soul."[12] Alerting man that imagination and emotion were part of his endowment, they called attention to the development of the individual self. Many of the Romanticists' significant contributions serve as stimuli for the Christian thinker who views their writings from a Christian world and life view.

Naturalism

At the opposite pole of romanticism is naturalism, a movement in literature which began with the novels of Emile Zola. Beginning during the second half of the nineteenth century and running into the twentieth, naturalism brought a scientific and deterministic temper into literature. For example, Zola made clear that he was substituting for the study of abstract or metaphysical man the study of the natural man subject to physiochemical laws and governed by environment. Regarding the responsibility of the writer as one who must operate upon characters, passions and actions as the chemist and physicist operate on inorganic bodies, and as the physiologist operates on living bodies, Zola went on to conclude that determinism governs all people and all things.

The Zola theory places man in a pathetic condition. By being made a mere product of heredity and environment, man becomes a machine controlled and guided by physical and chemical laws. His reason, considered so powerful in the eighteenth century, has now

[11]Stewart, *op. cit.*, p. 51.
[12]Edmund Fuller, *Man in Modern Fiction* (New York: Random House, 1949), p. 163.

lost its dignity and potency. Man is simply a helpless creature driven by chemical compulsion to act out his folly and fulfill his desires. He is a biological pawn rather than an agent of free will. Natural laws and environmental influences are more powerful than the human will; consequently man is stripped of his uniqueness as a person, and the expression of the individual, God-given self is either stifled or denied.

Readers of naturalistic literature can usually expect modern industry and the industrial worker to play an important role in the naturalistic novel. A large amount of social and economic facts fills this type of fiction because these serve as excellent documentation for deterministic circumstances. Individuals with some potential for leadership but without opportunity, or individuals with opportunity but with serious hereditary or environmental problems, are usually the leading characters. So the parts are put together, and the formula looks something like this: certain people living in certain circumstances will definitely act in a definite, fixed way.

Several American writers of the later nineteenth and early twentieth centuries were influenced by naturalism. Writers such as Stephen Crane and Frank Norris are frequently cited as examples of naturalistic authors. There may be traces of naturalism in their works, but the most thoroughgoing naturalist in the Zola sense was Theodore Dreiser.

Observing life with the closest scrutiny and intensity, he recorded his detailed observations by the thousands. Brevity is never the characteristic of any of the six Dreiser novels, and often the reader gets the impression that the writing of the book entailed the expenditure of undirected energy. But within these sprawling works there is a rather well-defined and coordinated picture of the amoralism of naturalistic thought. Perhaps the clearest demonstration of the literary method and naturalistic philosophy of Theodore Dreiser is *The American Tragedy* which appeared in 1925. This novel traces the story of Clyde Griffiths, the hero, from his questionable boyhood background to his death in the electric chair for murder at the age of twenty-two. Dreiser spared no detail to show the manner in which the environment of Clyde Griffiths combined with his biological urges was responsible for defects in his character that caused him to change from a sensitive adolescent into a socioeconomic opportunist, ambitious but spineless. But what does Dreiser say about the circumstances and urges of his main character?

Clyde Griffiths is reared in poverty. He is underprivileged. He hardly has any formal education. He aspires to rise in the world and to be a success as measured by money and social position, for money and social position are the standards of the new social set he enjoys after he becomes the head of the collar-stamping department in his uncle's collar factory. Before the glittering possibility of marrying a rich society girl enters Clyde's mind, he becomes involved with an unsophisticated girl who has come from her father's farm to work in the factory. The farm girl becomes pregnant by Clyde, but this would never have happened had it not been for Clyde's loneliness and urges. Faced with the dilemma of his wanting to marry a society girl, and the farm girl's refusal to stop pleading that he save her name by marrying her, Clyde becomes the opportunist and plots the murder of the farm girl. Yet Dreiser would have his readers believe that Clyde is in no way to blame for the actual death of the girl. To be sure, he lures her into a boat, but it overturns accidentally. She cannot swim; Clyde can, but is he obligated to save her? Clyde is brought to trial, and there the defense attorney calls him a "mental and moral coward," but he immediately adds, "Not that I am condemning you for anything you cannot help. After all, you didn't make yourself, did you?" And one of Clyde's last reflections while he awaits the electric chair sounds the same note: "Would no one ever understand—or give him credit for his human —if all too human and perhaps wrong hungers—yet from which so many others—along with himself—suffered?"

In concise summary, Dreiser's created world in *The American Tragedy* shows that Clyde Griffiths is not responsible for what he is and does. He did not make himself; he did not choose his parents or his place to live. He is simply a pawn pushed about by his inner drives and circumstances. Given certain inner compulsions and environmental conditions, what happens must happen; and man is not morally responsible. Ethics obviously play no role if life is nothing more than a series of physical and chemical reactions. Pushed to its conclusion, Dreiser's deterministic outlook leads him to hold that the universe is neutral, indifferent to the destiny of mankind. Consequently there are no final truths, no sustaining purposes, no absolute principles.

A depiction of naturalistic tendencies in Dreiser's novel should not close without one further observation. Portraying a man completely without moral responsibility seems difficult on occasion even for Dreiser. For example, the memories of the strong, Christian faith of Clyde Griffith's mother would sometimes cause Clyde to reflect on his moral responsibility. He could not push completely out of his mind the remembrance of his mother's strength and endurance which came from her belief in God. Also, a reader cannot forget some of Clyde's own reactions during those days when the idea of possibly murdering the farm girl began to flash through his mind. One of these reactions Dreiser describes this way:

> His hand shook, his eyelids twitched—then his hair at the roots tingled and over his body ran chill nervous titillations in waves. . . . An icy perspiration now sprang to his forehead; his lips trembled and suddenly his throat felt parched and dry.[13]

This simply does not appear to be the behavior of one in whom all sense of moral responsibility is dead. Dreiser has trouble in his naturalistic outlook in explaining the intricacies of the human personality created in the image of God.

Zola and Dreiser and other representatives of the naturalistic theory convey partial truth but not the whole truth. Undoubtedly men are in part governed by environment and heredity. These are factors that markedly affect the temperament and attitudes of man, and they need to be studied with discernment and understanding. A look, however, at any number of biographies reveals the triumph of many individuals over inherited disabilities and unfavorable surroundings. Major achievements are accomplished against enormous odds. On the authority of the Scriptures there is the clear declaration that man is inherently imperfect, but he has the possibility of reconciliation with his Creator. On the one hand, he is not able to lift himself by his own good works; on the other hand, he is not deterministically fixed in his predicament. Rather than inhabiting a morally neuter universe, he inhabits an orderly universe; and both man and the universe are subject to God's concern and His laws. It is interesting and stimulating to know that most of Western literature depicts this view of man rather than the naturalistic concept of Dreiser or Zola. Deeply concerned about the view of man in modern fiction, Edmund Fuller makes the observation that within the Western historical-literary tradition from the early Greek period until the latter part of the nineteenth century,

> . . . man is seen as, or tacitly understood to be, a created being, with an actual or potential relationship to his Creator. Each man is a unique person. Man is not portrayed as *either* good *or* bad, but as *both* good and bad. . . . His fundamental moral laws are commands of his Creator, not just social contracts between him-

---

[13]Theodore Dreiser, *An American Tragedy* (Cleveland, Ohio: World Publishing Co., 1946), II, 45.

self and his fellows. . . . Thus man, so seen within this vast,
varied, but basically consistent tradition, is individual, responsible, guilty, redeemable.[14]

To some readers, contemporary literature contains far more
bleakness and helplessness than naturalistic writings. Referring to
the contemporary scene, Hilda Graef says, "Except for a few 'silver
linings,' the picture is dark, indeed. If Christianity has often seen
this world as a 'vale of tears,' modern thinkers and novelists seem
to picture it generally as a lunar landscape of unmitigated despair."[15]
This view is perhaps too pessimistic, for there are writers such as
Alan Paton, C. S. Lewis, Graham Greene, Charles Williams and
J. R. R. Tolkien whose works are surely not pictures of "unmitigated
despair." Yet one must admit that there are skilled contemporary
literary artists who assert the meaninglessness and emptiness of life.
In light of this trend, Christians should objectively read and study
these authors. Perhaps there is no clearer depiction of the predicament and anguish of unregenerate, contemporary man than in some
of the artistically sound, modern novels.

Existentialism

The present scene in literature, as in other eras, is an integral
part of the cultural climate. Two great wars, combined with the
dreaded possibilities of a third, have shaken man's faith in an optimistic future. Technology and industrialism have reduced the significance of man and his creative individual power. Society has become more and more impersonal and anonymous, and the individual
more and more alienated and impotent. Contemporary man feels
lost and alone in a world that means nothing to him. He has lost
his own identity, his belief in God and in moral values. He is his
own god; and there is no one to whom he can turn for help, so he
thinks. He is sure only of the primacy of death and the meaninglessness of life. This type of thinking in modern literature is essentially
what contemporary scholars have titled atheistic existentialism. As
Charles Glicksberg points out, "Existentialist fiction is essentially
a literature based upon a philosophy. At the heart of the existentialist philosophy is the belief that man makes himself and that in
this consists his fundamental freedom.[16] Man is saddled with a

---

[14]Fuller, *op. cit.*, pp. 9-10.
    [15]Hilda Graef, *Modern Gloom and Christian Hope* (Chicago: Henry Regnery
Co., 1959), p. 127.
    [16]Charles I. Glicksberg, *Literature and Religion* (Dallas: Southern Methodist
University Press, 1960), p. 192.

dreadful freedom to choose—to make his own life even though he is caught in an impasse of nothingness.

Students of modern literature must be very careful not to categorize all writers as atheistic existentialists whose work may contain flashes of philosophical nihilism. To come from the reading of Albert Camus' *The Stranger*, for example, one may have one view of the author. But, if one goes on to read *The Plague* and *The Fall*, he cannot help having another view of Camus. When one reads *The Stranger* and observes that nothing, whether life or death, or God or love, is of any genuine significance to the chief character, he might immediately want to conclude that Camus is the epitome of the extreme in atheistic existentialism. But there is more to Camus than what is unmistakably in *The Stranger*. As one continues with *The Plague*, which appeared in 1947, he discovers that Camus faces more significantly and realistically large metaphysical questions such as the meaning of life for man and how man meets the problems of evil in the world for which he is not responsible. As Camus in *The Plague* wrestles with the question of why individuals suffer in a situation not of their own making, he seems to move from the nihilistic note in *The Stranger* at least to a more humanistic position. Appearing in 1957, his latest work, *The Fall*, depicts an even more serious attempt to discover values by which man can live in a world that no longer accepts and affirms the old verities that give a basis for faith. This is not to say that Camus becomes a Christian and demonstrates that he is a Christian writer in *The Fall*. However, it does seem valid to contend that although

> *The Fall* would scarcely qualify, in either subject matter or treatment, as a religious novel, it does voice a number of specifically religious attitudes and insights. . . . Here is a writer who, leaving behind him the metaphysics and absurdity, has now formulated an ethic that emphasized the need to develop a sense of human limitations.[17]

Therefore Camus hardly deserves to be categorized with those who commit themselves to absolute nothingness if, indeed, a human being ever really does.

Nihilism

Perhaps one of the clearest and most symptomatic expressions in contemporary literature of atheistic existentialism is found in the writings of Jean-Paul Sartre. His novels, his plays and his essays

---

[17]*Ibid.*, p. 220.

reveal his story of man's meaninglessness in a world of nothingness. Man is alone, faced with himself, and he must act, for man's "hopeless discovery" in Sartre's works is "that the world is absurd and his acts the unjustified creations of his freedom."[18]

Pursuing further this facet of Sartre's existentialism, Jacques Guicharnaud writes:

> The traditional idea that man commits such or such act because he is thus and so, is replaced with its opposite; by committing such or such act, man makes himself thus and so. Nothingness to start with, man spends his life giving himself an essence made up of all his acts. And it is through action that he becomes conscious of original nothingness. The anguish that grips him is provoked by that nothingness, that absence of justification, and the metaphysical responsibility which makes him the creator of his own essence. The idea . . . is uncomfortable to start with. But more important it eliminates the notion of human nature . . . and treats human destiny in itself as meaningless and useless agitation, in other words, absurd.[19]

Consider now Jean-Paul Sartre's play *The Flies*. The burden of freedom (in the Sartrian sense) and the incomprehensibility and absurdity of life are projected in this play.

Orestes, the "hero," tired of his lack of uncharted purpose, combats the superstitious attitude of man's religious consciousness and his belief in a divine order. Orestes will take orders from no one, neither divine nor human. By murdering his mother and her lover, Orestes discovers his freedom and *makes* himself. Further, he discovers that the only way to assert his freedom is to rebel against established, oppressive order. In *The Flies* Orestes is a liberator of mankind, and he is not under the domination of Zeus. He is a *man among men*. He is not guilty of murder; he has simply acted under the burdensome compulsion of freedom. Near the closing section of *The Flies*, Zeus says to Orestes, "But, you Orestes, you have done evil, the very rocks and stones cry out against you." Orestes defiantly replies, "Your whole universe is not enough to prove me wrong. You are the king of gods. . . . But you are not the king of man." The arguments continue and Zeus interrogates, "So I am not your king? Who, then, made you?" To which Orestes gives one of his key existential replies, "You. But you blundered; you should not have made

[18]Jacques Guicharnaud, "Man and His Acts," *Sartre: A Collection of Critical Essays,* ed. Edith Kern (Englewood Cliffs, N.J.: Prentice-Hall, Inc., 1962), p. 65.
[19]*Ibid.*

me free." Zeus simply answers, "I gave you freedom so that you might serve me." After a few more remarks in the dialogue, Orestes affirms, "I am my freedom. No sooner had you created me than I ceased to be yours." And later he adds, "I am doomed to have no other law but mine. . . . I am a man and every man must find out his own way. . . . You are God and I am free; each of us is alone. . . ."

Man grows up, according to Sartre, when he recognizes he is alone in a universe in which he must make himself by significantly acting under the compulsion of the burdensome responsibility of freedom. Man in the loneliness of his absurd, irrational existence is free— and free for nothing.

Jean-Paul Sartre's novels manifest much of the same type of thinking as his play, *The Flies*. His novel *Troubled Sleep*, for example, is intensely preoccupied with the problem of freedom. The third novel in a trilogy, *Troubled Sleep*, graphically describes the demoralizing conditions prevailing among soldiers and civilians in France after the Nazi victories. The disintegration of prominent characters in the book is unforgettable. Consider Mathieu. At one time a teacher of philosophy but now "existing" in the scattered French army, he finds existence almost unbearable. He wrestles with the burden of freedom and the problem of time. In deciding to fight against the Germans, he faces another question; could he at this decisive moment justify his thought, "I am going to die for nothing"? When Mathieu makes up his mind, Sartre has him pessimistically conclude, "Here and now I have decided that all along death has been the secret of my life, that I have lived for the purpose of dying. I die in order to demonstrate the impossibility of living."

The novels of Sartre, like those of other atheistic existentialistic writers, are filled with darkness, nothingness and a pervasive despair.

For Sartre, God does not exist. Yet, he has difficulty convincing himself and others that he really believes this. A study of Sartre led Charles Glicksberg to conclude, "Though Sartre declares himself to be an atheist, he finds it distressing that God does not exist, for then man stands alone in the emptiness of space, without a spiritual home, without a goal toward which to strive."[20] And Glicksberg goes on to say, "Indeed, Sartre himself in 1947 declared: 'God is silent and that I cannot possibly deny—everything in myself calls for God and that I cannot forget. . . .' "[21] However, this is not an attempt to explain away the nihilism of Sartre. He may be able to say, "Everything in myself calls for God and that I cannot forget," but

[20]Glicksberg, *op. cit.*, p. 221.
[21]*Ibid.*

he refuses to include God in his vision of life and substitutes for the Christian God a meaningless god, Nothingness. Sartre is a spokesman for many godless, unregenerate, yet spiritually hungry individuals of the contemporary world whose thinking is decidedly in the Sartrian context. Certainly the study of literature should not merely be utilitarian, yet at the same time, knowing Sartre and ascertaining how to meet the challenge he presents can be a sharp tool in coping with the attitudes of scores of individuals of the Sartrian world— many of whom are on college and university campuses. On this point, Elton Trueblood gives some sound advice:

> The way to recover lost territory, academic or otherwise, is to accept the challenge rather than to neglect it. A good example of such strategy may be seen in the Christian's reaction to the atheistic existentialism of Jean-Paul Sartre. . . . here we have a point of contact, in his brave acceptance of personal responsibility. . . . All that we ask of a man like Sartre is that he examine carefully what the concept of responsibility implies. To whom am I responsible? It is clear that responsibility implies. To whom am intrinsically transitive in character; it requires an *object*. . . . But I cannot reasonably be responsible to myself, for I am not good enough to warrant it. . . . Therefore, if responsibility is to be understandable, it must involve responsibility to Almighty God, for only in God is there the adequate personality and worthiness. It is possible—and even likely—that many of those existentialists who are also atheists would not be willing to follow this logical procedure, but they at least deserve the opportunity of examining it. It would be the function of a Christian academic task force to meet such opposition, to take it seriously, and to go on from there.[22]

It is emphatically true that the Christian affirms the fact of freedom just as readily as Jean-Paul Sartre. The real issue is not whether Sartre is for freedom and the Christian is for something else, but the crucial point is freedom with God or freedom without God. Despite the errors that the Christian reader sees in him, Sartre still "compels both atheists and theists to re-examine their accounts of the relationship between being and freedom. . . . The question he makes central deserves the place he gives it, even though, . . . he fails to distinguish between desiring to *become* God and desiring to be restored to fellowship with God."[23]

---

[22]Elton Trueblood, *The Company of the Committed* (New York: Harper & Bros. Publishers, 1961), p. 84.
[23]David E. Roberts, *Existentialism and Religious Belief,* ed. Roger Hazelton (New York: Oxford University Press, 1959), pp. 224-25.

This study of Sartre is necessarily brief, but his thinking deserves far greater attention, for his influence has made its impact on the contemporary mind.

Literature then, as stated earlier, is the dynamic interrelationship of "substance . . . distanced by form." It is an integral part of the world of thought. To be sure, it is not philosophy nor is it any other academic discipline. Literature is *literature* even though, as the works surveyed have suggested, it contains philosophical, psychological, historical and social implications. It wrestles with all human concerns; and in its own created world, it has molded and reshaped these concerns into a form which releases keen insights. Literature should be read, studied and appraised. It must be scrutinized in the dynamic relationship of all its parts. It must be probed as a unity, and the appraiser should remember, "Truth, the absolute, forms in every integrated work of art the invisible center around which everything in it coheres and in relation to which it becomes a communicator of value."[24] And this value is inescapable if the writer is more than a mere craftsman. The authentic literary artist seeks for meaning and pattern in the midst of the changing and the relative and discloses in his own aesthetic way truth about God, man and the world. For the Christian such truth is particularly significant and meaningful in the light of biblical revelations as illuminated by the Spirit of the God of truth.

FOR FURTHER READING

DREISER, THEODORE. *An American Tragedy*. Cleveland: World Publishing House, 1946.

EMERSON, RALPH WALDO. *Essays and English Traits*, ed. CHARLES W. ELIOT. New York: P. F. Collier & Son Co., 1909.

FULLER, EDMUND. *Man in Modern Fiction*. New York: Random House, 1949.

GLICKSBERG, CHARLES I. *Literature and Religion*. Dallas: Southern Methodist University Press, 1960.

GRAEF, HILDA. *Modern Gloom and Christian Hope*. Chicago: Henry Regnery Co., 1959.

KERN, EDITH (ed.). *Sartre, a Collection of Critical Essays*. Englewood Cliffs, N. J.: Prentice-Hall, Inc., 1962.

MacIVER, R. M. (ed.). *Great Moral Dilemmas*. New York: Harper & Bros. Publishers, 1956.

---

[24] D. S. Savage, Preface to *The Withered Branch* (New York: Pellegrini and Cudahy, 1952), p. 3.

PAINE, THOMAS. *Age of Reason.* New York: Wiley Book Co., 1942.

ROBERTS, DAVID E. *Existentialism and Religious Belief,* ed. ROGER HAZELTON. New York: Oxford University Press, 1959.

SARTRE, JEAN-PAUL. *Troubled Sleep.* New York: Alfred A. Knopf, 1958.

SAVAGE, D. S. *The Withered Branch.* New York: Pellegrini & Cudahy, 1952.

STEWART, RANDALL. *American Literature and Christian Doctrine.* Baton Rouge, La.: Louisiana State University, 1958.

TRUEBLOOD, ELTON. *The Company of the Committed.* New York: Harper & Bros. Publishers, 1961.

ZYLSTRA, HENRY. *Testament of Vision.* Grand Rapids: Wm. B. Eerdmans Publishing Co., 1958.

PHILOSOPHY

Arthur F. Holmes

Arthur F. Holmes is professor of philosophy at Wheaton College. He holds the B. A. and M. A. degrees from Wheaton College and the Ph. D. from Northwestern University. In addition to numerous journal articles he has authored *Christianity and Philosophy*, which has appeared also in British and French editions.

3

PHILOSOPHY

Arthur F. Holmes

Eᴀʀʟʏ Cʜʀɪsᴛɪᴀɴɪᴛʏ made its debut in the highly developed culture of the Hellenistic world, a culture in which Greek ideals found continued expression through such media as literature, the arts and philosophy. Before the close of the Apostolic Age, an inevitable interaction between Christianity and philosophy had begun. While warning their readers against being deceived by prevalent nontheistic views and while combating the inroads of various heretical viewpoints into the church, the New Testament writers nonetheless used profitably the language, the categories and even the concepts of Hellenistic philosophy. These provided the tools for reflection upon the meaning of the Christian revelation, the form for argumentation in defense of the gospel, and the means for communicating it to the mind of the ancient—all of which were indispensable to the effective establishment and expansion of the early church. Paul's address at Athens, for instance, and his handling of the Colossian heresy stand as major examples of such early interaction. John's *logos* doctrine, for all its Hebrew background, is a remarkable parallel to Hellenistic ideas.

Similar activity has persisted to the present. Throughout the history of the West, the developing ideals and changing problems of our culture, together with advancing scientific knowledge and new philosophical methods, have produced new and different philosophical positions. Such fresh positions stimulate continued Christian interaction. The unchanging truth of Christianity must be oriented to changing intellectual climates, and its implications for both old and new philosophical problems must be explored without cessation.

RELATIONSHIP BETWEEN CHRISTIANITY AND PHILOSOPHY

It is this perennial demand for proper orientation, continued interaction and fresh exploration which poses the oft-recurring problem of revelation and reason and of the precise relationship between Christianity and philosophy.[1] Some individuals, deeply impressed with the seeming congeniality of nonchristian thought, have compromised biblical revelation. The Christian Gnostics of antiquity, the deists of Enlightenment days, and the theological liberals of the last few generations exemplify this rationalistic tendency. In each case Scripture was deprived of its final authority, and nonchristian philosophical viewpoints outweighed biblical truth. On the other hand, some individuals, reacting against rationalistic compromises, have swung to an antiphilosophical fideism. Tertullian (c. A.D. 165-220) avowed faith even in what seemed absurd; Pascal (1623-62) refused to give weight to any philosophical arguments concerning God, creation or the human soul; Kierkegaard (1813-55) ridiculed the historical scholarship and abstract philosophy of his day. These men have their present-day equivalents.

Others again, avoiding both the rationalistic and the fideistic extremes, have attempted to effect a working relationship between Christianity and philosophy without compromising the legitimate claims of either. Calvinists, Franciscans and others, following the example of Augustine (A.D. 354-430), insist that faith begets both theological and philosophical insight. They maintain that divine illumination offsets the effects of sin on the human intellect so that faith, far from being irrational, is a step taken by the enlightened understanding, a step rewarded by a still fuller comprehension of the truth. They therefore grapple with current problems and positions from a biblical perspective, developing in the meantime a more complete understanding of Christianity and its philosophical implications, often by the use of categories and concepts drawn from past and present philosophies. Thomas Aquinas (1225-74) effected a different kind of synthesis of faith and reason which is preferred by

---

[1]For a further discussion of this question see the author's *Christianity and Philosophy* (Chicago: Inter-Varsity Press, 1960). Also Etienne Gilson, *Reason and Revelation in the Middle Ages* (New York: Charles Scribner's Sons, 1938); J.V.L. Casserley, *The Christian in Philosophy* (New York: Charles Scribner's Sons, 1951); H. Richard Niebuhr, *Christ and Culture* (New York: Harper & Bros., 1951); Gordon H. Clark, *Religion, Reason and Revelation* (Nutley, N.J.: Presbyterian & Reformed Publishing Co., 1961); Herman Dooyeweerd, *In the Twilight of Western Thought* (Nutley, N.J.: Presbyterian & Reformed Publishing Co., 1960); and Maurice Nédoncelle, *Is There a Christian Philosophy?* (New York: Hawthorn Books, Inc., 1960).

the Dominicans and by some Protestants. Disclaiming any direct effect of sin upon the intellect, Thomas could regard philosophy as competent apart from special divine revelation or illumination. Philosophy is a valuable propaedeutic to theology, and in many regards precedes it in the order of human thought. It is able, for instance, to establish such premises of theology as the existence of God and the immortality of the soul. This means that philosophy and theology have different premises and objectives and somewhat different methods and subject matter.

The problem is often complicated by misunderstanding and over-simplification. Is philosophy irrelevant speculation? Is faith an emotive response devoid of sound judgment? Concerning the first question, it should be recognized that philosophy is an indispensable cultural expression which serves both as the critic of prevalent ideas and ideals and as the explicit systematizer of a given view of man and the world. Philosophers, that is to say, serve two functions: (1) In their analytic and critical activities, they search relentlessly for meaning and truth, they explore the presuppositions of life and thought, and they evaluate the methods and activities of both science and society. (2) In their synthetic and speculative activities, philosophers develop the implications of our governing ideals for every phase of human life and thought—systematic world views which seek to interpret art and morality, science and history, religion and ordinary life in terms of basic postulates and values.[2] Philosophy in both senses is a legitimate and necessary Christian activity. Particular analyses and world views may be unacceptable to the Christian and may create problems for him, but he will still be compelled to think both critically and systematically. Such is inevitable in mature and alert, committed and responsible individuals; and it becomes a special obligation for those who seek to harness every ability for the glory of God.

The concept of faith requires similar clarification. Some writers, particularly since the Enlightenment, have regarded faith as emotive and therefore distinct from rational activity. Many contemporary existentialists regard faith as an ultimate concern devoid of cognitive beliefs. This is both biblically and psychologically unsound. Psychologically it implies that the intellect and the emotions are separate

---

[2]Some philosophers have emphasized one aspect of philosophy at the expense of the other. For instance, nineteenth century rationalism stressed the systematic function at the expense of the analytic and critical. Twentieth century philosophers have reacted against the resultant speculative extremes, some by acknowledging only the analytic task, and some by swinging to purely pragmatic and existential concerns. Some of these reactions will be discussed later in this chapter.

faculties, that thought is entirely void of either feeling, freedom or choice, and that emotive states arise in intellectual vacuums. This is contrary to fact. Man functions as an integrated personality and, biblically, faith does not exclude rational activity. The extent of understanding, the adequacy of evidence, and the conclusiveness of argument may vary from one subject and person to another. But faith always involves some understanding, and is both related to observable facts and open to rational investigation. The term "faith," rather than being antithetical to knowledge, denotes the fact of personal commitment and involvement in what is known. It refers to a basic attitude which guides and motivates the whole of life, including philosophical life; Christian faith guides and motivates the Christian as he interacts with the philosophical thought of his day, and as he himself philosophizes.

In what follows, certain leading strains of current philosophy will be considered. Space prevents fuller coverage, more detailed explanation or thorough interaction and criticism. This study can attempt only to pose what seem to be some basic positions as they bear on Christian thought, and to suggest some lines of possible criticism. For more thorough treatments the reader must look elsewhere.

RECENT METAPHYSICS

Twentieth century philosophy both continues earlier trends and reacts thereto. Metaphysics, the quest for an understanding of reality, nature, man and God, has been profoundly affected by modern science and its insights into the processes of nature. Earlier metaphysicians, for example, often regarded permanence as more real than change. They talked of unchanging substances and forms and of universal qualities that present changing manifestations. The essence of a man is unchanging throughout the processes of growth, maturation and degeneration. Indeed, the essence of man is changeless throughout human history. Changes are incidental. So it was with everything. But recent metaphysicians have challenged this concept; they tend to invert the order, to regard change as more ultimate and permanence as secondary or only apparent. There are no eternal and universal essences; there is no permanent order or direction to the world process.[3]

Among the factors which have contributed to this rise of process metaphysics, three will be mentioned: nineteenth century histori-

---

[3]"Process philosophies" are not altogether novel. Heraclitus (c. 566-470 B.C.) and Leibniz (A.D. 1646-1716) are outstanding cases from earlier years.

cism, theories of biological and cultural evolution, and modern physics.

Historicism

Historicism is the view, signally evident in Marx's materialism,[+] that a description of origins and processes exhausts all possible explanation of any phenomenon. The difficulty, of course, is twofold: first, even origins and processes are phenomena which must be accounted for; second, historicism assumes that historic antecedents are always causes and indeed the only causes. This is the logical fallacy of *post hoc ergo propter hoc*, which arises from confining oneself to a historical *description* of *what* transpired, in place of looking for a causal *explanation* of *why* it happened.

Evolution

Evolutionary theories were given philosophical status in the writings of men like Herbert Spencer. John Dewey (1859-1952) is a good example of the influence of such philosophies. His *Reconstruction in Philosophy* is a plea for such a consistent application of scientific methods and conclusions as would reduce all knowledge and values to temporary and relative instruments in the natural processes of biological and sociological adjustment. The emergent evolution of Samuel Alexander's *Space, Time, and Deity* provides a further example. Alexander (1859-1938) did not regard either life or mind as realities distinct from matter, as was often done before, but rather he saw life as a quality of certain highly complex chemical compounds, and he viewed mind or consciousness as a quality of highly complex organisms. Life and consciousness are, therefore, dependent on physical processes for both their existence and their operation, and both cease with those processes.

From a Christian theistic viewpoint, the difficulty with both Dewey and Alexander is not so much their openness to theories of biological and cultural change but their naturalistic presuppositions. Both the scientific data and the Christian doctrines of creation and providence allow the possibility of the gradual development of a variety of living things and human cultures. But logic cannot consistently argue that a description of such processes exhausts their explanation; this was the fallacy of nineteenth century historicism into which Dewey now appears to fall. Nor can Christianity grant such a supposition; nature and its processes, for the theist, are neither self-explanatory, self-operating, nor self-existent. God is the first and sustaining cause of all things.

On Marxist philosophy see also the final section of this chapter.

Physics

Modern physics also has exerted a profound influence on metaphysics. The interpretation of matter as a form of energy has forced many thinkers to the dynamic rather than the static view of nature. As early as the seventeenth century, Leibniz anticipated this; he discarded traditional notions of an unchanging substratum in favor of energistic explanations of nature's orderliness and apparent permanence, which he found more consonant with his Christian theism. Some contemporary philosophers have seen energy as a manifestation of mind rather than vice versa and so have favored idealism above naturalism. But the majority have preferred naturalism, sometimes speaking of "energistic materialism" as distinct from the earlier "mechanistic materialism." The term "philosophy of organism" is sometimes used in this context, especially with reference to A. N. Whitehead (1861-1947), who tried to develop the metaphysical implications of the theory of relativity.[5] If there is no absolute location in space or time, there can be no permanently located and immutable spatiotemporal objects. Reality is to be understood in terms of events rather than substances; it is a concrescent process of intimately related space-time events. "God" is a religious name for the governing principle of natural selection which produces novelty and gives direction to the process.

The problem for the Christian is not with either energistic physics or relativity theory. Scripture presents an immutable God, not an immutable creation. The problem is rather with the naturalistic interpretation given to these scientific findings and with the extension of the notions of change and relativity to the Creator as well as creation. While Whitehead does not fall into the historicist fallacy and content himself with mere description, his explanation still involves naturalistic presuppositions that are unacceptable to Christian theism. In place of a personal and transcendent God, he has a Deity subject to the same processes as nature—a Deity whose destiny is therefore tied to that of the universe. Man too is related more closely to the physical in this view than in Christianity, and the image of God in man loses much of its uniqueness. Despite the attractiveness of his interpretation of physical and biological processes, Whitehead's extrapolation of these findings to man and God is surely not required by modern physics.

This, in fact, is the difficulty with philosophical naturalism in

---

[5]See his *Science and the Modern World* (1st ed. 1925; New York: Mentor Press, 1948). His principal work is *Process and Reality* (New York: Macmillan Co., 1929).

general. While its concern with the natural sciences has been extremely profitable, it oversimplifies the situation when it reduces man and God to physical proportions. Human rationality, human freedom and creativity, moral and aesthetic values, religious and political concerns—the naturalist must explain all of these as the products of an unconscious, unreasoning, amoral nature, which uniformly appears to be causally determined rather than free and purposeful. He must explain man's hunger for God and righteousness, his sense of guilt and love of beauty, his lofty aspirations and his shattering frustrations. This is not all. Nature itself poses the historic problem of existence and essence. The naturalist must say that nature is self-existent, needing and having neither originator nor sustainer. He must say that nature is self-operating and self-explanatory, accounting completely for the essential nature of every form it takes. Cosmologists, however, can only speculate as to the origin of matter and the universe; and if biologists succeed in synthesizing primitive organisms in the laboratory, they will only have reproduced a phenomenon of nature whose utimate origin will remain a mystery. The naturalistic position is not demonstrable. On metaphysical grounds alone, theism commends itself for the coherence, scope and adequacy of its explanation as well as for its compatibility with the assured results of scientific investigation.[6]

POSITIVISM AND ANALYSIS

Many contemporary philosophers profess no interest in metaphysics. The twentieth century has reacted against nineteenth century dogmatism and speculation in that area. Logical positivism is one such reaction, a skepticism about the meaningfulness of metaphysical questions. Formulated in the Vienna Circle of the 1920's, its proponents have been concerned most with logic and scientific method. Starting with Ernst Mach's assertion that a scientific theory is an economical way of describing the relationships between sense data, Moritz Schlick (1882-1936) and others insisted that all empirical statements, all statements of fact, purport to describe sense data. If upon examination an empirical statement is found to have no

[6] For a somewhat nontechnical criticism of philosophical naturalism, see the author's article "Christianity and Naturalism," *Christianity Today,* June 8, 1959, p. 10; also C. S. Lewis, *Miracles* (New York: Macmillan Co., 1947), chaps. 2-5. More complete discussion, still at an introductory level, is given in W. E. Hocking, *Types of Philosophy* (3d ed., New York: Charles Scribner's Sons, 1959), chap. 6; and M. Rader, *The Enduring Questions* (New York: Henry Holt, 1956) pp. 222-28. For one developed theistic metaphysic, see W. Temple, *Nature, Man and God* (New York: Macmillan Co., 1934).

such reference, then it has no meaning. To be meaningful it must be verifiable by reference to the data of sense experience. In the course of subsequent discussion, A. J. Ayer *(Language, Truth and Logic)* and others explained that the verifiability principle need not require actual substantiation but only its hypothetical possibility. Verification procedures must be conceivable but not necessarily performable. Descriptions of historical or fictitious events are therefore meaningful but not metaphysical statements. Metaphysical statements refer not even to hypothetical sense data but only to universal qualities or abstract concepts. Most theological statements fell under the same condemnation, as did normative ethical judgments. To say that stealing is wrong is to say nothing about sense data; therefore nothing significant is said except that the speaker or his society disapproves of stealing. It is an emotive expression that makes no cognitive reference to objective facts or norms.

The task of philosophy, for logical positivism, is accordingly one of analysis alone, rather than one of systematic metaphysical inquiry. The philosopher analyzes the logic and the language of purportedly meaningful and scientific discourse. Pseudoproblems are exposed as vacuous, and the meaningful problem is relegated to an appropriate empirical science. Admittedly the empirical sciences are based on descriptions—but this is the only meaningful language in any case.

Opponents have accused logical positivists of abdicating from philosophy in bypassing problems and assuming their meaninglessness of a priori grounds. Certainly the philosophical enterprise has been radically restricted. It seems presumptuous to declare all at once that discussions, which intelligent people for 2,500 years or more found both meaningful and essential, are in effect irrelevant nonsense. On prima facie grounds such a declaration tends to discredit the positivistic theory of meaning rather than traditional metaphysical discussion.

Verifiability Principle

Considerable discussion has accordingly been focused on the verifiability principle itself. Is it an empirical statement? If so, can it be reduced to sense datum language? The positivist usually replies that it is not an empirical but a formal statement—a matter of definition, of language rules. But then *whose* definition of meaning, *whose* language rules are to be accepted? And how is this decided? The verifiability principle is now widely recognized as far too restrictive. Not all meaningful judgments are either formal or strictly sensory, nor are empirical statements purely descriptive.[7]

Logical positivism, moreover, makes three assumptions which have been much debated in the history of philosophy, and which ought not to be settled simply by stipulating how some people want to use the term "meaning." One is the phenomenalist theory of perception brilliantly propounded by David Hume (1711-76), to the effect that empirical knowledge is restricted to subjective impressions (sense data) and so to the world of appearances; no legitimate inferences can be drawn concerning the world of reality; therefore metaphysics is impossible. Phenomenalism is by no means an assured conclusion. On other epistemological and psychological premises than Hume's, it is possible to construct a more realistic theory of perception which does at least as full justice to both science and common sense. The second assumption is that of nominalism, the view that general terms refer only to groups of physical particulars and not to either general concepts or universal realities. If, as many contemporary philosophers believe, one of these alternatives to nominalism can be successfully defended, then it becomes possible to talk meaningfully about something other than sense data, namely, about general concepts or universal realities. Metaphysics, theology, normative ethics and related subjects may accordingly be reinstated. The third assumption is the thesis of Auguste Comte (1798-1857) that the evolution of scientific thought has rendered infantile the earlier theological and metaphysical stages of intellectual development. This thesis presupposes, among other factors, that scientific thought has neither assumptions nor implications of a metaphysical or theological nature, a presupposition which is by no means evident.[8]

Ordinary Language Movement

As these issues, together with the overoptimism of the verifiability principle, have been increasingly recognized, so philosophers have tended to move from the logical positivism of a few decades ago toward other types of philosophical analysis. Of growing importance in America is the British "ordinary language" movement which has its roots in G. E. Moore (1873-1958) and Ludwig Wittgenstein

---

[7]On the failure of positivists to formulate the verifiability principle satisfactorily, see Alvin Plantinga, "Analytic Philosophy and Christianity," *Christianity Today*, VIII: 78 (1963); also C.E.M. Jood, *A Critique of Logical Positivism* (Chicago: University of Chicago Press, 1950).

[8]See, for instance, A. N. Whitehead, *Science and the Modern World* (New York: Macmillan Co., 1926) and E. A. Burtt, *The Metaphysical Foundations of Modern Science* (Garden City, N.Y.: Doubleday & Co., 1955).

(1889-1951) and is represented by men like Gilbert Ryle, John Wisdom and J. L. Austin. Working on the supposition that philosophical disputes arise from linguistic confusions and that philosophical problems are created by verbal puzzles, these men first conceived of philosophy as a form of intellectual therapy. They tried to resolve problems by improving philosophical language and clarifying the ways in which ordinary language operates. Later some of them, notably J. L. Austin, became interested in functional analysis, the attempt to map out areas of language that are especially troublesome to philosophers. Gradually it was recognized that not all philosophical problems are misconceived and linguistic in origin, and analysts like P. F. Strawson are now bringing their functional studies to bear on traditional metaphysical questions.[9]

Ordinary language philosophy has escaped the positivist preconception that all cognitive statements must fit a scientific mold, and has recognized rich diversity in linguistic functions. The tendency is now to ask how words operate in discourse. This view, however, assumes that language is a form of overt behavior rather than a vehicle for personal reflection; it gives scant credit to the role of language in abstract thought, important as this is in traditional philosophy and theology. Yet the movement has undoubtedly been helpful, both in releasing philosophy from its positivistic straightjacket and in admitting the possible meaningfulness of metaphysical, ethical and theological language.

Religious and theological language in particular has received respectful attention by analytic philosophers—attention of a kind and extent that is unprecedented in this century. Some with positivist leanings still deny religion any reference to reality, and some regard it as a psychological projection of a Freudian sort. On the whole, it is noticeable that the various analyses of religious language reflect various views of religion and of divine revelation. Reflecting Schleiermacher's theology of experience, some analyze the language of faith as referring to religious feelings. Others reflect Ritschl's emphasis on human values and set forth religious language as expressing moral ideals in theological form. True to existential theology, others find religious utterances to express ultimate concern of a nonpropositional sort. Still others recognize the propositional content

---

[9]See G. J. Warnock, *English Philosophy Since 1900* (New York: Oxford University Press, 1958); Vere Chappell (ed.), *Ordinary Language* (Englewood Cliffs, N.J.: Prentice-Hall, Inc., 1964); D. F. Pears (ed.), *The Nature of Metaphysics* (New York: Macmillan Co., 1957). Ludwig Wittgenstein, *The Blue and Brown Books* (New York: Harper & Bros. Publishers, 1958) was one of the prime inspirations for ordinary language philosophers.

of revelation and so of religious discourse, which is essential to historic Christianity.[10]

One problem arising from this development is that of the logic of religious belief. If verification is not as empirical as the positivists supposed, yet if religious belief has some factual and propositional content, what sort of evidence or argument would serve to confirm or deny what is believed? Some, of course, refuse to accord any factual or propositional content to faith and interpret religion either existentially or in terms of psychological projections. Others, admitting factual content, either deny that this can be verified or suggest that confirmation comes only after death, when one will discover for certain whether or not the faith is true. Others again speak of confirmation of a belief by virtue of its "good fit": it neither cramps the facts nor fails to grasp them clearly, but handles adequately every relevant consideration.[11] This is a problem which will directly affect apologetics: how contemporary Christians handle it will determine the method used in arguing for the truth of the Christian faith.

PRAGMATISM

Pragmatism is a native American philosophy which arose as a reaction against the speculative idealisms of the last century. Being indigenous to America, it captures the spirit of optimism, practicality and individual freedom. As a reaction it shares the scientific and empirical spirit of positivism. These characteristics are represented in both William James (1842-1910) and John Dewey (1859-1952).

James' Relativism

James began his professional career in experimental psychology and moved more and more into philosophy.[12] An interest in the in-

---

[10]For a general discussion see Frederick Ferré, *Language, Logic and God* (New York: Harper & Bros. Publishers, 1961). Also helpful are Ian Ramsey, *Religious Language* (New York: Macmillan Co., 1963) and *Models and Mysteries* (New York: Oxford University Press, 1964); William Hordern, *Speaking of God* (New York: Macmillan Co., 1964); E. L. Mascall, *Words and Images* (New York, Ronald Press, 1957); and David H. Freeman, *A Philosophical Study of Religion* (Nutley, N. J.: Craig Press, 1964), pp. 224-39.

[11]See, for instance, Kent Bendall and F. Ferré, *Exploring the Logic of Faith* (New York: Association Press, 1962); John Hick, *Faith and Knowledge* (Ithaca, N.Y.: Cornell University Press, 1957); Ramsey, *op. cit.*

[12]His early medical training interested him in physiology and then in psychology. At the turn of the century psychology was just gaining independent status as an experimental science. It was several years thereafter, for example, before *The Journal of Philosophy, Psychology, Etc.* assumed its present title, *The Journal of Philosophy*. This meant that psychology and philosophy were so closely associated that James made the transition with seemingly little difficulty, even though without formal philosophical training.

fluence of personality and temperament, which led him to write his famous *Varieties of Religious Experience*, guided the development of his pragmatism. Philosophers, he argued in a well-known lecture,[13] are of two general types—tough-minded and tender-minded. The former become empiricists and materialists: pessimistic and fatalistic, skeptical and irreligious. The latter become rationalists and idealists: optimistic and indeterministic, dogmatic and religious. In fact in many problems temperament decides the issue; that view is accepted which provides the greatest personal satisfaction. In *The Will to Believe* he applied this principle to religious faith, claiming that the inconclusiveness of the evidence leaves one to choose on psychological grounds.

James fully recognized the implications of such a position. No theory is meaningful, he insisted, unless it makes a difference in practical (i.e., psychological) matters; as a result many abstract metaphysical questions become meaningless. The truth of a statement also is to be decided by its cash value—whether it actually makes the practical difference intended. This test for truth suggests the very nature of truth. Truth is simply workability, expediency.

Problems arise. The pragmatic theory of truth is oriented toward future experience rather than toward the past. It tends to detach expectations of the future from both experiences of the past and the understanding of what logical consistency demands. Is it not an oversimplification to think logical and historical considerations can be minimized instead of being made prime requisites of valid inquiry?

Undergirding his futurism, however, are a practicalism and a relativism. Knowledge emerges in man as a practically oriented being, concerned more with his own needs than with abstract theory or former eras. Because consciousness is in a state of flux, there is neither a guarantee that abstract theories hold nor an assurance of what they refer to; nor is it known whether past eras serve as a trustworthy guide to the future. Truth becomes entirely relative to the particular situation of the individual. In this view there are no absolutes.

Such an expression of practicality and individuality has much to make it appealing. The pragmatic *test* for truth has some usefulness; and much so-called human knowledge is plainly relative and subject to change. But James went far beyond these truisms. He viewed not merely knowledge but truth itself as changing and relative. This is

---

[13]"The Present Dilemma in Philosophy," Lecture I in *Pragmatism* (New York: Longmans, Green & Co., 1907).

an odd use of the term "truth"; and although James regarded himself as a theist, it is plainly incompatible with historic theism's belief in God whose knowledge and wisdom are the unchanging source and standard of all truth. It conflicts with the conviction that both the historical and doctrinal statements of Scripture are unchangingly true.

Moreover, James' theory of meaning as practical implication may be compared with the positivists' verifiability theory. Whereas James takes a statement to refer to an implied set of psychological data, the positivist takes it to refer to an observed set of sense data. In both cases meaning is denotative; it is to be founded in specific, observable and predictable events. Consequently the criticisms leveled at positivism—criticisms of arbitrariness, of nominalism, of phenomenalism—are adaptable to pragmatism.

Dewey's Naturalism

Such a comparison points up the empirical and scientific spirit which pragmatism shares with positivism. It is assumed that the methods of empirical science are fully applicable to all subject matter, to all realms of thought. Twentieth century positivists and pragmatists have cooperated in attempting to unify all human thought under scientific procedure. John Dewey, for example, regards all thinking as basically scientific, experimental. It arises in the process of biological and social adjustment when habitual behavior is disturbed by problematic situations.[14] Thinking invariably takes the form of problem solving and therefore includes hypotheses, experiments and verification. Ethical problems are not questions of right and wrong in any normative sense but rather questions of proper adjustment. Their solution is to be found in hypotheses that can be successfully acted upon, rather than in an understanding of ultimate standards or a sensitivity to proper motivation. Insofar as a religious attitude assists life adjustment, it is valuable; but religion as such can lay no claim to absolute truth. Scientific thinking precludes absolutes. Religious and ethical ideas and values are to be regarded as instruments, as means, not as true or valuable in themselves.

Here again one detects the futurism, the practicalism and the relativism discernible in James. One may wonder at the arbitrary disjunction of the future from the past, of the practical from the the-

---

[14]Dewey is perhaps most famous in nonphilosophical circles for his educational theory, which viewed the school as a community in which the child learns by resolving problem situations. This view illustrates succinctly Dewey's experimental theory of knowledge. See his *Reconstruction in Philosophy* (New York: Henry Holt, 1920), for his view of how man thinks.

oretical, of the relative from the enduring.[15] But one is faced more plainly than before with a universal extension of scientific methods. Experimental procedures may indeed be adaptable to any realm where experience can be controlled, repeated or predicted—as is necessary for experimentation—but it still has the following limitations. (1) It is notoriously difficult to control or predict human behavior with accuracy or to experiment with human values. Huxley's *Brave New World* and Orwell's *1984* illustrate this admirably. (2) Dare one assume that all which is potentially knowable is exhausted by one way of knowing, that there is no other way of knowing and that there is no supraempirical reality? Here both pragmatist and positivist make wholly unwarranted assumptions. On a priori grounds they exclude speculative and abstractly conceptual thought, as well as the possibility of divine revelation. The reason seems to be that, while disclaiming metaphysics, they retain the metaphysical assumption that the world of empirical data is the totality of reality, self-sustaining and self-explanatory. They are naturalists, as Dewey himself and other pragmatists are quick to acknowledge.

For the Christian then pragmatism is unsatisfactory because of its relativism and its naturalism, with all that these imply regarding God, man and values. But the Christian must not suppose that pragmatism makes no worthwhile contributions to religious thinking. Its practicalism, though overdrawn, is a welcome counterbalance to earlier extreme, opposing tendencies. Its futurism, though excessive, is a healthy preventative against that preoccupation with the past which hallmarks alike the sterile society and the uncreative mind. The pragmatic *test* for truth, as scientific advance readily attests, is a useful if fallible guide to both knowledge and action, even though Christians may regard it as fallacious to define truth pragmatically. The limitations of human knowledge, after all, are such that one is frequently compelled to decide both theoretical and practical issues on the basis of probability. Much can be learned by experience, by trial and error.

EXISTENTIALISM

Like both logical positivism and pragmatism, existentialism rose in reaction against rationalistic extremes. Although its roots reach even deeper, it stems in part from the influence of the Danish writer,

---

[15]For further development of this type of criticism see W. P. Montague, *The Ways of Knowing* (New York: Macmillan Co., 1925), chap. 5; and Brand Blanshard, *The Nature of Thought* (New York: Macmillan Co., 1939), Vol. I, chap. 10.

Sören Kierkegaard (1813-55). Repudiating alike the dead orthodoxy
of the established Lutheran church and the seemingly sterile ab-
stractions of Hegelian metaphysics, he argued that religion and philosophy alike had alienated men from reality, from their true existence before God.[16] Religion did so by its overconcern with historical
and critical questions and by its furtherance of the image of Christianity as simply moral and social responsibility. Philosophy
estranged men from reality by its "essentialism," a concern with
universal concepts to the neglect of the specific involvements of individual existence. Hegel in particular erred by forcing on reality
a rationalistic system that purported to explain exhaustively the
whole of history as the logically necessary unfolding of the Absolute.
This universal determinism robbed men of their individuality and
freedom and denied life its spontaneity and uncertainty. By contrast, Kierkegaard emphasized freedom rather than determinism,
the individual rather than the universal, *existence* rather than abstract essence. As a result, "existentialism" has become known for
its focus upon human freedom and the predicament of the individual.

Subjectivity

How can a man alienated from his true existence regain it? How
can he become authentic and freely assume responsibility for himself? To Kierkegaard this query asks how one becomes a Christian,
and he responds by asserting that faith means passionate involvement, a leap in the dark that transcends the paradoxes which rise
when human logic is confronted with the unique and the eternal.
Kierkegaard has been accused of irrationalism, of failing to accept
any obligation to the laws of thought. But he regards paradox as
inevitable when eternity breaks into time. God does not violate His
own character, but He transcends the limited expectations created
by human logic and morality; He asked Abraham to murder his son,
an inconsistent and immoral act by human standards. But God is
not logically or ethically restricted. He is free, and when He con-
fronts a man with the demands of faith, that man too must passionately transcend impersonal law.

Some dissatisfaction with Kierkegaard nonetheless seems justified.
If God is a rational and moral being, if the attribute of truth means

---

[16]Notice that, in keeping with Kierkegaard's intent, philosophers now speak
of men as individuals rather than of man in general. Kierkegaard presents his
case most fully in *The Concluding Unscientific Postscript* (Princeton, N. J.:
Princeton University Press, 1944). See also Kierkegaard's *Fear and Trembling*
(Garden City, N.Y.: Doubleday & Co., Inc., 1954).

that He cannot contradict Himself, if divine moral law is a valid expression of His holy character, and if man is made in the image of this rational and moral God—then man must bow to the demands of reason and true morality as to the demands of God Himself. Kierkegaard errs in that, while stressing the need for subjective involvement, he fails to relate it constructively to the objectivity of truth and goodness. If on the other hand he intended to present a caricature rather than a description, then one must still aver that he exaggerates in a very misleading fashion.

The imbalance of his position stems from his subjective method. Kierkegaard and existentialists generally engage in personal introspection. They explore the anguish of a morbid soul before God or the dreadful freedom of a man without an anchor. They take what they find to be normative. They tend to universalize what may well be the abnormal psychology of a frustrated individual in a grossly abnormal age.

By doing this, they also yield to the very "essentialist" tendencies of which Kierkegaard accused other philosophers. Essentialist tendencies are unavoidable. Man inevitably reflects, generalizes, infers, conceptualizes, defines essences. To confine oneself to the particular is to abdicate from philosophy, from rationality, from the very image of God in man. The point is not whether one should be an essentialist or an existentialist. It is rather that one should maintain a relationship between essence and existence, between the universal and the individual, between subjective concern and objective truth, in both thought and action. An intelligent person cannot bypass the agelong problem of essence and existence. Nor can the legitimacy of the questions Hegel faced be denied. The objection to the existentialists then is not that they trespass into the realm of essence; if they did not, they would not be philosophizing. It is rather that the existentialists approach essences unwittingly and without sufficient consideration for what traditional philosophy teaches in this respect. Regardless of helpful insights their method may yield, by itself it is still a very inadequate basis for generalization about the nature of man, truth and God.

That this criticism holds is evidenced by the heterogeneity of viewpoints embraced in the existentialist movement. According to Jean-Paul Sartre, there is a unifying thesis: that existence precedes essence, that man faces the dreadful freedom of having to give meaning and purpose to his life while being immersed in existence. But beyond this thesis there is great diversity—from the theism of Kierkegaard, Marcel and Jaspers to the atheism of Nietzsche, possibly Heidegger and certainly Sartre.[17] Existentialism may have succeeded in analyzing one aspect of the human predicament, but it has neither given a complete diagnosis, nor traced the ultimate causes of distress, nor prescribed an effective remedy. Yet for all its limitations, the existentialist school continues to find ready acceptance in both Europe and America, whether in the novels and plays of Sartre, Camus and Simone de Beauvoir or in the theology of Bultmann and Tillich.

Phenomenology

Many existentialists themselves are well aware of these and other difficulties, and they attempt more rigorous descriptions of human subjectivity by the use of phenomenological methods. Phenomenology is a procedure devised by Edmund Husserl (1859-1938) for uncovering the essential structures of consciousness by suspending judgment on the usual philosophic questions about the reality of man's surroundings. By this means he hoped to be able to describe more directly and objectively areas which the sophisticated experience and thought of the ages had obscured or misconstrued. He himself was no existentialist, but his method was introduced into existential philosophy by his students such as Martin Heidegger.

Recognizing both the impossibility and undesirability of a complete suspension or *epoche*, Heidegger tried rather to apply the phenomenological method to human existence with all its historical uniqueness, concern and sense of foreboding destiny; and he attempted to describe the structure of the historical consciousness of the individual. Jean-Paul Sartre pursued this further, stressing the totally unstructured nature of human freedom and the persistent tensions between the self and its environment. His novels and plays dramatize what his philosophy describes phenomenologically. Gabriel Marcel (1887 ——) heartily disagrees with Sartre's radical views, and offers more informal descriptions of phenomena such as faith, hope and love which he finds are given new significance and content by Christianity. Maurice Merleau-Ponty (1908-61) has tried to avoid one-sidedness by stressing the lived-world as a whole rather than just its subjective component. His descriptions of bodily existence and world-consciousness have disclosed relationships between existential philosophy and sciences like psychology and linguistics.

---

[17]See J. P. Sartre, *Existentialism* (New York: Philosophical Library, 1947). Significant selections from this and other important existentialist writings are available in Walter Kaufmann (ed.), *Existentialism from Dostoevsky to Sartre* (New York: Meridian Books. 1956). Helpful critical commentaries may be found in John Wild, *The Challenge of Existentialism* (Bloomington, Ind.: University of Indiana Press, 1955) and James Collins, *The Existentialists* (Chicago: Henry Regnery Co., 1952).

The principal difficulty seems to be that phenomenological descriptions of man and his life tend to be relative to the experience and perspective of those who do the describing. Phenomenology does not provide indisputable facts nor can it decide between conflicting world views. Absolute truth eludes it. Yet one does well to heed Paul Ricoeur's reminder that the Christian regards absolute truth, as far as complete human knowledge of it is concerned, as an eschatological ideal toward which history is moving, rather than as a present achievement. The biblical revelation illuminates the human predicament and gives direction to thought, but man still knows only in part. One stands to learn much from existential insights and phenomenological descriptions, as can be experienced from disciplined work in the sciences and humanities generally.

Existentialism has had repercussions in religion. Theologians like Tillich and Bultmann, along with popularizers like Bishop John A. T. Robinson of *Honest to God*, have tried to translate the Christian message into existential terms. In doing so they have largely robbed its initial historical events of the unchanging significance to both God and man which is recounted by the biblical writers. They deny the possibility of either conceptualizing God or defining the essential nature of man. They construe the Christ-event as awaking in men the courage to exist: this is an existential impact, not propositional truth; it triggers personal authenticity rather than disclosing the nature of a redeemer-God to needy men. Revelation, in other words, is neither propositional (as in orthodox theology) nor is it a universal presence (as in liberal theology). It is rather the traumatic experience of realizing the emptiness of life and discovering the ground of all being.

* * *

It becomes apparent that philosophies of reaction tend to exaggerate and oversimplify. This is true, for instance, of the positivist and analytic reaction against the idealistic systems of the last century—reactions which eliminated the whole of metaphysics in order to dispose of one particularly distasteful variety. It is true of the pragmatist reaction against detached speculation unrelated to the problems of life; creating an uncrossable gulf between the theoretical and the practical, pragmatism attempts to outlaw all but the practically valuable. It is true of the existentialists; in reaction against the cold objectivity of Hegel's philosophic method, they have exaggerated the individual and the subjective and thereby have oversimplified the interpretation of man, his freedom and his responsibilities.

It also becomes apparent that by their tendency to exaggeration and oversimplification, philosophies of reaction often become inconsistent. Positivism has its unrecognized and unscrutinized presuppositions, and analysis has its systematic concern with the language and concepts of metaphysics. Pragmatism's attempt to universalize scientific thinking recalls the binding force of absolutes where relativism should reign. Existentialism's concern with a man's existence has led to new interest in the essence of the human situation.

MARXISM

A similar pattern—reaction leading to exaggeration, oversimplification and inconsistency—may be detected in the philosophy of Karl Marx (1818-83) and Friedrich Engels (1820-95).[18] Their "dialectical materialism," as has been observed above, is one expression of nineteenth century historicism and seeks to explain man and history by describing traceable origins and processes. They accepted Hegel's view that all world processes, whether physical, logical, psychological or social, follow a dialectical pattern; that is to say, history proceeds through the conflict of an initial form, the thesis, with its antithesis, to the emergence of a higher synthesis which in turn becomes the starting point, the thesis for a new dialectical conflict. Marx described this pattern as he saw it in social and political history and came to the conclusion that progress is always achieved through the conflict of basically economic antitheses, through class struggles. The conflict of capitalism with the proletariat will eventually be synthesized in the classless society of true Communism. Underlying this supposedly empirical description are a number of crucial philosophic assumptions.

Historicism

Historicism assumes that description exhausts explanation, with its own naturalistic assumption that the processes described are self-explanatory, self-operating and self-sustaining.

---

[18]Marxism pursues its objectives on every front, including the philosophical. In Europe, Marxism, existentialism and neo-Thomism (usually Roman Catholic) seem to be the leading contenders. Some existentialists are also Thomists; others have had Marxist sympathies. A readily available source is Lewis S. Feuer (ed.), *Basic Writings on Politics and Philosophy—Karl Marx and Friedrich Engels* (Garden City, N.Y.: Doubleday & Co., Inc., 1959). For evangelical reactions see Lester de Koster, *All Ye That Labor* (Grand Rapids: Wm. B. Eerdmans Publishing Co., 1956); also E. J. Carnell, *A Philosophy of the Christian Religion* (Grand Rapids: Wm. B. Eerdmans Publishing Co., 1952), chap. 4.

Dialecticism

Dialecticism is the generalization that all processes necessarily follow the thesis-antithesis-synthesis pattern.

Determinism

Determinism covers the view that all events are controlled by other events within the same overall process, and that man is no exception to this general rule; freedom of thought or action is an illusion.

Economic Determinism

Economic determinism deals with the assertion that economic processes ultimately control all others, that the juxtaposition of such factors as labor, materials and wealth explains fully every other aspect of history. Ethical standards reflect the interests of one class or another and its struggles. Religion is a tool of the capitalist classes, an "opiate of the masses." Philosophical argument is a weapon for class warfare. Art and literature portray the economic viewpoints of one class as against another.

Materialism

Materialism reflects the view that all of reality is ultimately reducible to the material, that consequently there are no more ultimate factors than the economic which could control the course of history—no God, no free man in pursuit of values.

Each of these assumptions manifests some degree of oversimplification. Does historical description *fully* explain everything? Can *every* process—logical, physical, biological, and historical—be poured into a dialectical mold? Can one safely assume that there are no transcendent (i.e., supernatural) forces to direct the inner determinism of nature, and that man's creativity and freedom are not exhibited in his rational control of natural forces or in transcending what appears to be inevitable—in having dominion over creation? Do impersonal economic factors really dominate history, even in twentieth century America where the workers are often capitalist shareholders or profit-sharers? Can matter and motion satisfactorily explain the rich diversity of nature and man, man's quest for happiness and freedom, his hunger for beauty and righteousness?

Doubtless the generalizations involved in Marxist assumptions arise from exaggeration during reaction. Marx wrote in the aftermath of the industrial revolution, incensed by the exploitation, injustice and inequalities of those days. He was a man with a mission, a polemicist rather than a research scholar. His conclusions are understandably hasty and one-sided. Yet this opens the way to inconsistency. Present-day Marxists see the class struggle as one between imperialism and nationalism, yet Western accusations of Marxist imperialism ring strangely true when capitalist powers have recently granted independence to one nation after another while the Iron and Bamboo Curtains stay intact. One wonders in which directions Marx would today level his charges of exploitation and injustice.

The fact remains that for all its exaggeration, oversimplification and inconsistency, Marxism must be taken seriously. Its appeal is widespread. It gives to modern man a utopian goal, a sense of personal mission in a world filled with international tension and impersonal technology. The Christian must face honestly the issues Marxism poses, developing clearly and explicitly, without oversimplification, with consistency that stems from Christian integrity and philosophical rigor, the implications of biblical revelation for these days. A careful philosophy of history, as well as an understanding of nature, personality and human values in a technological age, becomes essential. Social ethics must again capture our attention, the voice of the regenerate conscience echoing the concern of the Hebrew prophet amid the political, social and philosophical conflicts of these times.

These conclusions could be generalized with reference to contemporary thought as a whole. The Christian should be concerned not only to understand other positions, not only to proclaim and defend the faith he cherishes, but also to explore its contributions to the world of thought. Endless tasks face the Christian in philosophy today, tasks which lead him into every branch of the discipline and which call for the dedication of every intellectual resource. If Christ is Lord of all, and if all truth is ultimately His, then it is the Christian's responsibility to discover and express this message in detail and with discipline.

FOR FURTHER READING

The following list is not intended to represent the most important philosophical literature of recent years, but to guide the interested reader to fairly introductory works.

AYER, ALFRED J. *Language, Truth and Logic*. New York: Dover Publications, Inc., 1936.

BRETALL, ROBERT W. *A Kierkegaard Anthology*. New York: Modern Library, 1946.

CASSERLEY, J. V. L. *The Christian in Philosophy.* New York: Charles Scribner's Sons, 1951.

CHAPPELL, VERE (ed.). *Ordinary Language.* Englewood Cliffs, N. J.: Prentice-Hall, Inc., 1964.

CLARK, GORDON H. *Religion, Reason and Revelation.* Philadelphia: Presbyterian & Reformed Publishing Co., 1961.

COLLINS, JAMES. *The Existentialist.* Chicago: Henry Regnery Co., 1952.

DEWEY, JOHN. *Reconstruction in Philosophy.* Boston: Beacon Press, 1957.

DOOYEWEERD, HERMAN. *In the Twilight of Western Thought.* Philadelphia: Presbyterian & Reformed Publishing Co., 1960.

FERRE, FREDERICK. *Language, Logic and God.* New York: Harper & Row, 1961.

FREEMAN, DAVID H. *A Philosophical Study of Religion.* Nutley, N. J.: Craig Press, 1964.

HORDERN, WILLIAM. *Speaking of God.* New York: Macmillan Co., 1964.

HUSSERL, EDMUND. *Phenomenology and the Crisis of Philosophy.* New York: Harper Torchbooks, 1965.

JAMES, WILLIAM. *Pragmatism.* New York: Longmans, Green & Co., 1907.

KAUFMANN, WALTER (ed.). *Existentialism from Dostoevsky to Sartre.* Cleveland: Meridian Books, 1956.

MASCALL, ERIC L. *Words and Images.* New York: Ronald Press, 1957.

NEDONCELLE, MAURICE. *Is There a Christian Philosophy?* New York: Hawthorn Books, Inc., 1960.

WALSH, W. H. *Metaphysics.* London: Hutchinson University Library, 1963.

WARNOCK, G. J. *English Philosophy Since 1900.* London: Oxford University Press, 1958.

WHITEHEAD, ALFRED N. *Science and the Modern World.* Mentor Books, 1948.

WILD, JOHN. *The Challenge of Existentialism.* Bloomington, Ind.: University of Indiana Press, 1955.

WITTGENSTEIN, LUDWIG. *The Blue and Brown Books.* Oxford: B. H. Blackwell, 1958.

THEOLOGY

R. Allan Killen

R. Allan Killen is lecturer in apologetics at Covenant Theological
Seminary in St. Louis. He has previously taught at Faith Theological Seminary and was vice-president of Toronto Bible College.
A graduate of Wheaton College, he holds the B. D. from Faith
Theological Seminary, the Th. M. from Dallas Theological Seminary and the D. Th. from the Free University of Amsterdam, Holland. He is author of *The Ontological Theology of Paul Tillich*.

4

THEOLOGY

R. Allan Killen

A GOOD DEFINITION of theology is not easily found. The term comes from the two Greek words *theos*, "god," and *logos*, "study of," so that the simplest definition is "a study of God." The following is a more comprehensive definition: a methodical study of God—who He is, the proofs of His existence, His relationship to the world and man—which gathers its materials inductively from the Bible, the facts of physical science, psychology, history, the other sciences and philosophy, and then examines, evaluates and organizes all these in the light of the Bible, as God's revealed source and norm of the truth.

Theology must draw its basic materials from the Bible (the field of biblical theology). Since it expresses the development of doctrines in a systematic manner, it adds, however, to the above a consideration of tradition and the creeds and confessions of the church, along with comparative religion, in the formulation of a systematic presentation of truth.

Six clearly defined theological movements are already evident in the twentieth century: (1) Modernism or Liberalism; (2) Neoorthodoxy; (3) Bultmannism; (4) American Realism; (5) the grand synthesis of Ontological Theology; (6) the New Theology, which is also called Radical Theology and the God-Is-Dead Movement. The first three followed each other in a chronological sequence, liberalism having its strongest influence from 1900 to 1920, neoorthodoxy from 1920 to 1941, and Bultmannism from 1941 to 1960. The fourth is a synthesis of liberalism and neoorthodoxy; the fifth is an eclectic synthesis of the other four. The sixth, an acknowledgment that all the rest have failed, is a return to Hegel and Nietzsche. Tillich's influence (fifth) has extended from 1933 till the present. The new theology (sixth) has come to the fore since about 1960.

LIBERALISM

Liberalism, or modernism, had its beginning early in the nineteenth century. It is chiefly the product of a philosopher and a theologian. Its philosophical father is Hegel, with his view that progress rests upon a triadic dialectic; its theological father is Schleiermacher.

Hegel worked out a system in which good and evil were set in opposition to one another, and out of this contradiction there developed a synthesis or unity. The triadic dialectic of Hegel runs thus: (1) *thesis*, or first proposition; (2) *antithesis*, the contradiction or opposite of the thesis; (3) *synthesis*, a combination of elements of thought from both the thesis and antithesis.

Hegel's basic triad, from which existence starts, is Being, Nonbeing and Becoming—the latter standing for God as active and creative. His all-embracing triad, which covers God, the world and man, is Becoming (God, or the Absolute), objective being (the material world) and subjective being (rationality and self-consciousness in man). Hegel taught that the rational is the real and the real the rational—in other words, whatever is at a particular time is the rational or dialectical development of Being, or God, for that time, and therefore right for that time.

Schleiermacher is the theological father of modernism. He followed Hegel very closely at several points but was also influenced by Immanuel Kant. Kant had come to the conclusion that God cannot be known; He can only be assumed to exist. The world, the soul and God, he reasoned, are only "regulative knowledge" or ideas. They cannot be proved. His reason for saying this will be considered a little later on. Man has, however, an inherent categorical imperative, a *Du Solst*, that is, a "thou shalt," which urges him to act in such a manner that whatever he does as an individual could be chosen to become a universal law for all mankind. This *Du Solst* demands a soul, God and immortality, in order that it fulfill its goal. Its existence in man is the only direct evidence man has for God or for a future life.

Cut off by Kant from the use of the theistic arguments to establish a knowledge of God, and from all possibility of a knowledge of God by discursive thought,[1] Schleiermacher decided that there was still another way to know God, namely, a psychological approach. Man has a feeling of absolute dependence and this is a psychological condition from which he can build up a knowledge of God by inference. This feeling forms the basis of theology and of a knowledge of God.

Schleiermacher's convictions became the foundation for much of the liberalism and modernism which followed. He personally confined the possibility of his psychological theology to Christianity. However, some other theologians soon realized that pagan religions could just as well qualify, since they also exhibit the feeling of absolute dependence upon some heavenly being. As a result, the men who comprised the Comparative Religions School attempted to argue for the uniqueness of Christianity, on the basis of a comparison of different religions. Ernst Troeltsch with his great work, *Die Absoluteit des Christentums und die Religionsgeschichte* and Gerardus Van der Leeuw in his symposium, *De Godsdiensten der Wereld (Religions of the World)*, investigated the uniqueness of Christianity. Troeltsch thought that he made one finding: the Christian has a higher moral consciousness than the heathen. But Van der Leeuw's symposium claimed to find all the significant concepts of Christianity scattered through primitive as well as other religions.

Liberalism, or modernism, is a very diversified movement. Its followers have certain common characteristics and also wide areas of difference. This movement is characterized by eight general assumptions.

1. *The scientific method is to be applied to everything at all times.* "Modernists are Christians who accept the results of scientific research as data with which to think religiously."[2] New empirical evidence is accepted in the place of and as superior to all other evidence, particularly historical and personal. When science comes to a conclusion, this is to be accepted, even if it conflicts with the Bible.

The first problem this empirical procedure raises is that science and the scientific method fail to reveal the moral law with the same accuracy and clarity with which they disclose physical law. When man attempts to base his moral code on scientific investigation, this mode of inquiry proves inadequate, not having any way

---

[1]See section on neoorthodoxy in this chapter.
[2]Shailer Mathews, *The Faith of Modernism* (New York: Macmillan Co., 1924), p. 23.

of explaining the origin and the presence of sin and evil. Therefore the scientific method, while satisfactory for the laws of the physical realm, fails when applied to the spiritual. The situation which is to be examined, the present life and condition of man, is abnormal because of the entry of sin into God's creation.

Again, in order to be truly scientific, the scientist should consider all the facts. These include not only physical laws and empirical knowledge but also the Bible and all contained in it, and particularly its attestation to God, the incarnation of Christ, miracles, the nature of man, man's fall, sin. But many secular scientists are not ready to weigh all these factors. They will not admit that science is inadequate, without revelation, to explain dysteleology— the apparent lack of purpose—in the universe and in sin in man.

Nor are the secular scientists willing to give historical and personal evidence their proper place. This proves very devastating to the formulation of a theology since the Bible presents both a history of salvation and a plan which is dependent upon and interwoven with historical events. The facts and truths taught in God's Word rest upon the integrity and credibility of the biblical witnesses. Laws of evidence, therefore, become as important to apply as the laws of science in the examination of what the Bible teaches. When approached as a reliable historical record and examined according to well-established laws of evidence, the Bible meets and satisfies the highest standards.

2. *The assumption of the complete rationality of the universe.* The second basic premise of liberalism states that everything runs according to physical laws and that man can therefore explain everything rationally once he can find the laws. When this concept is assumed, the presence of the supernatural and of the realm of higher laws is excluded. Miracles are denied. Pure naturalism takes the place of supernaturalism.

The very fact that God is a self-conscious personal being demands that, if He be the Creator of all, He also be the creation's Sustainer and Ruler. The universe must be subject to His direct fiat and will, or else He is controlled and ruled by the universe. The Bible teaches that God created everything (Gen. 1:1; John 1:2-3; Col. 1:16), that moment by moment He continues to uphold all by His word and will (Col. 1:17; Heb. 1:3), and that all is subject to His direct command and control (II Peter 3:5-7).

Back of all constructive action lies will. Behind the universe lies the will of God. This divine volition alone explains the direct personal control of the universe by God. While God's will is governed by His holy character, still it is personal and therefore free. Even as man can control and command his body and its actions directly through his will, so God can control His universe directly by His own will. Miracles are accomplished as He imposes His will, either through the imposition of higher laws or through His power to control the atoms which He sustains by His direct power (Col. 1:17; Heb. 1:3).

3. *The view that the Bible shows man coming to know God rather than God revealing Himself to man.* God is regarded by the modernist as immanently present in the world—present everywhere in a real, immediate sense. No special revelation is needed in order to come to know Him. Man can find God in himself (e.g., in his feeling of utter dependence [Schleiermacher] and in his feeling of "ultimate concern" [Tillich]).

An immanental view of God always leads finally to the pantheism of a Paul Tillich or a Bishop John Robinson (e.g., *Honest to God*). It comes to the conclusion that God is in all, and all is somehow permeated by Him and is in some way a part of Him and of His own self-development. This position sees evil either as a necessary waste in the process of creation, which God cannot prevent, or as the unrestrained breaking forth of that negative contradictory force which makes God active and creative (cf. Hegel and Tillich).

The Bible teaches, in contrast, that God is transcendent as well as immanent. He is entirely holy and separate from both the world and evil. He is not in any sense continuous with or part of the world and man, even though He is present everywhere—or perhaps it is better to say everything is equally present to Him. When theologians start with a God who is entirely immanent, they cannot explain Him without including evil in His self-development. Only a God who creates ex nihilo, from nothing, and is entirely separate from His universe can remain clear of evil. If God is in any sense a part of His creation or of the creature, He becomes involved in the origin and development of evil and is thereby responsible for it.

If man is to know God, it must be by divine revelation. Though God's handiwork is to be seen in the whole of creation (Ps. 19:1 ff.), this can merely lead man to the conclusion that God exists and has the power and knowledge to cause such a creation. Since man is a sinner, such a disclosure cannot meet his real needs. Direct special revelation is required if man is to know God personally and to find salvation.

4. *Progress.* The modernist holds that things are steadily progressing from the less developed to the more complex, from the

primitive to the fully developed, from the imperfect to the perfect. A steady march of evolutionary development and progress is assumed in nature, in man and in morals. Hegel was the philosopher of progress, Charles Darwin the anthropologist, the liberals the theologians.

This theory of progress would be wonderful if it could be proved true. In the moral realm World War I was sufficient, however, to disillusion Karl Barth and most of the European existentialists about any real progress. The purges of the Jews in Germany, the Communist bloodbaths in Russia and China, and the horrors of World War II have proved to the Western world that there is no such thing as moral progress. Man in his heart is as evil as ever. "The heart is deceitful above all things, and desperately wicked: who can know it?" (Jer. 17:9, cf. Rom. 3:9-18). The Bible's view of man's fallen nature has been vindicated.

5. *Miracles are only natural events as seen through consecrated eyes.* This tenet of modernism is somewhat refined and changed in neoorthodoxy and the other later systems as they say miracles are forms of myths, or symbols, used to express divine transcendent truth.

In denying miracles, the modernist fails to leave any place or possibility for divine control by a personal God. If he does believe in a personal God, the liberal binds Him to the iron laws of the universe He has made; if he does not so believe, he makes God into a part or ingredient of that universe, such as the Absolute materializing Himself in the physical universe and coming to consciousness in man (Hegel) or the Power of Being present in man and all that exists (Tillich).

6. *Religion is the awakening of the human consciousness to the presence of the divine consciousness.* This postulation states that God is seen as present everywhere—as immanent—and all man needs to do is to become conscious of His presence. Man finds God through feeling—the feeling of absolute dependence (Schleiermacher), through having "ultimate concern" (Tillich).

Such a god has no face or form. He is only subjectively experienced and known. The objective revelation in the Scripture is ignored or denied, and one is left with a subjective experience supported by no divine data or propositional revelation. How can the Christian distinguish between his feeling of dependence (saying that it reveals the God of the Bible and Christ) and the pagan's feeling of dependence upon his gods? It is impossible to prove that the Christian's experience is the only one, and the correct one, apart from some objective, revealed standards and truth. The works of the Comparative Religions School have shown this to be true.

The Bible states that man has the "work of the law" written in his heart, as witnessed by the manner in which his conscience reacts and his thoughts accuse or excuse his actions (Rom. 2:14-15). The Word of God declares man responsible with the use of his divinely given reason to come to the conclusion that God exists, that He has the eternal power to create this world and man, and that He possesses a glorious personal character (Rom. 1:18-20; Ps. 8:3; 19:1 ff.). It states man once knew God through the revelation given to him at the beginning, but deliberately turned away from Him (Rom. 1:18 ff.). The Bible makes it clear that man is utterly lost and needs a special revelation from God of His plan for man's salvation in Jesus Christ if he is to be saved.

7. *Christ was only a sinless man.* Jesus Christ is seen as a man who distinguished Himself from all other men in the sense that He, like an evolutionary mutation, attained the full development to which man is destined (Schleiermacher). He was more conscious of His dependence, and of God, than any other man, and more transparent to the Divine; and thus He mediated the "new being" and eternal life (Tillich). The ontological biblical Trinity is denied in such views, along with the existence of Jesus Christ as the second Person of the Godhead and His incarnation. At the same time Jesus Christ is only unique in the sense that He was the first man to attain essential being, or what man ought to be ("God-manhood" Tillich calls it).

Liberalism ignores the major stress of the New Testament upon the preexistence and full deity of Jesus Christ. This deity is not only stated by the New Testament writers as they describe the person of Christ (John 1:1; Rom. 9:5; Titus 2:13), it is also claimed by Christ (John 8:58; 10:30-33) and acknowledged by those who heard Him (Matt. 27:54; John 1:49: cf. Luke 5:21; 7:49).

8. *Man is inherently good.* Liberalism holds that if man is given the right environment and opportunity, he will become good. This is the view of the so-called social gospel. If the heathen are taught how to grow crops, exercise good hygiene and rule themselves, they will become enlightened and free. The concept of the fatherhood of God and the brotherhood of all men lies behind this view. Men are just naughty, rebellious children who need to learn that they are dependent upon God and must obey Him, and all will be right.

The Bible teaches—and modern wars, persecutions and purges

have illustrated—that man is inherently evil rather than good. Christ insists a man must be born again to be saved—he must become a child of God by regeneration (John 3:7: cf. John 1:12-13; I John 5:1), because the unsaved are children of the devil (John 8:44). Paul adds that they are children of darkness (I Thess. 5:4-5) and of disobedience (Eph. 2:2).

The Three Mainstays of Liberalism

The three factors which contributed to the growth and spread of liberalism will now be discussed.

Organic Evolution. The idea that everything in the world can be explained by some theory of progressive evolution found its first proponents in Heraclitus and Anaximander followed by Aristotle with his theory of the Unmoved Mover—Aristotle's concept of God. Though he was like a man in a space capsule with all the windows closed, the Unmoved Mover drew all the potentialities out of pure unformed matter in a series of mounting evolutionary steps from inorganic to organic, sentient, and on to rational life. Hegel, the German philosopher who reached his prime about 1824, had a very different view. Aristotle had started with two principles, the Unmoved Mover and matter. Hegel started with one, God alone. First, God developed in a triangular triadic manner as Being (thesis) was opposed by its negation, Nonbeing (antithesis); and the clash between the two resulted in Becoming (synthesis)—God as creative. But no sooner did God develop into Becoming than a new negation or contradiction developed and so on until reason appeared in man, as the final step, only to return back to Becoming.

However, the biggest boost to the theory of evolution came with the appearance of Charles Darwin's *Origin of Species* (1859) and his presentation of the theory of organic evolution. Later evolutionists struggled with the ideas of adaptation to environment, mutations and survival of the fittest in endeavors to explain the progress which evolution claimed to find in the universe, starting with the simple cell and progressing up to man as the climax of the process.

Evangelical Christian anthropologists handle evolution in several different ways. Some have adopted what may be called theistic evolution. These accept the evolutionary theory but see it as developed by a self-conscious personal God. In the upward development from the simple cell through animals to man they see a point at which a developing organism receives a living soul and becomes a man. This view proves difficult, however, in the light of the

Genesis record where man is presented as possessing a living soul at the very time of the forming of his body from the dust of the ground.

Others feel that theistic evolution raises too many great problems concerning the biblical revelation, the time of innocence, responsibility and the fall. They see the possibility for much and wide development but not of organic evolution. God created phyla or original classes of animals from which many species have developed. Man, however, as a separately created phylum appeared quite late upon the earth.

Higher Criticism of the Bible. Lower criticism endeavors to establish the original text of the Scriptures and is accepted by all scholars, evangelical and otherwise, as necessary and legitimate.

Higher criticism attempts to find the meaning and truth of the Bible by the application of so-called scientific methods of investigation. Secular history is applied to historical facts and predictions, and literary methods of examining the sources and authorship are utilized in relation to the composition and content of the different books of the Bible. Some seeming contradictions are pointed out, some anomalies, such as Moses' death being recorded at the end of his own book in Deuteronomy 34, and some prophecies which do not appear on the surface to have been fulfilled. Criticisms of this nature demand much painstaking work and study to refute. Some of them can be quickly answered; others cannot be answered until the biblical archaeologist uncovers the needed evidence with his spade. One by one, problem by problem, however, at whatever point the accuracy of the Bible has been tested, it has again and again proved to be true. The recent finds in Palestine are adding new evidence.

Higher criticism launched a devastating attack on the Bible from the standpoint of sources and authorship of the text. The higher critics claimed that the Pentateuch, the first five books of the Bible, was composed from four sources: a Jahweh, an Elohim, a Priestly and a Deuteronomic writer (the JEPD theory). Portions, paragraphs, and even verses were divided where, for example, the words *Jahweh* and *Elohim* appeared in the same sentence or paragraph. One critic allotted Genesis to sixteen distinct writers or sources by using such a method. A similar approach was made to the New Testament also on the basis of *Formgeschichte*, or historical forms.

Careful, thorough study on the part of such scholars as James Orr *(Problem of the Old Testament)* and William Henry Green

(Unity of the Book of Genesis) convinced many Christians of the weakness and inapplicability of the theory to the Pentateuch. Their studies are exacting and difficult, but convincing and conclusive. There is no reason why an able man like Moses could not have written the first five books of the Bible. The subject matter of these books covers such differing fields and such a breadth of experience that the variety of expression and content found in them is only natural and appropriate. The mention of Moses' death at the end of the book of Deuteronomy, though it may appear strange, forms a necessary part of the Suzerain-vassal form of covenant revealed in that book. The Mosaic Covenant is sealed by the death of Moses, its representative testator, even as the New Covenant is sealed by the death of Christ (cf. Heb. 9:16-17).[3]

The attacks upon the New Testament can be easily understood by reading *The Gospel Before the Gospels* by Burton Scott Easton, in which a clear description is given of *Formgeschichte*, or "form criticism." A lucid straightforward analysis of the origin of the Synoptic Gospels and an answer to form criticism is to be found in Ned B. Stonehouse's *Origin of the Synoptic Gospels*. The writers of the original Gospels agree in their basic materials, and much can be gained by a study of the origin and use of the same, but each author writes the same story from a different viewpoint and in order to attain a different goal, and yet they all agree.

Study of Comparative Religion. The intense study of the religions of both the East and the West, plus that of the primitive religions, led to many books on comparative religion. The works of two men are of particular significance, namely, the book by Ernst Troeltsch and the symposium by Gerardus Van der Leeuw of Groningen, already mentioned.[4] Men tried to single out just what it is that makes Christianity unique. Troeltsch almost reached a dead end in this regard when he failed to find anything more significant than a deeper sense of morality. Van der Leeuw did reach the end when he found all the main concepts of Christianity in the primitive religions (the new birth, sacraments, myths, confirmation, etc.). One Dutchman, J. Vesdijk, in his book *De Toekomst der Religie (The Future of Religion)* prophesied a resurgence and return to Buddhism; and as shall be seen later, this appears to be happening both in the pandeism in Roman Catholicism and in the ontological theology of the Protestant theologian, Paul Tillich.

---

[3]Meredith G. Kline, *The Treaty of the Great King* (Grand Rapids: Wm. B. Eerdmans Publishing Co., 1963), p. 40.
[4]See p. 81.

Along with these attempts to compare Christianity with other religions, there arose a theory of a seven-step evolution of religion through dynamism, animism, fetishism, manism, totemism, polytheism and on to monotheism.

The theories of comparative religion fail to explain how it is possible that the most primitive tribes and religions still have concepts of the true God in their myths and worship of a "High God" or a "Sky God," who is loving, holy, perfect, and who never does any evil; a concept of creation, the flood and other biblical events. Further, these hypotheses cannot account for the advanced full-blown revelation of morals and of a holy, wise, just, loving God, as presented from the very beginnings of the race, in the book of Genesis. In no other place, in no other race than the Jewish, has such knowledge and wisdom appeared. From it alone have come the only other monotheistic religions, Christianity and Muhammadanism. Preconceived attitudes of criticism and negativity have prevented these critical students of religion from grasping the high moral tone and the sublimity of the religion of the Old Testament patriarchs and from seeing its continuity and progression and fulfillment in the New Testament and Christianity.

NEOORTHODOXY

Much of what has been said concerning liberalism also applies to neoorthodoxy. Two of the three mainstays of liberalism, evolution and higher criticism, remain. The view of miracles is essentially the same except that they are not simply regarded as ordinary events seen through consecrated eyes but as mythological ways of expressing ineffable (i.e., inexpressible) divine truth. Christ is the "raising the dead" Jesus and the "multiplying the loaves and fishes" Jesus for Emil Brunner. According to this Swiss theologian, Jesus never really raised the dead or multiplied the loaves and fishes, but this is the only way the early believers could express what Jesus meant to them. Miracles do at least teach and convey some meaning. They are no longer to be utterly ignored. They are instrumental.

However, there is a radical change. Man is no longer seen as simply progressing inevitably toward perfection. The social gospel has failed to show that man is a sinner. There is a renewed effort to analyze sin. World War I proved to the neoorthodox that liberalism was bankrupt. Man is entirely vile and a sinner. Every man commits "original sin" by repeating Adam's sin of pride. Brunner states, "I am Adam, you are Adam." God too is seen differently; He is not regarded any longer as immanent. He is wholly transcendent, *"totaliter aliter."* There is no direct line of communication open any longer between God and man. God must communicate with man by sovereign grace. Man must reach God by a "leap of faith," through believing the absurd, the contradictory, the paradoxical. Man does not find God by looking inside himself, by examining his feeling of utter dependence. Revelation is an event which occurs as man reads a Bible which is full of faults and errors. This fallible Bible becomes the very Word of God, in a "here and now" revelation, and a person receives Jesus Christ either as he reads the Bible or as he hears it in the gospel proclamation.

What were the causes of this entirely new approach to the Bible? There were mainly two: first, disillusionment concerning liberalism's social gospel because of the evil revealed in man by World War I; second, a Kierkegaardian existential approach to God and His relationship and self-revelation to man.

In order to understand the neoorthodox position, one has to look back at Sören Kierkegaard's philosophy of God and revelation, and in order to understand Kierkegaard, a person is required to go still further back to Kant.

God, for Kant, is timeless and spaceless. How did he come to this conclusion? Kant argued that only one Infinite can exist. However, if time and space are also infinite, then there are three. This appeared to him to be impossible. Therefore, he concluded, God is infinite but time and space are finite and confined to the physical creation.

If God and all eternal truth are timeless and spaceless, Kant reasoned that man cannot know God as he knows external objects and events. Man can assume He exists, he can postulate God, but he cannot prove He exists. The same can be said of the world and the soul. Yet in order to think things through and put things in order, man needs the three—the world, the soul and God. They are "regulative ideas" which enable man to make sense of things. With the concept of the world, one can unify the diversity of things which exist in the physical universe; with the idea of the soul, one can unify the phenomena of individual human experience; and with the concept of God, man can bring unity into these phenomena and all else that exists.

When such a view of God and of the knowledge of God is adopted, it is easy to see that He must be considered as totally different from man. He is *totaliter aliter.* Further, divine knowledge, heavenly truth, is also then entirely different from man's knowledge. In fact, man possesses no mental containers in which to receive eternal timeless and spaceless heavenly truth. There is then a complete disjunction between God and man. A towering wall exists between them. Kierkegaard developed the concept of this disjunction in revelation with his theory of "indirect communication." Man, he reasoned, can only receive, witness and record revelation in the form of symbol or myth.[5] Kierkegaard added the view of "original sin," already mentioned, which makes every man the inevitable originator of his own sin. Both these concepts—of revelation and of sin—are adopted by the neoorthodox. Barth, however, was the first to make the disjunction between God and man the basis of a whole theological system.

While the liberals failed by making God immanent and God and man continuous, the neoorthodox fail by making them wholly discontinuous and separated. No real knowledge of God is any longer possible. Propositional revelation, that form of revelation in which God speaks directly to man in the words of human language, is denied and excluded. Man's knowledge of God too is entirely subjective and can at best only be expressed in symbols, myths, sagas; because, while language represents something divine, it cannot possibly express it in intelligible terms.

The basis of the neoorthodox problem is twofold: the adoption of the first two mainstays of liberalism and the acceptance of Kant's mistaken view of time and space. The first has been considered, and now the second will be examined somewhat further.

It is not necessary, nor do some feel it is even sound thinking, to consider time and space to be created relations, created categories. If one defines time as the mere possibility of the relationship of before and after, that is, of sequence, and space as the mere possibility of a relationship between objects, then these two are not finite in nature at all. Certainly one can think of mathematics and counting without counting apples. A person can surely conceive of the mere possibility of counting countables. Mathematics is merely the means of measurement of time and space. And since it is theoretically and a priori possible, so also are time and space.

The biblical view of revelation reveals a God who is not limited by time—He is omniscient and omnipresent. Nor is He limited by space—He is omnipresent and omnipotent. What more does He

---

[5]Barth speaks of saga, rejecting myth as something which never happens, in contrast to saga, which records a truth that is repeatedly stated.

need than the three incommutable attributes of omniscience, omni-presence and omnipotence to distinguish Him from man! At the same time He can and does communicate with man through the gift of the languages which He Himself has given to man. Repeat-edly the Scriptures state, "Thus saith the Lord," "The Lord said" and "God said."

The neoorthodox maintain that they have entirely rejected the subjective idea of revelation presented by liberalism. Nevertheless, because of their denial of direct propositional revelation, their teach-ing that man receives revelation—even the Word of God which is Christ—as he reads a fallible Bible is itself an extreme form of subjectivism. Ineffable truth, truth which cannot be put even into the form of words, is the most subjective experience possible to man.

In neoorthodoxy faith and reason are entirely separated. By this is meant that while reason and the laws of reason are regarded as proper and applicable to all scientific and secular everyday knowl-edge and truth, they are considered inapplicable to religious and divine truth. Revealed truth must appear as absurd, contradictory and paradoxical because it can only be witnessed by man, cannot be received in time-space terms, and cannot be communicated in written Scripture. Faith is a leap, and it demands the acceptance of the absurd, the contradictory and the paradoxical.

This is of course just the opposite of what the Bible teaches. According to the Scriptures, faith is based upon reasonable evi-dence rather than acceptance of the absurd and a leap in the dark! Christ offers historical and biblical evidence when demanding faith in John 5: the witness of John the Baptist (vv. 33-35), His miracles (v. 36), the corroborating testimony of God the Father (vv. 37-38) and the prophecies of the Old Testament (v. 39). John says he has recorded the facts in his gospel in order "that ye might believe that Jesus is the Christ, the Son of God; and that believing ye might have life through his name" (John 20:31). Christ tells Thomas, "Reach hither thy finger, and behold my hands; and reach hither thy hand, and thrust it into my side: and be not faithless, but believing" (John 20:27). Faith and reason are united in these scriptures. And, if this is not enough, Christ maintains in John 8 that God can and is giving direct propositional revelation through Him, for He teaches what He has seen (v. 38), heard (v. 26) and been taught by the Father (v. 28). He states that except a person believes in Him on this basis, he cannot have eternal life. His view of revelation demands a grammatical-historical exegesis of the Bible and the admission of direct special revelation from God, in contrast to the neoorthodox philosophy of indirect communication.

BULTMANNISM

With the appearance of Rudolf Bultmann's *Theology of the New Testament*, an even more drastic approach was introduced to theology. Bultmann maintains that man in our present mechanized, scientific age can no longer accept the biblical ideas of a three-story universe and a heaven filled with angels and demons. He intends to produce a theology which can be accepted by existential man living in a scientific industrial age. At the same time he is convinced that Barth and the neoorthodox have not gone all the way with their theory of the dialectic between finite and infinite, temporal and eternal. Everything of value to be found in the Bible is myth. They have made the mistake of accepting much in Scripture as direct revelation. It is Bultmann's pride that he carries dialectical theology through to its full logical conclusion: all in Scripture is myth.

Bultmann has introduced the modern philosophy of existentialism into his theology. He is very much influenced by Heidegger with his view of the "mass man," the everyday man, who is merely acting like the machine. He teaches that man must transcend himself, he must cease to be mere *sarx*—the New Testament view of unregenerate man—and become *pneuma*, or spirit—the New Testament view of regenerate man.

There is a "life outside faith" which is characterized by sin, flesh and fear (anxiety and death). This is contrasted by a life of self-transcendence, a "life inside faith" which is characterized by freedom from sin, flesh and fear, and by openness to the forgiving grace of God. The "life inside faith" is true eschatological existence, even though it is not a possession such as a new nature but rather an experience based on a constantly renewed decision and obedience to God. And yet, as in Barth and neoothodoxy, this occurrence, this attainment to the authentic existence, spoken of by Heidegger, occurs only through an act of God that is brought about outside man. God is the originator of this authentic existence by His sovereign grace. The heart of the gospel is the secret of self-transcendence; it is going from the unauthentic existence of the "mass man" to the authentic one of the Christian.

Bultmann's view of the sayings of Christ falls far below Barth's concept. Time after time Bultmann speaks of the disciples and the gospel writers, putting words in the mouth of Jesus. At these points he returns to the position of liberalism.

In one other sense Bultmann claims originality. He teaches demythologization. This consists in detecting and interpreting myth in the Scriptures. Tillich also makes much of this concept. It follows as a necessary consequence out of the fact that man, according to Kant, has forced all truth into time-space categories. In demythologization these categories are to be removed so that the eternal truth can really appear.

The difference between Barth and Bultmann cannot be properly understood unless allowance is made for the fact that these two theologians have very different views of Christ. For Barth the true deity of Christ is not in question. Jesus is the Word of God, one of three *"Seinsweisen,"* or forms of being of God; and all of God is in Him as much as in the Father and in the Spirit. For Bultmann, Jesus, if He really existed historically at all, is just a man upon whose lips the disciples and the early church placed the greater part of His sayings. Barth can, because of his unitarian modalism, quite consistently use the words of Christ and quote them as the Word of God. This opens a way of direct communication between God and man, for him, which is entirely closed for Bultmann. Therefore Barth's "inconsistency"—in Bultmann's eyes—regarding revelation received from a *totaliter aliter* does have a certain justification.

This does not mean that the evangelical can wholeheartedly side with Barth at this point. The very fact that he rejects the ontological Trinity revealed in the Scriptures separates Barth from the orthodox by an uncrossable gulf. It raises all the main problems which adhere to unitarianism: a God who is less than man in His major relationships: subject-object, I-thou or personal encounter, and We-you or the social relationship—until He has a world and man—because Barth has a God who needs man to complete His full personalization.

Bultmann's consistent application of the dialectic seen between God and man, infinity and finitude, timelessness or eternity, and time or temporality, leads to an anthropological interpretation of man and his relationship to God and even of God Himself. There is no other place from which he can get a source of content for his myths. How can man find any interpretation for myths—if this is all the Bible offers—except by looking at himself? Myth cannot interpret myth. This new approach leads to anthropology rather than theology. There is no divine light from heaven shining through the Bible. The Bible reflects only man's autonomous or personal conclusions about God, and these conclusions man bases on his own experiences and finds within his own mind.

If the historical Christ is vague in Barth, in Bultmann both His historicity and His deity have vanished. The sole importance of Christ is His exemplification of transcendence. The end of the trail in the denial of both the divine personage and the historicity of Christ has been reached with Bultmannism, and theology must now either return to a reconstruction of the historical Christ and the admission of direct communication and revelation from God to man or simply cease to exist.

AMERICAN REALISM

While Karl Barth insisted upon the complete transcendence of God, his early colleague Emil Brunner was not ready to go so far. Brunner saw at least one point of contact between God and man, namely, general revelation. This modifies the antithesis between time and eternity. The image of God in man is not so completely destroyed by the fall that he cannot grasp some natural theology through God's self-revelation in creation. Reinhold Niebuhr agrees with Brunner in this regard but wants to extend the point of contact between God and man much further. Man is a sinner but not a total sinner as Barth says; otherwise how can he know he is a sinner at all? God is transcendent but not "wholly other"; otherwise how can He reveal Himself to man? Revelation is an offense to reason, but not a total offense; otherwise how can man ever recognize the truth in it? God's law is above anything man can attempt or accomplish but not wholly so; otherwise how can man distinguish right from wrong, and the voice of God from that of the devil? The theology of Reinhold Niebuhr can well be called American realism. It refuses both to accept the neoorthodox disjunction in its entirety and to reject the possibility of doing something with life as it finds it. Niebuhr's theology distinguishes itself from Bultmannism in its decision to make a synthesis between the Kierkegaardian disjunction—the discontinuity between time and eternity insofar as this discontinuity applies to man's ability to know, that is, to epistemology—and life as it finds it. Bultmannism, on the other hand, made a synthesis between the absolute disjunction and the philosophy of existentialism per se, that is, in itself. Bultmannism accepts Kierkegaard's problems of communication between God and man and applies them to realism, namely, to the fact that man is able to think (rational), does know good from evil (moral), has difficulties knowing God, and still has some knowledge concerning Him.

Niebuhr's realism leads him to face very squarely the fact that man, as composed of body and soul, lives in two environments, the physical and the spiritual, and experiences two worlds, that of time and that of eternity. As a result, science and practical living in time must have their places along with revelation and a regard for the demands of eternity. There is a fluid coupling between time and eternity for Niebuhr. They cannot be mixed nor can one absorb the other. Sin is that condition in which man remains in anxiety over mediating eternity in time, either because man wants to transcend himself but cannot, or does not want to and therefore cannot. Salvation is the mediation of eternity in time.

This view certainly does not apply the theory of the disjunction between time and eternity as consistently as neoorthodoxy. It admits some possibility of communication between God and man, at least to the extent that it maintains there is evidence of common ground; but having already assumed discontinuity between heaven and earth, it cannot explain how man actually receives a revelation from God that has any real meaning. Whatever meaning Niebuhr may claim to give to the Bible is inconsistent to the extent it rests upon the assumption that some of what the Bible says is sufficiently direct to be understood, even if the rest is myth.

ONTOLOGICAL THEOLOGY

The ontological theology of Paul Tillich (1886-1965) could well prove to be the most significant movement of the twentieth century. In many ways it is the most difficult of all, even if, at the same time, it is the most thoroughly worked out and consistent. It rests upon a complete philosophical system, or perhaps one should say a systematic synthesis of several systems, developed into an ontological explanation of God, the world and man.

While Tillich maintained that he did not produce a *Summa Theologica*, perhaps he came closer to doing so than any man since Thomas Aquinas. Philosophy, anthropology, psychology and comparative religion all have a place in his theology. From each of these he winnowed the views of many thinkers and combined them, after a searching analysis and correction, into one new system.

Evolution plays a large part in Tillich's views. He adopted Aristotle's view of evolutionary progression from the inorganic through organic, sentient life, up to spirit, and on up to the new being. To this he added, however, Hegel's view of a triadically developing God with Being as the thesis, Nonbeing as the antithesis, and Power of Being as synthesis. God as Power of Being, however, has both creative and destructive elements or inclinations which need to be resolved in another triad. Power of Being as synthesis of the first triad, therefore, becomes the First Principle in "the Trinity," and the thesis of a triad in which the *Logos* is the Second Principle and Spirit is the Third Principle. The Spirit is creative and from it flows all that exists. From this point on, Tillich appeared to switch to Aristotle, though shadows of Hegel's triadic thinking appear in his theory of dialectical movements, which climb from pure matter stepwise to the new being.

Such a system must lead to a form of pantheism similar to Hegel's. Tillich revealed this in his view that the Power of Being is present in everything that exists, whether it is a stone, a person or even a word.

Jesus Christ is just a man, but a man who denied all of self—His words, His works and His commands—and became entirely transparent to the divine. In this lucid state He received into Himself the "God-man," a force composed of the *Logos* united with essential being—what man ought to be and is in the mind of "God"—to become Jesus who is the Christ. Christ mediated the New Being completely and is an example to man of how he can have the New Being and salvation. Christ is unique in the sense that He was the first to attain to such a condition, but according to Tillich He is not the only one.

If and after a man has become "new being," he will at death return to Being-itself or the Power of Being. A man could possibly sink into Nonbeing and become lost, but the gate is so wide and the conditions so lax—merely to be concerned with the ultimate or to have ultimate concern—that to all intents, salvation is universal.

When he described revelation, Tillich drew upon all of the concepts of Kierkegaard; the disjunction, indirect communication, symbol, myth (and demythologization) are all parts of his theory. But he added a new source of revelation, a depth found in man which he called the "depth of reason." It appears in works of art, such as painting and sculpture.

Tillich, as already mentioned, taught that one can observe a steady evolution in religion. Each stage of this evolution expresses elements of truth and is therefore significant. Theological doctrines also progress or evolve for Tillich. Each expression, such as justification by faith for Luther, predestination for Calvin, the synoptic

Jesus for modern Protestantism, followed by the Kingdom of God, is right for its time but becomes obsolete as another age takes its place.

What can be said of such a system? It certainly endeavors to assimilate into one whole the main points of every other theological system. Liberalism contributes immanence; neoorthodoxy, the disjunction present in revelation; and Bultmannism, demythologization. The different philosophical systems too are made to contribute their parts: Hegelianism supplies the view of God's inner development; Aristotelianism, the theory of organic evolution; Kierkegaardian existentialism, the Kantian view of God and knowledge of God; existentialism the insistence upon making man the starting point as much as Being or God.

In doing all of this, however, ontological theology has gone even further astray than liberalism and neoorthodoxy in that it has not only lost direct propositional revelation but also any personal God. Being is not an object or a person and does not exist, yet it permeates all. There is no God to whom to pray. Eternal life or heaven is merely a return to the bosom of Being, the Plotinic All, the Buddhist Nirvana.

THE NEW THEOLOGY, ALSO CALLED RADICAL THEOLOGY OR THE GOD-IS-DEAD MOVEMENT

This latest development in theology is largely an American phenomenon or event. It is new in that, though it has developed out of the preceding movements mentioned, it has gone beyond them to declare that the God presented in the Old Testament is now a thing of the past and dead. It is radical in that it urges extremely revolutionary theological ideas and social actions.

The roots of the new theology are to be found in the historical and philosophical struggles which occurred because of Kant's mistaken theory of knowledge concerning God and Hegel's synthesis of good and evil through dialectical triads in which good and evil, as thesis and antithesis, were synthesized, or united, to form progressive solutions, each of which in turn proved to be ambiguous and dissolved into a new triad.

Three things in particular characterize the new theologians. First, they are men who are dissatisfied with the conclusions of their immediate predecessors. Finding no place for social action in Karl Barth they make social action all-important. Seeing Bultmann using Christ as merely the basis for an existential decision, they claim to restore Him to a place of supreme importance by teaching that

Christ has become united with fallen man in the form of universal humanity. Christ is to be seen in every human face and felt in every human hand. They make much of Bonhoeffer's concept that man has reached maturity, as seen in the fact that he can solve all of his problems by science and the scientific method.

Second, these radical theologians continue in the train of the Hegelian dialectic as it pertains to good and evil. Good and evil are not seen, by them, as being self-exclusive but as synthetized, united, whenever moral decisions are based upon love. This explains the philosophical nature of situation ethics, as decisions to break the laws of God are justified when made in love. Euthanasia is permissible if it is called for by love.

Third, the problem which the God-is-dead theologians are struggling with and trying to solve is "How can man be really free?" Since freedom is a question which we all must face, their search is not something which is wrong in itself. It is their answer which is wrong. How to have total freedom was the problem faced originally by Adam and Eve in the Garden of Eden. Satan urged them to seek it by rebelling against the restraints of God's revealed will, in contrast to accepting the freedom offered within the confines of a holy law which revealed the very character of God. Undoubtedly the positive law of loving God and one's neighbor had been given to Adam and Eve (cf. Matt. 22:36-40; Rom. 13:8-10).

Friedrich Nietzsche, who can be called the father of the God-is-dead theologians, was obsessed with the question of freedom, absolute arbitrary freedom, for himself and for man. Because such lawless freedom led to the deepest of sin, he could not bear to have God looking into his "dirtiest corners"; therefore he murdered God through his writings. Then he cried, "God is dead!" and went on to present the idea of the superman who would live "beyond good and evil."

The new theologians have different ways of expressing and explaining "the death of god." Paul Tillich, who greatly influenced such men as Thomas J. J. Altizer and William Hamilton, only urged that the name of God be dropped for a generation until men could adopt a new concept of God. Tillich spoke of the "God beyond God" who, while absent, is still present as the power of being in everything that exists. Bishop John Robinson aired the same view in his *Honest to God*. Altizer knew Tillich and his view, but returned to Nietzsche through the Hegelian triadic dialectic. He says that God has died over and over again—even in our day—to appear in constantly new epiphanies. Through his last triadic development God has become "The Great Humanity Divine." William Hamilton though, like Bonhoeffer, with increasing uncertainty, only sees God as having withdrawn Himself to reappear at a later time. Paul Van Buren applies linguistic analysis and argues that the word *God* is contentless and meaningless and that therefore we must say that God is dead.

What is it that holds men of such varying opinions together? They are united on eight points: (1) All demand total arbitrary freedom for man. (2) They hold an optimism that the new theology can lead man to this freedom. (3) All place stress upon the need for social action. The Christian is to go into the secular city (taking no eternal norms with him since this is to be secular Christianity) and help the people there work out their problems—whether ethnic, social, economic or political—pragmatically, that is, on the basis of functionalism, namely, finding out what works. (4) Revolutionary activism is the ideal of the movement as seen in such things as freedom marches and rental strikes. (5) The movement is aware that the church has failed to reach secular man where he is. From this flows the next point. (6) The new theologians insist on the secularization of man. Man can now meet all his needs without God's help. This he has learned from science. Therefore Christianity must meet man on the secular plane. (7) Ethical decisions are to be made on the basis of each particular situation. This is what is called situation ethics. The seventh commandment, "Thou shalt not commit adultery," does not hold, or any other for that matter, when love overrules it! (8) The God of the Old Testament, who is absolutely holy and changeless, has ceased to exist—has died—and in His place we have a Christ who has now become universal humanity.

The answer to this movement entails a thorough study of the place of the law of God, both the physical and the moral law, in relation to the attainment of the fullest true freedom for man. When man lives within the physical laws of the universe, and uses these laws effectively, he experiences the blessings made possible by modern twentieth century progress. Only as he lives within the sphere of "the perfect law of liberty," which encompasses the Ten Commandments (James 1:25; 2:10-12), will man know the blessings of spiritual and moral freedom. Life can be beautiful and wonderful when it is lived in freedom from guilt and from the bondage of sin. Of course, since man is fallen to begin with, he must be saved through the substitutionary work of Christ as his Redeemer from sin, if he is to know freedom in its eternal dimensions. And yet, through God's common grace, all who live within the sphere of the moral laws of God do enjoy particular blessings, apart from salvation, until their death. After that, common grace can no longer help the unsaved.

Functionalism does have its place in the discovery of methods for the organization of social groups and unions, for instance; but it should go hand in hand with the tenets of God's revealed moral law. It cannot give the guidelines needed for ethical decisions without the help of the moral principles revealed in the Bible.

CONCLUSION

It is clear from the above outline of the course of theology since 1900 that there has been no improvement in the theological situation, no real reversal of the trend first to modernism, then to neoorthodoxy, and finally to thanatology (the death of God), and no return to orthodoxy. The devastating work of the early liberals has continued its effects in neoorthodoxy; the effects of Bultmannism are seen in Tillich's ontological synthesis; the tenets of Hegel and Nietzsche are mirrored in the new theology. The attempt of the neoorthodox to present a Kierkegaardian theory of revelation has failed to bring theology back to an improved view of the Bible since it denies all propositional revelation. Tillich's grand synthesis of theologies and philosophies has proven even more bankrupt. He lost prayer, a personal God and a future life. With their new theology the radical theologians have done away with the God of the Bible and substituted a Christ united fully with fallen humanity.

A return to the Bible can alone offer the answers. The Scriptures reveal a God who can communicate with man. They present a personal God who can offer a sufficient redemption for fallen man, followed by fellowship through prayer. They tell us of a God who is moral and holy and who can therefore show man the way to a true freedom gained by following and living according to the revelation of His character as given in the promulgation of the Word of God.

FOR FURTHER READING

General

EASTON, BURTON SCOTT. *The Gospel Before the Gospels.* New York: Charles Scribner & Sons, 1928.

FLINT, ROBERT. *Agnosticism.* New York: Charles Scribner & Sons, 1903, pp. 171-206. An analysis of Immanuel Kant.

MACKINTOSH, HUGO ROSS. *Types of Modern Theology: Schleiermacher to Barth.* London: Nisbet & Co., Ltd., 1954.

ORR, JAMES. *The Problem of the Old Testament.* New York: Charles Scribner & Sons, 1931.

SCHMIDT, WILHELM. *The Origin and Growth of Religion.* New York: Dial Press, 1935.

SOPHER, DAVID WESLEY. *Major Voices in American Theology.* Philadelphia: Westminster Press, 1953.

VAN DER LEEUW, G. *De Godsdiensten Der Wereld.* Amsterdam, Holland: Meulenhoff, 1948.

VAN TIL, CORNELIUS. *The New Modernism.* Philadelphia: Presbyterian & Reformed Publishing Co., 1947.

Neoorthodoxy

Neoorthodox Theologians:
KARL BARTH:
BARTH, KARL. *Church Dogmatics.* 8 vols. London: T. & T. Clark, 1962.

————. *Epistle to the Romans.* London: Oxford University Press, 1933.

————. *Dogmatics in Outline.* New York: Philosophical Library, n.d.

AN ANALYSIS OF KARL BARTH:
CLARK, GORDON. *Karl Barth's Theological Method.* Nutley, N. J.: Presbyterian & Reformed Publishing Co., 1963.

KLOOSTER, FRED H. *Significance of Barth's Theology.* Grand Rapids: Baker Book House, 1962.

RUNIA, KLAAS. *Barth's Doctrine of Holy Scripture.* Grand Rapids: Wm. B. Eerdmans Publishing Co., 1961.

VAN TIL, CORNELIUS. *Barth and Evangelicalism.* Nutley, N. J.: Presbyterian & Reformed Publishing Co., 1964.

————. *Barth's Christology.* Nutley, N. J.: Presbyterian & Reformed Publishing Co., 1964.

————. *Christianity and Barthianism.* Nutley, N. J.: Presbyterian and Reformed Publishing Co., 1960.

EMIL BRUNNER:
BRUNNER, H. EMIL. *Man in Revolt.* Philadelphia: Westminster Press, 1947.

————. *Revelation and Reason.* Philadelphia: Westminster Press, 1946.

————. *The Mediator.* Philadelphia: Westminster Press, 1947.

AN ANALYSIS OF EMIL BRUNNER:
JEWETT, PAUL KING. *Emil Brunner.* Chicago: Inter-Varsity Press, 1961.

RUDOLF BULTMANN:

BULTMANN, RUDOLF. *Theology of the New Testament*. Translated by Kendrick Grobel. New York: Charles Scribner's Sons, Vol. I, 1951; Vol. II, 1955.

AN ANALYSIS OF RUDOLF BULTMANN:

HUGHES, PHILIP E. *Creative Minds in Contemporary Theology*. Grand Rapids: Wm. B. Eerdmans Publishing Co., 1966.

PAUL TILLICH:

TILLICH, PAUL. *Systematic Theology*. Chicago: University of Chicago Press, Vol. I, 1951; Vol. II, 1957; Vol. III, 1963.

————. *The Courage to Be*. New Haven: Yale University Press, 1952.

AN ANALYSIS OF PAUL TILLICH:

FREEMAN, DAVID. *Modern Thinkers: Tillich*. Nutley, N. J.: Presbyterian & Reformed Publishing Co., 1962.

————. *Recent Studies in Theology and Philosophy*. Nutley, N. J.: Presbyterian & Reformed Publishing Co., 1962.

KILLEN, ROBERT ALLAN. *The Ontological Theology of Paul Tillich*. Kampen, Netherlands: J. H. Kok, 1956.

MCKELWAY, ALEXANDER J. *Systematic Theology of Paul Tillich: A Review and Analysis*. Richmond: John Knox Press, 1964.

TAVARD, GEORGE H. *Paul Tillich and the Christian Message*. New York: Charles Scribner's Sons, 1961.

THOMAS, J. HEYWOOD. *Paul Tillich: An Appraisal*. Philadelphia: Westminster Press, 1963.

GENERAL ANALYSIS OF MODERN THEOLOGY:

FREEMAN, DAVID. *Recent Studies in Theology and Philosophy*. Nutley, N. J.: Presbyterian & Reformed Publishing Co., 1962.

HUGHES, PHILIP E. *Creative Minds in Contemporary Theology*. Grand Rapids: Wm. B. Eerdmans Publishing Co., 1966.

RAMM, BERNARD. *Handbook of Contemporary Theology*. Grand Rapids: Wm. B. Eerdmans Publishing Co., 1966.

The New Theology

God-is-dead Theologians:

ALTIZER, THOMAS J. J. *The Gospel of Christian Atheism*. Philadelphia: Westminster Press, 1963.

ALTIZER, T. J. J., and HAMILTON, W. *Radical Theology and the Death of God*. Indianapolis: Bobbs-Merrill Co., Inc., 1966.

BONHOEFFER, DIETRICH. *Letters and Papers from Prison*. New York: Macmillan Co., 1962.

COX, HARVEY. *The Secular City*. New York: Macmillan Co., 1965.

FLETCHER, JOSEPH. *Situation Ethics: The New Morality*. New York: Macmillan Co., 1966.

HAMILTON, WILLIAM. *The New Essence of Christianity*. New York: Association Press, 1961.

VAHANIAN, GABRIEL. *The Death of God*. New York: George Braziller, Inc., 1961.

VAN BUREN, PAUL. *The Secular Meaning of the Gospel*. New York: Macmillan Co., 1963.

ANALYSIS AND REFUTATION OF THE NEW THEOLOGY:

GIROD, GORDON H. *God Is Not Dead*. Grand Rapids: Baker Book House, 1966.

HAMILTON, KENNETH. *God Is Dead*. Grand Rapids: Wm. B. Eerdmans Publishing Co., 1966.

MONTGOMERY, JOHN W. *The "Is God Dead?" Controversy*. Grand Rapids: Zondervan Publishing House, 1966.

OGLETREE, THOMAS W. *The Death of God Controversy*. Nashville: Abingdon Press, 1966.

RAMM, BERNARD, *et al*. *Is God "Dead"?* Grand Rapids: Zondervan Publishing House, 1966.

WOLFF, RICHARD. *Is God Dead?* Wheaton, Ill.: Tyndale House, Publishers, 1966.

EDUCATION

Cornelius Jaarsma

Cornelius Jaarsma is a late professor of education at Calvin College. Previously teaching posts were held at Montclair Teachers College, Slippery Rock Teachers College, Taylor University and Wheaton College. He received the A. B., A. M. and Ph. D. degrees from New York University. In addition to numerous articles, he authored *Educational Philosophy of Herman Bavinck, Fundamentals in Christian Education,* and *Human Learning, Growth and Development.*

5

EDUCATION

Cornelius Jaarsma

T HE FUNDAMENTAL REASON why children do not act right is because
they do not have the conditions for right action." This quotation
from Francis W. Parker, educator of the latter part of the nineteenth
century, opens a chapter on discipline in a book written for pros-
pective secondary school teachers.[1] The authors of this book, Schorling and Batchelder, state the significance this quotation has for
them in their view of education:

> It is probably the most important sentence in this book.[2] Parker's
> idealistic guide will tend to transform depressing episodes into
> challenging problems that you can attack with professional zest
> and handle with necessary objectivity. Do you accept it as
> the cornerstone in the structure of your educational philosophy?
> We urge you to hold on to this idealistic statement whatever may
> happen in the turbulent exigencies of classroom situations. With-
> out it a lifetime devoted to teaching is not likely to yield the
> greatest satisfactions, for you would be sailing the pedagogical
> sea without a true compass.

Can a Christian sail the "pedagogical sea" with this compass in
the confidence that it is reliable because it is true? Is it the "cornerstone" in the structure of his educational philosophy?

This statement by Schorling and Batchelder is quite representative of current thought and practice in education. To say that it is
representative does not mean that upon close examination one would

---

[1]Raleigh Schorling and Howard T. Batchelder, *Student Teaching in Secondary Schools* (New York: McGraw-Hill Book Co., 1956), p. 90.
[2]In addition to discipline, the authors discuss pupil study, curriculum, methodology and professional development of the teacher.

not find differences of conceptual articulation and of emphases in practice. Quite to the contrary, there is considerable debate on educational issues today among those who in substance subscribe to the Parker dictum. The Christian, however, finds no place in the Parker pronouncement for the reality of sin, redemption, regeneration, and call to holiness as revealed in the Scriptures. The denial of these basic doctrines of the Christian faith is common to all current theory and practice in education, despite the differences among men who hold to the Parker statement.[3]

A survey of educational theory during the past generation or two discloses some interesting developments which a Christian should not ignore in his interpretation of education today. As long as philosophical dualism or theological dichotomy of two distinct substances (mind and body or soul and body) prevailed in psychology, education was understood to be some kind of shaping, forming, structuring or training of the mind or soul as entity. The shaping or structuring was thought to be accomplished by exercising the faculties or powers of the mind or soul. What throughout the centuries had become known as liberal education consisted of a selection and structuring of subject matter which was thought to be inherently appropriate to the process of forming the mind or soul. When toward the close of the nineteenth century philosophical dualism gave way in psychology to a functionalism and behaviorism, concepts of education began to change accordingly. A developmental concept of mind and education began to prevail. Education came to be viewed increasingly as a growth and development process which has its analogy in plant and animal life. In the thinking of some students of education the structuring and patterning of the nervous system became the focal point in learning and teaching. At the same time others understood education in more organismic terms, as a process of the whole organism in its growth and development from infancy to maturity. When in later studies psychology began to speak more in terms of personality change and personality adjustment, education turned its attention increasingly to the shaping, structuring or forming of the whole person. Of late there has been a reaction to the wholeness concept in education (especially since Russian space achievements) by those who think that the intellectual area of human personality has been subordinated to an adjustment theory that tends to level all human productivity to a common mediocrity. A cry has arisen, calling for a rescue of the schools from current

---

[3]Cf. J. Donald Butler, *Four Philosophies of Education* (New York: Harper & Bros. Publishers, 1957).

"wastelands" to a restored or new excellence,[4] a return to fundamentals in subject matter. Under the impact of current philosophies
which view man as engaged in a titanic struggle, not merely for survival but to create meaning for himself in what is in itself a meaningless reality, the educative process has come to be understood increasingly as getting meaning from and giving meaning to experiences
in all situations.[5] The "new mathematics," the "new biology," and
the "new approach in social studies" that one reads and hears about
today have their inspiration in part in this development in philosophy.

What can a Christian student of education say in the middle of
these changing concepts of the past half century? If he is a discerning student of the history of education, he will recognize that
theory and practice in education early in the history of western
civilization and throughout the Middle Ages were a deduction from
the premise of a philosophical dualism of mind and body. Educational
reformers like Quintilian (A.D. 35?-95), Comenius (1592-1670),
Pestalozzi (1746-1827), Froebel (1782-1852), and Herbart (1776-
1841) demonstrated insights in education without the benefits of
scientific studies of more recent vintage in child development and
learning. Only very recently, and then often hesitatingly, Christian
education has begun to break through restraining influences of earlier
philosophies. It is one thing, however, to recognize that a Christian
view of education must deliver itself from limiting concepts of the
past; it is quite another to view education aright when one views
man vertically, a spiritual, heavenly being, not merely horizontally
or structurally continuous with the world of nature. Anthropological,
psychological and sociological studies have transformed the understanding of man to such a degree that a Christian student of education returns to the Scriptures with new insights gained. In the spirit
of Psalm 36:9, "In thy light shall we see light," he asks with new
urgency, "What, then, is man?" In the language of John Calvin,
he puts on the glasses of revealed truth in the Scriptures to examine
facts and principles of these sciences for lines of thought that he can
follow. Answers will not be readily forthcoming. To be dogmatic and
doctrinaire will be to obscure his vision. Light is available to him
who will walk in the Light. Christians are called to be humble seekers
for truth in the light of the Truth. In this seeking too God pleases

---

[4]Cf. John W. Gardner, *Excellence* (New York: Harper & Bros. Publishers,
1961); Max Rafferty, *Suffer Little Children* (New York: Devin-Adair Co.,
1962).
[5]Cf. George F. Kneller, *Existentialism in Education* (New York: Philosophical Library, Inc., 1958).

to work in and through His own if they acknowledge Him in all the details of their lives.

This chapter will be devoted to this very subject, namely, seeking clearer insight into a Christian view of education.

CRITERIA FOR DETERMINING
A CHRISTIAN VIEW OF EDUCATION

Universality of sin. Reference was made earlier to the reality of sin as the mark of distinction between current thinking in education and that of the Christian. This was not a reference to sin merely in terms of the doctrine of total depravity which educational theory and practice of early New England days seemed to make a central and controlling concern. Nevertheless, the sin question looms large in a Christian's thinking about education. The Scriptures teach clearly that men are conceived and born in sin and are by nature "children of wrath." Wrongdoing common to all can be understood only in light of this revelation about man. The non-Christian may scorn this revealed truth, but this does not alter its reality. The Christian recognizes sin for what it is and takes it into account in seeking to understand and to control the ways of men. A Christian's theory and practice in education are affected fundamentally by what God has said about sin, what He has done and is doing about it, and how He will ultimately resolve it. The fundamental reason (not the only reason) children do not act right is because, as members of the human race, they too are sinners. No statement is more anathema to the modern mind in education than this assertion.

The sin question is at the very root of the human predicament and points to the very nature of man. Man is the kind of being who can sin, that is, deny the very purpose of his being by disowning his origin and purpose. By disobedience to God's clear command, man voluntarily estranged himself from God as the very ground and source of his well-being. Created in God's image, given a clear mandate by his Creator, namely, to function as vice-regent over all God had created, conscious of a clear choice of alternatives and the consequences of these alternatives, man voluntarily chose the way of self-fulfillment independent of God. Ever since this tragedy, man as a Godlike being estranged from God has been groping for understanding and control which he had all but lost. He remains educable because he is man, but basically he needs transformation and restoration by divine invasion of his very being if education is to accomplish anything truly meaningful in him as man.

At the very dawn of human history God promised transformation and restoration by what He would later accomplish in the suffering, death and resurrection of His Son, Jesus Christ. The penitent sinner can have redemption full and free (grace) in Christ by faith through commitment to God.

Organic unity of the human race. The fact of sin points to another truth concerning man clearly taught in the Scriptures, namely, the organic unity of the human race and a corresponding unity of the individual person. Sin became man's lot universally and affected the whole person in all dimensions of his being. Redemption is also organic in effect because it restores man by faith to organic unity in Christ and redeems the whole man in resurrection. A Christian view of education, therefore, has at its very center the transformation and restoration of the person estranged from God.

Man's responsibility to God. At least one more criterion determining a Christian view of education should be added. Man as made in the image of God was given a clear mandate. God commanded him to take charge of the creation that He had declared good. A great stewardship became man's privilege and responsibility. The urge for understanding and control of the subhuman creation inherent in man by creation is evident throughout human history. But man, being fractured in the totality of his person, has in the crossroads of human endeavor tried to make his own way. Despite his amazing accomplishments, he gives all the evidence of groping rather than being able to read the road signs. A Christian view of education, on the other hand, takes into account God's original charge which has been called man's cultural mandate, and affirms that in Christ as Lord of all, this mandate takes on new significance for the Christian.

MEANING OF EDUCATION

With the forenamed criteria clearly in mind, the next consideration will be the meaning of the education concept. Education has been variously defined depending largely on how one views the educand, the one to be educated. As long as the educand was viewed as dichotomy, a two-substance being, education was understood to refer to a filling, training or disciplining of the mind. When functionalism and behaviorism in psychology replaced a dichotomous view of the educand, education came to be thought of more as a patterning of the organism to function successfully in a given environment. When more recently the wholeness of the person in interpersonal and environmental relations gained prominence, education was defined more in terms of shaping or forming of personality.

One should be grateful to such sciences as biology, psychology and sociology for having delivered society from dichotomies and dualisms that kept man from developing a philosophy of education more in harmony with the scripturally oriented view of man. But one cannot follow these sciences in their failure to recognize the nature of man in the vertical dimension of his being. The criteria for a view of education grounded in the Scriptures call for another concept.

How shall education be defined in keeping with the criteria mentioned? For practical and functional purposes one may say that education is the process of bringing about changes in the behavior of free, self-directing persons that enable them to exercise their potentials in an integrated way to the fullest degree possible. This definition takes account of the organic wholeness of the person as a dynamic, self-acting being, free and responsible. The changes referred to cannot make one a Christian. Only a supernatural, divine invasion of the person, known in theology as regeneration, can accomplish this basic reorientation.

THE PROCESS OF EDUCATION

Nurture. In a limited sense education has its analogy in the development of plants and animals. Education is a development process. The person is an organism, and by interaction with and nourishment from the environment he maintains and unfolds himself in his potentials. Education is nurture.

As the potentials of a tulip bulb and those of a bird dog can be spelled out, so can the potentials of a person as human being. Likewise as the unfolding of the potentials of a tulip and of a bird dog involve their total structure, so is the total structure of a person involved in the unfolding of his potentials as human being. In another work[6] the writer has described the potentials of the person as human being in these terms: rationality, morality, sociality, aesthetic sensitivity, freedom and responsibility. These are the distinctive qualities of man as made in the image of God. Subhuman organisms share none of these qualities which involve an ego, I, or self-identification capacity unique in man. These qualities make the use of the concepts of sin, redemption, regeneration, justification, sanctification and glorification relevant to human experience.

[6]See Cornelius Jaarsma, *Human Development, Learning, and Teaching* (Grand Rapids: Wm. B. Eerdmans Publishing Co., 1961), pp. 66-68.

Fruition. As these distinctively human qualities come to fruition through the developmental process of the person, he is being or becoming educated. Such fruition, however, is more than the result of a developmental process as observed in subhuman organisms. It is the result of a self-directing striving for fulfillment of Godlike qualities inherent in a personal being. In a subhuman organism the nurturing environment makes possible the unfolding process of the organism which produces the realization of its potentials. The person, however, becomes capable of seeking, selecting, organizing and controlling his environment for the purpose of self-fulfillment. Education as a process involves this self-directing, purposeful effort of the person. Therefore "training" and "education" are not synonymous terms. A bird dog is trained by the channeling or canalizing of his behavior toward a given end of which the organism is capable. A person is being educated when he develops the unique, distinctive qualities of his being. As organism the person is subject to training, but training is educative only to the degree that it facilitates genuine self-fulfillment of the person.

The educative process, then, should not be thought of in terms of receiving something or giving something. Rather should it be thought of in terms of achievement by the person. The changes man attempts to effect in a person become educative as they contribute to the fulfillment of the unique, distinctive qualities of the educand's being.

Though education is a developmental process, the development concept that became characteristic of educational theory during the nineteenth century and was known as developmentalism cannot adequately portray a Christian's view of education. In the developmental process of the person, the unique, distinctive qualities of the Godlike being come to fulfillment. The person is achieving the shaping or forming of his personality when in self-expression these qualities come to fruition.

When one understands the educative process as here stated, the inadequacy of the quotation from Francis W. Parker at the beginning of this chapter is evident. Not conditions for right or wrong action constitute the fundamental reason for right or wrong conduct, but the person understood as a Godlike being (religious being) in his estrangement from God.

How does a Christian view of education—the shaping or forming of a personality as religious being—affect one's view of the school, the curriculum, discipline in the classroom, and what is generally known as religious education? These crucial issues in modern education will be discussed next.

The School

The modern school, elementary and comprehensive secondary, as known in the United States, is essentially an innovation of the past hundred years. Until a century ago elementary schools were largely private and locally supported institutions for instruction in the basic tools of learning known as the three R's (reading, 'riting, and 'rithmetic). Secondary schools were almost entirely structured to prepare students for college or university levels of learning. Both elementary and secondary schools of today function as agencies of the state that provide universal educational opportunity consonant with demands made upon citizens in a democratic society. Private and parochial efforts are legally permitted, and lately they have increased because religious issues with reference to education in public schools have become a matter of concern to many citizens. But these efforts must compete instructionally with public schools to survive. Whether private and parochial schools should share in tax money raised for public schools is becoming a hotly debated issue. Elementary and secondary schools, whether public, private or parochial, are by consensus regarded as social institutions that seek to orient youth in our democratic society.

A Christian recognizes that as a citizen in a pluralistic,[7] democratic society he is obligated to promote schools that seek intelligent participation of youth in a free, self-governing society. Whether he can be satisfied with the instructional program of the public school for his children is another matter. A parent committed to Christ as Saviour and Lord cannot escape this issue.[8] He is forced to face this question: What is a Christian view of the modern school?

For an answer to the question the parent needs a Christian view of education similar to that which has been explained. The Christian recognizes that the school as a social institution organized for educational purposes is a necessity in the current social order. The school provides the youth orientation to our culture, an orientation a Christian also needs in order to function as Christian in the modern world. A Christian recognizes that he is responsible to God for the education of his children. There is no adequate substitute for the modern school in the task of the orientation of youth to the cultural advancement of modern times. The Christian parent must

---

[7]"Pluralistic" here refers to variations in religious views.

[8]Cf. Frank E. Gabelein, *Christian Education in a Democracy* (New York: Oxford University Press, 1951); Edward K. Worrell, *Restoring God to Education* (Wheaton, Ill.: Van Kampen Press, 1950).

also look to the school for an instructional program that provides the educative process described earlier.

What instructional program does the task of orientation require? It demands a curriculum that is consonant with a Christian's view of culture.

The Curriculum

What is a Christian view of culture? Culture consists of what has been produced by human ingenuity and effort through the centuries. Man has worked with God's creation and providence to produce that which he can use and enjoy. This creative capacity, divinely given him as Godlike being, lay fractured after his estrangement from God through the fall. Man's ingenuity produced human language, social institutions and organizations, economic systems, means of transportation and communication, systems and bodies of learning and knowledge. In the cultural endeavor of man, God has not left Himself without witness. God works in and through man by His providence. The terms "common grace" and "general revelation" have been used to designate this work of God in and through man. To the unbeliever, unenlightened by the Word of God through the work of the Holy Spirit, the cultural product represents the fruit of an indigenous potential in man as an organism continuous with nature, or as representative of a divine immanence. The Christian, restored to his original relationship to God in the redemptive work of Christ, recognizes the Creator at work to accomplish His purpose according to His revealed will in the Word of God.

A Christian view of culture calls for a curriculum, a program of instruction in the school, consonant with it. What can constitute such a curriculum? A curriculum of any elementary and secondary school consists of the organization of culture for effective learning with the purpose of having young people develop to maturity. For a beginner the organization of that which is to be learned is very general in the sense that there is very little differentiation among facts and principles in terms of specific studies such as science, mathematics and history. As learners advance, facts and principles are increasingly differentiated in terms of specific subjects. For example, the growing of plants in the classroom window box of a first grade becomes elementary science in the third or fourth grade; it becomes general science in the eighth grade, biology in senior high school, and botany on even more advanced levels. For the non-Christian, subject matter involves facts and principles of man-man and man-world relationships. For the Christian, it involves a three-fold relationship: God-cosmos (including man and world), man-man, and man-world. A Christian's treatment of subject matter is centered in the God-cosmos relationship. Subject matter as organization of facts and principles is not in itself Christian or non-Christian. It is right or wrong, true or false, or more or less so. Interpretation of acts and principles in relationship makes the difference for a Christian. When one speaks of Christian culture, he actually means an overt expression or embodiment of Christianity in institutions and patterns of thought and action. People live in a mixed culture from a Christian's point of view; that is, modern culture more or less embodies a Christian's view of life. Modern curriculum, therefore, comes from a mixed culture. Subject matter from this mixed culture can be made appropriate learning for a Christian's development to maturity. This is done by selecting, organizing and interpreting facts and principles for effective integration in a Christian's total personality.

The question arises whether a curriculum consonant with a Christian's view of culture can be expected in and advocated for a school that in a pluralistic society must of necessity view education from a nonchristian perspective? The answer is obvious. For a curriculum congruous with a Christian's view of culture the only solution is a school committed to a Christian's philosophy of education and staffed by Christian teachers who can implement this view in all instruction and school activity in general.[9]

Discipline

It is in the exercise of discipline that many Christians think public schools in recent years have generally been weak. Discipline in this case is referring to external control of the conduct of young people. There is indeed ground for serious misgivings concerning the modern school's effectiveness in the administering of such discipline. Whether the chief source of this apparent ineffectiveness lies with the school is another question. Any appraisal of a school's competence in the exercise of its disciplinary function should take account of one's interpretation of discipline as an aspect of education. How is discipline to be interpreted in the context of a Christian's educational philosophy?

A Christian's view of discipline has its distinctiveness in his view of authority. A Christian's view of authority is founded on the claim of Christ as recorded in Matthew 28:18, "All power is given unto

[9]Worrell, *op. cit.*

me in heaven and in earth." All authority among men originates with Him. He reminded Pilate of this fact when Pilate claimed to have the power to put Him to death or to set Him free. All authority among men is delegated authority to be used responsibly. All men will be held accountable to Jesus Christ. The right to discipline is not inherent in any man or in any institution.

Authority being what it is, according to the Scripture, which is the divine prerogative of control of all things, human and subhuman, there can be only one right response to all duly constituted authority; and this response is voluntary conformity or obedience. The Scriptures link authority and obedience. There is only one absolute, original authority; it is the authority of God. Obedience, without reserve or exception, can be the only right response. All other than divine authority is delegated and subject to human failures. The only right response to duly constituted human authority too is obedience, but subject to the reservation as expressed by the apostles: "We ought to obey God rather than men" (Acts 5:29).

What duly constituted authority operates in the school, and what should be expected of a child with reference to it? Authority in school, it would seem, is of three kinds: parental, legal and pedagogic.

Parental authority. A teacher's and administrator's authority in the modern school is first of all and primarily parental in character. It follows from their *in loco parentis* position. This fact originates with the divine mandate that all authority and responsibility for nurturing children to maturity (responsible independence) rests wholly with parents. Until a youth has reached maturity, the school serves as an extension of the home in his nurture. A teacher's right to control child behavior and his duty to exercise control originate in the home-school relationship. Effective discipline depends largely upon the integrity of this relationship. When a school becomes a "baby-sitter" for delinquent parents, it cannot function in its rightful obligation as an instructional institution. On the other hand, if a school fails in its instructional task, parents, no matter how faithful and competent, cannot adequately execute their educational task in the complex social order of today. In either case the educational effectiveness of discipline is weakened.

Legal authority. The authority of the school is also a legal one. The modern school is a social institution: it arises out of social conditions and has become an arm of the state designed to enforce a minimum formal education for the youth of the nation. The teacher and adminstrative officer occupy a legal position as agents of the state in the exercise of authority in the classroom and in the school as a whole. A Christian's view of the state (government) as a divinely ordained agent to administer justice among men also circumscribes a teacher's authority and responsibility. However, in the administration of justice the teacher functions as one who nurtures youth to maturity, not as a policeman, because a school is an educational institution, not a penal institution.

Pedagogical authority. The third kind or source of authority of the school is pedagogical. In addition to representing the parent and the state in the control of child behavior, the teacher is an interpreter of the culture from which the curriculum of the school is drawn. He has been trained in the use of the tools and content of the culture, in the understanding of child development and learning, and in the expertise of guiding this development. To the immature learner the teacher is the very embodiment of the best of the culture. In keeping with a Christian's view of culture, a Christian teacher helps youth understand culture as a disclosure of God in His works. Such a teacher will help youth walk in the light which he himself reflects as a student of culture. Thus culture as subject matter becomes disciplinary.

How is a teacher to exercise this threefold authority: parental, legal and pedagogic?

First, the teacher should exercise his authority with reference to the supreme and absolute authority in his own life, the lordship of Jesus Christ. He must bring his thinking, feeling and his will captive to this lordship. This is not first of all a legal relationship but a personal loyalty to his Saviour who set him free to love and serve God.

In the second place, a Christian teacher recognizes divinely ordained authority among men. There is authority in Christ's church on earth. Parental authority is of God. So is the authority of the magistrate. A Christian's response to all rightful authority is obedience. Obedience to duly constituted authority should be exemplified in his life in order for him to have any claim to authority in his position as a teacher. To obey God rather than men is the only exception he allows himself. As teacher and as person he is under authority, and he exercises his rightful authority as such.

Third, a Christian teacher is conscious of his failures with reference to a life of obedience. These failures on his part call for penitence and contrition. A teacher who is very conscious of having been saved by grace will humbly and penitently exercise his rightful authority. Arbitrary authoritarianism should be foreign to a Christian teacher.

What can and must be expected of youth with reference to rightful authority in the school? Should unquestioned obedience be enforced? Obedience must be required, to be sure, for humble submission to rightly constituted authority follows from one's acceptance of the lordship of Jesus Christ. Obedience, however, is genuine only when voluntary, when it comes from the heart and is motivated by love. But the way of obedience is learned as every other way of life is learned. Discipline in the school aims at establishing the way of obedience in child behavior.

How is discipline to be administered to accomplish this objective? Not according to rule or formula. Tricks and devices will serve as momentary restraints which are sometimes very necessary. More lasting and developmental ends are attained otherwise. In other works the writer has given some specific suggestions for Christian teachers.[10]

In the references given, distinctions are made among constructive, preventive and remedial measures. Constructive measures should be interpreted as practices which follow from a student's becoming purposefully involved in the learning process. When a teacher sets up an instructional program designed to accomplish desired educational ends in a way that meets a learner's felt needs in a challenging, attainable endeavor, he promotes a feeling of meaningful accomplishment which brings satisfaction to the learner. The disciplinary effect on the student is a constructive one in the sense that it directly promotes self-discipline. The best of constructive measures, however, are beset by many limiting factors and circumstances, frequently beyond a teacher's control. Insofar as these can be anticipated, a teacher can use preventive measures. A well-organized classroom that promotes the security and self-respect of every pupil is an example. Cooperative behavior is expected, and every pupil recognizes and feels this from the start. But despite all constructive and preventive measures which a resourceful teacher may devise, infractions will occur. Remedial measures are in order that a learner may be brought to the realization of right and wrong, and to a voluntary effort to choose the right. Momentary coercion and required conformity may be necessary. Punishment may be in order to help a learner to greater self-restraint. These must all be selected, however, to enlist a learner's self-activity toward more constructive effort on his part.

---

[10]See Cornelius Jaarsma, *Guide to Directed Teaching on the Secondary Level* (mimeographed) (Grand Rapids: Calvin College, 1960), chap. 4; also Jaarsma, *Human Development, Learning and Teaching,* pp. 249-52.

Only a Christian who has achieved a mature, integrated personality in his own development can administer discipline that accomplishes a life of obedience in youth. But being this kind of Christian is not enough. Insight into the needs of youth on their respective developmental levels is indispensable.

Freedom

Closely related to the concepts authority and discipline in education is the concept freedom. Freedom, as stated earlier, is a distinguishing characteristic of man because he is Godlike in his being. Freedom has reference to the right and ability of self-determination. Only God is free in the absolute and original sense. He is wholly self-determining as absolute, personal Being. Man's freedom is contingent and defined with reference to his relationship to the Creator. Estranged from his Creator, he loses the right and competence of self-determination. To help man in this awful predicament, God has established authority among men that enables them to achieve some semblance of order and control. In the man-to-man relationship no one has a right to exercise authority over another except it be divinely ordained for the purpose of restraining and guiding men in the exercise of their freedom. Human freedom in general rests in the dignity of man as Godlike being. Immediately following the fall, God took action to protect man against himself and against others in the indiscriminate and irresponsible outworking of his drive for self-determination. On the other hand, a Christian is conscious of a new freedom; it is the restored freedom in Christ. He subjects himself to all divinely ordained authority for Christ's sake. Voluntary obedience is of the essence in his freedom.

What place has freedom in education? A child is born with the right of self-determination as far as his man-to-man relationship is concerned. But his competence for responsibility is limited. No one has a right to freedom among men unless he can exercise it responsibly. Acting responsibly is an achievement. No child can become a mature personality without the exercise of freedom in the process of becoming. There is no education without a responsible exercise of freedom. It follows that the exercise of self-determination is an essential ingredient in human development and learning. A youth must learn the way of freedom as he learns every other way of self-expression. He has a right to self-determination, but only insofar as he can use it responsibly. It is important, then, that a classroom provide the kind and amount of freedom that youth in a given situation and on a given level of development can exercise responsibly to the good of all concerned. Responsible self-expression is learned more by guided exercise of it than by precept. Authoritarianism inhibits a youth's inherent right of and need for freedom. Rightly constituted authority and respect for it as being authoritative in a youth's conduct are essential to the development of responsible self-determination.

A Christian view of education has a place for authority, freedom and responsibility as essential ingredients in the development of a person to maturity. Education that is Christian aims at a God-man relationship, a man-man relationship and a man-world relationship that make genuine self-realization possible. A person's self-understanding can have its true dimensions only in the perspective of these relationships as designed by the Creator.

RELIGIOUS EDUCATION

This chapter speaks of a Christian's view of education rather than of Christian education. This is done advisedly. It is not only more in keeping with the theme of this symposium but also more consistent with the meaning of education as stated in this chapter.

What is Christian in education? Is it in the process that the distinction of Christian and non-Christian is to be found? Is it in the curriculum? Or is it in the ends to be accomplished? In keeping with the views developed in this chapter, the distinction between Christian and non-Christian is to be found primarily in the ends achieved, namely, in the total personality which is the person in action. A Christian teacher seeks ends which should characterize a Christian in the personality formation of pupils. A Christian teacher selects content for instruction, organizes it in a chosen structure, and directs the entire learning process with aims in view that accomplish ways of thinking and living which should mark a Christian, a person in Christ. The same content of instruction and the same method or technique may accomplish different results in different learners. The ends turn out to be Christian for one and non-Christian for another. Education cannot make Christians; it can shape or form a personality that manifests qualities which should mark a Christian. In a Christian view of education, what is being taught is important with reference to end results. The how of teaching is likewise significant. Content of instruction, method employed, the climate of a classroom, and the atmosphere of the school in general are all conducive to the end results which promote the maturing of persons as Christians.

What is religious education in the context of this discussion? For a Christian the distinction commonly made between religious and nonreligious experiences, or the sacred and the secular, is erroneous. For a Christian all of life is religion, and all things are sacred. In the language of Paul, "All things are yours; . . . and ye are Christ's" (I Cor. 3:21, 23). The distinction is not in things, but in what men do with things. Men are either godly or ungodly. In the lives of godly men all things are sacred, and all of life is religion. If all of life is religion for a Christian, then all education is religious. What, then, is meant by religious education?

If by speaking of religious education one infers that for a Christian there is education that is nonreligious or secular, he betrays a dualism in his thinking contrary to the teachings of Scripture. It is this dualism, so common in evangelical literature, that the writer is trying to correct in this chapter. In a general, universal sense, all education is religious because it is the process of forming or shaping personality; and persons are religious beings in distinction from other organisms. So-called secular education too is religious. A Christian should not speak of things as sacred or secular. Things have no other relationship to God than objects of His creation and His providence. Men are sacred or secular in their use of things. The distinction should be drawn between truth and error, good and evil, beauty and ugliness. In the experience of men, things may contribute to one or the other, commonly to both in a world of sinful men. Of foundational importance is the fact that the Christian seeks to use things to contribute to the true, the good and the beautiful according to norms or standards of God's Word.

Notwithstanding the fact that all of life is religion and all education religious in a Christian's view, one may use the concept "religious education" with some constructive significance. Surely the study of arithmetic, history, physics and all other subjects generally included in a curriculum should be a religious experience for a Christian learner; that is, he should come to grips with truths and realities as disclosing God in His creation and providence. There are also areas of subject matter, however, that deal with God's Word to men and with God's work in salvation of men more directly. If one means by religious education that these areas of subject matter are selected and methodology is organized for the purpose of concentrating on a learner's personal relationship to God as a sinner saved by grace, the concept has genuine significance in a broader view of education. Daily vacation Bible schools, Sunday schools, catechetical classes and released-time instruction do exactly this. The church will be constantly engaged in religious education in her teaching ministry.

Conclusion

A Christian teacher needs a true compass to sail the "pedagogical sea," especially today. Shoals, crosscurrents and stormy seas make navigation difficult and precarious. His true compass is a view of God, man and world unfolded in the Word of God and centered in Christ. With the Holy Spirit testifying in his heart to the veracity and reliability of this record, the Christian teacher can sail the pedagogical sea with confidence that his compass will never fail him. It is for him to read and interpret the compass aright in his scholarly and pedagogic pursuits. He has no Messianic conception of education as a process, but he will center all educational endeavor in the Messiah who is the Light of the world.

FOR FURTHER READING

BOUMA, CLARENCE (ed.). *God-Centered Living, A Symposium*. Grand Rapids: Baker Book House, 1951.

BRUNER, JEROME S. *The Process of Education*. Cambridge, Mass.: Harvard University Press, 1962.

BRYSON, LYMAN, and FINKELSTEIN, LOUIS. *Goals for American Education, A Symposium*. New York: Harper & Bros. Publishers, 1950.

BUTLER, J. DONALD. *Four Philosophies of Education*. New York: Harper & Bros. Publishers, 1957.

CREMIN, LAWRENCE A. *The Transformation of the School*. New York: Alfred A. Knopf, Inc., 1962.

EAVEY, C. B. *History of Christian Education*. Chicago: Moody Press, 1963.

FALLAW, WESNER. *Church Education for Tomorrow*. Philadelphia: Westminster Press, 1962.

FULLER, EDMUND. *The Christian Idea of Education*. London: Oxford University Press, 1957.

GAEBELEIN, FRANK E. *Christian Education in a Democracy*. New York: Oxford University Press, 1951.

HAKES, EDWARD (ed.). *An Introduction to Evangelical Christian Education*. Chicago: Moody Press, 1964.

JAARSMA, CORNELIUS. *The Educational Philosophy of Herman Bavinck*. Grand Rapids: Wm. B. Eerdmans Publishing Co., 1935.

————. *Fundamentals in Christian Education.* Grand Rapids: Wm. B. Eerdmans Publishing Co., 1953.

————. *Human Development, Learning, and Teaching.* Grand Rapids: Wm. B. Eerdmans Publishing Co., 1961.

KNELLER, GEORGE F. *Existentialism in Education.* New York: Philosophical Library, Inc., 1958.

LeBAR, LOIS E. *Children in the Bible School.* Westwood, N. J.: Fleming H. Revell Co., 1952.

————. *Education That Is Christian.* Westwood, N. J.: Fleming H. Revell Co., 1958.

MILLER, ALEXANDER. *Faith and Learning.* New York: Association Press, 1960.

MUNRO, HARRY C. *Protestant Nurture.* Englewood Cliffs, N. J.: Prentice-Hall, Inc., 1956.

PHENIX, PHILIP H. *Education and the Common Good.* New York: Harper & Bros. Publishers, 1961.

————. *Realms of Meaning.* New York: McGraw-Hill Book Co., 1964.

RUSHDOONY, ROUSA JOHN. *The Messianic Character of American Education.* Philadelphia: Presbyterian & Reformed Publishing Co., 1963.

UNGERSMA, A. J. *The Search for Meaning.* Philadelphia: Westminster Press, 1960.

What, Then, Is Man? Symposium. (Graduate Study III.) St. Louis: Concordia Publishing House, 1958.

WISE, JOHN E. *The History of Education.* New York: Sheed & Ward, 1964.

WORRELL, EDWARD K. *Restoring God to Education.* Wheaton, Ill.: Van Kampen Press, 1950.

THE TREND OF IDEAS
IN THE
HISTORY OF ASTRONOMY

Karel Hujer

Karel Hujer is professor of astronomy and physics at the University of Chattanooga and is director of Jones Observatory at the University. He has previously taught at Iowa Wesleyan College and Michigan State University. He studied at Imperial College of London University, Yerkes Observatory of the University of Chicago, and received the D. Sc. degree from Charles University, Prague, Czechoslovakia. Dr. Hujer has written numerous scientific papers and articles and has contributed chapters to the *Encyclopedia of Physics* and to a new volume published by the Italian National Research Council and marking the 400th anniversary of the birth of Galileo. Dr. Hujer's professional concerns have taken him to many international science congresses in recent years, including those held in Warsaw and Cracow, Poland; Florence, Pisa, Vinci and Turin, Italy; Barcelona and Madrid, Spain; and Oxford, England. His study of the history of astronomy and participation in solar eclipse expeditions have taken him to India, China (including Tibet), Peru, Mexico, Siberia (three times), and elsewhere.

6

HISTORY OF ASTRONOMY IN THE THE TREND OF IDEAS

Karel Hujer

NEWTON THEORY

Isaac Newton, the pioneering genius in astronomy, the great founder of mathematical physics and a symbol of an era in the history of science and civilization that established the age of technology, in 1687 wrote in his masterpiece, *Principia:* "This most beautiful system of the sun, planets and comets could only proceed from the counsel and dominion of an intelligent and powerful being."[1] Newton's devoutly religious approach was not followed in the subsequent growth and evolution of the new astronomy of this age, upon which this mathematical giant impressed his name.

LAPLACE HYPOTHESIS

On the threshold of that scientifically most prolific nineteenth century, one encounters a sharp and acidic mathematical genius, Pierre S. Laplace, who formulated a brilliant hypothesis on the origin of the solar system boldly outlined behind the gossamer of deterministic equations. Laplace's sensational work, *Exposition du Système du Monde*, published in 1796, became a keynote of the triumphal march of scientific thought of the nineteenth century. Even before the English biologist made himself known to the world, Laplace became a Darwin in astrophysical sciences. An incident is symptomatic of what was in the ferment. It is said that Napoleon, the jealous supporter of intellectual activity in his short-lived revolutionary and aggressive empire, commented while he was about to

---

[1] *Philosophiae Naturalis Principia Mathematica* (London, 1687).

confer the title of marquis on Laplace that he could not find God mentioned once in his book on this subject—*Exposition of the World System*—as would be expected. Laplace proudly retorted: "Your majesty, I did not need him." This attitude became inherently typical during the ensuing growth of physical science with its vast philosophical consequence in the apostatic tendency of scientism. It is, however, curious that this hypothesis sometimes carries the dual designation of Kant-Laplace because the famous Königsberg philosopher, even before Laplace, fathered its purely philosophical speculative foundation. Unlike Laplace, Kant, the son of a pietist mother, is known for his religious leanings, particularly by his oft quoted statement: "There are two things that constantly bring me into the state of admiration: The star-filled heavens above me and the moral law within me."[2]

LEVERRIER COMPUTATION

Yet it was the personality of Laplace which set the course that scientific thought with its philosophical world view was to take through the formative nineteenth century. This agnostic and materialistic tendency, a marked feature of the French revolution, was signalized by another intellectual triumph, Leverrier's mathematical discovery of Neptune in 1845. Although computed previously by the young English astronomer J. C. Adams, the result of the proud and arrogant director of Paris observatory obtained the prompt attention of the educated world, and Leverrier's computation was soon confirmed by J. G. Galle in his telescopic location of the planet Neptune at Berlin observatory. Even Halley's first prediction of the comet's return was applauded previously, so the discovery of Neptune was hailed as an unprecedented victory of Newtonian mathematical physics. The crux of this course of scientific progress was that some leading philosophers of the time interpreted this trend as a distinct and final trail leading toward man's solution of cosmic creation. It was supposed that it was only a question of time before the human intellect would unravel all the mysteries which were formerly ascribed to God. Astronomy, asymptotically merging with a rising physics, was ever more explicitly instrumental in shaping this course that was upheld by the triumphal strides in physics by such scientific wizards as Kelvin and Helmholtz in their deterministic world view. This picture presented our universe merely as a more complex machine that engineers would be capable of building in its

[2]Immanuel Kant, *Allgemeine Naturgeschichte und Theorie des Himmels* (Koenigsberg, 1755).

model scale when once formalized by the equations of mathematicians.

The triumphant progress of applied science, technology and technocracy, which alarmingly superficialized man's apprehension of cosmic mysteries, was perhaps primarily responsible for the secularist tendency in the philosophy of science. Although there were some outstanding, devout and religious scientists after the example of Newton, they could not even in their fame produce a moderating influence. On the contrary, they became innocently instrumental in this course of estrangement or growing hostility between science and religion. Michael Faraday is an example. His mental organization, which made it possible for him to erect an absolute barrier between his science and his religion, was indeed an unusual one. John Tyndall, a famous physicist and friend of the genial founder of modern electromagnetism, once described this attitude of mind in his own trenchant way by saying that "when Faraday opened the door of his oratory, he closed that of his laboratory."[3] Yet, it was this very attitude of complete separateness of science and religion which is still observed by most scientists and technicians of today—the aloofness to face the supreme problems of life—that even in Faraday's faithful devotion to religion and to his Sandemanian Christian sect was responsible for the growing crisis between science and religion. As yet it is not possible to visualize the climax of this crisis.

Thus, in the nineteenth century there arose a philosophy of science which considered the world of sense perception the only and ultimate reality. The triumphant strides of Galilean experimental science—empiricism—and the incessant stream of discoveries of towering magnitude encouraged and supported this bold view. Materialism, the belief in the primacy and objective reality of matter, under the circumstances found a favorable climate after a long period of inaction extending from the time of such a school of philosophy of ancient Greece as that of Heraclitus. By the eighteenth century this doctrine became fashionable among French materialists who progressively refined it until eventually it found expression in the popular system of Auguste Comte's positivism. This occurred in the middle of the golden era of physical science in which astronomy played the crowning role. Determination of distances, sizes and masses of the planets in the solar system and, above all, the first measurement by Struve and Bessel of stellar parallax, revealing by 1838 the fantastic abyss of interstellar space, produced an overwhelming impression on man's mind and became a most powerful catalyst in the world of

---

[3]Sylvanus Thompson, *Life of Michael Faraday* (London, 1898), p. 299.

thought. Indeed, nothing in the present century can be compared to the glowing hopes and expectations that animated all humanity in the middle of the nineteenth century.

MARX AND ENGELS' DIALECTICAL MATERIALISM

Yet, despite the lingering idealistic views, the progress of science oriented a trend toward such popular schools of thought as that of Feuerbach and Bauer, until among the many personalities, two portentous figures, Friedrich Engels and Karl Marx, began to cast their silhouettes over the Western world. They challenged the very foundation of Christianity and shaped the destiny of the twentieth century. The very fact that Marx and Engels appeared on the world scene at the time of triumphant physics and astronomy is symptomatic, for they both claimed the scientific age to be the age of material redemption and the age of the proletarians. This prophecy of the previous century was suitable preparation for the idolatry of technology in either the promises or in the fulfillment of an air-conditioned paradise of automation on both sides of the Iron Curtain. Dialectical materialism, the official dogma proudly promoted as the final wisdom in any Communist state, is only a natural outcome of successful technology. All modes of life indicate that this philosophy is very much alive in its original Western home where it flourishes in its universities and, above all, in its laboratories. Only recently at a scientific conference, the chairman of the physics department of a university on the eastern coast of the United States made a frank Laplacian admission that he neither believed in any God nor needed any. It was the writer's deep concern to observe the lack of religious interest of various astronomers and to note that an agnostic attitude is prevalent among them.

As did Laplace and Leverrier, astronomers today still largely assume that the universe is made of matter and space regulated by some deterministic laws and that is all there is to it. Accordingly, the philosophy of Psalms 8 and 19 is a quaint relic of the past. Naturally Christian scholars are compelled to ask questions: Is this attitude justified or is it only the present position of the philosophy of science? What is it in classical physics and astronomy that has caused this alarming undermining of the Christian faith to the extent that it would arouse the envy of Julian the Apostate? One should bear in mind that at present a large percentage of the inhabitants of this planet are under the control of governments theoretically organized on the tenets of Marx and Engels, who once were inspired and guided by the triumphant physical science.

What are these qualities of astronomy and physics which appeal so much to materialists and supposedly encourage their agnostic world view? Behind the Iron Curtain, astronomy is considered a most effective scientific tool for the indoctrination of dialectical materialism. These materialists maintain that the universe is knowable and deterministic, and that functionally it is dialectically materialistic. Therefore, they hasten to conclude, there is nothing supernatural about it. In their minds they create a picture of a universe without God. Moreover, this means that in due time man will inevitably solve all the mysteries which in the past have been described as the handiwork of God and revealed by the prophets. It is undeniable that the victorious march of science, together with the industrial revolution, produced a forceful impact on the social and intellectual life of man. These two movements were seen to foreshadow a new redeeming age in which man himself was to become the coordinator and finally the master of the laws of the universe.

This view is boldly stated in the significant work *Life in the Universe*, recently published by the Soviet Academy of Science. It was written by two outstanding Soviet scientists, the biochemist A. I. Oparin and the astrophysicist V. G. Fesenkov. These two authors first refer in an affable and patriotic manner to the eighteenth century Russian pioneer scientist, M. V. Lomonosov, pointing out that from the style of his writing it is evident that Lomonosov was at that time a tributary of the masters of his day. Apparently Oparin and Fesenkov are not aware that they too are subservient to the new masters of this age when they quote from Engel's *Dialectics of Nature*, a work little known among Western scientists but a universal and obligatory textbook for any student in the Communist world. The views of Oparin and Fesenkov consistently coincide with this context. They maintain that life, including any higher state of consciousness and the subsequent moral qualities it involves, is only the natural result of the cosmic evolution of matter. Both authors maintain that life began in the complex vibrations of ultimate particles of physics, such as electrons, protons, neutrons, and that any idea of a divine origin as a result of God's work is merely a relic of man's primitive mythology. They feel the implication here is obvious. It is only a question of time and systematic research until man's intellect, itself a product of spontaneous and accidental chemical processes, will discover these delicate vibrations and be able to create life in a test tube.

Our Western world's synthetic picture of life is not dissimilar when voiced by so outstanding a scientist as the distinguished former director of Harvard observatory, Dr. Harlow Shapley, who defines life as "self-perpetuation of certain macro-molecules"[4] and who continues by saying that the origin of life on this planet has lost its mystery when in Dr. Harold Urey's laboratory, chemist Stanley Miller has succeeded in synthesizing twenty-one amino acids merely by directing electric discharges into atmospheres of methane, ammonia, hydrogen, and water vapor, thus reproducing hypothetical primeval conditions on earth. Man still asks the question: Does this solve the riddle of life?

In Russia, it is indeed very impressive to witness this iconoclastic attitude reenacted as a victorious social doctrine of the new Soviet society in Leningrad's permanent exposition. It is located in one of the largest churches, in Kazansky Cathedral on Nevsky Prospect. The prominent inscription above the former sanctuary's portico reads: "Museum of the History of Religion and Atheism of the Academy of Science of the U.S.S.R." The pervading theme of this museum and exhibition is to present religion as a survival of mythology which, as such, is doomed to die, withering by itself without any unwise persecution. They maintain religion is bound to be replaced by progress and by the ultimate victory of science, the true savior of humanity. So the climax of this museum's exposition is intentionally centered in an appropriately located gallery of science, implying the elimination of anything supernatural, because it is now science, such as astronomy and man's conquest of space, that on a rational basis produces something greater than the "miracles" of the past. Gazing at a huge painting of Lenin which has sacrilegiously replaced the altar picture of the Lord Jesus, one realizes God's boundless patience with man.

What actually is in the background or foundation of this agnostic or outright atheistic philosophy that appears to stem from scientific cognition of the physical world? Is this view justified on the basis of that same scientific thought? This particular *Weltanschauung*— the faithless world view—does not flourish merely behind the Iron Curtain. As indicated before, it is also popular in the Western world, in the scientific laboratory and university classroom, although society here has claimed official adherence to Christian traditions.

The foundation of this philosophy rests on the conviction that only *a posteriori* knowledge—knowledge derived from laboratory experimentation—is the guarantee of reality and therefore constitutes pragmatic truth. This means that man's sense perception and

[4] *Of Stars and Men* (New York: Washington Square Press, 1958), p. 116.

experimental verification provide the only channel to the cognition and realization of the existence of the world outside the frame of finite senses. A positivistic or materialistic philosopher who claims that his views are firmly established on scientific foundations can say, "I recognize only that to be real and true which I am able to see, touch, hear or otherwise perceive by my senses." Superficially this appears quite reasonable; and backed by actual, successful accomplishments, this empirical view became the cornerstone of pragmatic philosophy which, in its striking affinity to dialectical materialism, continues to dominate the mentality of the major part of the society of this technological civilization. Whether experiments of pure physics by Galileo or Faraday or those of a practical nature by James Watt, Edison or Steinmetz, they established an experience that seemed to become an unfailing source of invaluable usefulness for material welfare. Thus, according to the generally accepted pragmatic view, anything that brings results and provides practical service is inevitably considered true and real. Yet it is this very philosophy of science and materialistic, pragmatic *Weltanschauung*, that has been questioned by some aspects of the latest phases of Einsteinian physics and the riddle of cosmogony.

ELECTRON AND QUANTUM

It is possible to trace the change in the philosophy of scientific thought to the last decade of the nineteenth century. The century that saw the unparalleled boost of materialistic doctrines also planted the seeds of future reversal. At the occasion of the Columbian Exposition in Chicago in 1893, the venerated physicist, Albert Michelson, made a historic statement in which he described physics as an accomplished science that had reached the final degree of perfection and whose further progress was to consist only in "the position of decimal point," that is, in the increasing precision of measurement. Yet it was symptomatic that this view was expressed on the very eve of great events which precipitated such a revolution in physical science that its ends cannot be apprehended even in the second half of the present century. According to the doctrinal views of classical physics, the discovery of such startling phenomena as X rays and radioactivity by 1895 did not at all fit into the scheme of Newtonian physics. The need for revision of seemingly well-established ideas was even more intensified when J. J. Thomson identified the smallest known particle, the electron, and Max Planck by 1900 discovered the ultimate rationed parcel of energy whose name, quantum, impressed itself on modern physics. Finally the edifice of orthodox views of classical physics was exposed to shattering blows with the publication of Einstein's first paper on relativity in 1905. Each of these major discoveries contributed to the relentless change of the tide that philosophically blazes the trail toward a new era.

EINSTEIN'S PRINCIPLE

Initially the novelty of X rays consisted in their ability to penetrate opaque material. The revolutionary blow of radioactivity crumbled Daltonian indivisible atoms into smaller, ever more enigmatic particles. Exact and copious rationing associated with electrons and quanta inspired man's ideas about an orderly universe down to the minutest frame of space and time in terms of ultimate cosmic constants. The wave of the future, however, was most precipitously stirred by Einsteinian ideas. So far, it has never been sufficiently indicated that the philosophic aspect of the principle of relativity will increasingly influence the changing tide of thought from the barren desert of agnosticism toward new vistas beyond all imagination. The reason for this view rests on the fact that Einstein's principle places such an outlook on a very reasonable and logically justified basis, from which it is possible to affirm that man can never possibly grasp the absolute and the ultimate; and in his utterly imperfect frame of sense perception he will only observe appearances, limitations and delusions. Romain Rolland said it in a poetical way when he stated, "The Universe will jealously conceal from man ultimate mysteries of creation."[5] The statement that the Einsteinian universe is finite refers inevitably to the universe of man's limited and foggy sense perception; and, indeed, such universe is inevitably finite as is the universe of an ant. There is a universe beyond and above all and everything, inconceivably outside the level of our perceptibility—a universe whose existence can never effectively be denied, a universe that passes all human understanding.

Undoubtedly the macrophysical and macrocosmic world in which such pioneers of classical physics as Galileo, Kepler or Newton exclusively operated, turned out to be widely different from the microphysical or microcosmic world of atoms and its constituent ultimate particles that is the sole operational region of the present relativistic and quantum physics. Thus, one recent Nobel laureate in physics, C. F. von Weizsaecker observes:

> Physics began with the determination of the laws which satisfy the events immediately perceptible by the senses, but now its goal is precisely to investigate the atomic world, which is no longer

[5]Stefan Zweig, *Romain Rolland* (Prague: Orbis, 1934), p. 91.

perceptible by the senses, and to reduce all other types of order to the laws of atomic processes.[6]

It is indeed a most prophetic statement by the grandson of Charles R. Darwin, Sir Charles G. Darwin, Cambridge University physicist, when he maintains:

> The general point of view of questioning the reality of anything unobservable is one of the greatest revolutions in scientific thought that has ever occurred. . . . The great idea which Einstein contributed to scientific philosophy was the principle that if a thing is essentially unobservable then it is not a real thing and our theories must not include it.[7]

Atoms and electrons definitely belong in the category of unobservables and as such could be considered as unreal; yet nothing has influenced the life of modern man more than these supposedly unreal concepts. This is certainly a very poignant indication of the dilemma brought about by a revolutionary reversal in the realm of physical ideas. Nevertheless, the facts should be stressed that such incidents are far from unique in the history of ideas and in man's eager search for peace and security.

How firm, glorious, reliable and unfailing appeared the homocentric Ptolemaic system that placed the earth in the center of the universe. A careful investigation of this geocentric world picture, which once nurtured the medieval philosophy of the venerable church Father, Thomas Aquinas, will reveal that there was enduring pragmatic value in this *Weltanschauung* that actually prompted the revival of the modern Thomistic school of thought. Yet the most dramatic events in the history of ideas have shown that the cherished geocentric system was only a mirage of an incomprehensible cosmic reality that is the true nature of phenomena beyond the variety of misleading sense perceptions. The once established and conventionalized world views of Euclid, Ptolemy, Copernicus and Newton, to mention only a few, all have served their turn in their accepted reasonability; yet each in turn reveals a series of delusions. Nevertheless, human inertia and conservatism allowed these delusions because of their temporary usefulness or anthropomorphic, self-centered flattery to be petrified into dogma or even idolatry. This could be seen when the Christian faith was associated with the geocentric world picture and its leaders condemned to the flames those who discovered the extended glory and majesty of God's universe.

---

[6] *The World View of Physics* (Chicago: University of Chicago Press, 1952), p. 14.

[7] *The New Conceptions of Matter* (Cambridge: Cambridge University Press, 1931), pp. 23, 81.

The story of the description or explanation of celestial movements, the strife between the geocentric and heliocentric world views that also played a major role in the history of religious ideas, reveals the most outstanding drama of man's struggle between delusion and what he called reality. The ancient Greek philosophers, who already encountered the complexity of epicyclic movements, called for *diasozein ta phainomena* ("saving of appearances"), an appropriate designation of the perennial dilemma in the relation of the observed phenomenon to the observer, the external world to the inner world of the perceiving mind. Man's interpretation of what he observed must have been reasonably in agreement with what he physically perceived. In other words, he must save, not discard or disregard, the phenomena. There are, however, a number of ways by which the same phenomenon can be explained. As the noted astronomer and mathematician J. Henri Poincaré stated, it is a matter of convenience as to which explanation is accepted.

History has shown many times that it was also a matter of tradition or prejudice that dictated the interpretation of some phenomenon. Thus, a sensational intellectual controversy was occasioned by Poincaré in 1906, when in one of his learned articles published in *L'Astronomie* he insisted that it is a matter of convenience to say the earth is spinning about its axis since the earth's rotation is not a scientific fact because the earth's spinning is not directly perceived by our senses. Poincaré defined a scientific fact as a raw and direct result of human experience. This line of thought had a medieval forerunner in Ossiander who expressed this view in his apologetic introduction to the first edition of Copernicus' radical *De Revolutionibus Orbium Coelestium* in 1543. Ossiander attempted to tone down the disturbing novelty of the heliocentric doctrine and maintained: "It is neither necessary an hypothesis be true nor even probable but it is sufficient if it renders calculations consistent with observations."[8]

If one carefully examines this startling statement of a medieval mind in the preamble to the most revolutionary book in the history of scientific ideas, he will realize that man, formulating hypotheses, is actually an inventor of so-called reality. This was virtually the case in the history of all hypotheses in which man tried to reconcile the phenomena perceived by his sensory framework with what he described as reality.

---

[8]N. Copernicus, *Des Revolutions des orbes celestes,* translated into French by A. Koyré (Paris, 1934), p. 28.

IDEALISM VS. MATERIALISM

In the history of philosophy there have been two schools of thought, each in its own way attempting to explain the observed phenomena: one was idealistic, the other materialistic. The idealistic, usually associated with Pythagorean traditions, assumed man's ultimate inability to comprehend the supreme mystery of creation. Therefore, this line of thought recognized the existence of a supernatural plane which man, so long as he was prisoner of his imperfect body, would never be able to penetrate or comprehend. Nearly two millennia later Johannes Kepler, like Pythagoras, perceived the manifestation of God through the harmony and orderliness that permeate our universe. Back in the sixth century B.C., Pythagoras was known for his enthusiastic exclamation "God must be a Geometer." Kepler, guided by the same kind of ideas, was led to the discovery of his three laws of planetary motion that paved the way for Newton. Kepler was particularly jubilant about his third law, and he, as a Pythagorean philosopher, named it the Law of Harmonics. As an idealist, he associated no property to matter. His laws were an expression of cosmic geometry, everything else including matter being subservient and obedient to this supreme order. Newton, however, changed the interpretation when he generalized Kepler's laws into the Universal Law of Gravitation and stipulated that it is the property of matter to exude a force which has been called gravitation. When this law is expressed in a mathematical formula that can be interpreted as a form of geometry, Newtonian physics emerges as an entirely new idea in the supremacy of matter.

For a quarter of a millennium Newton's world picture appeared to be an unfailing and unchallenged representation of reality, and the reasonableness of the Newtonian universe was never so firm as throughout the nineteenth century. Yet at present, in the light of relativistic and quantum physics, the picture of its reality is rapidly fading. Man now appears to be farther from reality than in the time of Ptolemy or Copernicus. It was indeed a historic scene at the session of the Royal Society in London, November 6, 1919, presided over by the brilliant physicist of the age, Sir J. J. Thomson, when the confirmation of Einstein's theory was announced in the results of the first solar eclipse expedition. "It is not the discovery of an outlying island but the whole continent of new scientific ideas," declared the presiding physicist. Alfred North Whitehead as a mathematician, a philosopher, and a man endowed with excellent historical and religious sense, recorded his personal impressions of this dramatic session:

It was my good fortune to be present when the Astronomer Royal made the announcement. . . . The whole atmosphere of tense interest was exactly that of Greek drama. We were the chorus commentating on the decree of destiny as disclosed in the development of a supreme incident. There was dramatic quality in the very staging—the traditional ceremonial, and in the background the picture of Newton to remind us that the greatest of scientific generalizations was now, after more than two centuries, to receive its first modification. . . . This remorseless inevitableness is what pervades scientific thought. The laws of physics are the decrees of fate.[9]

What is actually in the background of these changing scenes of human opinion? The crux of the historical development rests in the growing feasibility of the revolutionary reversal from empirical, materialistic views to the opposite philosophical outlook in which a logical, pure idea not necessarily supported by experimental evidence reveals its startling reasonableness. In other words, an aprioristic, assumed idea may lead to results equal in value to that which is the outcome of aposterioristic experience—experimental verification. From the point of view of idealistic philosophy this trend is extremely important, if only in reference to the claims of dogmatic tyranny of a seemingly triumphant materialistic philosophy.

LORENTZ-FITZGERALD CONTRACTION

At the dawn of Einsteinian physics, the Michelson-Morley experiment (1887) used an ingenious mathematical fiction in order to "save the phenomenon" in the form of the Lorentz-Fitzgerald Contraction. In the language of Ossiander, this mathematical formula merely attempted to render the calculation consistent with observation. It was, however, an idea that was to shape a new world view in face of the most enigmatic situation: the Michelson-Morley experiment was inconsistent with the previously experimentally established view of the earth's motion through cosmic space! So again a question was raised: Is the Lorentz-Fitzgerald Contraction a mere mathematical fiction or is it a reality? Yet, if one inquires about the reality of this mathematical contraction, he is in the same position as when he asks: Is the architect's scaffold a reality, or the cathedral, for which the scaffold is only a temporary means to an end? There are a number of famous examples such as Bohr's picture of the planetary hydrogen atom in which an idea is pictured as a reality. In fact, Einstein pointed out:

---

[9]Philipp Frank, *Life of Einstein* (New York: Alfred A. Knopf, 1947), p. 140.

Physics really began with the invention of mass, force and inertial system; these concepts are all free inventions. They led to the formulation of the mechanical point of view. Science is compelled to invent ideas corresponding to the reality of our world. Science is not a collection of laws, a catalogue of unrelated facts, it is a creation of the human mind, with its freely invented ideas and concepts.[10]

Einstein himself invented a mathematical fiction of equivalence of mass and energy which he first published in 1905. He could then hardly foresee the dramatic as well as tragic circumstances in August, 1945, when the correctness of an idea shattered the entire city of Hiroshima and adumbrated a new era in human history. Long before this occurred, Einstein stated in his 1933 Herbert Spencer lecture delivered at Oxford University:

It is my conviction that pure mathematical construction enables us to discover concepts and the laws connecting them, which give us the key to the understanding of the phenomena of nature. Experience can, of course, guide us in our choice of serviceable mathematical concepts; it cannot possibly be the source from which they are derived. In a certain sense, therefore, I hold it to be true that pure thought is competent to comprehend the real as the ancients dreamed.[11]

From the classical experimental point of view, it is heretical indeed to maintain that experience cannot possibly be the source from which serviceable mathematical concepts are derived. This statement of Einstein is the most radical that could have been given by a highly esteemed and recognized scientist. It opens the door to a consideration of the validity of subjectivism. In other words, as against knowledge acquired by experimentation, which is the inviolable and unswerving creed of present empirical science and scientific method— the gospel of dialectical materialism—Einstein goes so far as to use the language of idealistic philosophy which advocates the guidance of an aprioristic knowledge—pure thought—the mysterious realm of man's mind that appears in the role of weaver of reality. Thus in physics the center of gravity, temperature, climate, density, vector and latitude are some of the mental concepts or constructs that appear very real; yet actually they do not exist.

PHYSICS OF COLOR VISION

Another and perhaps the most significant aspect of an explorer's

---

[10]Albert Einstein, "On the Method in Theoretical Physics," Herbert Spencer lecture delivered at Oxford, June 10, 1933.
[11]*Ibid.*

dilemma between reality and sense perception is encountered in the physics of color vision. Actually it is a matter of unending philosophy as one may find from the historical controversy between Goethe and Newton, both valid and famous representatives of their age. As a physicist, Newton maintained that the origin of colors is entirely outside the human eye; it is in the sunlight and in the prism that produces the spectrum. Goethe, remembered primarily as a poet, dedicated forty years of his life to an ardent study of the nature of colors and color vision and reached the conviction that color vision is in the human eye, in man's mind. Despite his fame as a poet and philosopher, Goethe was not (and still is not) taken seriously in the field of science, especially while the scientific fame and authority of Newton remained undisputed. Newton advised that to learn about colors, man must study the spectrum of sunlight produced by a prism. Goethe, on the other hand, urged an investigation of the human eye and above all of man's mind. This investigation was inadvertently done by Goethe's contemporary, the founder of physiology, J. E. Purkinje, of Breslau and Prague universities, whose work aroused the enthusiastic interest and support of the Weimar poet and philosopher. In his time, Purkinje's research was considered a dangerous novelty. Present development, however, tends to liberate Goethe from his philosophical isolation as is well indicated in Sir James Jeans' remark where he discusses a physiologist examining the brain of a patient: "Most people's opinion is that the physiologist sees the brain of the patient but the philosopher insists that actually it is the brain of the physiologist himself."[12] Sir Arthur Eddington in a similar line of thought writes: "The beautiful hues which flood our consciousness under the stimulation of the waves have no relevance to the objective reality."[13] Goethe would surely be pleased to hear these views from the twentieth century successors of Isaac Newton in London's Royal Society.

Purkinje Effect

The case of Purkinje is very important in the object of this search and needs additional comment. Purkinje, known in physics for his Purkinje Effect, can be described for this discovery alone as the founder of exact subjectivism. The Purkinje Effect stipulates that the physiological sensation of any specific color is not associated with

[12]*Physics and Philosophy* (Cambridge: Cambridge University Press, 1953), p. 87.
[13]*The Nature of the Physical World* (Cambridge: Cambridge University Press, 1929), p. 94.

a fixed wavelength, as the physicist's spectrum mathematically or numerically indicates, but is dependent on the human eye. As other scientific explorers, Purkinje was in search of reality, scientific truth; and his idea to trace the origin of colors in the physiology of the human eye was sound. Philosophically, according to the present outlook in modern atomic physics, he was nearer the goal of the desired reality when he examined the human eye than was Newton who examined sunlight with his prism. However, as Eddington states in *The Nature of the Physical World*, the physiologist can trace the stimulus of the nerve mechanism up to the brain, "but ultimately there is a hiatus which no one professes to fill up. Symbolically, we may follow the influences of the physical world up to the door of the mind; they ring the door-bell and depart."[14] Thus, the problem remains suspended between the subjective world which speaks in terms of colors, and the objective, external, scientific world which in its quantitative language displays its electromagnetic wave. Naturally, the latter claims to be nearer to the description of reality; but the first, the color, may be described as the fancy of the mind, "mind-spinning." The physiologist, on the other hand, examining the human eye, claims in turn to be nearer that spinning wheel of the human mind which, in response to various stimuli at the end of the nerve, "creates the fancy that it is turning the reel of a cinematograph."

As one follows this train of ideas to the full consequence and considers the evasive concepts of microcosmic, utterly imperceptible, ultimate particles such as electrons or quanta, he cannot be surprised by Sir James Jeans' radical and unorthodox view calling this universe "a great thought." The universe is whatever idea man creates of it inside the frame of his sensory system and in the realm of his intellectual level and degree of consciousness. The discovery of the atom's nucleus is associated with Ernest Rutherford, yet Eddington exclaims that Rutherford did not discover the nucleus or proton inside the atom; "he has put it there." After all, this challenging mathematical astrophysicist maintains that although scientific progress eliminated any fantasy of the spirit in order to clear the trail toward reality, yet it arrived at the conclusion that the most valid reality is inseparably associated with the ability to arouse those very fantasies. How remarkably testified to in Einstein's original fantasy! Apparently, according to Eddington, that is only because "the spirit or mind, that mysterious weaver of illusions, is the only warrant of reality and also that it is possible to find reality in the foundation of

---

[14]*Ibid.*, p. 319.

each fantasy."[15] It is the writer's belief that the history of concepts and theories in physical science amply justifies and will continue to substantiate Eddington's opinion.

The evolution of astronomical concepts apparently reveals there is no detached objective and unrelated picture of the external universe, world or phenomenon that could be declared an absolute and authoritarian doctrine. In the present state of astrophysical knowledge, there cannot be another exclusive hypothesis like that of Laplace which once dominated for an entire century. Conceivably even the system of Einstein, Schrödinger, Heisenberg, will give way to some new world realization in the ever changing drama of man's vision of inscrutable eternity.

The Laplace hypothesis was followed by the Chamberlin-Moulton hypothesis with its amendment of some of the untenable fallacies of the French mathematician's highly popular ideas. But hardly a quarter of a century had elapsed before the Chamberlin-Moulton hypothesis encountered its own difficulties confronted by the increasingly complicated facts of the steadily advancing observational astrophysics. At present, the principal interest of cosmogonical investigation is directed toward the search for the origin of matter in the universe. Although highly complex, this question of the origin of such advanced forms as this solar system is not inconceivable once the origin of the constituent substance is established. Yet this very substance—the origin of matter—is the most enigmatic riddle in contemporary astronomical as well as atomic physics. Once such substance enters into the realm of cosmic observable phenomena, even then no complete theory is possible which, as a panacea, would be capable of explaining the original formation of a large number of permanent condensations in interstellar gas or diffused matter so profusely recorded throughout galactic space.

Of various fragmentary hypotheses, there are two outstanding views of the nature and origin of the universe that attempt to respond rationally to the external world of observed phenomena. In their theory Bondi and Hoyle advocate that the dissipative effect of constant annihilation of matter through radiant stars is balanced by a continual creation of new matter. "It should be clearly understood," Bondi emphasizes, "that creation here discussed is the formation of matter out of nothing, 'ex nihilo.' "[16] No doubt a philosophical implication here is evident: the maintenance of the universe

---

[15]*Ibid.*, p. 319; chap. 15.

[16]G. J. Whitrow, *The Structure and Evolution of the Universe* (New York: Harper & Bros. Publishers, 1959), p. 137.

as a whole in a steady state. The second theory, that of Abbé Lemaître supplemented by George Gamow, envisions the beginning of the universe in a cataclysmic original explosion of a primeval atom, an inconceivable impulse that is presently still perpetuated by the observed expansion of external galaxies.

Neither of these theories can claim the explanation of the ultimate origin of matter. Both operate with *fait accompli*—with matter emerging from the mysterious unknown. Bondi's "ex nihilo" indicates only the rational impasse while Lemaître's faith is able to produce a vision of primeval, spaceless atom, a form of ultimate cosmic particle, that once contained the entire universe. How seemingly real the electron, presently known as the smallest particle of microphysics, appears in our daily usage to the point that the genial astrophysicist Eddington speaks confidently of its behavior in his description of physical ideas. Yet in the next breath he confides that the electron is "something unknown . . . doing we don't know what."[17] Eddington's humble admission does not take him to the preposterous claim of creation "ex nihilo" but indicates that the transphenomenal level is apparently forever inaccessible to both man's perception and imagination. Clearly, man's knowledge will advance, but whatever level of understanding and consciousness is attained will, in turn, contain its own new, transposed boundary separating man from the supreme Unknown.

The weakness of the present scientific method and its aposterioristic, empirical knowledge lies in its insistence upon investigating or analyzing the phenomena of cosmic activity apart from the only reality—the reality of the universe drawn on the mind of man, recorded by traditions of untold ages through each individual's sensory system. The strict objectivism claimed by the scientific method is not only a philosophical fiction but produces additionally a serious one-sidedness. Through what is called scientism the present century has witnessed the process of alarming dehumanization, an inevitable consequence and eventual end to which man's strictly objective and amoral scientific method leads. While this procedure piles up cherished and flattering successes, it becomes another delusion because it entails fragmentation of mind, fragmentation of knowledge, and fragmentation of the social body, all of which undermines and eventually dissolves the very foundation of human society and its culture in the realm of the spirit. It intensifies the hopelessness of human isolation in a universe with its primacy of matter

---

[17]Herbert Dingle, *The Sources of Eddington's Philosophy* (Cambridge: Cambridge University Press, 1954), p. 20.

alone, and human society is consequently brought to ends opposite
to the original purpose of science—which is actually man's libera-
tion through the vision of eternal oneness. On the contrary, this
type of science cannot arrest the chronic warfare of the present
century but, through servile, scientific, agnostic robots in the service
of a pagan state, makes the art of warfare ever more scientifically
dehumanized. Science, as such, not only finds no place in the sanctuary of compassion, but as science without philosophy—lacking
the true light of wisdom—it becomes more readily a social menace.

The only valid reality for man's individual life, as it appears, is
the world picture impressed upon his mind by his sensory framework.
The consequences of the Principle of Relativity have reasonably indicated the plausibility of this realization. The new physics, whether
Einsteinian or quantum physics, which brings man to the borderland
between what is "real" and what is "sense delusion," has undeniably
shattered the foundation of materialism or Comte's positivism. Even
the law of causality is challenged by such aspects of microcosmic
phenomena as implied in Werner Heisenberg's principle of indeterminacy that is beyond the range of man's ordinary perception. In-
strumentalism, that is so cherished by our technological convictions,
does not at all remove the dilemma of man's bondage to the misleading sense perception. Whether it be the spectroscope, telescope,
microscope, cloud chamber or any other clever laboratory device,
they only magnify, extend or alternate the field in which all the
phenomena still have to be processed through our sensory framework.

At the time of Galileo, it was a startling novelty to observe the
four satellites revolving about Jupiter instead of around earth, suggesting the weakened authority of the illusory geocentric universe.
Yet, since the earth's motion was established by Galileo's eloquent
pleading in his *Dialogues*, it remains an ever greater enigma for the
very Galilean experimental science to interpret the negative result
of Michelson's experiment. In replacing one illusion of "reality" by
another, man erroneously attempts to explain one external event
by another external event, disregarding the imperfection in the very
framework of the human sensory system. In this type of search,
man is like a person who seeks the cause of the projected image
on the screen while disregarding the projection machine which produces the image. It is man himself, the least-known reality, who
fathers the changing, projected thought images of this universe, and
these he tries to intercommunicate, although imperfectly. Scientific
truth evolves extremely slowly and, in addition, each change of

scientific thought is a mere creation of new words applied to the old tune. Or, to put it another way, the old image is not destroyed but merely refocused. Yet therein rests the value of science—through the realization of ever recurrent errors and illusions along the pathway toward an ever higher consciousness. New light that is now being gathered around the problem of physical reality is that new factor which promises to lift human beings out of the isolation of their material oblivion and bring rays on the boundless value of moral truths. Once again, after his Babylonian delusion, man is bound to realize that "in the beginning God created the heaven and the earth."

FOR FURTHER READING

BERDYAEV, NICOLAS. *The Fate of Man in the Modern World: A Prophetic Warning Against the Dangers of Modern Science.* Ann Arbor: The University of Michigan Press, 1961.

CHAMBADAL, PAUL. *La Physique Moderne et Son Interpretation.* Paris: Librairie Arman Colin, 1956.

COUDERC, PAUL. *The Wider Universe.* ("Science Today Series.") New York: Harper & Bros. Publishers, 1960.

COULSON, CHARLES ALFRED. *Science and the Idea of God.* Arthur S. Eddington Memorial Lecture. Cambridge: Cambridge University Press, 1958.

CROMBIE, ALISTAIR CAMERON. *Science from Augustine to Galileo.* London: Mercury Books, 1961.

DINGLE, HERBERT. *The Scientific Adventure: Essays in the History and Philosophy of Science.* London: Sir Isaac Pitman & Sons, Ltd., 1952.

————. *The Sources of Eddington's Philosophy.* Cambridge: Cambridge University Press, 1954.

DREYER, JOHN LOUIS EMIL. *A History of Astronomy from Thales to Kepler.* Reprint. New York: Dover Publications, Inc., 1953.

EDDINGTON, ARTHUR. *The Nature of the Physical World.* Cambridge: Cambridge University Press, 1929.

————. *New Pathways in Science.* Messenger Lectures. Cambridge: Cambridge University Press, 1935.

————. *The Philosophy of Physical Science.* Cambridge: Cambridge University Press, 1939.

————. *Science and the Unseen World.* New York: Macmillan Co., 1930.

HEITLER, WALTER. *Man and Science.* London: Oliver & Boyd Ltd., 1963.

HOYLE, FRED. *Frontiers of Astronomy*. New York: Harper & Bros. Publishers, 1955.

————. *The Nature of the Universe*. New York: Harper & Bros. Publishers, 1951.

JACKS, LAWRENCE PEARSALL. *Sir Arthur Eddington: Man of Science and Mystic*. Cambridge: Cambridge University Press, 1949.

JEANS, JAMES. *The Mysterious Universe*. Cambridge: Cambridge University Press, 1932.

JONES, H. SPENCER. *Astronomer Royal: Life on Other Worlds*. New York: Macmillan Co., 1940.

KOESTLER, ARTHUR. *The Sleepwalkers: A History of Man's Changing Vision of the Universe*. New York: Macmillan Co., 1959.

KOYRE, ALEXANDRE. *From the Closed World to the Infinite Universe*. New York: Harper Torchbooks, 1958.

MUNITZ, MILTON KARL (ed.). *Theories of the Universe from Babylonian Myth to Modern Science*. "Library of Scientific Thought." New York: New York University, 1957.

ORR, M. A. (MRS. JOHN EVERSHED). *Dante and the Early Astronomers*. New Edition. London: Allan Wingate, Publishers, 1956.

PANNEKOEK, ANTONIE. *A History of Astronomy*. New York: Interscience Publishers, Inc., 1961.

SANTILLANA, GEORGE DE. *The Crime of Galileo*. Chicago: University of Chicago Press, 1955.

SCHROEDINGER, ERWIN. *What Is Life?* Cambridge: Cambridge University Press, 1947.

STRÖMBERG, GUSTAF. *The Soul of the Universe*. Reprint. North Hollywood, Calif.: Educational Research Institute, 1967.

TOULMIN, STEPHEN, and GOODFIELD, JUNE. *The Fabric of the Heavens: The Development of Astronomy and Dynamics*. New York: Harper Torchbooks, 1965.

WEIZSAECKER, C. F. VON. *The World View of Physics*. Chicago: University of Chicago Press, 1952.

WHITROW, G. J. *The Structure and Evolution of the Universe*. New York: Harper Torchbooks, 1959.

ZINNER, ERNST. *The Stars Above Us*. New York: Charles Scribner's Sons, 1957.

CHRISTIAN FAITH

AND

HISTORY

Earle E. Cairns

Earle E. Cairns is professor of history and chairman of the department of history and political science at Wheaton College. A graduate of the University of Omaha, he holds the A. M. and Ph. D. degrees from the University of Nebraska and the Th. B. from the Presbyterian Seminary of Omaha. Previous teaching posts were held at Western Bible College (Manitoba, Canada) and Presbyterian Theological Seminary of Omaha. An ordained minister of the United Presbyterian Church, U. S. A., he served churches in Nebraska, Illinois, and Wisconsin. Dr. Cairns is the author of *Christianity Through the Centuries* (also produced in a Japanese edition), *Saints and Society* and *Christianity in the United States,* in addition to numerous journal articles and chapters of symposia.

7

CHRISTIAN FAITH
AND
HISTORY

Earle E. Cairns

CHRISTIAN FAITH AND HISTORY are unrelated in the thinking of many so-called scientific historians in the tradition of Leopold von Ranke. They claim that history is scientific in method and can have no relationship to final causation. Unfortunately for them, philosophy, which they exclude at the front door, creeps in the back way through their exaltation of geography, economics or some other factor as the explanation for historic phenomena. Their philosophy is implicit and often unrecognized by them.

The Christian historian does not exclude these secondary horizontal earthly factors but seeks to relate them to ultimate causes. Thus explanation in history involves a horizontal and a vertical orientation of scientific and philosophic elements. The Christian historian gathers his data by the best scientific procedures that the nonchristian historian uses but goes on to use the biblical frame of reference in interpretation rather than some man- or nature-centered world and life view. It is clear that any interpreter has concepts that determine his interpretation of data no matter how scientific he may have been in its collection.

This approach becomes particularly relevant in the light of the failure of purely scientific history in this age and the rise of historical relativism. It is now clearly recognized that, while history may be scientific in its method, it is, implicitly or explicitly, philosophical when one begins to interpret it.

The approach is also important as one faces the modern crises of history. The vastness and impersonality of natural catastrophe, such as the Japanese earthquake of 1923, and the constant enlargement of the universe by science leave the individual with a sense of weakness and inadequacy in the face of a universe which without God is apparently hostile to man. This cosmic problem is intensified by the social problems created by impersonal, total, global and mechanized war, uncontrollable economic crises, such as the Great Depression of 1929, genocide and now the threat of nuclear annihilation. The personal problem of sin cannot be answered by merely scientific history. Therefore one cannot divorce Christian faith from history without sacrificing the possibility of deriving any meaningful understanding of it.

Four ideas are inherent in the word *history*. It may mean the events which are the raw data of history. The historian cannot know events directly except for the existential moment of historic happenings in which he may participate. History in this sense is absolute and occurs only once in time and space. The event cannot be repeated. In this sense history does not repeat itself. The German word *geschichte* conveys this meaning.

History may also mean the material which the historian uses in his reconstruction of the past. This is the raw material of actual relics from the past, such as buildings, furniture and documentary remains. Thus the historian is confined to indirect data from the past rather than the direct and present data with which the exact sciences work. Furthermore, history involves the process of inquiry or investigation of the data. *Historia* as used by Thucydides, the father of scientific history, conveys these two ideas. Our word *history* is also derived through the Latin and the French from *historia*.

The Greek word *historikos* refers to a fourth meaning: the final product of the historian's activity, the written narrative. Thus history may be thought of as event, remains, method or research and reconstruction.

This necessitates an attempt at a definition of history as man can know it. History is the interpreted reconstruction of socially significant human activities based on facts gained by scientific methods. Thus any historian, including the Christian, must give attention to the philosophic as well as the scientific and literary elements in his work. Luke in his prologue to his gospel (1:1-4) mentions all of these elements. There he gives an organizing framework for the relation of Christian faith and history. In fact, Luke's statement is a cogent epitome of the best advice to be found in the finest modern manuals of historiography, as is shown below.

THE SCIENTIFIC ASPECT OF HISTORY

History can never be an exact science in the sense that physics is, although it can be scientific in its method of using materials. It cannot be an exact science because it does not have the fixed vocabulary of science. The word *ohm* means the same to scientists around the world, but *progress* has many meanings, depending on the historian. Scientific experiments can be repeated and become the basis of law or prediction; historical events are not repeatable nor the basis for exact prediction. History deals with past activities of dynamic man which are to be found only in remains, whereas science deals with the present objects of nature operating under uniform laws. The scientist can work directly on his objects, but the historian must use the indirect record of the past. The scientist is outside his data; the historian cannot disassociate himself from history. His work is personal rather than impersonal. In addition, the free will of man operates in history in a way that makes repetition, except in very general patterns, impossible. Bias, either personal or environmental, prevents attainment of complete objectivity. For example, sixteenth century histories of the Reformation by Cardinal Caesar Baronius and Matthias Flacius are marked by contrasting religious biases. Because Edward Gibbon lived in the rationalistic climate of eighteenth century thought, he was unable to properly assess the role of Christianity in his *History of the Decline and Fall of the Roman Empire.* Moreover, evidence may be incomplete or forged. The *Donation of Constantine*, used to buttress papal power from the eighth to the fifteenth centuries, was a forgery. Finally the Christian historian cannot ignore the role of God in history. The books of Habakkuk and Jeremiah reveal that God may even use pagan nations to punish His sinful people.

The above points make ridiculous the claims of Von Ranke and his modern followers to objective or exact scientific history. One should also keep in mind that the presence of implicit or explicit conceptions in the interpretation of history introduces another element of subjectivity into the process. Must the Christian historian then become a historical relativist, or can he use scientific methodology in gathering his data and, recognizing his limitations of bias and his frame of reference in interpretation, reconstruct history as accurately as possible within these limitations?

By way of answer, one can turn for illumination to Luke's selection of materials. In his gospel (1:1), he states that he made use of the best secondary materials available to him from existing narratives of the life of Christ. Luke associates himself with these writers by the use of the words "also" (v. 3) and "us" (v. 2). Furthermore, he does not condemn these writers but uses them to construct a more adequate account of Christ's life. He also uses the primary contemporary accounts of "eyewitnesses" (v. 2) of the words and deeds of Christ. He had many opportunities to talk with such contemporaries of Christ as Philip the evangelist, the "old disciple" Mnason, James the brother of Christ, and most likely Mary the mother of Jesus. From whom else would he have obtained the clinical account of the virgin birth (Luke 1-2)? Men such as Sir William Ramsay and William Hobart have demonstrated the accuracy of Luke's geographical, nautical, political and medical terminology. Like any modern historian, he used the best primary and secondary sources which were available to him and thereby set a high standard for the present Christian historian.

Luke also sets a pattern of careful historical methodology. He uses the word *parakoloutheō* (Luke 1:3) which means "to follow, trace or investigate a thing." The same word is used in I Timothy 4:6 and II Timothy 3:10 to suggest the idea of personal investigation to get full information. In addition, Luke claimed that he had investigated "all things" from "the very first" (Luke 1:3). This suggests an orderly chronological account of his information from the account of the virgin birth of Christ to His death. Luke's further use of the adverb *accurately* suggests his attempt to be objective. He would not falsify, withhold, or manufacture evidence but would follow his work to its logical conclusions. The use of the words *in order* also suggests a consecutive and logical treatment of the data derived from his sources by this scientific technique. No better summary of the best elements of modern historical method can be found in the accepted modern manuals on historical method.

The modern historian uses external criticism to establish the authenticity or genuineness of the document he is studying. This process is known as historical criticism. Then textual, or lower, criticism is used to find out whether the text has integrity. This involves discovering whether the text came complete from the hand of the author or whether there have been interpolations. The historian finally employs techniques of internal criticism to see whether the document has credibility as a statement of historical *fact*. This is the goal both of the Christian and the secular historian.

While it is clear that the historian cannot accept the contention that history can be an exact reconstruction of the past, the Christian historian, as did Luke in his day, will use the best scientific methods to obtain his facts. In this regard he will be as honest and as fair a workman in the gathering of his data as the secular historian.

When, however, he turns from the scientific aspect of history which may be said to make history a general although not an exact science, he will admit to a problem. This is created by the fact that all come to the task of selecting and interpreting data with a general frame of reference out of which comes a philosophy of history. This philosophy may not be recognized but is implicit. The historian who recognizes his underlying assumptions about life and history will be better able to approximate Luke's motivation to present truth concerning the past—in Luke's case, the life and work of Christ (Luke 1:4). Truth is the final goal of history, and this leads the historian into the realm of philosophy of history. There should be room here for knowledge which revelation throws on what has happened, so that one can construct a broad view of the past which will be as relatively accurate as human beings can make it in the light of the limitations already discussed.

THE PHILOSOPHIC ASPECT OF HISTORY

Any reconstruction of the past involves the question of the meaning of history. What truth does it offer concerning the past? In the process of answering this question, historians have tended to create schools and philosophies of history. Adherents of schools of history claim to base historical meaning upon descriptive facts attained by scientific methods, but the philosophers of history recognize the subjective deductive aspects of their work. The former deal with the data of time and space concerning man or nature; the latter seek wholeness by the relation of the data of time and space to the ultimate, which for the Christian historian includes the data of revelation. Schools of historical interpretation limit meaning to secondary and temporal data of man or nature within history, such as geography, economics or great men. The Christian philosopher of history recognizes that consideration of historical data cannot be effective without relating history to a vertical dimension. The data of time must be related to eternity to achieve wholeness. The origin, scope, course and goal of history cannot be ignored. Actually some historians who represent schools of history really have an implicit philosophy of history which they do not recognize. Thus the difference between a school and a philosophy of history is more one of scope than of essence because those in the schools do give an ultimate though unrecognized interpretation to their data.

The economic determinists constitute a school of historical interpretation. The idea of the importance of the economic factor in history is derived from Karl Marx, although economic determinists are not necessarily Marxian socialists. Charles Beard in his book, *An Economic Interpretation of the Constitution of the United States*, asserts that the holders of bonds and currency issued during the American Revolution created a strong federal government to protect their investment. The economic determinists have done a service in demonstrating that how men make a living is equally significant with politics in historical interpretation. The Reformation, one must remember, had an economic factor as one of its causes. The error consists in making economics the main causal factor rather than a secondary contingent factor. The Christian historian like Paul (I Thess. 4:11-12) will not ignore economic considerations, but he will not make them ultimate in his interpretation.

Nor will he follow the geographic school which makes geography the final cause in history. Frederick Jackson Turner's assertion of environment or the frontier as the causative factor in American history led him to credit the influence of the frontier American with the development of democracy, thrift, energy, nationalism and institutions. This interpretation ignores the fact that American democratic culture was carried to the West by settlers whose ancestors had brought it from England. Turner forgot that geography is a static factor above which dynamic man can rise. Geography is an important conditioning factor in human history, but it is not an adequate, final explanation of the data of history.

Some historians subscribe to the great man school of history which makes great men the causative factor in history. Accordingly, German history in the twentieth century is to be explained in terms of Kaiser Wilhelm and Hitler. This ignores the fact that leaders are more often clever men who take advantage of environmental conditions favorable to rise to power. Man is a finite creature who is often as much a victim of history as a maker of history.

The schools of interpretation do give us partial truth in asserting the importance of human or natural factors on the horizontal level. The Christian historian must recognize economic, human and geographic factors as secondary, contingent and conditioning elements in human affairs, but he must not expect to find final answers in the historical process. The schools provide no answer to the problem of sin, the role of God in human affairs, or ethical norms. The economic factor in the Reformation in Pope Leo's desire, as Luther put it, to milk Germany "now that Italy is sucked dry," did anger Germans; but it is only a partial answer to the causes of the Reformation.

Luther's *Ninety-Five Theses* were the occasion for the German Reformation, but this does not mean there would have been no Reformation without Luther. The historian must relate these secondary factors to the final cause. Partial answers are in the temporal historical process, but the ultimate answers are beyond the historical process. The Christian student must take into account the eternal God who is transcendent to history as its Creator but immanent in it as providential Ruler and Redeemer. Philosophy of history is essential.

Philosophers of history seek to relate the data within the process of history to some ultimate or transcendent source of reality. Organization of these various views into pessimistic, optimistic and pessimistic-optimistic categories has in the opinion of this writer been most fruitful in understanding their basic thrust. Categories of time, such as cyclical and linear, are inadequate because men such as Arnold Toynbee combine cyclical and linear views. Other categories are equally open to objection at various points.

Pessimistic View

The pessimistic view of history with roots in classical philosophy is illustrated by Oswald Spengler's famous work, *The Decline of the West*, which was published just after World War I. Time is linked with deterministic cycles in his thinking. This view is best symbolized by a treadmill or by a free-spinning wheel.

A culture, according to Spengler, constituted the basic unit of history instead of the class division of Marx.[1] These cultures recur in history as self-contained entities. Like biological organisms or seasons, they go through a life cycle.[2] Each is a closed unit and there is no progress from one to the other. Each of the eight cultures, of which he discusses only three in detail, in its life cycle moves from a peasant-dominated, primitive historyless phase to a culture which degenerates into a civilization[3] marked by a money economy and urban democracy. This is followed by a universal state after a period of wars in which a dictator takes control. Then comes a return to the historyless rural society. There is no progress from cycle to cycle, and man cannot guide history. History has no meaning, is not relevant.[4]

---

[1]Oswald Spengler, *The Decline of the West*, trans. Charles Atkinson (2 vols.; New York: Alfred A. Knopf, 1957), I, 21.
[2]*Ibid.*, I, 107 and Table I.
[3]*Ibid.*, I, 31.
[4]*Ibid.*, II, 44.

Spengler's theory has not appealed to Americans because of their activistic buoyant spirit. One cannot deny that there has been technological progress and that one civilization has borrowed from the other. Love as well as force has influenced the course of history. More serious from an evangelical viewpoint is Spengler's cyclical pattern of degenerative determinism which clashes with the orthodox concepts of human responsibility to God and man's temporal freedom of choice expressed in free will apart from the matter of salvation. Cultures or civilizations are the result of the interactions of individuals with each other, nature and Deity. Spengler's stress upon force as the dominant factor in history leads him to relativism in truth and morals.[5] The Christian, because Christ is Lord of history, rejects cycles. With Augustine in *The City of God*, he concludes that the circular maze of cyclical interpreters is the only circular item in history.[6]

Optimistic View

A much larger group of interpreters adopt an optimistic philosophy of history which may be symbolized by spirals, the upward-moving line of a graph or the progressive forward movement of the wheels of a chariot. Such interpreters tend to base their thinking upon biological and social evolution. God's immanence, if He is allowed in history at all, is emphasized. Social action, education and science make possible a golden age in history on earth. Progress toward a golden age is elevated to a dogma. Many of these optimistic interpreters owe much to Hegel's *Philosophy of History*. He believed that the Absolute mind or spirit was seeking to realize freedom through purposeful evolutionary development in nature or space and time or history. This realization involved the conflict of opposites which resulted in a final synthesis.

One of the best-known nontheistic optimistic interpreters of history is Karl Marx. He eliminates Providence from a history in which matter in motion is the ultimate. Because "man is what he eats," economic forces of production in the hands of an exploiting class determine all the institutions and culture of society; and because the capitalistic producer deprives the worker of "surplus value" in the form of profits, monopoly concentration of wealth takes place and the poor become poorer. A dialectic tension occurs between the worker and the capitalist who deprives him of "surplus value." This class conflict will end in a dictatorship of the proletariat as the

[5]*Ibid.*, I, xiii, 23, 25, 46, 315.
[6]Augustine, *The City of God*, XII. 13.

workers seize power in an economic or military crisis. In time, after the threat of capitalism has been ended, the state will wither away and a classless society will emerge. This is an earthly millennium in which each man produces according to his ability and is rewarded according to his need. Nearly one-third of the world's population is under the sway of this creed, and it is presently the gravest threat to Christianity and Western democracy.

This sytem is abhorrent to the Evangelical because it has no room for love or faith in history and also denies God as an ultimate. Neither the historical facts of sin in the world nor the sacredness of personality inherent in Christianity is given any room in this theory. Its repellent atheistic materialism blinds it to any higher force in history.

There are other optimistic interpreters who also subscribe to the dogma of progress and are under the spell of evolutionary theory but who are theistic in their approach to history. God becomes the guarantee of earthly progress in history. Following the lead of Hegel, in many cases, men such as Sherwood Eddy, Shirley Jackson Case and Shailer Mathews look to a golden age through the work of Christians in society. These systems are basically postmillennial in eschatology and naïvely optimistic concerning sin and the perfectibility of human nature because of rooting their thinking in the philosophy of the Renaissance, the Enlightenment and nineteenth century evolutionary idealism.

Arnold Toynbee, the great contemporary philosopher of history, offers a secularized version of Augustine's *City of God* in his various writings, such as *Civilization on Trial*, which is the best summary of his thinking. With Spengler his impression of recurrence in history leads him to adopt cycles of civilizations, but unlike Spengler, he asserts these civilizations may make progress, especially along spiritual lines from one to the other. A civilization, which he thinks is the basic unit of history, rises when a creative minority leads a group of people in a favorable response to a physical, social or moral challenge. The civilization grows as it meets moral and spiritual challenges successfully, but it suffers breakdown when the creative minority do not renew the springs of creativity by temporary withdrawal from and then a return to the society. They then try to hold their privileged position by force, and a schism occurs in which the people passively submit but give their allegiance to a new religion. At this point external barbarians destroy the civilization, but the religion may become the chrysalis of a new civilization. At least thirty civilizations have gone through this cycle, but the religion in each has contributed to the successor. Toynbee thinks our present civilization might survive if man develops a synthetic religion from Christianity and Mahayana Buddhism, a more collectivistic society, and a democratic world order. Then earth will become a province of the kingdom of God.

While the Evangelical deplores Toynbee's slavish adherence to evolution, his destructive biblical criticism and his syncretistic higher religion, he is glad of his emphasis upon the universality of sin, the possibility of technological and cultural progress and the necessity for religion in society. The Evangelical is not quite so sure that man will achieve Toynbee's grand synthesis, especially when Christ's deity and work are minimized. Toynbee, like all optimistic interpreters, is under the spell of the natural law conceptions of Newton and the idea of genetic development to an earthly Utopia by human effort. Sin to him is Pelagian rather than Augustinian because it seems to be more a matter of bad environment than heredity. The historical process rather than Christ is savior.

Pessimistic-Optimistic View

Pessimistic-optimistic philosophers of history admit that there are recurrent parallels in history but, unlike Spengler, do not view them as deterministic. They also admit that there is cultural and technological progress in history. Faith creates active love in the present, and hope energizes service until Christ consummates human history by His appearance.

Such interpreters owe much to the inspiration of Augustine's *City of God*, which was his answer to the crisis of Roman civilization in the sack of Rome in A.D. 410. Augustine asserted that a sovereign God created history over which His Son became Lord. Augustine saw the unity of the human race in sin and salvation in the course of history. The individual, by love of God or by self-love, chooses his city. The consummation will come, according to Augustine, in the cataclysmic advent of Christ to establish final order. Augustine's influence has been strongest among pessimistic-optimistic interpreters of history.

One group of such interpreters seems to cling to the optimistic approach but holds to the possibility of progress through spiritual dynamism until Christ comes. Herbert Butterfield, a Methodist professor at the University of Cambridge, in such books as *Christianity and History* develops such a view. He claims that scientific, academic or technical history can only yield secondary causes. Human personality which is spiritual and free exists for the glory of God, and the purpose of history is "the manufacture of souls." Because man is free, universal sin results, and no man or nation is in a position to make moral judgments upon others. The dynamic of history is love, such as Christ demonstrated by His suffering and which will help man to make progress as he loves and suffers. Butterfield is somewhat indefinite concerning the nature of the end of history. Unfortunately, he and others like him, such as John Baillie and Kenneth S. Latourette, do not sufficiently relate their view to the person and work of Christ. Also, they still accept the ideas of evolution and biblical criticism.

The neoorthodox group constitutes another class of pessimistic-optimistic interpreters. This group is in revolt against reason, the liberal overemphasis upon the divine immanence, and the cult of progress because of the demonstration of the sinful in human history in two world wars in this century. Most neoorthodox theologians owe much to Karl Barth, the Swiss neoorthodox authority, and in turn to Sören Kierkegaard, the Danish existentialist theologian.

Reinhold Niebuhr's *Faith and History* will serve as a typical illustration of the neoorthodox approach to philosophy of history. God is wholly other than man, and time is separate from eternity. Thus divine history is separated from secular history in a thoroughgoing dualism which is not biblical. Only as God pierces history and discloses its meaning in Christ's life, death and resurrection is there any way that man can cope with universal sin. In this crisis man is related to God by the leap of faith. He asserts the relativism of our historical knowledge, of progress to the goal of moral perfection because of sin, and of the solution of history by the dogma of progress. Unlike the other neoorthodox thinkers, Niebuhr, perhaps because of the social problems encountered in his pastorate among automobile workers in Detroit, thinks social progress is possible through love made actual in deeds. The Christian can participate in the limited development of a more Christian social order without expecting to create a final perfect social order by human effort.

Niebuhr's view of the holiness of God, the universality of sin, rejection of the cult of progress and the need for divine intervention to save man and consummate history pleases the Evangelical, but he is distressed by Niebuhr's too ready tendency to accept biblical criticism and to reduce biblical accounts, such as the fall, to the category of myths which are mere stories to explain historical facts.[7]

[7]Reinhold Niebuhr, *Faith and History: A Comparison of Christian and Modern Views of History* (New York: Charles Scribner's Sons, 1949), pp. 33-36, 121.

The conservative Christian takes exception to the neoorthodox dualism between holy and secular history which denies the unity and continuity of history under the lordship of Christ. While God is transcendent Creator, He is also immanent in history in providence, redemption and the work of the Holy Spirit. Except for Niebuhr, neoorthodox interpreters weaken man's sense of responsibility to show in the social order the implications of his faith in Christ by loving service. Their view of the Bible becoming the Word of God in the confrontation of the soul with God in the existential crisis leads to subjectivism and mysticism by which one has immediate intuition of God. The role of reason in apologetics to buttress the faith is depreciated. Such a philosophy or theology of history does not do justice to the biblical and historical materials.

The evangelical interpreter in the biblical and Augustinian tradition of philosophy of history agrees with the pessimist concerning the presence of evil in history but disagrees with his cyclical view of time. With the optimist he is hopeful concerning the outcome of history, not through human effort but because God is controlling the process for His eventual glory and man's final good. His interpretation is general because he does not know enough to say of each detail whether it is or is not God's action.

The Evangelical's *source* of history is the act of the sovereign will of a transcendent self-existent and self-sufficient God (Rom. 11: 36). This rather than chance accounts for the origins of nature and man. God is declared to be the Creator of nature for man's use (Gen. 1:28; Ps. 8:3-8; 24:1-2; Jer. 27:5; Heb. 11:3). Man is the result of a creative act of God for His own glory (Gen. 1:26—2:25; Job 33:4; Ps. 8:4-6; Isa. 43:7; Jer. 27:5). Apart from God's activity there is nothing; Christ is related to the work of creation as the causative agent of Deity in John 1:1-3, Colossians 1:16 and Hebrews 1:2-3. Thus in addition to the data of history, achieved by the scientific study of documents, there is the data of revelation as in God's self-disclosure through men inspired by the Holy Spirit. God reveals Himself in words as well as in the divine acts of which neoorthodox thinkers make so much. The historian must add the data of revelation to the data of science and history or else he will be limited to a horizontal limited view of history as of no concern to God.

In addition to these ontological and epistemological considerations, the historian must take account of absolute values, revealed in the human consensus as to what is right and wrong through the universal condemnation of such acts as murder and adultery. This forces him to give some consideration to the role of conscience in history (John 8:9; Rom. 2:15). God is seen as the source both of conscience and moral values. Perhaps this is why man in history has been haunted by frustration and guilt in failing to achieve what he knows is his better destiny. His achievement is limited by finitude and moral inability caused by the fall.

Consideration of the historical and biblical data concerning the *scope* of history leads one to reject the parochial view of the favored proletariat of Marx or the favored Prussian state of Hegel. Both the biblical assertion and the record of man's grasping after unity in history suggest the unity of the race. Alexander, the Caesars, Charlemagne, Napoleon, Hitler and now the Communist leaders seek to unify the world and to achieve the oneness of man in history.

Consistent failure to achieve such unity points to the dualism in history which comes because of the fall (Gen. 3; cf. Ps. 51:5; Rom. 5:12-19) and the external solicitation to evil by Satan. It is little wonder that Spengler could see no progress in history or that the neoorthodox thinkers are pessimistic concerning secular history. There are indeed two cities among men. The presence of original sin through heredity and actual sin by transgression creates the flaws in the tapestry of history. Both history and the Bible document "man's inhumanity to man." This must be taken into account if one is to understand Hitler's attempt at genocide in the killing of over a third of the Jews in the world during World War II. Yet history is still one because Christ is the Lord of history, and in this period of grace God is allowing man to exercise his free will in choosing to reject or accept Himself.

Succession of events in time or the course of history must also be related to the Divine Being. Providence is seen in the laws of nature which govern God's creation. The functioning of these laws is related by the writers of Scripture to Christ (Col. 1:17; Heb. 1:3). The uniformity upon which the scientist and farmer equally count is a result of this contention. Without it experimental science could not function.

Human institutions such as the family (Gen. 1:28; 2:20; Matt. 19:4-6) and human government (Gen. 9:5-6; Rom. 13:1-7; I Peter 2:13-14) are empirical phenomena which the Bible attributes to God. Even the Russian attempt to destroy the family by easy divorce after their revolution has given way to an almost Puritanical conception of that institution. These are tools for the good of man but, in the case of the state, they may become perverted when the state becomes an end in itself and the individual a means.

God is also linked with the control of historic events within the Bible. The Hebrews' Babylonian captivity for seventy years under the Chaldeans was said to be "for their good" (Jer. 24:5). The Chaldeans were a divine instrument to punish a sinful people and were in their turn judged by God for their sins. God is said to control the existence of nations as well as their power and their movements (Deut. 32:8; Dan. 2:21; Amos 9:7; Acts 17:26). The persistent retention of the Jew's identity through two thousand years of dispersion cannot be accounted for by scientific historical techniques.

Above all, Christ is related to meaningfulness in history. His coming was related by Paul to a providential preparation in the Roman Empire (Gal. 4:4) in a way that cannot be ignored when one considers the unity created by Roman citizenship, law and roads; the universal Koine language which the Greeks under Alexander had developed; and the assertion of a coming Messiah in the dozens of synagogues in the empire. God through the incarnation (John 1:14, 18) entered into time and history. The calendar is an empirical witness to this event.

The cross serves as another empirical demonstration of the self-sacrificing love of God to man in order that man might have salvation from sin and from the limitations of history. God in Christ is immanent in human affairs as Redeemer. The divine approval of the atoning work of Christ is declared to be the resurrection (Rom. 1:4; I Cor. 15:14), a historical fact as certain as the existence of the Emperor Tiberius.

Finally, a Christian philosophy of history must take into account the historical fact of a chosen people in both the Old and New Testaments. This community of the redeemed cannot be ignored by any historian when he considers its ongoing impact on human affairs. The cosmic function of the church is to reveal the divine wisdom (Eph. 3:10). The church also functions as the light of the world in proclaiming the saving power of its Redeemer in order to fulfill His major commission (Matt. 28:18-20) to it. It also has a cultural function in serving as salt to preserve culture. It was the church, imperfect though it may have been, which converted and civilized the Teutonic barbarians when they moved into the Roman Empire between A.D. 375 and 476. The Reformation era becomes meaningless without study of the work of the Reformers. The historian will only confuse his understanding of American culture if he ignores the role of Puritanism in English and American life or the social reforms of such Evangelicals as William Wilberforce and the seventh Earl of Shaftesbury in nineteenth century England. Modern missions, as Latourette in his scholarly volumes on missionary history in the nineteenth century demonstrates, have played as important a role in the Europeanization of the world as modern science and technology.

The summation or conclusion of history, toward which man seems to be moving ever faster with the compression and acceleration of historical events in an era of modern technology, must be related to God by the historian unless he is to neglect some essential data. The integration of redeemed humanity is suggested by such passages as Ephesians 1:10. When one considers the flourishing Jewish state since 1948 and the importance of the Middle East with its strategic Suez Canal and air routes and great resources of oil, he wonders how near man is to the climax of history in the cataclysmic coming of Christ to consummate human affairs.

This coming also suggests the moral element in history to which the British historian Acton called attention. The resurrection of Christ is a testimony to the fact of the responsibility of men ultimately to give an account to God of their human pilgrimage. Judgment is as sure as the resurrection of Christ (Acts 17:31; 24:15; John 5:28-29; Heb. 9:27-28).

In such a framework the empirical data which the historian gathers by scientific techniques will have more than a secondary economic, geographic or personal meaning. It will be related to the ultimate source of history which is God Himself who finally becomes all in all with even Christ subject to Him when Christ completes His work in time (I Cor. 15:28). Moreover the revelational data gives an insight one cannot gain from the empirical facts.

History also has didactic and moral value. Polybius asserted the didactic[8] and moral value of history.[9] Plutarch's *Lives* demonstrated the danger of evil and the value of moral conduct. Paul (Rom. 15:4; I Cor. 10:6, 11) and medieval historians agreed with this. Only modern historians, carried away by the supposed autonomy and sufficiency of reason and intoxicated with the possibilities of the scientific method to achieve a perfect order, have forgotten this.

Evangelical historians should shoulder the task of making philosophy of history as relevant to the contemporary crises as Augustine did in his day. Views such as those of Spengler lead to despair in society, while the optimists mistakenly look for a Utopia by human effort. The Christian historian, who honestly uses the scientific method to establish his facts and then puts them into a biblical

[8]*Histories,* I:1; IX:2; XII:25.
[9]*Ibid.,* I:35.

perspective, is more realistic in his assessment of human origins, sin nature and destiny than his nonchristian colleagues. With Luke he uses the best materials and methods to arrive at the meaning of history in terms of truth. He will seek to present this truth in artistic literary style so that it will be clear to the reader. Neither cyclical motion nor indefinite spiraling progress answers the dilemma of man's destiny as well as eschatological linear direction in history by God. The goal of history is the ultimate triumph and rule of God in history as well as beyond. History thus considered is a revelation of the working in time of God "of whom, through whom and to whom are all things."

FOR FURTHER READING

AUGUSTINE. *The City of God*. Still the classical exposition of a Christian philosophy of history.

GARRAGHAN, GILBERT S. *A Guide to Historical Method*. New York: Fordham University Press, 1946. The author, a Roman Catholic, develops a detailed study of historiography with more than usual attention to a theistic philosophy.

GOTTSCHALK, LOUIS. *Understanding History*. New York: Alfred A. Knopf, 1950. This author clearly presents the scientific aspect of historical writing.

LOWITH, KARL. *Meaning in History*. Chicago: University of Chicago Press, 1949. Lowith traces the major ideas of the main philosophers of history from Marx back to Augustine and, finally, to the Bible which he seems to interpret along neoorthodox lines.

MASTERS, DONALD C. *The Christian Idea of History*. Waterloo, Ontario: Waterloo Lutheran University, 1962. This is an able evangelical approach to the philosophy of history.

BIOLOGY

John W. Klotz

John W. Klotz is professor of natural sciences and chairman of the division of natural sciences at Concordia Senior College, Fort Wayne, Indiana. He has also taught at Concordia Institute, Bethany Lutheran College, Mankato, Minnesota, and Concordia Teachers College, River Forest, Illinois. A graduate of Concordia Collegiate Institute, Bronxville, New York, and Concordia Seminary, St. Louis, he holds the Ph. D. from the University of Pittsburgh. His publications include *Genes, Genesis and Evolution; Modern Science in the Christian Life;* and *The Challenge of the Space Age.*

8

BIOLOGY

John W. Klotz

Biology may well be standing on the threshold of amazing break-throughs. There are some who believe that in the next generation biology will occupy the prestigious position that physics occupies today, and they may well be right. In the past, man has witnessed some remarkable achievements. He is learning more and more about the ways in which life processes occur. The work of Watson and Crick in determining the structure of DNA (deoxyribonucleic acid, the basic "genetic code" material of the chromosomes) has promise of an immense increase in the understanding of inheritance.

On the other hand it should be recognized that biology has traditionally lagged behind the physical sciences in the adequacy and comprehensiveness of its theories, and the social sciences have traditionally lagged behind the biological sciences. This is not because of an innate lack of intelligence on the part of biologists; it is a part of the nature of the subject matter. As Warren Weaver has pointed out, physical science seems to be loosely coupled.[1] So far as cause and effect are concerned, there are in the physical sciences many one-to-one relationships, that is, many instances in which a given effect or result can be analyzed as related to a single or a few causes. This is not the case in biology. Living things are more complicated than nonliving materials in the sense that a given effect can rarely be analyzed as a result of a single or a few causes. It is more difficult to study biological phenomena than it is to study the phenomena of the physical sciences.

[1] Warren Weaver, "Science and People," *Science,* CXXII (December 30, 1955), 1256.

THE NATURE OF BIOLOGY

One of the effects of this is that biology is much more a descriptive science than are the physical sciences. The latter are largely explanatory; biology is partly explanatory and partly descriptive. In the physical sciences the common practice is to develop hypotheses and then to conduct observations and experiments on the basis of the hypotheses in order to test them. The experiments and observations conducted are largely experiments of proof rather than experiments of discovery.[2]

In biology, on the other hand, much of the work involves experiments of discovery. Biologists are still attempting to discover facts; they are not yet at the point where they can fully test their explanations. They are still getting information and classifying it; they have not yet advanced to the point where they can explain much of the information they have gathered.[3]

Biology is also handicapped in that it has very few general theories such as the atomic theory which serve to cover the whole area of the discipline. This slows progress in this field of study. About the only generalized theory that the biologist has is the theory of evolution, and that is one of the factors which accounts for the strong appeal of evolution. The biologist is constantly searching for these general theories, but so far he has not been as successful as his colleagues in the physical sciences.

Actually the biologist has much to contribute to society and to the understanding of the world in which man lives. There is nothing more important than a study of life itself. Man has gained a large amount of information about life processes, and this has been translated into substantial practical benefits. The research scientist ordinarily seeks generalized knowledge for knowledge's sake; his purpose is not practical outcomes but a better understanding of the nature of things. Many of the leading biologists both of past centuries and of this age have been motivated by nothing more than an outstanding curiosity, but inevitably the information and understandings they have gained have had practical outcomes. It is this that Warren Weaver had in mind when he spoke of "the incapacity of science to be impractical."[4]

Biology is an outstanding example of Weaver's phrase. The practical progress that has been made is reflected in the extended life

---

[2]Stephen Toulmin. *The Philosophy of Science* (London: Hutchinson & Co., 1953), pp. 54 ff., 66 ff.
[3]*Ibid.*
[4]*Op cit.*, p. 1257.

expectancies and in the huge increase in food production. Here in the United States the average life expectancy has increased from thirty years in colonial America to over seventy years today. Most of this increase has come since the turn of the century; the average life expectancy in 1900 was a mere forty-seven years.

Today, too, the American society is feeding more people than ever before. A single development, that of hybrid corn, has made it possible to support millions more here in the United States. It is estimated that an area such as Licking County, in central Ohio, supported five thousand people under an Indian economy; today that same county supports eighty thousand people.

EVOLUTION

It is apparent that biology has been a real tool for blessing. Through it God has brought practical benefits to His children. Yet biology has had its conflicts with evangelical Christianity. Chief of these has been the controversy over the theory of evolution. There are many definitions of the theory. Some equate it with change, and if this is meant by the term "evolution," then certainly evolution has taken place, for it is apparent that today's world is one of change; only God is changeless (Ps. 102:25-27). Most biologists, though, have in mind a change of much larger magnitude. By evolution they mean the theory that nonliving matter became alive, that this original living material was simple in its organization, and that the world of living things known today, including man, gradually developed from these originally simple forms.

This theory is an old one. The Greeks had well-developed theories of evolution which the Romans later adopted. Because the Middle Ages overemphasized the use of the deductive method, most of the science of that period consisted of a study of ancient scientists' writings. There was little independent observation and consequently little speculation on the origin of the diversity to be found among living things. With the Renaissance, speculation started again, but with the frame of thinking of those days, it was hard to come to the idea of an evolution. An admiration for Greek and Latin learning developed in the early days of the Renaissance. To the people of the day looking back on the golden age of learning, it seemed that deterioration and not development had taken place. For that reason the people of the day simply could not conceive of progress.[5]

---

[5]Herbert Butterfield, *The Origins of Modern Science* (London: Bell, 1957), pp. 210-14.

Theories of evolution began again in the eighteenth century. Buffon (1707-88), the outstanding biologist of that period, sought natural explanations for all biological phenomena and did not hesitate to reject special creation. Erasmus Darwin (1731-1802), grandfather of Charles Darwin, presented his ideas of origins in *Zoonomia*. None of the eighteenth century scientists suggested a mechanism whereby the changes they postulated might take place. It remained for Jean Baptiste de Lamarck (1744-1829) to suggest such a mechanism in his theory of the inheritance of acquired characteristics, a theory which today is almost universally rejected.

Charles Darwin, more than any other person, developed the modern theory of evolution. The time was ripe in his day for such a development. If he had not reached the conclusions he did and published them, someone else would have done so. Indeed, Alfred Russel Wallace reached the same conclusions as Darwin did at approximately the same time and presented a paper with many of the very same ideas at the very meeting of the Linnaean Society of London at which Darwin first broached his ideas. Darwin had more experimental evidence to support his position, so he usually receives credit for the theory. Actually, though, Wallace and Darwin had come to identical conclusions concurrently.

Darwin and those who have followed him based their conclusions on a number of assumptions. They assumed that this world was the result of natural processes and that it continues to exist through the operation of natural processes. They posited uniformitarianism, believing that the present was the key to the past. They believed that the changes they witnessed on their time level could be extrapolated to the indefinite past. The theory of evolution is not only the logical but the inevitable consequence of these assumptions.

Darwin was a careful worker. The theory of evolution which he developed was not the result of a sudden inspiration, nor was it the work of a sensationalist, nor of a man who hastens to publish. Darwin had made a series of careful observations during the five-year around-the-world voyage of the British frigate H.M.S. "Beagle" on which he served as biologist. On his return to England in 1836, Darwin very carefully reworked his notes. It was only after ten years that he reached the conclusion that his observations could best be explained by assuming the gradual development and evolution of organisms. Moreover, he was such a careful worker that ten more years elapsed before he was ready to publicize his conclusions.

Once more it should be noted that the theory which Darwin developed was the natural consequence of his assumptions. Logic gave him no choice; if natural processes are to be employed to explain the origin and development of living things, if the present is the key to the past, and if it is proper to extrapolate from the past, then evolution is a reasonable explanation of the diversity of living things.

Almost all biologists use the same premises today, and it is for this reason that evolution has such an appeal. Yet these are assumptions and nothing more. Why should God be made so small that He cannot use His power directly either in the creation or preservation of the universe? Recognizing that He ordinarily works through natural means, why should man insist that He works only in this way? Why assume that the present is the key to the past and that man can describe the past accurately by extrapolation? It is just as logical and reasonable to postulate a creation by God at some point in time, a creation in which living things were brought into being by the direct action of God without the use of the natural laws by which He ordinarily governs the universe today. True, this is a matter of faith, but so are the assumptions on which evolution is based.

There is another point that deserves to be considered—a factor which explains the emotionalism which surrounds any discussion of evolution. Few scientific theories are discussed objectively. The scientist becomes emotionally involved in the theories he embraces, and is rarely unbiased and unprejudiced. Dr. Conant put it this way: "The notion that a scientist is a cool, impartial detached individual is, of course, absurd. The vehemence of conviction, the pride of authorship burn as fiercely among scientists as among any creative workers."[6] The theory of evolution developed in an especially highly emotional atmosphere. Charges and countercharges flew. Darwin, the mild-mannered man that he was, was deeply disturbed by the controversy that his theory raised. When the theory was discussed in 1860 at the Oxford meeting of the British Association for the Advancement of Science, Darwin was not even present because he did not want to become embroiled in the controversy which a discussion of his theory was bound to arouse. Unfortunately it was a British bishop who assumed the responsibility for attacking the theory; and, what was even worse, he chose to launch a personal attack on Thomas Huxley who, in Darwin's absence, found himself cast in the role of apologist for the theory.

Later the teaching of evolution was forbidden by law in some parts of the United States. Most of these state laws were passed at

---

[6]James B. Conant, *Modern Science and Modern Man* (New York: Columbia University Press, 1952), p. 67.

the insistence of churches and churchmen. When the Tennessee law, which forbade the teaching of evolution in the public schools of the state, came under attack and John Scopes was arrested for teaching evolution in the schools of Dayton, Tennessee, it was a Christian layman, William Jennings Bryan, who assumed the responsibility of prosecuting Scopes. Bryan was poorly prepared for the task; he had not tried a case for twenty-five years. Moreover, he was in poor health at the time, and died five days after the trial's conclusion. He assumed a very grave responsibility in agreeing to represent the church, and did a poor job in the role which he accepted. Both these episodes reflected unfavorably on the church. The church was placed in the position of using personal attacks and the authority of the state to interfere with science and to hamper the search for scientific truth. Consequently any attack on evolution, even today, raises a red flag and resurrects the controversies of the past. It is very difficult to find an objective discussion of evolution; the subject continues to be an emotional one.

What attitude should the Christian student of biology take toward evolution? As has been pointed out, the theory permeates biological thinking today. It is the one overall principle which many biologists believe necessary to correlate their discipline. Certainly the theory of evolution, as it has developed today and as it is generally taught and accepted, cannot be reconciled with the biblical account if this account is accepted historically. This is not to deny the fact of change or the development of new species; both can readily be demonstrated. But to accept the biblical record is to deny the gradual development from the nonliving to the living entirely by natural processes. The Bible teaches that living things came into existence by God's almighty power and that from the beginning, life existed in a wide variety of forms. It also teaches that man was specially created and that all human beings are the descendants of a single Adam and a single Eve. It denies the gradual development of all living things by natural processes from one or a very few ancestral forms, and rejects the idea that man developed from lower organisms.

In rejecting evolution the writer is not suggesting that the Christian is required to accept the chronology of Archbishop Ussher. The age of the earth is a separate problem. It is not the same as the problem of organic evolution though the two are certainly related. In any case the Bible binds no one to the acceptance of 4004 B.C. as the date of creation. Indeed there is clear evidence from the Scriptures that Ussher was wrong, though no one can determine by how much. In any circumstance, the use of genealogical tables to establish a chronology is a hazardous undertaking, and Ussher in his calculations omits at least the time between the birth of Cainan, the son of Enos, and that of Cainan's oldest son, Mahalaleel.

Can the Christian student loyal to the Scriptures hope to study biology with the idea of disproving evolution? The premises and assumptions on which this science is based do not lend themselves to scientific examination. When one uses the assumptions of the evolutionist, evolution is inevitable. It may be that sometime in the future a new paradigm or point of view will develop, and then evolution will be replaced. That has happened in the past. The Ptolemaic point of view was replaced by the Copernican, and the phlogiston theory of combustion was replaced by the modern theory of combustion. Uniformitarianism in geology is being challenged, and it could be that the theory of evolution will one day be replaced. However, the nature of the theory is such that it cannot be disproved. Nor as a matter of fact can any scientific theory be disproved; it can only be replaced by another which correlates better with the observable facts.

There is another matter that should be noted. The Newtonian scheme with strict cause and effect relationships has had its day in the physical sciences, but biology is still based on rigid cause and effect relationships. While there are aspects of the philosophy of modern physics which run counter to the Christian faith, the passing of strict cause and effect permits God to enter once more and play a part in the governing of the universe. It may be that biology will one day move away from the strict causal determinism which governs it today.

Can biology be studied fruitfully without accepting the theory of evolution? If it is the overriding principle in biology, is it worthwhile to study biology or to work in the area? Can an individual who does not accept the theory of evolution make significant contributions to the discipline? Actually there is no basic controversy between science and the church on our time level. As Dr. Conant points out, the controversies deal chiefly with phenomena of the past.[7] The Christian who does not accept evolution takes the same approach to the biological phenomena of our time level as does the evolutionist. The Christian recognizes that God ordinarily works through cause and effect relationships, and he seeks to determine the nature of these cause and effect relationships. As a Christian,

---

[7]James B. Conant, *Science and Common Sense* (New Haven: Yale University Press, 1951), pp. 259 ff.

he is committed to the idea that God can work outside the cause and effect relationships by which He governs the universe; but he recognizes that as a scientist these possibilities are outside the realm of his study. As a human being, he must work with and through the cause and effect relationships which God has established; while he recognizes that God can suspend these, he must work through them. Therefore, he finds himself operationally working in the same way as the evolutionist and as the man who denies the existence of God.

It should also be emphasized that the Christian in rejecting evolution is doing so on the basis of a set of assumptions different from those of the evolutionist. They are just as logical and reasonable as those of the evolutionist. Why should God not have stepped into the picture at a point in time and brought a functioning universe into being? Is this any less reasonable than the suggestion that the present be extrapolated back into the past? How far back into the past is one to go? If one postulates the origin of life from nonliving materials, he must violate the principle of uniformitarianism; for it is a fact that living things are not originating from nonliving things today. One can only suggest that conditions of the past were different from those which exist today. The only alternative is to suggest that life is originating today but that no one has been able to observe it, and this seems unlikely. Moreover, man is faced with the problem of the origin of the original matter—energy. Where did it come from? How did it come into being? One is forced to accept some modification of the steady state universe theory which holds that matter and energy are constantly being created, and this is only a step removed from the idea of the creation of a functioning universe instead of only its raw materials.

THE PLACE OF THE CHRISTIAN BIOLOGIST

Should Christians interest themselves in and promote biology? Clearly the answer is yes because the biological sciences face towering challenges in the years that lie ahead. It is highly desirable that Christian influences interact with nonchristian thinking in determining how the discoveries of the days ahead are used. Science in itself is basically amoral, neither good nor bad. This is not to say scientists are amoral; they certainly are moral creatures with moral responsibilities. The moral standards of scientists as they affect their work are of the highest. Deviations from the highest standards of honesty and truthfulness are simply not tolerated. However, the basis for scientific morality as such is pragmatism; these standards are demanded because they work and because they are necessary for the continuing progress of science. Christian morality has a different basis: the demands of a Creator God and love for a redeeming Christ that is to be shown in love for one's fellowmen. This morality goes beyond the pragmatic morality of those scientists who are not Christians. It extends beyond the laboratory and beyond relationships with fellow scientists into the private lives of individuals. It is not satisfied with a morality that works, but it seeks a morality that is based on love for the fellowman. Thus it is the principle of conduct that goes the second mile.

Christian influences are also needed to counteract the increasing depersonalization that is found not only in the biological sciences but in all the sciences. Indeed this is a trend not only of all science but of modern society itself. It is reflected in the team research which is so much the vogue today. Because work is the effort of a team, the individual is often lost and feels little more than a cog in a giant machine. Moreover, science is also practiced as a team discipline (e.g., the present form of medical practice with its specialization). The family doctor has given place to a group of specialists practicing in a modern clinic. While the increase in medical knowledge is a good reason for the specialization and makes it virtually a necessity, there is danger that the individual will lose his identity.

Christian love will be needed to meet the challenges and solve the problems which automation will bring. There is no doubt that modern man is in the throes of a second industrial revolution. The first industrial revolution supplied machines to do the work formerly done by men; the second industrial revolution provides computers to supervise machines. This has resulted in economic dislocations when some persons find their services no longer in demand. These men and women will need help in finding their place in society once more. Moreover, the computer has come into its own to the extent that, in many human relationships, the individual is a number, not a person. While automation has been a blessing in many respects and has increased the goods available to man, it must also be recognized that it has brought an increasing depersonalization and substantial economic dislocation. With depersonalization there has come increased emphasis on the importance of the society of which the individual is a part. The individual counts for less and less. His welfare must be subordinate to that of the society of which he is a part. However, Christianity is a world view in which both the individual and the society of which he is a part are important. In the language of Scripture, God has written His children's names on the palms of His hands (Isa. 49:16). He knows all men as individuals, not as numbers. Particularly in medicine and in the allied health sciences there is need for the Christian emphasis on the dignity and worth of the individual.

Christian influences are also needed to counteract the overemphasis on man's position as a part of nature. He cannot, of course, claim immunity from the natural laws by which the universe is governed; he is indeed a part of nature. However, by virtue of the uniqueness of his creation, man holds a position of special responsibility. He is to rule over the earth and subdue it. Modern science has enabled him to exercise that rule in a way unknown in previous generations. Now, by virtue of the control he exercises over the natural world, he has a responsibility to care for the rest of creation. He cannot exploit the rest of creation for his own selfish ends. He cannot slaughter animals just for the joy of killing; he cannot upset the balances of nature out of sheer perversity.

God has given twentieth century man powers unknown in previous generations. He must use these wisely and intelligently. The Christian will want to recognize that man has this obligation to the God who has permitted him to gain this knowledge. Nature is made up of a series of intricate balances, and man has the power to alter some of these. He needs to be wise enough to recognize the hazard of indiscriminate alterations of the balance of nature, a danger modern biology has clearly demonstrated. If he poisons the atmosphere, not only other living creatures but he himself will be adversely affected. If he dumps wastes into streams and lakes, not only will he destroy aquatic life but he will harm his own best interests. The control which man has gained demands responsible stewardship. He needs to be reminded repeatedly that he is steward, not master; and this reminder is more in order today than formerly. As Sharp points out, men in primitive groups seem to understand the relationships between themselves and plants better than men in more advanced cultures. There seems to be an almost direct correlation between the degree of civilization of a society and its failure to appreciate this dependence.[8] Christian biologists who recognize God as the Master and man as the creature are needed to emphasize this relationship.

The rise of modern biology has created new ethical and moral problems, problems which did not exist in previous societies and earlier generations. Modern medicine has given rise to some of them. One example is the problem of the individual who is critically ill.

[8]A. J. Sharp, "The Compleat Botanist," *Science,* CXLVI (November 6, 1964), 746. This article is an adaptation of an address delivered on December 30, 1963.

To what extent is society obligated to keep an individual alive as long as possible? There was a time when this was no problem; the major battle was against death, and death was usually the victor. Today the situation is somewhat different. Today it is possible to keep individuals alive who, humanly speaking, would be better off dead. These are those who are terminally ill, who will not recover permanently and whose death is only being postponed. These are also the living vegetables who can be kept breathing but who will never regain consciousness.

It is clear, of course, that the doctor has the obligation to keep alive the individual for whom there is some hope of complete or substantial recovery. It is also clear that the doctor has no right to administer a drug or take some affirmative action which will effect death. It is also clear that he and those working with him must supply the ordinary needs of his patients. But to what extent is the physician obligated to supply oxygen, blood and plasma, glucose, and electrolytically balanced solutions to those who will never recover? Questions such as these require careful consideration and consideration within a Christian framework. At first the idea of withholding things necessary for the survival of a given individual is repugnant. Such inaction seems to conflict with the general medical tradition and with the total obligation of Christian love. But is it love when a person is kept alive in severe pain when death might bring a merciful end to his suffering? Is it love to keep a person alive for months and even years in a comatose state?

Christians must recognize that the goal is not length of days but rather the bliss of heaven. For the Christian, life is only a pilgrimage. He has no abiding city here; his real home is in the presence of God. Idealistically, death holds no real terrors but serves as the gateway to a blessed eternity with Christ. It may not be love at all to keep a cancer patient alive in acute agony for a few days when he might be delivered to the joys of heaven. It may not be love at all to keep an unconscious son or daughter of God from the full conscious bliss of heaven. Yet no one can presume to know what the inscrutable purposes of God may be in these situations.

It is not suggested here that a physician is under obligation to withdraw extraordinary means and thereby bring about the individual's death. But the author does believe there may be reasons why extraordinary treatments should not be employed. Perhaps these decisions should be left to the Christian conscience and judgment of the Christian physician or the patient himself, whenever possible.

Another problem which requires Christian consideration and concern is the frantic race between growing food supplies and growing populations. The United States has often had a real problem with its agricultural surpluses; in some other areas the problem is one of near starvation. Ironically enough, modern medicine has contributed to this problem by saving the lives of many thousands of people who in former days would have succumbed as infants or as children. Because in so many places there has been a marked death control without any corresponding birth control, the problem continues to grow.

There is no easy solution to this dilemma. American surpluses will not always be such that they can be shared with the less fortunate. Sometimes there are problems with transportation of goods. In other cases there are national and racial food preferences which make these surpluses useless. Those who do not want to eat the foods that the United States has in surplus should not be criticized. Americans have their own prejudices which cause them, for instance, not to eat horsemeat.

Probably the greatest assistance which Americans can provide is helping the underdeveloped countries to help themselves. Where United States know-how will actually improve the situation in these countries (and it does not necessarily follow that it will), the acquired information should be shared. In this way the United States will provide adequate help in solving this critical problem.

Sometimes increasing knowledge raises problems that were not formerly known to exist. This is certainly the case with the increasing comprehension of the hazards of radiation. When natural radiation was first discovered and when the first X rays were produced, few people, if any, had an understanding of the hazards involved. It was only in 1927 that scientists discovered that radiation brings about mutation. When this new knowledge was added to the knowledge that most mutations are harmful, scientists realized how potentially dangerous all forms of radiation are. While this author sees no peculiarly Christian aspect of the radiation problem, he would prefer to know that Christian biologists are familiar with it and are advising regarding its solution. In the light of what is now known about radiation hazards, man needs to take another look at the whole problem of war. There are just wars; one must recognize that the government bears the sword as a minister of justice. But man's war-making ability has increased along with his abilities in other areas, and today it is possible for him to destroy himself and to poison the atmosphere, soil and water for long periods of time. Certainly the Christian must not only pray for peace but also work for peace as a disciple of the Prince of peace.

BIOLOGICAL QUESTIONS WITH THEOLOGICAL IMPLICATIONS

Is the Christian biologist limited in the research areas in which he may engage? Are there some areas which by virtue of his Christianity are off limits to him? What about research designed to create life? Will the biologist ever succeed? Would success not be a denial of God? Can the Christian participate in such research? Might such participation be blasphemous? Certainly there is nothing in the Scriptures which would deny the possibility of man's creating life. The Bible does state that life was originally created by God and that it came into existence by God's almighty power. But this does not mean God will never permit man to learn this secret of His. In a sense, men and women participate in the creation of life each time a baby is born. God has permitted His creatures to learn many of His secrets. Man has gained insights into the way in which God works in other areas; there is no reason why God should not permit man to learn the wonder of creating life.

Another question that frequently rises is the possibility of extra-terrestrial life. Is it possible that there is life of high order, similar to human life, on some other planet somewhere in this universe? Is it in order to study this question? Can the Christian participate in space exploration designed to study this question? Is the entire space program, on the other hand, an affront to God, a challenge similar to the one hurled in the teeth of God by those who attempted to build the tower at Babel?

There are those who point to the command given to the father of man that he was to rule over the earth and subdue it. They claim that the attempts to leave the earth are a violation of this command-ment. Others believe the exploration of space is only an extension of this command God gave Adam, and this author is inclined to agree with the latter group. It seems apparent that if God does not want man exploring the vast reaches of space, He is perfectly capable of making this known by providing insurmountable barriers. Mean-while it seems that man is justified in exploring space. God has made man a curious creature who seeks to meet challenges. Space is another frontier that man rises up to conquer.

Scientists are generally agreed that there is no life similar to hu-man life anywhere in the solar system. Conditions on the sun's planets, as scientists now know them to exist, are such that they would not permit the existence of complex life such as characterizes man. Some suggest there may be simple plant life on Mars and bacteria in the Venusian clouds, but they agree on the absence of humanoids elsewhere in the solar system.

At the same time there are many scientists who suggest there may be life on some planet revolving around a distant star. There are some who believe that from a statistical standpoint, intelligent life is not only possible but probable. To establish the existence of such life is a difficult if not an almost impossible task. At the present time man cannot conceive of being able to travel fast enough through space to make exploration of such planets (if they exist) feasible. Scientists have listened for signals from such planets; in 1960 the radio telescope at Green Bank, West Virginia, was aimed at Tau Ceti and Epsilon Eridani, two stars 11.8 and 10.8 light-years away respectively, which were thought to be the nearest stars that showed the possibility of life. No signals were heard, but even this does not disprove the existence of intelligent life. They may be clever enough to reason as some of our scientists did when it was suggested that signals be sent in addition to listening; these men cautioned against the procedure, reasoning that these people might have solved the problem of interstellar travel, might be cannibalistic, and might be moved on hearing earth signals to attempt an invasion of the earth.

Modern biology has its challenges. Like the other sciences it has been a means used by God to shower blessings upon His people. All these sciences, however, are, like the rain, for the benefit of both the just and the unjust. They are meant for everyone; they are good; God wants all mankind to have and use them.

The future is indeed bright. There are many contributions to be made by the discipline of biology. The fact that some biologists are not Christians should not disturb God's children, nor should they be shaken by the fact that some are led away from the faith by what they learn in modern biology. A little knowledge is dangerous, and that is exactly the case in biology. Man is looking through a glass darkly. There is no reason to abandon biology to the ungodly. Christians need to learn more and more about the living world that God has created. There is a need for Christian biologists who will see God's glory in the world of living things and who will provide leadership in suggesting how these gifts of God that are acquired through the understanding of biology are to be used.

FOR FURTHER READING

BECK, WILLIAM S. *Modern Science and the Nature of Life*. New York: Harcourt, Brace & Co., 1957.

CONANT, JAMES B. *Modern Science and Modern Man*. New York: Columbia University Press, 1952.

————. *Science and Common Sense*. New Haven: Yale University Press, 1951.

DAMPIER, SIR WILLIAM. *A History of Science and Its Relations with Philosophy and Religion*. Cambridge: Cambridge University Press, 1943.

HEIN, KARL. *The Transformation of the Scientific World View*. New York: Harper & Bros. Publishers, 1953.

KLOTZ, JOHN. *Genes, Genesis, and Evolution*. St. Louis: Concordia Publishing House, 1955.

————. *Modern Science in the Christian Life*. St. Louis: Concordia Publishing House, 1961.

MIXTER, RUSSELL (ed.). *Evolution and Christian Thought Today*. Grand Rapids: Wm. B. Eerdmans Publishing Co., 1959.

RAMM, BERNARD. *The Christian View of Science and Scripture*. Grand Rapids: Wm. B. Eerdmans Publishing Co., 1954.

SMETHURST, ARTHUR. *Modern Science and Christian Beliefs*. Nashville: Abingdon Press, 1955.

ZIMMERMAN, PAUL (ed.). *Darwin, Evolution, and Creation*. St. Louis: Concordia Publishing House, 1959.

ANTHROPOLOGY

James M. Murk

James M. Murk is presently completing his Ph. D. at the University of Chicago in the division of the social sciences. A graduate of the University of Chicago, he holds M. A. degrees from the University of Chicago, the University of Minnesota and Bob Jones University. He previously served on the staffs of Missionary Internship, The Navigators and Wycliffe Bible Translators, and taught at Bob Jones University and Wheaton College.

9

ANTHROPOLOGY

James M. Murk

ALTHOUGH anthropology, now approximately one hundred years old, is one of the youngest of the academic disciplines, it is also the broadest and most ambitious in scope. It may be defined as the study or science of man, and bridges all major categories of knowledge which deal with human life in the natural and social sciences and the humanities.

Anthropologists investigate both the physical aspects of man's past and present and also man's patterns of behavior or cultures. The important contributions of physical anthropology have been in the areas of (1) the discovery, analysis and classification of human and humanlike fossils, (2) theoretical descriptions of human evolution, and (3) the definition and evaluation of race.

Principal emphases of cultural anthropology include (1) the development of the concept of culture, (2) the study of the influence of culture on personality and some attempts to analyze human nature, (3) a massive amount of information compiled about non-Western cultures or ethnographic studies, (4) cross-cultural comparisons of this material demonstrating similarities (universals) and differences in human behavior with the resulting philosophical perspective of cultural relativism, and (5) studies in the processes of culture change, especially the dynamics involved when peoples of disparate societies come in close contact.

Another specialized area of much interest to Christian scholars, and one in which they have made significant contributions, is linguistics. This has been a major field of endeavor for missionary linguists, such as those of the Summer Institute of Linguistics or

Wycliffe Bible Translators and members of the translations department of the American Bible Society. These Christian scholars have also helped immeasurably to interest the contemporary evangelical church in applied anthropology as it can be used to make the message of Christ and its implications more relevant and constructive to non-Western peoples.[1] This has also been a continuing endeavor of many workers in Roman Catholic missions.[2]

Whereas there are a number of positive contributions to the Christian ministry from the scientific study of man, there is potentially major conflict between anthropology and Christian theology. This is to be expected because both disciplines deal with many of the same subjects, such as religious and moral behavior, values, and the origin and nature of man; and both interpret the evidence from different points of view or from conflicting sets of presuppositions. The conflict that exists today is not between scientific fact and Christian revelation so much as it is in the different frames of reference from which the facts are interpreted. Faith is involved in all positions.

Conflicts between orthodox Christianity and science show a greater intellectual maturity today, a point of view which recognizes the validity of the leap of faith. Most anthropologists, furthermore, have a very tolerant attitude toward all religions including the theistic frame of reference, for it is characteristic of the nature of man that he seems to need some kind of religious faith or expression.[3] Also behavioral scientists no longer idealize man but recognize his many shortcomings, such as his rebellion and aggressions, his irrationality and his selfishness, and on the whole portray a rather pessimistic picture of his character, which is much in keeping with the biblical revelation of man's sinful nature.[4]

There are, on the other hand, major differences between the scientific study of man and evangelical Christian thought. It is often in areas of conflict like these, which some unfortunately prefer to sidestep or sometimes dismiss with irresponsible statements and conclusions, where Christians can learn the most and are most challenged in the faith. Three typical problem areas in anthropology

---

[1]See especially Eugene A. Nida, *Customs and Cultures* (New York: Harper & Bros., 1954); also the bimonthly journal *Practical Anthropology,* ed. William A. Smalley.

[2]See e.g., Louis J. Luzbetak, *Church and Cultures: An Applied Anthropology for the Religious Worker* (Techny, Ill.: Divine Word Pubns., 1963).

[3]William W. Howells, *The Heathens: Primitive Man and His Religions* (Garden City, N.Y.: Doubleday & Co., 1948).

[4]Bernard Berelson and Gary S. Steiner, *Human Behavior: An Inventory of Scientific Findings* (New York: Harcourt, Brace & World, 1964), pp. 659-67.

have been (1) human evolution and fossil man, (2) race, and (3) human nature and cultural relativism.

HUMAN EVOLUTION AND FOSSIL MAN

Anthropological investigations into the origin of man present a two-pronged problem for evangelical Christians who believe that Genesis 1-3 is a part of an authentic revelation from God the Creator concerning his entrance into time and history: (1) researches seeking to demonstrate and explain the development of modern man from lower forms of life, and (2) the study and interpretation of hominid, or manlike, fossils.

When faced with evidence put forward for evolution, conservative Christians, when not ignoring this theory completely, have usually chosen one of two alternatives. One group has dismissed the problem with the easy solution that the evolution of man's body was God's method of creation. This is the position, for example, of most Roman Catholic scholars. It is faced with the immediate difficulties of the exegesis of Genesis 1-3, on the one hand, and the question of the proposed evolution of man's intellectual capacity and culture, on the other. Another group has entirely discounted the evidence as too fragmentary or unreliable. Those who take this latter position tend to do so a priori, seldom giving the evidence a thorough, careful scrutiny.

The general theory of evolution is admittedly not without its obvious problems, gaps and inconsistencies. It is only fair to say, however, that it would not be accepted by intelligent men without considerable evidence in its favor. On the other hand, it must be affirmed that those who reject the creationist position as an outlandish solution to the origin of life are predisposed to accept the theory of evolution as the only reasonable alternative no matter what its problems may be, and there are many such difficulties. Perhaps again it is a matter of presupposition and faith. The evolutionist tends to exalt the evidence and ignore the problems; the creationist usually emphasizes the problems and too often avoids the evidence.

How many creationist critics are aware of the support for evolution in the paleontological, or fossil, record? For example, do they know how specific the skeletal evidence actually is for *nonsapiens* manlike creatures which, taken together, gives credence to the view that there once existed the "missing links" between modern man and more animallike creatures? How many understand, furthermore, the significance of the fact that built into the very fabric of life is a mechanism permitting constant change, namely, the possibility of slight alterations in the structure of the DNA molecule known as gene mutation? It is this ability which makes the adjustment to different environments possible for biological life through time, and this has been absolutely necessary for life to survive.[5] Evolution in a general sense simply means change, and minute changes are occurring all the time.

If Christians are going to take the Genesis creation account seriously, however, there must be some limitation to these changes since the record does not say that God created a single cell and sent it on its way to produce all the fruits of the tree of life. There is an interpretation which is a middle ground for the theist and which lies between the thoroughgoing theistic evolutionary position and older, static creationist views. This position faces up to what facts can be mustered from paleontology and laboratory experiments in genetics. It accepts what change can be demonstrated, and at the same time preserves the distinct activity of God's creative acts revealed in Genesis; in fact, there is no contradiction of this interpretation at all in the Genesis record. God created the large subdivisions designated *min* (Hebrew), or "kinds," which were the species of their day. The capacity for a certain amount of change and proliferation was built into the fabric of life of these "kinds" enabling them to survive and adapt to changes in environment. Today the biologist recognizes these family likenesses and classifies life into orders and families. It would appear that these are the subdivisions as they exist today which are referred to in the phrase "after their kind." This logical and hermeneutically possible solution was suggested several years ago by biologist Russell L. Mixter of Wheaton College, and has gained a wide acceptance.[6]

This point of view, when applied to man and the Primate order of which he is physically a part, recognizes, first of all, that there is no reason to preclude the existence of creatures more manlike than the anthropoid apes. It is also obvious that man is made of the same substances as the animals and after the same basic pattern. It asserts too, however, that man is not simply a product of an impersonal, chance evolution but that he is a unique creation of God,

---

[5]Theodosius Dobzhansky, "The Genetic Basis of Evolution," *Scientific American,* 182 (January, 1950), 36.
 [6]*Creation and Evolution* (Mankato, Minn.: American Scientific Affiliation, 1953).

a separate "kind" as implied by Genesis 1-3. This uniqueness is obvious to any who study man objectively today. Anthropologists declare that the gap between man and even the most intelligent animals is so great that it amounts to a difference in kind and not in degree.[7]

How was this uniqueness developed? How did this difference in kind come to be? Physical anthropology, of course, is committed to the only naturalistic alternative feasible for the origin of man, that he is the product of a gradual evolution from lower forms of life. From where else could man have come if he developed by natural process on this planet? Human evolution is considered a fact, a closed issue, is virtually axiomatic and is taken for granted by physical anthropologists. The only concerns are where, how and why this occurred, especially when one comes to the singular human endowments of language and culture.

Today there is ample fossil evidence of manlike creatures, none of which was known to Darwin when he published his controversial *Descent of Man* in 1872. Since Darwin propounded his theories, many fossils have been found which could be hailed as missing links. The picture is more complex than Darwin suggested, and anthropologists have never insisted that man evolved from anything exactly comparable to the living apes, because they of course have been evolving too. It is suggested, however, that somewhere in the past— perhaps twenty-five to thirty million years ago, which paleontologically speaking is really quite recent—man shared a common ancestor with our anthropoid "cousins." Fragmentary evidence indicates that perhaps twelve to fifteen million years ago creatures of the hominid (man's) family were in existence (a fossil known as *Ramapithecus*). And as early as one to two million years ago there were tool-using or even toolmaking creatures who normally walked, or at least ran, upright—a distinct characteristic of man among the animals today. Man's foot, in fact, is his most specialized organ.

This one- to two-million-year date is suggested by recent discoveries in East Africa which have been estimated by the new potassium-argon radioactive dating method. The better-known carbon 14 dating technique, furthermore, indicates that men exactly like ourselves lived on earth at least 35,000 to 40,000 years ago. In between these absolute dates there is evidence for many varieties of hominids, or manlike creatures, in a relative time sequence.

The question of the validity of radioactive dating methods has

[7]Leslie A. White, "The Symbol: The Origin and Basis of Human Behavior," *The Science of Culture* (New York: Farrar, Straus & Co., 1949), p. 25.

been raised by some Evangelicals who are bothered by the vast amounts of time involved. Though this is the domain of the geo-chemist and physicist and cannot be discussed thoroughly here, one must note that radioactive decay is a constant which is not in-fluenced by any known physical force or chemical substance. Radio-actively determined dates, furthermore, are cross-checked by many other methods of dating, and there is no legitimate reason at present to doubt their validity. If evidence for the shortening of the geologi-cal time sequence is what one is seeking, it should be noted that carbon 14 dating, for example, has halved earlier estimates based on traditional relative dating techniques of geology, such as sedimenta-tion and erosion rates.

Including modern man, the hominid fossils may be classified into three major groups with the following approximate time schedules: (1) Australopithecines—perhaps two million to 600,000 years ago; (2) *Homo erectus*, or the Java and Peking fossils—600,000 to 100,000 years ago; (3a) *Homo neanderthalensis*—250,000 to less than 40,000 years ago (including both Neanderthaloids and the more recent Classic Neanderthal variety of southwestern Europe); (3b) *Homo sapiens*, or modern man—perhaps 45,000 years ago to the present. Dr. L. S. B. Leakey of the Coryndon Museum of Nairobi, Kenya, suggests another division between (1) and (2) called *Homo habilis*, a recent fossil find from the Olduvai Gorge in Tanzania. It ranges from 1.8 to .8 million years ago. Other scientists have classified this new creature simply as a variety of Australopithecine.[8]

The major physical difference in these creatures, and really the only significant difference in (1), (3a) and (3b), is in the size of the brain. Approximate ranges are as follows: (1) 450-650 cubic centi-meters; (2) 750-1250 cc.; (3a) 1250-1700 cc.; (3b) Normal indi-viduals have ranged from 1000 to 2000 cc., though the average European male is 1450 cc. The extensive overlapping of Neanderthal and modern man should be noted. Because of this, many biologists have reclassified them as subspecies or major races of the same species (*Homo sapiens neanderthalens* and *Homo sapiens sapiens*). There are greater physical differences than exist between any two races living today, but these discrepancies are not outside subspecies limits according to standards for biological classification of animals.

The correlation of the size of the brain with intelligence or human-

    [8]L. S. B. Leakey, P. V. Tobias and J. R. Napier, "A New Species of the Genus *Homo* from Olduvai Gorge," *Nature,* No. 4927 (April 4, 1964); James O. Buswell III, *"Homo habilis:* Implications for the Creationist," *Journal of the American Scientific Affiliation,* XVII (September, 1965), 74-78.

ness is very difficult to analyze, and the complexity of the brain is only very imperfectly known from an endocranial cast. Anthropologists assume that there was increasing facility in the use of mental faculty in the development of the hominids. The clues supporting this belief, however, are in the extraphysical, or what are termed cultural, remains. There is a very gradual development in the complexity and variety of tools. This takes a fantastically long time, however, compared to cultural developments of modern man.

The first tools appear in the archaeological record, according to potassium-argon dating, almost two million years ago. According to a currently accepted definition of man as "the toolmaker,"[9] all of these hominid varieties might classify as man. It is likely that even the small-brained Australopithecines could fashion crude implements. This explains why just a few years ago Louis Leakey hailed the Australopithecine *Zinjanthropus* as the world's earliest man.[10] In spite of very primitive physical characteristics including an ape-size brain (525 cc.), numbers of crude tools were found on the site with this fossil which was dated by potassium-argon at 1.75 million years ago. More recently Leakey has suggested that his *Homo habilis* with a slightly larger cranial capacity may have been responsible for the tools, but he was also a very primitive hominid.

Recent discoveries about chimpanzee behavior by Jane Van Lawick-Goodall in Tanzania suggest that the definition of man as the toolmaker is premature, for these anthropoid apes were observed modifying natural objects to create crude tools.[11] Language and the accompanying reasoning powers, which have been identified as distinctly human characteristics, are therefore not necessary for simple toolmaking. What is necessary perhaps is the mental capacity to abstract images in the brain plus a retentive memory.

Where is the threshold then which separates true man from the intelligent animals? Where in all of this long period of time is there any satisfactory evidence for the entrance of man made in the image of God? The following alternatives have been suggested: (1) Some Christian scholars have accepted the assumptions of the anthro-

[9]Kenneth P. Oakley, "A Definition of Man," *Science News,* ed. A. W. Haslett (Harmondsworth, England: Penguin Books, 1951), XX:69-81; reprinted in *Culture and the Evolution of Man,* ed. Ashley Montagu (New York: Oxford University Press, 1962), pp. 3-12.

[10]L. S. B. Leakey, "Exploring 1,750,000 Years into Man's Past," *National Geographic,* 120 (October, 1961), 564-71; "Finding the World's Earliest Man," *National Geographic,* 118 (September, 1960), 420-35.

[11]Jane Van Lawick-Goodall and Hugo Van Lawick, "My Life Among Wild Chimpanzees," *National Geographic,* 124 (August, 1963), 305; Jane Van Lawick-Goodall, "New Discoveries Among Africa's Chimpanzees," *National Geographic,* 128 (December, 1965), 813, 817, 828-29.

pologist and have held that all the hominids who were toolmakers descended from the first true man. This would, however, take one back perhaps two million years. (2) Others identify true man with *Homo erectus* (half a million years ago or more) with his larger brain size, his more finely wrought tools, his use of fire and his supposedly more complex society. (3) Some would recommend that with the appearance of the less brutal Neanderthaloids, such as Steinheim and Swanscombe about 250,000 years ago, the beginning of the special human creation may have been discovered. Some anthropologists identify these finds as the first evidence of extreme types of *Homo sapiens*. The are definitely, however, of the Neanderthal variety.[12]

These first three suggestions all stand on two assumptions: (1) that since the "image of God" really has no reference to any physical appearance, it makes no difference what Adam or his immediate descendants looked like; and (2) that the time of the creation of man is not an important consideration since Genesis cannot be used to support any certain chronology before Abraham.

It certainly is not necessary to insist that the first true man looked exactly like modern man; however, it must be assumed that he had language and at least the rational capacity (if not more) of his twentieth century descendants. The second assumption presents the major problem for orthodox Christians, namely, how to squeeze all of the hundreds of millennia into the first eleven chapters of Genesis.

The best answer to this was suggested over seventy years ago by W. H. Green of Princeton Seminary in his article "Primeval Chronology."[13] He demonstrated that exact chronologies cannot be determined from Hebrew genealogies which were not constructed for the purpose of recording time. This is perhaps true to an even larger extent in Genesis 1-11 than in the more detailed historical records of the Old Testament. The primary purpose for the Genesis revelation is obviously to set forth the beginnings of God's chosen people, the Hebrew nation. Extensive, detailed history does not begin until Genesis 12. The first eleven chapters are a very compressed account of the ages before Abraham, detailing to some extent the major works of God in creation, judgment and salvation, and recounting the human predicament. One might call this kind of compressed

---

[12]Sergio Sergi, "Morphological Position of the 'Prophaneranthropi' (Swanscombe and Fontechevade)," *Ideas on Human Evolution: Selected Essays, 1949-1961,* ed. William Howells (Cambridge: Harvard University Press, 1962), pp. 507-8.

[13]"Primeval Chronology," *Bibliotheca Sacra,* XLVII (April, 1890), 285-303.

record theological history; some exegetes have suggested that it even be examined under a different hermeneutic category from the rest of the book.

A popular solution which avoids this problem of the vast period of time has been to assume that the fossil hominids are remains of pre-Adamic manlike creatures, and that man made in God's image does not appear until just before the civilizations of postglacial times, or about 10,000 B.C. This position is more easily harmonized with previous interpretations of Genesis 1-11, but it ignores the archaeological record of earlier civilizations of modern-type man, for instance, the Upper Paleolithic, which are at least 35,000 to 45,000 years old.

A more recent suggestion for a solution to the problem of the time of the origin of man made in the image of God is stated in the author's article "Evidence for a Late Pleistocene Creation of Man."[14] This theory avoids many of the above problems and is a possible interpretation of the archaeological evidence. In summary it includes the following propositions:

1. Man's capacity for complex symboling, illustrated best by language, is a unique capacity of human beings and is an external evidence for the image of God.

2. The creation of simple stone tools requires a symboling process but can conceivably be executed on a much more elementary level than is required for language.

3. Artistic creativity exemplified in graphic and plastic arts is another expression of the capacity for complex symboling, and its appearance in the archaeological record is evidence also for the existence of language at that time and hence for man made in the image of God.

4. The first appearance of art and ornament is coincident with the cultural efflorescence of the Upper Paleolithic, which has been called the world's first great civilization.[15] It also marks the beginning of more complex developments in toolmaking. Coincidentally this is the culture identified with the first men who are certainly of modern type, or *Homo sapiens sapiens*.

5. This culture and these men seem to originate in the Near East in the vicinity of the land of Palestine something in excess of 40,000 B.C. Archaeological evidence leaves no doubt of their superior capac-

[14]James M. Murk, "Evidence for a Late Pleistocene Creation of Man," *Journal of the American Scientific Affiliation,* XVII (June, 1965), 37-49.

[15]Francois Henri Bordes, "Evolution in the Paleolithic Cultures," *Evolution After Darwin,* Vol. II: *The Evolution of Man,* ed. Sol Tax (Chicago: University of Chicago Press, 1960), p. 110.

ity. Of this period the great geneticist Theodosius Dobzhansky writes:

> Mutation, sexual recombination and natural selection led to the emergence of *Homo sapiens*. The creatures that preceded him had already developed the rudiments of tool-using, tool-making and cultural transmission. But the next evolutionary step was so great as to constitute a difference in kind from those before it. There now appeared an organism whose mastery of technology and of symbolic communication enabled it to create a supraorganic culture.[16]

Exactly how God created this first true man may never be discovered. That it was a special act of God and not the impersonal end of a gradual process is a necessary conclusion if one is to take the Genesis account seriously. The obvious question is what relationship is there, if any, between near man and true man? Did God use previously existing genetic material (e.g., hominid DNA) in the special creation of Adam, or did He simply approximate closely the existing hominid pattern?

The special creation of Eve (Gen. 2:21-24) presents a definite problem for those who might like to generalize the Genesis record. She was built up or fashioned by the Creator out of something specific taken from Adam's side. With our present knowledge there is no basis even for conjecture as to how the Creator might have done this. It is certainly not outside the pale of contemporary genetic thinking, however, since we know that within the nucleus of every human cell there is all the genetic material required to create another human being. The traditional translation declares that it was a rib which God took from Adam's side, and it is a fact that this bony structure does contain much of the living tissue necessary to the human organism. All the Creator really needed, however, was one cell with its forty-six chromosomes. With certain slight alterations to avoid duplicating Adam, here was all the necessary genetic material with which to fashion a related being. Perhaps now we have slipped beyond the scientific or the theological into the realm of fantasy. It really is not so fantastic, however, when we consider that geneticists today are seriously contemplating the time when they may be able to duplicate a man from his own DNA, the molecular structure in each chromosome containing the genetic code for that particular person. How God actually did it, or how human

---

[16]"The Present Evolution of Man," *Scientific American*, 203 (September, 1960), 89.

scientists may be able to do it in the future, we do not know now; but some day we shall, without much doubt, know and understand.

It is finally very interesting to note that biologists are now suggesting that since the appearance of *Homo sapiens sapiens* there has been no evolutionary improvement in the human stock but rather a degeneration.[17] This parallels theological assumptions concerning the results of the fall. Apart from divine grace, natural man will never achieve the purpose for which he was created.

THE CONCEPT AND SIGNIFICANCE OF RACE

There are several new developments in the investigation of the living races of man, an area in which anthropology has made one of its major contributions to knowledge. More exact analyses and differentiations are being made by means of genetic studies, and a whole new perspective on the concept of race has resulted.

It is hoped that race can someday be defined in terms of gene frequencies in a population rather than by the external phenotypic characteristics, such as skin color and hair texture. The genetic composition of a population, of course, includes much more than is apparent to the eye. Much greater attention is being paid to those traits for which specific genes have been isolated, such as blood types, Rh factors and haptoglobins (hemoglobin-binding proteins in the blood). Most of the traits thus far studied are distributed widely across population boundaries and do not correlate with older racial categories.

The causes for racial differences are still not completely understood. Generally speaking, the variety in physical characteristics is due, first of all, to the alternative genetic makeup of the prehistoric human population and, secondly, to slight changes or mutations in the gene pool since prehistoric times. Those changes in individual genes, which for some reason were spread around small isolated populations by inbreeding, became racial traits. The most common reason given for the continuance of certain physical changes is natural selection, namely, that these new traits had greater survival value in the particular ecological or cultural environment in which they were found. Professors Coon, Garn and Birdsell, for example, have argued convincingly that the extreme Mongoloid type— opaque skin, epicanthic fold, depressed nasal root—is a selection of

[17]Ernst Mayr, *Animal Species and Evolution* (Cambridge: Belknap Press of Harvard University Press, 1963), pp. 658-59.

traits for a very cold environment.[18] Also the extent of the concentration of the ultraviolet rays of the sun may be one of the selecting factors for the amount of melanin in the skin which causes the varying degrees of dark coloration. The mutation causing sickle-shaped red cells has adaptive significance in a malarial environment. These are, however, only a few examples. Natural selection cannot at present be demonstrated as the only reason for many racial differences. Some permanent changes are doubtless due to a fortuitous selection of gene mutations or to factors which are not yet understood.

Such possibilities of change in this physical world may simply be expressions of its finiteness as assumed by Christian theology; however, it is this capacity for genetic mutation which makes it possible for biological life to survive through time in a changing physical environment.

This new genetic approach to the study of race has contributed to some general skepticism concerning the validity of the concept of race itself when applied to *Homo sapiens*. A few anthropologists would like to discard the designation entirely.[19] Human races today do not vary from each other as much as most subspecies of animal life. It is the extreme types of physical difference which are popularly designated races, but there is almost every variety of graduated difference in between. Where one draws the boundary lines to indicate racial divisions is therefore somewhat arbitrary. This means, for example, that one could divide all human beings into two groups —straight-haired and non-straight-haired—or one could differentiate hundreds of races.

Many thousands of years ago the extreme examples of so-called races developed in marginal areas of the great world island as illustrated in Figure 1.

In between all of these extreme margins, however, the same process was going on in neighboring environments. Also there was always some overlap, a migration or two, a mixing or interbreeding of tangent populations, giving rise to gradual changes from one extreme to another.

When mapping the geographical distribution of genetic traits, this overlapping is very apparent. Blood types, for example, do not correspond with hair texture and certainly not with skin color. Very few traits have common boundaries, thus well-defined lines cannot

---

[18]Carleton S. Coon, Stanley M. Garn and Joseph B. Birdsell, *Races, A Study of the Problems of Race Formation in Man* (Springfield, Ill.: Charles C. Thomas, 1950), pp. 65-75.

[19]C. Loring Brace *et al.*, "Discussion and Criticism: On the Race Concept," *Current Anthropology*, V (October, 1964), 313-20.

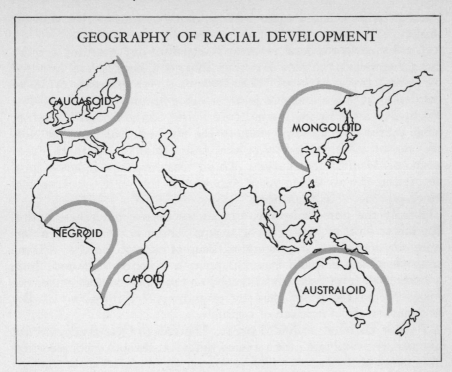

GEOGRAPHY OF RACIAL DEVELOPMENT

CAUCASOID

MONGOLOID

NEGROID

CAPOID

AUSTRALOID

be drawn. One must simply classify in terms of percentages since a racial type is merely an average of a population. It is obvious then that "race" is an ambiguous term and needs some redefining.

One of the best summaries of recent research is Stanley Garn's *Human Races*.[20] He broadly defines race as a breeding population where enough time has elapsed to make the assembly of genetic lines in the population somewhat uniform. (No statistical analysis is yet possible here to make exact distinctions.) Garn recognizes three kinds of breeding populations and defines race more specifically in three different ways relative to the size of the group and the length of time involved. These three kinds of populations are (1) geographical races, (2) local races, and (3) microraces.

Geographical races are the large mixed groups including those that are thought of as races today: Negroid, Caucasoid, Mongoloid, but also Capoid (Bushman-Hottentot), Australoid, Polynesian, Melanesian and Amerindian. There are about ten of these. Their genetic

[20]Springfield, Ill.: Charles C. Thomas, 1961.

relationship is believed to go back as much as tens of thousands of years.

Local races correspond more to the present-day breeding populations themselves, the genetic relationship going back several hundred or several thousand years. The Australoid, for example, could be divided up into a number of local breeding groups of this type. The Pygmy, or little Negro, in the Ituri Forest of the Congo is another local, inbred group. More generally the northern European, or Nordic, can be distinguished by several traits from the southern European, or Mediterranean, type. These dissimilarities indicate local separation thousands of years ago within the major geographical stock designated as Caucasoid.

Finally the term "microrace" indicates genetic differences within the larger local or geographical groups. There is a very real difference, for example, in the genetic makeup of cities in Europe. A Dane from Copenhagen would thus belong to a different microrace from a Norwegian from Oslo. This is based on the fact that though genetic insularity has been breached by migrations, interbreeding usually is a mathematical function of distance.

Race is therefore a fluid concept. The races of yesterday are not necessarily exactly like the races of today. Anthropologists recognize that many of the factors which produced racial variations in the past are still at work in the present, although most populations are much larger and no longer isolated.

For Christian theology the major implication of this recent research on the subject of race is that it reiterates even more emphatically the unity of all men. Anthropologists have concluded for a long time that biologically all men everywhere were of the same genus and species. They have also believed that so-called racial differences were only superficial and that there were no significant qualitative differences between major populations. This is in harmony with the biblical writings which place no importance on race; in fact, there is hardly any reference made to it in Scripture. One cannot conclude that the biblical writers were unaware of racial differences, but it seems that these had no cultural or theological significance for them. Rather the Scriptures stress the unity of mankind, revealing a single origin for man. The Apostle Paul also stated specifically in his address to the Athenians, "And he made from one every nation of men to live on all the face of the earth, having determined allotted periods and the boundaries of their habitation" (Acts 17:26, RSV). The second half of this passage has sometimes been used to support a segregationist position, but there is no necessary correspondence between *nation,* which is a political or cultural unit, and *race,* a biological concept. A nation may include more than one race.

At various times other Scriptures have been distorted by even some devout, orthodox Christians who have attempted to rationalize their prejudices or sanction a particular social structure. Old wives' tales such as "God's curse on Ham" have been the salve for not a few Christian consciences since the days of slavery. This curse, however, was by Noah on Ham's son Canaan who was the father of the Canaanites, doubtless nations of Mediterranean Caucasoids. Ham's other sons were Mizraim, Phut (Put) and Cush, identified respectively with Egypt, Libya and Nubia (Ethiopia). Of these three sons only the last-mentioned might conceivably be related to Negroid stock. However, it is noted that Cush had a son Nimrod who was the founder of cities in Mesopotamia (Gen. 10:8-11). No one suggests the "land between two rivers" as a Negro homeland.

Nowhere except at the Tower of Babel did God separate men from each other as a general principle; and this occasion was on the basis of language and eventually culture, but not race. There is ample evidence, furthermore, that it is God's ultimate purpose in the new creation to reverse what He did at the Tower of Babel and unite all men who are committed to Jesus Christ as Lord into a single family without any kind of barriers—linguistic, cultural, national or racial. In the example of Christ one finds the particular national or racial prejudices of the Jews toward Gentiles and Samaritans reprimanded. Peter was instructed by the conversion of Cornelius and his household that "God is no respecter of persons: but in every nation he that feareth him, and worketh righteousness, is accepted with him" (Acts 10:34-35). Paul also instructed the churches that no barriers were to separate Christians: "Here there cannot be Greek and Jew, circumcised and uncircumcised, barbarian, Scythian, slave, free man, but Christ is all, and in all" (Col. 3:11, RSV). After a similar passage in his letter to the Galatians, he concluded, "For you are all one in Christ Jesus" (3:28, RSV).

Even as the anthropologist finds no biological justification for discrimination, so also the Christian can find no theological grounds. In fact, both imply the potential unity of man. The anthropologist does not state dogmatically that there are no qualitative differences in the races at all, such as intelligence or athletic ability, which, of course, are genetically based. He does say, however, that in all his researches he has not been able to identify any; and, even if they did exist, they would be insignificant. It should be realized, furthermore, that even if there were racial differences in intelligence or any other quality, this would be no more reason for discrimination than differences in ability which are obvious within racial groups themselves.

Finally the racial issue is not simply a biological or social problem to the Christian. Man is seen as created originally in the image of God. The reconstitution of this image is God's goal for each member of His new creation. This engenders a deep sense of the potential worth of Christians and all others, and has profound implications for interpersonal relations.

If racial barriers should be eliminated anywhere, it ought to be in the community of those who are committed to Jesus Christ. His disciples are to be trailblazers in a new ethical relation among men which brings God's reconciliation to earth. God's children are to show the world what He is like and what His ultimate purpose is for men, namely, by regeneration to unite them all in a likeness to Jesus Christ who is the exact likeness of God. Christians are to learn their revolutionary ethic from Christ and set the pace for the world, not conform their ethic to the world for fear of offending society. Followers of Jesus are taught to please men for love's sake but only in the context of pleasing God first (I Cor. 10-31—11:1).

Because they are human beings, however, Christians are no strangers to prejudice nor to the pressures of society. Raw prejudice has its roots in self-centeredness which is the essence of the biblical concept of sin. It may be said that one is prejudiced in favor of that which supports the self (sympathy) and prejudiced against that which threatens the self (antipathy). The individual learns in the enculturation process how to properly control or express his own self-centeredness. Usually observable differences in people have permitted men to erect barriers to maintain their uniqueness and try to assert their superiority. From the earliest times these differences were national or cultural, such as dissimilarities in language, religion and economic pursuits. However, as these differences became symbolized by skin color, hair texture, nose form or any of the other superficial characteristics which identify the races, reaction against them resulted in race prejudice. This identification of racial difference as an object of prejudice certainly is acquired, but the selfishness which permits it is a part of the nature of man.

When the irrational focus of prejudice is race, one must either change the focus or eliminate the prejudice. Education can expose our irrationalities and misinformation about race, but the only ultimate answer to prejudice is the radical and continuing change accomplished by the redemption of man by our Lord Jesus Christ and by the infusion of His love. A Southern Baptist minister has written a most helpful book on this subject. He states:

> Race prejudice is learned; religious bigotry is learned; social snobbery is learned; but they can be learned only because they have an apt and eager pupil in the inherently prideful and instinctively prejudiced will of man. We do not have an inherent antipathy for certain colors or particular physical attributes; what we do have is a dominant, built-in preference for self over all that is not-self.[21]

The only final solution for Christians is for self to be replaced by the life of Christ at the center of the being. All other solutions are simply expedient, external and social, substituting one scapegoat for another.

THEORIES OF HUMAN NATURE AND CULTURAL RELATIVISM

Two of the subjects in cultural anthropology which have been most provocative for Christian thought are the discussions on human nature and cultural relativity. Statements of anthropologists on these subjects have often been in direct conflict with orthodox Christian theology. In the last few years, however, the scientific study of man has drawn conclusions which harmonize very closely with the biblical view of man and society.

Human Nature

In the nineteenth century most anthropologists assumed the unity of man and attempted to explain similarities among the world's cultures as the result of something innate in the human mind. Phrases such as "elementary ideas" and "psychic unity" were popular. This assumption was a necessary presupposition underlying theories of the evolution of societies. Much of anthropological thinking was an effort to show that all human societies went through the same stages of development, such as from animism to monotheism or from promiscuity to monogamy. This was inevitable because all men were psychologically alike underneath, though at different levels in their progress.

When it was finally proved that these evolutionary theories did not fit the facts, they were discarded and with them went the premise of the unity of man. What was emphasized next was the tremendous

[21]Kyle Haselden, *The Racial Problem in Christian Perspective* (New York: Harper & Bros., 1959), p. 80.

variety and divergence of human cultures; and by the 1920's human nature was being considered a formless, plastic blob susceptible to any kind of development. There were therefore many human natures; in fact, there were as many kinds of men as there were cultures creating them. It was almost an established tenet of behavioral science that there was "no such thing as a universal human nature."[22]

This belief in the unlimited variability of man stimulated the optimistic humanism of that day. It was hoped that scientists might somehow finally reconstruct a better environment and then improve human nature. This was the dogma which spurred many radical idealists who wished forcibly to rebuild the societies of the world and thereby remake man.

The upheaval of World War II demonstrated that human nature is not so easily shaped. It can only change within certain limits. The emphasis has shifted today from a belief in unlimited human flexibility to a search for the underlying psychobiological structure which all men hold in common. Most behavioral scientists now admit that man shares a common humanity—an inherent nature of some kind. It is a very vague concept, however, and scientists know little about it. In fact, "the intuitions as to this reality are stronger than the demonstrations of its content." Common sense recognizes it, but no scientific discipline completely describes it. Though confronted daily, it is "almost indescribable." It is simply what must be there because of what is observed concerning man's behavior.[23]

Anthropologists have long recognized the many similarities among men. They were first listed as nine or ten broad categories, such as religion, technology and social organization, under which each culture in the world may be cataloged. More recently the Human Relations Area Files, a classified collection of all the known information about human societies, listed seventy-three items common to all men, such as cosmology, division of labor, etiquette, folklore, gift-giving, incest taboos, law, magic, personal names, property rights, sexual restrictions, soul concepts, trade, and weather control.[24] Even within this refined classification, however, there is room for a large variety of behavior. It is recognized today, nevertheless, that there are limits

[22]Richard T. LaPiere and Paul R. Farnsworth, *Social Psychology* (New York and London: McGraw-Hill Book Co., 1936), pp. 198-200, 261-86.

[23]Robert Redfield, "The Universally Human and the Culturally Variable," *Human Nature and the Study of Society,* ed. Margaret Park Redfield (Chicago: University of Chicago Press, 1962), p. 448.

[24]George P. Murdock, "Universal Aspects of Culture," *Exploring the Ways of Mankind,* ed. Walter Goldschmidt (New York: Holt, Rinehart & Winston, 1960), pp. 654-55.

to cultural variation, and that there are recurring themes underlying all of the vast differences among men.

This unity of man is better experienced than explained. Anthropological field workers, in spite of being exposed to exotic differences in the behavior of human groups, find themselves invariably submerged in a common humanity. Even such seemingly aberrant practices as cannibalism and infanticide or such meaningless customs as matrilineal descent and the couvade[25] become reasonable in the context of the total way of life and philosophy of the people.

Margaret Mead, who thirty years ago was stressing the differences among men, wrote recently that there is a "layer of human behavior so basic and universal that cultural modification is minimal."[26] Eric Wolf, Professor of Anthropology at the University of Michigan, summarized this new emphasis in the field recently in his contribution to the Princeton Studies in Humanities. He said that there is an inherited design which causes men to seek answers to the same questions and solutions to the same problems of living. The answers and solutions may vary slightly from culture to culture, but the basic themes are the same.[27]

What can be known about the raw human nature by the scientist can only be known indirectly. It must be inferred from behavior which is common to all men everywhere—the cultural universals. The late Robert Redfield of the University of Chicago, whose research in this area was a major emphasis of his last few years, believed that one must think of man's innate nature as a state of mind. The most significant way in which man differs from other earth creatures is in his capacity to create and use symbols, and this is essentially a matter of thought. Given this capacity, "what mankind has invariably done, in each traditional group, is to develop more or less orderly ideas about a universe to which, in some way, man is significantly related, or of which he is a part, and to clothe these ... with feelings of inherent rightness and wrongness."[28]

What Redfield stressed here is that (1) all men have a world view and (2) all men have a moral sense. Men need a world view because they become conscious selves and must orient themselves to others

---

[25]In general, matrilineal descent refers to legal descent and inheritance on the female side of the family. The couvade is a custom where the father goes into seclusion and to bed after the birth of a child.

[26]Eric R. Wolf, *Anthropology* (Englewood Cliffs, N.J.: Prentice-Hall, Inc., 1964), p. 34.

[27]*Ibid.*, p. 33.

[28]Redfield, "Anthropological Understanding of Man" *Human Nature*, p. 465.

and to the universe around them. Man thus brings order out of chaos and gives a meaning to life. Man cannot just exist; he must fit somewhere, must be tied in. Is this an innate sense of purpose, that there must be a reason and a goal for human existence? Does not man sense his own incompleteness?

Man's moral sense is a capacity to be taught what ought or ought not to be or what one ought or ought not to do. "Everywhere there are recognized obligations, commitments, sentiments, and judgments of what is good and what is bad."[29] This is related to the broader capacity of man to make evaluations. All cultures have value systems which anthropologists are recognizing as perhaps the key to the way man chooses and orders his behavior. The heart of any culture is really a code of values and this is to the culture what the genetic code is to life.[30]

Redfield suggests a third point, that innate to all men is a creative urge which reaches out beyond the demands of survival or subsistence. It includes appreciation and discrimination beyond the merely useful. It is an expression of the imagination—a work of the mind.[31] One demonstration of this is the universality of myth, ritual and art.

Finally human nature seems to have a tremendous capacity for expansion or contraction. In the richer, deeper, more advanced cultures, man produces notable works, higher sentiments and greater mental accomplishments. The physical environment or mental attitudes (values) may not permit expansion or may cause a contraction of the developed human nature. The Scripture supports this idea of expansion in the area of man's capacity to accumulate knowledge and technique: "And the LORD said, 'Behold they are one people, and they have all one language; and this is only the beginning of what they will do; and nothing that they propose to do will now be impossible for them'" (Gen. 11:6, RSV). There is no recognition, however, of a capacity for moral progress until after the new birth. There is, on the other hand, much teaching concerning man's inevitable decline and inability to measure up to the purpose for which he was created.

Having this great flexibility, man as one kind of being only gives the impression of being modified to become many kinds of being. All men touch each other with likeness somewhere in their nuclear

---

[29]*Ibid.*, p. 464.
[30]Wolf, pp. 33, 39.
[31]Redfield, "Anthropological Understanding of Man," p. 465.

human nature no matter how different or mutually incompatible they may seem.[32]

Actually there is no contradiction here with Christian thought at all. The theological picture of human nature is not much more than what is claimed for it by anthropology today. Universally man is a reasoning being with a moral and evaluating sense and a capacity to create. The only areas where theology and anthropology do not touch directly, because they involve value judgments, are (1) the matter of the sinful nature and (2) the purpose or final destiny of man. Concerning the latter, behavioral scientists affirm man's quest for meaning, but none would venture to guess what the ultimate goal might be. Eric Wolf admits that they are not really sure what man should become: "Let us not forget that to this day neither psychology nor psychoanalysis possesses a satisfactory theory of maturation, only a sophisticated understanding of man's multiple immaturities."[33] There are many images of man's illness but none of man's perfect health. The Christian believes that redeemed man may become like God as pictured in Jesus Christ, and that He is the measure of maturity and health.

The behavioral sciences nowhere picture man idealistically. He is portrayed universally as a rebel who does not live up to his own ideals, an aggressive defender of self and a rationalizer. A recent summary of what science knows about man does not paint a very optimistic picture. Man is weak standing alone. He seeks approval and satisfaction through people far more than by virtue or reason. He is very willing to be deceived and depends upon illusions to make life bearable. He "maneuvers the world to suit himself." He does this primarily through words because this is how most desirable things, such as security and status, are bestowed. There is little effort, however, to seek the truth for truth's sake. Man is more concerned with that which will satisfy the self.[34] Here is a picture of the irrationality of man, his inability to control his drives and urges by his reason, and a disengagement between man's sentimental part and his reasoning part. A theologian could not make a better case for the "fallen Adam."

Cultural Relativism

In this context of the subject of human nature one is confronted

[32]*Ibid.*, p. 466.
[33]Wolf, p. 47.
[34]Berelson and Steiner, pp. 663-65.

with the doctrine of cultural relativity and its troublesome corollary, moral or ethical relativity. In studying cultures as whole units, anthropologists became aware, first, of the enormous variety of cultural expression and, secondly, that each traditional way of life had its own workable arrangement or integration of customs and beliefs. People trained in these cultures were living examples of these differences in thought and behavior, hence the emphasis on many human natures discussed above.

Since it was assumed that human nature was completely plastic, each culture was a valid expression in itself with its own inherent dignity; and was just as good as any other. Consequently, the foundations of morality were seen to be only in the judgments of each particular community, and theoretically anything wrong or bad in one culture might be considered right or good in another.

This extreme interpretation of the relativist position met with several serious objections: (1) Philosophers argued that it is a self-contradiction to assert a universal value of cultural relativity in order to deny the existence of universal values. (2) It was observed that the existence of a certain cultural system did not necessarily justify it. There is no logical connection between *what is* and *what ought to be*. (3) That there are different ways of behaving in various cultures does not preclude the possibility of universal values or underlying principles for human behavior which would be valid for all societies. (4) The fact that human beings are basically alike underneath implies that there are ways of behaving which are truer to man's nature or better for his fulfillment as man. In the face of arguments such as these, extreme relativism, professed by such men as W. H. Sumner and Melville J. Herskovits,[35] has been discarded by the majority of anthropologists today.[36]

Cultural relativism still is valid, nevertheless, when used as an objective point of view for the study of each culture in its own context. It is certainly true that there are different, workable ways to organize a society, to produce food, to show honor, to build a shelter and even to worship God, which ultimately satisfy the same need or fulfill the same goal for man. The perspective which cultural relativity maintains is that these many different ways of behaving must be evaluated in terms of the total pattern of the culture in which

---

[35]Sumner, *Folkways* (New York: New American Library Mentor Books, 1960); Herskovits, *Man and His Works* (New York: Alfred A. Knopf, Inc., 1948), pp. 61-78.

[36]For an analysis and list of references see David O. Moberg, "Cultural Relativity and Christian Faith," *Journal of the American Scientific Affiliation,* XIV (June, 1962), 34-48.

they appear. It is appreciated today, however, that this cannot be made to imply that all ways of behaving are equally valid or best for man even if they are sanctioned by a particular group. The extreme relativist has found it embarrassing to defend such actions as Aztec human sacrifice, Marquesan cannibalism, racism and the Nazi extermination of the Jews.

The popular idea which developed from the extreme point of view was that there is no moral standard and, because of the variety of man and cultures, any kind of conduct was permissible in any given culture. This was an unwarranted conclusion never taught by anthropology. In his prizewinning book *Mirror for Man*, Clyde Kluckhohn of Harvard University wrote:

> The concept of culture, like any other piece of knowledge, can be abused and misinterpreted. Some fear that the principle of cultural relativity will weaken morality. "If the Bugabuga do it why can't we? It's all relative anyway." But this is exactly what cultural relativity does not mean.
>
> The principle of cultural relativity does not mean that because members of some savage tribe are allowed to behave in a certain way that this fact gives intellectual warrant for such behavior in all groups. Cultural relativity means, on the contrary, that the appropriateness of any positive or negative custom must be evaluated with regard to how this habit fits with other group habits. . . . While breeding a healthy skepticism as to the eternity of any value prized by a particular people, anthropology does not as a matter of theory deny the existence of moral absolutes. Rather the use of the comparative method provides a scientific means of discovering such absolutes. If all surviving societies have found it necessary to impose some of the same restrictions upon the behavior of their members, this makes a strong argument that these aspects of the moral code are indispensable.[37]

Though behavioral scientists do not like to talk in terms of absolutes, they do recognize that, in spite of all the differences, rules of conduct in the world tend toward a very general similar content.[38] This could be predicated from the assumption of a common human nature. Man, being what he is, must approximate a certain standard of conduct if he is going to survive in society with other men.

Much that the moral codes of the world have in common is similar to or comes very close to biblical rules of conduct. Sociologist David Moberg, in an extensive and helpful analysis of cultural rela-

[37]New York: McGraw-Hill Book Co., 1949, p. 41.
[38]Redfield, "The Universally Human," *Human Nature,* p. 451.

tivity from the standpoint of evangelical Christianity, expressed his opinion in this way:

> Overt behavioral norms emerging from humanistic principles will, for the most part, coincide with those of the Christian Scriptures. In spite of the bewilderment that arises from first impressions of the earth's myriad moral codes, further analysis seems to indicate that there is a fundamental order and uniformity, with practically all peoples holding to precepts of respect for the Supreme Being or for benevolent substitutes, care for their children, control of sexual behavior, and reprehension of malicious murder, maiming, stealing, and deliberate slander against a friend.[39]

Christian theology has never suggested, however, that man could discover all the moral absolutes. There would be no purpose in the revelation of the will of God the Creator if man could discover all these truths by himself. Man has found out, however, that because of the way he is made and because he must live together with others, certain mores are more workable than others. Because of his nature he must live a certain way in order to survive. This is perhaps the underlying meaning of Romans 2:14-16 (RSV):

> When Gentiles who have not the law do by nature what the law requires, they are a law to themselves, even though they do not have the law. They show that what the law requires is written on their hearts, while their conscience also bears witness and their conflicting thoughts accuse or perhaps excuse them on that day when, according to my gospel, God judges the secrets of men by Christ Jesus.

This passage has sometimes been used to argue for an instinctive morality based on conscience. In the way that biologists use the term "instinct," however, man has no true instincts, and conscience is a product of training. But the fact that men are basically alike and have the same needs and problems, produces a large share of common conscience.

Because of the similarities among men, cultural relativism has been de-emphasized in the last decade, and, along with it, the glorification of the primitive society. Anthropologists no longer view every culture as a "qualitatively unique and irreducible monad." Regarding man as *one*, though with many expressions, they have returned to examining the culture process as universal—as a development, for example, from primitive to civilized society. The details of individual cultures may be very different, but the trend is the

---

[39]Moberg, p. 41.

same, and underlying it all is a common psychobiological nature of man.[40]

Another good influence of the cultural relativity principle is its check on man's selfish tendency to ethnocentrism. It is characteristic of every society of men to regard itself as the center of the world, to affirm its ways as the only normal and right ways and to judge others as peculiar, immoral or even inhuman. Man needs to be reminded that there are other ways of behaving which are not wrong, just different.

There is a recognition of this kind of relativism in the Bible.[41] Written over fifteen hundred years, its content bridges many different customs and cultures. Much of the antagonism of Jews to Samaritans and Gentiles, which was condemned by Jesus, had its foundation in ethnocentrism rather than piety (cf. John 4:1-42). The Christian reaction to this is expressed in the standard of the Apostle Paul: "I have become all things to all men, that I might by all means save some" (I Cor. 9:22, RSV). Out of context this could be interpreted as a thoroughgoing moral relativism; however, it is obvious that Paul was assuming the restrictions of the will of God and what he called "the law of Christ" (I Cor. 9:21).

The biblical standard for human morality is related directly to the purpose for which man was created, namely, to be like God. The nature of God Himself therefore is the only absolute by which human nature will be judged. The various laws and commands are simply expressions of the working out of God's being in the human situation. They are general principles which may be expressed or applied in different ways in various culture contexts. Humility and love, for example, are not usually demonstrated in our culture by washing the dusty feet of our friends. External standards may vary. The inner attitude serves as the key to moral fulfillment. "Man looks on the outward appearance, but the Lord looks on the heart" (I Sam. 16:7, RSV). One must not be careless in judging other ways of life, therefore, nor too confident of the virtue of his own.

The ultimate question which transcends all cultures is "What is the will of God?" This is the important supercultural principle which must find its specific application in every relative human situation.

---

[40]Wolf, pp. 22, 57-59.
[41]Moberg, pp. 44-47.

FOR FURTHER READING

BERELSON, BERNARD, and STEINER, GARY S. *Human Behavior: An Inventory of Scientific Findings*. New York: Harcourt, Brace & World, 1964.

BORDES, FRANCOIS HENRI. "Evolution in the Paleolithic Cultures," *Evolution After Darwin*. Vol. II: *The Evolution of Man*. Ed. SOL TAX. Chicago: University of Chicago Press, 1960.

BRACE, C. LORING *et al.* "Discussion and Criticism: On the Race Concept," *Current Anthropology*, V (October, 1964), 313-20.

BUSWELL, JAMES O. III. *"Homo habilis:* Implications for the Creationist," *Journal of the American Scientific Affiliation*, XVII (September, 1965), 74-78.

COON, CARLETON S.; GARN, STANLEY M.; and BIRDSELL, JOSEPH B. *Races, A Study of the Problems of Race Formation in Man*. Springfield, Ill.: Charles C. Thomas, 1950.

DOBZHANSKY, THEODOSIUS. "The Genetic Basis of Evolution," *Scientific American*, 182 (January, 1950), 36.

_____. "The Present Evolution of Man," *Scientific American*, 203 (September, 1960), 89.

GARN, STANLEY M. *Human Races*. Springfield, Ill.: Charles C. Thomas, 1961.

GREEN, WILLIAM HENRY. "Primeval Chronology," *Bibliotheca Sacra*, XLVII (April, 1890), 285-303.

HASELDEN, KYLE. *The Racial Problem in Christian Perspective*. New York: Harper & Bros., 1959.

HERSKOVITS, MELVILLE J. *Man and His Works*. New York: Alfred A. Knopf, Inc., 1948.

HOWELLS, WILLIAM W. *The Heathens: Primitive Man and His Religions*. Garden City, N.Y.: Doubleday & Co., 1948.

KLUCKHOHN, CLYDE. *Mirror for Man*. New York: McGraw-Hill Book Co., 1949.

LAPIERE, RICHARD T. and FARNSWORTH, PAUL R. *Social Psychology*. New York and London: McGraw-Hill Book Co., 1936.

LEAKEY, LOUIS S. B. "Exploring 1,750,000 Years into Man's Past," *National Geographic*, 120 (October, 1961), 564-71.

_____. "Finding the World's Earliest Man," *National Geographic*, 118 (September, 1960), 420-35.

LEAKEY, L. S. B.; TOBIAS, P. V.; and NAPIER, J. R. "A New Species of the Genus *Homo* from Olduvai Gorge," *Nature*, No. 4927 (April 4, 1964).

MAYR, ERNST. *Animal Species and Evolution*. Cambridge: Belknap Press of Harvard University Press, 1963.

MIXTER, RUSSELL L. *Creation and Evolution*. Mankato, Minn.: American Scientific Affiliation, 1953.

MOBERG, DAVID O. "Cultural Relativity and Christian Faith," *Journal of the American Scientific Affiliation*, XIV (June, 1962), 34-48.

MONTAGU, ASHLEY (ed.). *Culture and the Evolution of Man*. New York: Oxford University Press, 1962.

MURDOCK, GEORGE P. "Universal Aspects of Culture," *Exploring the Ways of Mankind*. Ed. WALTER GOLDSCHMIDT. New York: Holt, Rinehart & Winston, 1960.

MURK, JAMES M. "Evidence for a Late Pleistocene Creation of Man," *Journal of the American Scientific Affiliation*, XVII (June, 1965), 37-49.

————. "The Race Issue and the Christian College." Unpublished manuscript.

NIDA, EUGENE A. *Customs and Cultures*. New York: Harper & Bros., 1954.

OAKLEY, KENNETH P. "A Definition of Man," *Science News*. Ed. A. W. HASLETT. Harmondsworth, England: Penguin Books, 1951, XX: 69-81.

REDFIELD, ROBERT. "The Universally Human and the Culturally Variable," "Anthropological Understanding of Man," *Human Nature and the Study of Society*. Ed. MARGARET PARK REDFIELD. Chicago: University of Chicago Press, 1962.

SERGI, SERGIO. "Morphological Position of the 'Prophaneranthropi' (Swanscombe and Fontechevade)," *Ideas on Human Evolution: Selected Essays: 1949-1961*. Ed. WILLIAM W. HOWELLS, Cambridge: Harvard University Press, 1962.

SUMNER, WILLIAM GRAHAM. *Folkways*. New York: New American Library Mentor Books, 1960.

VAN LAWICK-GOODALL, JANE. "New Discoveries Among Africa's Chimpanzees," *National Geographic*, 128 (December, 1965), 813, 817, 828-29.

VAN LAWICK-GOODALL, JANE and VAN LAWICK, HUGO. "My Life Among Wild Chimpanzees," *National Geographic*, 124 (August, 1963), 305.

WHITE, LESLIE A. "The Symbol: The Origin and Basis of Human Behavior," *The Science of Culture*. New York: Farrar, Straus & Co., 1949.

WOLF, ERIC R. *Anthropology*. Englewood Cliffs, N.J.: Prentice-Hall, Inc., 1964.

SOCIOLOGY

David O. Moberg

David O. Moberg is chairman of the department of sociology at
Marquette University (1968 appointment). Previously he taught
at the University of Washington and Bethel College, St. Paul,
and was a Fulbright professor in the Netherlands and West
Germany. A graduate of Bethel Junior College and Seattle Pacific
College, he received an M. A. from the University of Washington
and a Ph. D. from the University of Minnesota. Dr. Moberg has
written *The Church as a Social Institution, The Church and the
Older Person, Inasmuch: Christian Social Responsibility in the
Twentieth Century,* and has contributed chapters to numerous
symposia and articles to more than thirty periodicals in the
United States and West Germany.

10

SOCIOLOGY

David O. Moberg

W HAT PROBLEMS do Christians face when they study sociology?
The writer's first reaction as a social scientist confronted with this
question was to ask for research findings on Christian students' experiences. Someone should make a survey of the subject to get the
facts! But to my knowledge, nobody has made such a survey. (It
would be an excellent topic for a term paper or thesis.) The writer
has found it necessary to rely upon his personal experiences as a
student and many years of observation as an instructor. Many relevant topics have come forward in discussions with other sociologists
and interaction with students.

Occasionally investigations have been made to compare what young
people like with what their religious education leaders or youth leaders think they like. There is often a wide discrepancy. (This, incidentally, is one of the reasons for the lack of success of many church
programs for young people.) This appraisal of the problems of sociology students may be no better. This essay may emphasize certain
points that have been resolved by the intelligent youth who are now
in colleges and universities. It may miss some problems which are
important to college students. It may misinterpret the reactions of
many Christians who for the first time are confronted with these
questions. (After all, no two reactions are identical!) It may present
as problems certain items that have been satisfactorily settled in
high school classrooms, young people's meetings, Sunday school
classes or Christian homes. Nevertheless, it is hoped that it will
stimulate thinking, discussion, Christian conduct and even some research on the subject.

WHAT IS MAN?

The science of sociology deals with man in his group relationships. The nature of man is therefore of special relevance to the discipline. Surprisingly, the typical introductory sociology textbook approaches this subject indirectly. No explicit statement is made about the fundamental nature of man. Yet the subject is discussed at length under such concepts as heredity and environment, "nature versus nurture," the development of social self, socialization, personality, social status, social roles and other topics. The student who has a basically religious orientation to man and the universe may feel that his religion is contradicted by the sociological approach to such subjects.

Instead of seeing man as, first of all, created by God and therefore responsible to Him, the sociologist tends to see man as a present fact in a nonsupernatural context. He emphasizes the social factors which have made any group of men what they are. He tends to look upon men as the product of social forces which operate upon their hereditary endowments; these forces have molded each person so that he conforms to the values of some reference group or subgroup within a society. If the group is at the core of the culture, these persons are conforming citizens; if it is on the fringes, the individuals in the group are deviant members of a subculture or a contraculture.

"Good" and "bad" as adjectives describing people are avoided by the sociologist because his definitions are relative to time, place and culture. They also are basically ethical or theological concepts. Yet in speaking about social deviants as well as about functions and dysfunctions in society, many sociologists have a disguised form of value-laden, or at least value-reflecting, language. The student who has come from a moralistic background, which tends to see people as either "good" or "bad," will not like the sociologist's insistence that functions and dysfunctions are intermingled, that well-intended and love-motivated deeds may have harmful results, and that either-or thinking fails to see the long continuum of varying shades of gray between the black and white poles.

Sociology may incline one to think that men are merely what their social groups have made them to be. For this reason the planned control of social forces which produce deviant behavior will make people conform to the values of society, that is, it will make them "good." Changing the group influences on people changes the people. This optimistic position may shock the evangelical Christian student who previously has led a somewhat sheltered life. He may consider it to be a direct attack upon his Christian faith, especially upon his belief that men can be justified (made "good") only through Jesus Christ. He may interpret the sociological view as the equivalent of the Social Gospel of the 1920's, with all of its factual and doctrinal errors. In fact it can be demonstrated, however, that men's outward actions can be changed by law and other social pressures. Furthermore, it can be demonstrated that Sunday school classes, evangelical services and other church programs are based upon the principle that group influences can be used by the Holy Spirit to change people.

Since sociologists tend to see man as primarily a product of the groups in which he is or has been a member, certain sociologists are inclined to accept a form of social determinism. Paradoxically, when this position is held in its extreme form, it fails to recognize that man is not only socialized by his groups but is also a modifier of these same groups. Modern developments in sociology therefore see man as not merely a socially imprisoned creature of society but also as an autonomous being with many opportunities to choose between alternatives. This is consistent with Christian doctrines of responsibility or stewardship.

The evangelical student may be tempted, however, to overemphasize free will, forgetting that man seldom is fully free. Every society puts restrictions on individual liberty to protect the liberty of other individuals. Choices can be made only between actual possibilities. One cannot choose to learn to play a piano if no piano is available. The Apostle Paul could not choose to go from Jerusalem to Corinth by railroad, automobile, jet airliner or steamship. Even faith in Christ can come only after some form of "hearing" God's Word (Rom. 10:17). Social circumstances therefore do indeed have a strong influence upon man's actions, including his spiritual life. They circumscribe the limits and prescribe the alternative opportunities within which and between which choices are made.

Sociological perspectives of man hence can be reconciled with evangelical Christianity. Sociology must not be confused with theology. This is not to deny that there is an implicit theological view in many of the basic underlying assumptions of the sociologist, if these assumptions are interpreted theologically. It is, rather, to assert that the sociologist's work is not that of analyzing the Scriptures to determine their philosophical and practical implications.[1]

---

[1]But a major need of Christendom today is for Christians trained in sociology who can combine the findings and insights of their discipline with scriptural values to give practical guidance to Christian work. Such persons are "applied" rather than "pure" sociologists. Their work is in the field of Chris-

It is not his task to study God, immortality, man's ultimate destiny in heaven or hell and related questions of theology.

SCIENTISM IN SOCIOLOGY

Some sociologists teach that empirical sociology can, through its application of the scientific method, cover *all* of social reality. This false conclusion can lead to the belief, sometimes labeled as scientism, that anything which cannot be scientifically observed is nonexistent. Hence, in the area of social life, the sociological and psychological aspects of man's religious behavior may be interpreted as being the totality of religion. That which lies beyond the observable, including God who is a "Spirit" (John 4:24), the "soul" or "spirit" of man, heaven, hell and other transcendent religious concepts which are presumed in Christianity to be "real," may be interpreted as totally nonexistent or assumed to be the figments of man's powers of imagination or the remnants of superstition from a prescientific age.

The basic error behind scientism is a form of parochialism which has been evident even in the writings of some professional sociologists, especially in the earlier stages of the historical development of the social sciences. They failed to recognize the philosophical and theological nature of many of their basic assumptions and postulates, and they did not fully realize how highly limited the scope of the scientific method really is.

It is true that basically belief in God, in the Bible as His revelation to man, and in other Christian doctrines must always remain an act of faith. The sociologist can study scientifically only that which is empirically observable by use of the five senses, aided and supplemented by various "measuring" devices. Sociological interpretations of scientific data may go beyond the immediate observations of the senses, however, through a process of intuitive insight and sympathetic understanding often referred to by the German word *Verstehen*. In any science, the logical analysis of data also involves a mental process of relating the phenomena observed with the senses to other observations and especially to explanatory hypotheses and theories. There is an empirically observable element of experience in a personal relationship with Jesus Christ to which any sincere believer can testify. Some aspects of this are on the level of "spirit bearing witness with spirit" and are not easily communicated to the

---

tian social ethics or church administration rather than in sociology as such, except when they engage in research to test sociological hypotheses or in analysis which develops sociological theories.

nonbeliever, so this may always remain outside the realm of a purely empirical behavioral science.

Because the totality of man's universe is so vast and so complex, it has been necessary to subdivide the labor involved in its study. The various scientific disciplines have separate although overlapping realms of investigation. Their techniques of study as they apply "the scientific method" must be adjusted to their unique tasks. (Sociologists do not use a cyclotron, and chemists do not use social distance scales.) The sciences, in turn, are in several respects different from the academic disciplines of music, art, literature, philosophy and theology, none of which depends directly upon the scientific method.

The student of sociology must recognize that none of the sciences, either alone or collectively, can cover the totality of human experience. Science can never take the place of theology. Sociological explanations of human experience, especially religious experience, are therefore limited and should never take the place of the Bible. Man is a spiritual being, not solely a sociological being. The sociology classroom is not the place for either a student or the instructor to preach metaphysical sermons.

Through their recognition of the many dimensions of man's religious behavior,[2] social scientists are now more cautious about their statements on religion than they often were in the past. Nevertheless, they still cannot include the totality of religion within the immediate empirical scope of their disciplines; true Christian faith involves something more than religious ritual, beliefs, knowledge, experience and consequences.

EVOLUTIONARY PERSPECTIVES

Many introductory textbooks in sociology still devote several pages to the evolutionary interpretation of the source of mankind and of man's social institutions. They use anthropological, archaeological, biological and geological resources for their discussions of certain aspects of evolution discussed in other chapters of this book. In addition, they may refer to some distinctly sociological theories of evolution. These were developed primarily by Herbert Spencer, Edward B. Tylor, Emile Durkheim, Max Müller and others, mainly in the late nineteenth century. They assumed that social institutions like the family, government and religion had developed through a succession of stages, each of which grew by natural processes out

[2]Charles Y. Glock, "On the Study of Religious Commitment," *Religious Education,* LVII, No. 4 (July-August, 1962), Supplement, S-98–S-110.

of another. In all societies the stages were presumed to be the same. Primitive peoples were therefore considered to be our "contemporary ancestors."

The student who is interested in this subject may be given an opportunity by his instructors to write term papers on evolutionary theories or theorists in sociology. He will find that these nineteenth century theories are now generally discredited because they rested upon tenuous assumptions and impeachable evidence. The theoretical structure was built in the mind of the scholar. He then gathered evidence to *illustrate* the theory. Instead of presenting it as a scientific hypothesis to be tested to see whether or not it was valid, he assumed its validity or truth and did his utmost to *prove* his idea was correct. Empirical facts were often taken out of context in order to fit the preconceived scheme.

The reputable social scientist today has more refined methods of research which rest upon a solid logical foundation. He gathers all available evidence on his subject, seeking evidence which does not support his hypotheses as well as that which does. He *tests* his hypotheses and as a result of his research either verifies, rejects or modifies them to fit the observed facts, instead of twisting the facts to fit the hypotheses. Today there is an abundance of available evidence on the errors of the evolutionary school of sociology.

This is not, however, to deny that there is development in the life history of social institutions. A careful student will learn from his studies of history as well as of sociology that there have been changes in government, patterns of family life, education, social welfare and church structure and activities. Social change is so extensive and pervasive in the modern world that some sociologists say, "The only thing permanent in society is change." When changes are viewed from a long-range perspective, they are sometimes called evolution.

RELIGION IN TEXTBOOKS

Many sociologists during the 1920's and 1930's believed that religion was a dying vestige of primitive and prescientific life. This opinion made them ignore its positive contributions to the welfare of mankind or led them to present it as something that would soon be replaced by a "scientific" view of the universe.[3] The midcentury "revival of religion" in the United States was a surprise to them.

---

[3]The best single example of this perspective is Harry Elmer Barnes, *The Twilight of Christianity* (New York: Vanguard Press, 1929).

The sociology of religion has developed rapidly since World War II. It has demonstrated clearly the important, even central, role religion plays in modern society.[4] No author of a current introductory textbook can afford to omit a section or chapter on religion. But how is religion treated? A study by Professor Denman of Stetson University is revealing. He found that two of the ten introductory sociology textbooks he studied gave the distinct impression that religion is directed merely toward conceptualizations which are developed in the mind of man and which refer to no objective reality. Two of the texts implied that the authors believe religion is directed toward a real supernatural entity called God. The other six had an unclear or noncommittal position on the reality of the supernatural. All ten were inclined toward a functional interpretation which sees religions as arising out of man's need to explain frustrations of death, suffering and other misfortunes. They presupposed that God is not a possible "intervening variable" in the explanation, prediction and control of religious behavior. They did not state that their discussion of religion was based upon their own epistemological and ontological positions and that alternative presuppositions could also serve as a basis for the sociological study of religion.[5]

The ten textbooks typically attempted to present a neutral value position in relationship to the desirability of religion. Three of the ten authors gave an impression that they were sympathetic to religious activity, and two indicated a positive attitude toward theological commitment. Two seemed to regard Christianity as superior to other forms of religion; the others implied that all religions have equal status, or they were unclear in their estimation. In the name of objectivity and neutrality the authors' personal value judgments were passed on to students. "No indication is given the student that one's commitment to the cult of objectivity or an anti-religious position may itself be a serious liability to the successful analysis of religious behavior."[6] Large bodies of recent research findings were ignored, so that many of the specific religious problems discussed were treated in terms of the situation a quarter century or more ago.

Students need to be critical in a wholesome way when they read their textbooks and do other assignments. But attacks which simply quote preachers or Bible verses without the support of sociological authority will only incur the disrespect of the unbeliever. Diligent

---

[4]Outstanding among the relevant research is Gerhard Lenski, *The Religious Factor* (Garden City, N.Y.: Doubleday & Co., 1961).
[5]Sidney B. Denman, "The Treatment of Religion in Introductory Sociology Textbooks" (unpublished manuscript, *c.* 1959).
[6]*Ibid.*, p. 6.

and wise students will use a different technique. By assimilating the essence of sociological methods of research and analysis, they will be able to use the tools and techniques of sociology itself to refute the errors of published resources. This approach will win the enthusiastic favor of most professors.

CRITIQUES OF RELIGION

Sociological criticisms of religion can help Christians to grow spiritually. If naïve religious groups are directly or implicitly attacked in the classroom or in reading assignments, the basis for the negative perspective or criticism can be determined. In most instances this will turn out to be certain unrealistic perspectives toward people, antiquated programs of activity, authoritarian mental perspectives or otherworldly attitudes which are not an essential part of biblical faith. Many, indeed, may be directly contrary to Christian social ethics.

Some research has demonstrated empirically that there often is a close relationship between fundamentalism and conservative political, economic and social perspectives, authoritarian personality traits, and certain forms of anti-Semitism and racial prejudice. Such studies need to be carefully evaluated by sociologists to determine whether the methodological problems of operational definitions, sampling, data collection and interpretation, measurement and analysis of the findings are satisfactorily handled. Their conclusions also need investigation from the theological perspective to determine whether sound Christian faith indeed *ought* to be related in the observed manner to certain social problems.

Christians can become more consistent by trying to overcome flaws revealed by sociological research—sins of ethnocentrism in missionary work, of class bias in evangelism, of indirect but vicious condemnation of Jews in religious education, of blind nationalism in political life, of wedding the gospel to a political party. Christians who sincerely try thus to put love into practice will win the respect of sociologists and others who have humanistic values.

Christians sometimes need to be driven back to an examination of the basic elements of their faith. Otherwise the accumulation of subsidiary practices and beliefs which has resulted from decades or even centuries of experience and tradition may be confused with the essence of the faith. Tradition can easily become a source of idolatry and hypocrisy (e.g., Mark 7:1-13; Col. 2:8). Modern missionary experiences and social research have helped Christians to realize that the kingdom of heaven does not consist of any given pattern of eating and drinking, clothing styles, church music, organizational arrangements or other institutionalized social processes and structures. The student of sociology should have a mind that is open to reexamination of his own religious beliefs and organizations so that they can be modified as necessary by the enlightening effects of sociology. If at the same time he retains a firm faith in Jesus Christ, he will not be shaken by efforts to explain Bible incidents with modern social science concepts.

The consequences of church programs and religious doctrines which are indirect and usually unobserved, those which sociologists call latent functions and dysfunctions as well as those which are manifest, lying on the surface, intended, and easily discerned, must be studied by the Christian who is anxious to please his Lord. The effects of human action are so complex that, while a person is doing good to ten men, he may be doing harm to a thousand without realizing it. On the level of practical action, Christians as persons and as members of religious and other groups needs to refine their principles of conduct by sociology and the other social sciences as well as by biblical theology.

The student should always keep in mind the fact that the ultimate values of society cannot come from sociology. From the Christian perspective, they ideally should rest upon the Scriptures. But in disclosing the truth of the Bible and showing its practical applications to life in contemporary society, the Holy Spirit can use the findings of sociology. The sociologist can help in the understanding of the specific ways in which man's pride, economic interests and self-centeredness tend to corrupt the actions of even dedicated Christians. The individualistic tendencies of orthodox Christians, which sometimes lead them to neglect their social responsibilities, need to be evaluated by both sociologists and theologians.

A major source of the widespread disrespect among sociologists for "old-fashioned" Christians is the inconsistency they observe between these Christians' verbal teaching and their worldly practice, especially on the level of group relationships and societal life. The critics thus teach that the social implications of the gospel must be given much more attention by conservative Christians than they have received in the past.[7] Even today God in His sovereignty uses "the heathen" to bring glory to His name!

---

[7]For guidelines to evangelical action, see David O. Moberg, *Inasmuch: Christian Social Responsibility in the Twentieth Century* (Grand Rapids: Wm. B. Eerdmans Pub. Co., 1965).

CULTURAL RELATIVITY

Woven into sociology as a result of observing many groups of people at different times and places is the perspective of cultural relativism. Each culture, indeed each subcultural group, has its own set of values—its own ideas of what is desirable and undesirable, good and bad, right and wrong, proper and improper, beautiful and ugly, legal and illegal. The wide variety of perspectives from one tribe or people to another has contributed to ethical and moral relativism as well. It is easy to reach the conclusion that there are no absolute standards which apply validly and unconditionally in any place and at all times, for each group has its own set of values, and those of one group often conflict with those of others.

Youth today may be confronted with this perspective long before they take their first course in sociology, but there they are apt to be confronted with it more directly and with a more solid intellectual basis than they have seen before. They may even discover that some social theorists have reduced God to a "collective respresentation" of human society; they make Him merely a symbolic figure standing for the social cohesion, integration or solidarity of the group. Since it can be shown that each major clan or cultural grouping of mankind tends to have its own conceptions of the deity, it is easy to conclude that all the gods of man are merely social products, hence even the God whom Christians worship is not objectively or ontologically real or true. Such interpretations must be recognized as being nothing more than theory.

Cultural relativity, on the other hand, is a fact. This can be demonstrated through the history of Christianity itself. Interpretations of Bible passages about the nature of the material universe have changed as a result of increasing scientific knowledge of the universe. Statements about the four corners of the earth were once taken literally, and the earth was viewed as a stationary center around which the sun rotated. Current interpretations of Bible references to footwashing, the "holy kiss," the place of women in the church, ornamentation and hair styles, slavery, the levirate, henotheism, keeping the Sabbath and the use of alcoholic beverages are considerably different from Christian interpretations of past centuries.

The wide variety of patterns of Christian ethics and of less rigid customs or folkways among the numerous contemporary Christian groups is further evidence of the fact that many standards of conduct are relative rather than absolute. The specific interpretations of "worldliness" by a religious group often are more closely linked to its social characteristics than to its theological stance. The divisions of Christendom therefore can be interpreted with the use of such sociological concepts as cultural relativity and cultural lag.

But this does not mean that there are no absolute virtues which all Christians should support and no universal evils they all should oppose. The *fact* of cultural relativism should not be confused with moral relativism as an *ideal*. Christian ideals are stated in the Scriptures, although careful study of them indicates that there are justifiable, even essential, variations in their specific interpretation and application. Being led by the Holy Spirit under the law of liberty, which also is known as the law of love, involves various limitations upon liberty which are essential to protect liberty. It also involves an accountability to God for all that one does. Each Christian is the judge of his own actions under the guidance of the Holy Spirit who enlightens the principles in God's Word. What is right for a child of God at one time may be wrong for him under another set of circumstances.

Christian relativism is not a vague anything-is-all-right moral philosophy. It rests instead upon the true Absolute, almighty God who reveals Himself and His will through Jesus Christ, the Holy Scriptures and the Holy Spirit. To be relevant, some judgments must be relative. Otherwise they could not apply in every age and place. Christians who fail to see this are enslaved by the errors of legalism which the Apostle Paul so strongly refuted in his epistles. Legalistic absolutisms make men distort the Scriptures to find support for culturally established beliefs. Instead Christians should go to the Scriptures to find out what the Bible really says and then modify their cultural traits to conform to these scriptural principles.[8]

"ERRORS" IN THE BIBLE

When the author was a high school student studying English, he became aware of several mistakes of punctuation and sentence structure in the King James Version of the Bible. For a while he was puzzled by statements that this translation is the greatest piece of literature in the English language, for it obviously seemed to have numerous flaws. (The most serious, perhaps, II Cor. 5:21: "For he hath made him to be sin for us, who knew no sin. . . ." According to the rules of modern English grammar and syntax, the clause "who

---

[8]For a more detailed discussion of this subject, see David O. Moberg, "Cultural Relativity and Christian Faith," *Journal of the American Scientific Affiliation,* XIV (June, 1962), 34-48.

knew no sin" should modify the immediately preceding pronoun "us.") The Bible itself was not a problem, for the author was never indoctrinated with the devastating rationalistic view that if one finds one error in the Bible, he must reject it all. But he was troubled with people's statements about the Bible which seemed inconsistent with the facts.

Gradually the writer came to a realization which is closely related to sociological understanding of such subjects. New rules of grammar have been developed, word meanings have changed and sentence structure has been modernized during the three and a half centuries since the King James Version was first published. Standards of "good English" in the 1960's obviously could not be applied by scholars living in 1611! Man's culture, which includes his language, is constantly changing. In order to understand the Bible as fully as possible, one must study the social context in which it was first written as well as that of its medieval and modern translators. Many of the so-called contradictions in the Bible are fully resolved merely by appeal to this fact.

"Facts" are always in a social context. What is accepted as true in one generation may be viewed as folklore or myth in another. Young people who throughout their lives have been indoctrinated with a series of erroneous "facts" about the nature of man, the universe or society, will face many difficulties when they get to college and discover that these alleged facts have been tested and rejected. If they have been reared in a naïve bibliolatry which does not face the problems of modern criticisms of the Bible sensibly, they may "make shipwreck of their faith" as one false interpretation after another is undermined.

It therefore is very important in all religious education to distinguish clearly between what God's Word says and what one interprets it to mean. Men's interpretations and opinions of the Bible must not be confused with God's Word. But unfortunately this happens often; it is a major source of the "loss of faith" among conservative Christians who attend college or university.

Sociology can help men to recognize that their "facts" are "culture bound." If the teaching of sociology is done in a spirit of pride and superiority, it may do more harm than good. But if it enables men to understand each other better, to sympathize with each other more and to respect the integrity of other people even if they do not agree with their opinions, then this approach contributes to the growth of Christian virtues.

CLASSROOM CLASHES

Students at times may be expected to learn theories with which they cannot agree. To memorize something is not the same as believing it; so the necessity to learn the prehistoric stages of man's cultural evolution, the distinctive doctrines and cultural features of a nonchristian religion, theories of the origin of religious institutions or the language and attitudes of the criminal underworld in order to pass an examination and gain a broad education should never be interpreted as an attack upon one's faith.

The church to which a student belongs may be referred to as a "sect." This may be taken as a slur against his religion. But if definitions of the concept are examined in sociological literature, "sect" will be recognized as a descriptive term that refers to a particular type of religious group. In most instances the student will be able to discover characteristics of other types of ecclesiastical organizations (church, denomination, cult) in his home church as well as the features of a sect.[9] Analyzing one's religious group in terms of sociological types can increase one's wisdom and reveal opportunities to improve the quality of his church.

The term "fundamentalism" is accompanied by a note of derision in many classrooms and publications. The person who has previously heard it only with an accent of approval and praise needs to discover the reasons why it is so often condemned. In other words, he must find the "operational definition" behind the use of the word in order to understand the message that is communicated. When he does so, he may discover that he himself is not a fundamentalist according to that definition.[10]

Effective communication can take place only when all parties to a discussion define their key concepts in basically the same way. When using emotion-laden terms like "fundamentalist," "liberal," "modernist," "old-fashioned," "evolution" or even "socialist," one should discover how the term is used by the audience he is addressing and make his own terms clear by context or definition. Failure to do so is the cause of many misunderstandings by both students and instructors.

SOCIOLOGY'S CONTRIBUTION TO PERSONAL FAITH

If the student copes successfully with religious problems of the

---

[9]See David O. Moberg, *The Church as a Social Institution* (Englewood Cliffs, N. J.: Prentice-Hall, Inc., 1962), pp. 73-126.
[10]*Ibid.*, pp. 280-84.

kinds mentioned here, he will find that sociology can help him grow in Christian grace. This is illustrated best by the writer's experiences.

Sociology has contributed to the writer's faith in several ways, although it is in no way a basic source of faith. The deeper one goes into the findings and theories of any science, the more he will recognize his own limitations. He can learn only a small portion of all the knowledge that has been accumulated even in his own discipline. He realizes that every research project which answers a few questions raises many more that had not been thought of previously. Sociology thus has helped the writer to realize that now we know only in part (I Cor. 13:12). It has increased the knowledge of personal ignorance and finiteness. In doing so, it has promoted the spiritual grace of humility. Sociology undermines the spirit of authoritarianism, which is a spirit of self-will, of egoism and of pride that assumes one has infinite knowledge and perfect wisdom.

Sociology has made the writer more honest. It makes one keenly aware of the subtle distortions in observation, interpretation and the reporting of experiences which make men see only the best, or even only an unrealized ideal, in their own organizations and activities and only the worst in those of disliked competitors. Learning sociological methods of research promotes the Christian virtue of honesty.

Sociology has helped the writer to understand certain theological concepts. Its insights into the formation of self-conceptions, social roles and statuses and the process of socialization help to clarify certain aspects of the human side of regeneration, known as being "born again." The conflict within oneself (Rom. 7; Gal. 5:17) is clarified by understanding the "marginal man" phenomenon and the relationships between cultural conflict, social deviation and personality problems.

The sinfulness of man is made very evident in the study of social problems like crime, juvenile delinquency, divorce, racial tensions, population problems, poverty and propaganda. Even within churches one can discover many inconsistencies and violations of Christian ethics. Sociology has made the writer more aware of the fact that "if we say that we have not sinned, we make him [God] a liar, and his word is not in us" (I John 1:10).

Sociology has helped the writer see how important social interaction with other Christians is for the nurture of one's own faith as well as for the Christian witness in the world. Personal religion cannot long endure without group support. Man must of necessity organize formally and informally in order to disseminate the Christian gospel at home and abroad.

SOCIOLOGY'S CONTRIBUTION TO CHURCH WORK

This means that any church on earth is a social institution, not only a divine establishment which is part of the mystical body of Christ. It has the strengths and weaknesses of other institutions. When this is not recognized, appeals to God can be abused to make the church even more resistant to wholesome changes and even more worshipful of tradition than other institutions which do not claim any particular divine support. In other words, sociology helps to clarify the process of goal displacement by which institutional leaders may become so concerned with self-centered ends or so preoccupied with bureaucratic machinery that they forget the basic purposes for which the institution exists. Churches are not exempt from "institutional diseases."

But diagnosis of ailments is a first step toward their treatment. As a sociologist, the writer may see flaws in the institutional church more quickly than others, but sociology also helps one see potential ways of correcting the flaws. It provides methods of research which can be used in the service of the church to study the effects of its programs of activity, organizational forms and social interaction patterns.

The findings of sociology also are helpful in church work. Applied sociology, as distinguished from "pure sociology," has a wealth of possibilities for church administration and Christian action. This is often referred to as religious sociology in Europe or Christian social ethics in America, but it goes beyond either of these academic specialties to touch upon every aspect of the life and work of the church. Of course this assumes that we should love God *with all our mind* as well as with all our strength, heart and soul. Only those Christians who have a lopsided (hence nonscriptural) view of the Christian life will resist the rational intellectual approach which calls for church planning in the light of the knowledge God has given us the ability and opportunity to acquire.

PROBLEMS AMONG CHRISTIANS

The hardest struggle of the Christian who is learning from sociology is therefore likely to be with his fellow Christians more than with his secular instructors and resources. If some Christians see sociology as an enemy or completely misinterpret it as a form of socialism, they will be suspicious of any suggestions which grow out of its insights. If they think of life as divided into two spheres, the "sacred" and the "secular," the "holy" and the "profane," or the "spiritual" and the "worldly," they will resist all insights of sociology and other sciences which point to life as a totality that is divided into disciplines of study only because man's finiteness makes him incapable of coping with the whole. If the sociologist sees the church on earth as a human institution, some Christians may suspect him of denying its nonempirical supernatural nature. If sociology implies that a church has faults, they will defend it instead of investigating it to discover whether or not the charge has a factual basis and, if so, to try to correct the faults. If sociologists say the church must change its activities or even its structural organization in order to remain contemporary, these Christians will hold that "the old-time religion" is best: "What was good enough for Grandma is good enough for me." By their obstructionism, they force many intelligent youth to leave their "old-time religion" and join "liberal" churches.

Rigid traditionalists in the church sin by knowing the good and not doing it (James 4:17). They sin by making the earthly structures and institutional programs of a church into absolute objects of worship which get between men and God instead of keeping them as mere instruments to bring men closer to God.

But the student who is enlightened by sociology may also sin. Knowing the methods by which men can be influenced effectively to serve God better than they have in the past, he may instead revolt against the "old fogies" and vested interests in his church, not even trying to work with them. He may display his command of sociological language when addressing them, not realizing that certain terms have vastly different emotional or intellectual meanings in everyday speech, and thus alienate his listeners. Knowing the decision-making process, he may ignore it or directly contradict it by words or deeds that alienate men from one another instead of reconciling them to each other and to God.

Repentance is needed on both sides of the differing perspectives and opinions. This repentance will come more readily when sociological insights into human conduct are diffused widely and not limited to those who have studied sociology in college. The sociology student and the college graduate in the church have the task of translating their academic knowledge into the language and daily life of their fellow church members. Doing so will help them to integrate their own life and personality around Jesus Christ. Making Him Lord gives a central direction and purpose. It promotes personal and group stability.

Sociology can clarify the way in which all people are interrelated, as well as how all activities in the life of any person are interrelated around a central philosophy of life, a world view and an implicit or explicit goal of living. Internalized values connected with this goal as well as with the group-life with other persons aiming at the same goal make one a better person as well as a better Christian. The highest, best and, for the Christian, the only ideal center of such an integrated life is a consistent recognition and application of the principle "For me to live is Christ" (Phil. 1:21). The student who has a solid faith in Jesus Christ will find that his spiritual life is strengthened through his study of sociology.

CONCLUSION

Sociology can be used as a basis for examining one's faith in order to determine which elements in it are essential and which are merely incidental cultural additions. It thus can drive men to a study of the cultural setting in which the Scriptures were first given to man. This will help to distinguish between what the Bible says and interpretations which have crept into its translations, traditions and theology. The limitations of sociology must of course be kept in mind; it can never be the ultimate source of moral and spiritual values. Christianity will always rest upon a biblical faith (Heb. 11:6).

Sociology raises basic questions which are addressed to the very core of man's being. It can increase the Christian understanding of man, a social being created in the image of God. Indirectly it reveals something of the complexity and wonders of God's methods of working with and through men. It can be used by the Holy Spirit to reveal sin and thus to convict Christians as well as non-Christians of their sinfulness.

Sociology shows how men typically assume that their own cultural perspectives on moral issues and social practices (folkways and mores) are the only correct ones and how they tend falsely to assume that these were divinely established by God. It makes men realize that they are limited by or even trapped in a cultural setting which has played an important part in molding their character and shaping their personality. Man no longer can indirectly establish himself or his group as a "god" when he has a thorough grasp of the insights of sociology.

Sociology can promote the dissemination of the gospel and the application of Christian principles in contemporary society if its lessons are heeded and applied. It can help Christians recognize the importance of men in the spread of the gospel (Rom. 10:17). It can give children of God an orientation to man and society which will enable them to be more effective instruments in the service of God. Its answers to man's problems are never final or absolute, but they can serve as a partial guide to action by clarifying the specific situations in which general scriptural principles must be applied.

The problems confronted by the student of sociology can be turned into spiritual blessings by all who have an abiding and sincere faith in Jesus Christ. These blessings will be evident in their own self-conceptions and feelings, in their work in the church, and in their service to their fellowmen.

FOR FURTHER READING

CASSERLEY, J. V. LANGMEAD. *Morals and Man in the Social Sciences.* New York: Longmans Green & Co., 1951.

GLOCK, CHARLES Y. "On the Study of Religious Commitment," *Religious Education*, LVII, No. 4 (July-August, 1962), Supplement, S-98–S-110.

LENSKI, GERHARD. *The Religious Factor.* Garden City, N.Y.: Doubleday & Co., 1961.

MOBERG, DAVID O. *The Church as a Social Institution.* Englewood Cliffs, N. J.: Prentice-Hall, Inc., 1962.

————. "Cultural Relativity and Christian Faith," *Journal of the American Scientific Affiliation*, XIV (June, 1962), 34-48.

————. "The Encounter of Scientific and Religious Values Pertinent to Man's Spiritual Nature," *Sociological Analysis*, XXVIII (Spring, 1967), 22-33.

————. *Inasmuch: Christian Social Responsibility in the Twentieth Century.* Grand Rapids: Wm. B. Eerdmans Pub. Co., 1965.

REDEKOP, CALVIN. *The Church Functions with Purpose.* Scottdale, Pa.: Herald Press, 1967.

SCHREUDER, OSMUND. "Church and Sociology," *Social Compass*, XI (No. 5, 1965), 5-19.

GEOLOGY

Douglas A. Block

Douglas A. Block is teacher of geology at Rock Valley College in Rockford, Illinois. A graduate of Wheaton College, he holds the M. S. from the State University of Iowa, the B. D. from Northern Baptist Theological Seminary and the Ph. D. from the University of North Dakota. He previously served as associate professor of geology at Wheaton College.

11

GEOLOGY

Douglas A. Block

INTRODUCTION

Geology is the science of the earth. More specifically, it is the application of distinctive principles that often involve aspects of chemistry, physics and biology to the problems of deciphering earth history, discovering supplies of necessary raw materials and fuels, and determining principles under which natural laws operate on and in the earth. It searches the atmosphere, hydrosphere, lithosphere and biosphere of the present earth in order to reconstruct ecological patterns of the past, and, in a sense, to foretell the earth's destiny. Oddly, geologists are generally historians more than prophets except where economic necessity dictates.

For the evangelical Christian, yet one more dimension is added to the study of the earth. This dimension involves a Christian philosophy of science that enables harmonization of natural phenomena with the Word of God. Implicit in such a task is the unmistakable testimony of Scripture that the God of creation and the God of redemption are one. There must not be contradiction between the works and the Word of God. There is a necessary harmony between general and special revelation.

Yet realistically, there are areas of supposed contradiction. The hyperorthodox challenge the validity of both principle and deduction under which the geologist works; the Christian strongly oriented in science concedes possible obscuring or at least regrettable silence

in the biblical text. Oddly, the same Evangelical dubbed fundamental in the university environment may find himself in the far
left wing of the liberal camp upon moving to the Christian campus.
It is the purpose of this chapter to focus attention on several areas
of geology with the intent that the reader may judge their assumed
opposition to the Word of God.

BASIC ASSUMPTIONS

It should be understood at the outset that this chapter is written
from the point of view that God exists, and that He is the First Cause
of the visible universe. Two denials and as many assertions are contingent upon this assumption:

1. The astronomic sphere that includes our sun and solar system
is not eternal. It had, however remote, a beginning in time and space.

2. The element of chance occurrence in nature is vetoed in favor
of system and order that emanate from the assumed existence of a
divine intelligence.[1]

The second basic assumption is that creation does not constitute
an end in itself. Rather, the burden of Scripture is that God first
conceived the existence of the highest object of His creative activity
—man in His own image—and what is counted as the created universe simply forms the suitable place of habitation for those who are
the prime objects of God's affection.[2]

These assumptions sharply distinguish the approach of the Evangelical to earth science from that of the naturalistic scientist who refuses to accept as valid the claims for the existence of an intelligent
God, and from that of the evolutionary paleontologist who says, in
substance, that if conditions on earth had been different, other forms
of life would have developed to fit those conditions.

It is the conviction of this writer that these evangelical assumptions are basic to a common ground of understanding. Empirical
data of many aspects of geology and paleontology can be reconstructed with equal logic from either the theistic or a nontheistic
point of view. Many alleged difficulties could be avoided if this diversity of starting points were recognized.

---

[1]One is assuming what one sets out to prove only if there is failure to separate cause from effect. One assumes the existence of the eternal One *revealed*
in Scripture. Our burden is to demonstrate not that the revelation is correct
but that creation is in harmony with the assumption of the revealed First
Cause.
[2]Cf. John 17:24; Eph. 1:4; Rev. 17:8.

BASIC DIFFICULTIES

At present, three concepts widely accepted in geology constitute major areas of difficulty for the Christian who is seeking to reconcile the Word of God and geological data:

1. the principle of uniformity in nature
2. the span of geologic time
3. the paleontological record of the sequence of living forms

Uniformitarianism Examined

Uniformitarianism, or the principle of uniformity in nature, as conceived by modern geologists grew out of the observation of natural phenomena. Its early proponents, James Hutton and Sir Charles Lyell, found themselves in sharp opposition to ideas accepted in their day, though each of these men was forced to answer different kinds of argument.

Karl von Zittel, reviewing Hutton's original treatise, expresses uniformitarian doctrine: "The events of past geologic ages can be most satisfactorily predicted from a careful examination of present conditions and processes."[3] In short, the present is the key to the past. Included in this principle is the notion that no process has operated in the past that is not somewhere in operation at the present hour. What the principle does *not* say is that processes have always operated at the same rate. Rather, geologists insist upon the converse: that processes at times are accelerated radically, acting catastrophically in a particular place and time. At other times the same processes seem to make imperceptible progress in their action upon the land.

Hutton's first paper, read before the Royal Society at Edinburgh in 1785, drew little attention because the learning of the schools had no part in Hutton's work. As a chemist successfully experimenting with innovations on his own farm, and as a wealthy, widely traveled country gentleman, he saw changes being effected on the surface of the land to which no one had earlier called attention. The publication in 1795 of his two-volume work seemed to receive most opposition from the disciples of Abraham Gottlob Werner who headed the Neptunist School. This school said, in substance, that all rock layers wherever found are precipitates from some primeval aqueous medium. Hutton, by contrast, showed that sediments derived from present continents were consolidated on the bed of the ocean and subsequently lifted by diastrophism to form new land masses.

[3]*History of Geology and Paleontology,* trans. Maria M. Ogilvie-Gordon (New York: Charles Scribner's Sons, 1901), p. 69.

Sir Charles Lyell, who published three volumes between January, 1832, and April, 1833, found himself cautiously vindicating his uniformitarian interpretation of nature against popular catastrophists: Buckland, Whewell, Sedgwick, Daubeny and Conybeare. The primary burden of these men was the defense of the Mosaic account of the flood. Significantly, neither Hutton nor Lyell was ever censured by the church for his views, though this is not to say that the writings of both failed to precipitate debate. Buckland and Sedgwick held the chairs of geology at Oxford and Cambridge; Daubeny was professor of chemistry at Oxford; Conybeare was a fellow of New College; and Whewell was senior tutor and, later, master of Trinity College, Cambridge. Charles Gillespie reports that nearly every meeting of the Geological Society appears to have resolved itself into a debate between Lyell's supporters and this Oxford School of Geology.[4]

Hutton wrote as a firsthand observer of natural processes and Lyell wrote as the interpreter of data discovered by field observation. Students today get the impression that pioneers in earth science deliberately set themselves to oppose and undermine biblical doctrine, when, quite to the contrary, they were fighting to advance the concept of order in natural phenomena wherein they perceived infinite wisdom. James Hutton himself remarked:

> It is with pleasure that man observes order and regularity in the works of nature instead of becoming disgusted with disorder and confusion. If the stone which fell today were to rise tomorrow, there would be an end of natural philosophy, our principles would fail, and we would no longer investigate the rules of nature from our observations.[5]

The modern geology student is not faced with the problem of reconciling Neptunism with current thought because observation and laboratory analysis have verified the variety of modes of rock origin. However, many modern evangelical students of geology find themselves still at odds with remnants of the old catastrophic school expressed by writers on "flood geology." George McCready Price's voluminous writings, Byron Nelson's *The Deluge Story in Stone*, A. M. Rehwinkel's *The Flood* and H. W. Clark's *The New Diluvialism* have exerted powerful influence among Fundamentalists during the first half of the twentieth century. On the other hand, their work has been discredited in university geology departments;

---

[4]*Genesis and Geology* (Cambridge: Harvard University Press, 1951), p. 140.
[5]*Theory of the Earth; or an investigation of the laws observable in the composition, dissolution and restoration of land upon the globe* (Edinburgh: Trans. Royal Society, 1788), p. 214.

and Christian students sitting in classes in these schools have found themselves also receiving the abuse sarcastically hurled at these writers.

In 1961, John C. Whitcomb, Jr., and Henry M. Morris published their strongly documented work *The Genesis Flood*. This book summarizes and updates the flood geology argument in concise fashion. Credit is due these men for comprehensively reviewing the Scriptures that describe the phenomena and significance of the biblical deluge. They review, as well, the attempts of the nineteenth century catastrophists to maintain their position against the growth of uniformitarian theory.

Their thesis is that two periods above all others in earth history are not compatible with the uniformitarian concept. These intervals are the Creation Week and the Noachian Deluge. The force of their argument regarding creation seems to lie in creation contra the first and second laws of thermodynamics. The first law is that of the conservation of energy which says that although its form can be changed, the total quantity is unaltered—energy is neither created nor destroyed in the present system. The second law of thermodynamics affirms that, although the total quantity of energy remains unchanged, there is always a tendency for it to increase in randomness and therefore to become less available for useful work. This is the principle of increase in entropy in nature. Whitcomb and Morris correctly maintain that in creation these laws cannot apply.

Moreover, Whitcomb and Morris posit from the biblical narrative of the flood that the nature and extent of such a worldwide catastrophe render the principle of uniformity invalid until after that event was completed.[6] Also, they say the uniqueness of such a supernatural catastrophe renders undecipherable the geologic activities that took place.

The geologic evidence they cite to harmonize their view is that of recent enlargement and overflow of ocean basins and increased volcanic and mountain building activity. It is true that postglacial eustatic rise of sea level and Pliocene-Pleistocene uplift associated with the Cascadian-Alpine revolution are unmistakable. However, the difficulty lies in attempting to systematize the vast store of geologic data within the boundaries set by their own presuppositions. Whitcomb and Morris say there was no death prior to Adam's fall, therefore the abundant fossil record that begins in the Cambrian must mark the onslaught of the deluge catastrophe. Thus the entire

---

[6]*The Genesis Flood* (Nutley, N. J.: Presbyterian & Reformed Pub. Co., 1960), p. 124.

Paleozoic, Mesozoic and Cenozoic record to the base of the Pleistocene was formed in the single year's period of inundation.

Each rock formation in the nearly eighty-mile thickness of sediments has its counterpart in some present environment and is subject to detailed comparison with current geologic processes. Whitcomb and Morris say this comparison is not valid, but they ask
rather that these sedimentary masses be attributed to catastrophic
submarine activity that can never be observed or repeated. In short,
they remove the entire body of observed geologic data from any
possible systematic analysis or description. This is the basic reason
why even Christian students of geology, who are equally zealous
for the defense of God's Word, are alienated from the views of flood
geologists.

Also, it is not known what disposition Whitcomb and Morris
would make of evidence of life in the Precambrian Era. Such evidence is admittedly not abundant, but it is unmistakable.

In sharp contrast are the views of a large number of evangelical
Christians who believe in a personal, omnipotent God who designed
and created the material world, but who believe, as well, that nature
constitutes a meaningful commentary on special revelation. These
men accept the principle of uniformity as valid. They believe that
the operation of natural law is a necessary concomitant to the recognition and definition of supernatural activity. What is produced via
the direct intervention of God should be recognizable if not unique.

Increasingly detailed study of the rocks formed from varieties of
sediments has enabled reconstruction of past environments in which
these sediments came to rest. Ripple marks, cross-bedding, degree
of sorting, composition of the sediments—each tells the story of its
formation. Laboratory experiment and analysis reveal temperature,
pressure and solubility conditions necessary for lithification. Not just
a single line of attack is involved; rather, geochemists, geophysicists
and marine biologists pyramid data upon the interpretations of the
geologists. Each researcher evaluates and criticizes the work of
others while augmenting the store of data by his own observations.
Students frequently fail to discern the keen competition that exists
between researchers and the laboratories of which they are a part.
No error escapes detection. Also, a whole new dimension in the study
of sediments has been gained from the mass of detail concerning subsurface layers derived from oil well borings. Many interpretations
made on surface exposures alone have been modified, and new questions have been raised.

From this reconstructed monument of the geologic past, only a few formations are unique to some environment that cannot be presently observed. It can be truthfully said that nearly every rock of the entire geologic timetable has its modern counterpart.

This is not to say, however, that uniformitarian geology is without problems. Oceanographic research has brought to light the existence of submarine canyons cut to depths of 15,000 feet below sea level; floors of deep ocean basins are sculptured by topography that dwarfs comparable features on the continents. Studies of paleomagnetism suggest, but do not prove, that continents have shifted their positions. Evidence for glaciation within the life-span of man on the earth is unquestionable, but adequate causes of necessary climatic shifts are subject only to speculation.

The Problem of Time

It is frequently said among geologists that the greatest contribution of historical geology to modern thought is a concept of the vastness of prehistoric time. If the entire span of the earth's assumed 4½-billion-year existence were to be represented by the twelve hours of a clock face, recognizable evidence of life appeared at 10:40; dinosaurs came on the scene thirty-three minutes before twelve; mammals arrived only nine minutes and thirty-six seconds before twelve; and man has been on earth for only ten seconds, or 1/4,500 of its total history.

For the Christian there can be two attitudes and as many basic questions: Either he will deny the interpretation of accumulated data, made on uniformitarian assumptions and argue that God supernaturally produced an appearance of antiquity either in creation or through the flood; or he will accept the geologists' picture of earth's life-span and attribute it to God's infinite wisdom in design.

The questions concern the validity of the geologic clocks. Is the gamut of geologic time based entirely on the theory of organic evolution, or can earth's longevity be substantiated by physical means? Also, are the physical means of time determination colored by interpretive prejudice or must the Evangelical accept their validity?

At this point the second basic assumption of this discussion should be recalled: The origin of the earth, in the biblical context, does not constitute an end in itself. We insist that, if indeed sequence can be ascribed to the creative mind of God, man in the image of God stands supreme in the creative fiat. Thus conceived, the antiquity of the earth, the solar system, the galaxies of stars magnify the imputed glory of created man.

God is extravagant—needlessly so by human standards. At nearly every level a hundred million seeds are sown to produce one new life. This is as true of the maple as of man. More than a billion galaxies, or of the order of 100 sextillion stars, can now be seen, the farthest of which is three billion light-years from earth. Scientists want to find life beyond the earth to give credence to its origin and existence in a multitude of conditions. No comparable need exists for purpose in time. Philosophic astronomers are satisfied to ascribe infinity to the existence of matter to escape the implications of a remote but finite creation.

The dilemma of the Christian is that of accepting time and space measurements based on physical means or of arguing that God created light already well on its way to earth from distant stars. Or possibly he will dare to risk the theory that light once traveled faster than at present! We believe that Christians need always be on guard against the temptation of ascribing within a theistic framework philosophical ideas that are as unfounded as those of the non-theist whom they consistently criticize.

Radioactivity constitutes a spontaneous uncontrollable nuclear reaction that presently cannot be varied at temperatures and pressures less than those on the surface of the sun. The dating of radioactive materials depends on determination of the ratios of originial materials to derived materials. If the rate of decay or disintegration of the material is known, the ratio of "parent" to "daughter" material will tell how long the "clock" has been operating. Geologists insist that care be taken that no material be lost or gained within a closed system. To allow such leakage would be comparable to operating a broken hourglass that allows sand to escape. Also, precise identification of end products of radioactivity is necessary and possible in order to distinguish them from comparable elements formed by normal mineral crystallization. In any event, leakage is of significance to the geologist because it would cause time figures to be less than actual.

The radioactive transformations that are most valuable in determining geologic age are uranium to lead, rubidium to strontium, potassium to argon, and carbon to nitrogen. Also, a recent method is to count the tracks or traces of fission particles formed by radioactivity that has been completed and then to bombard the specimen in a reactor to disintegrate the remaining uranium atoms. A comparison of the count of the second set of tracks compared with the first can be used to determine the age of the sample.

With the exception of the carbon-to-nitrogen transformation, many rocks and meteorites have been dated by several methods whose range of age determination overlaps sufficiently to provide mutual checks. On the basis of these tests, the age of the earth is presently believed to be 4½ billion years, and igneous rocks at other horizons in the geologic timetable have been placed in sequence by their determined radioactive age. No reasonable contradiction of these dates is possible through modern chemistry or physics. It should be noted that the catastrophists or flood geologists say nothing can be known of rates of decay in the antediluvian period. Here again, they place chronology in the limbo of indeterminacy.

The major difficulty encountered by the historical geologist is in making correlations between widely scattered local sequences that are dated unquestionably by absolute physical means. It is at this point that paleontology is pressed into service. The old idea of an index fossil representing a given layer or formation is now largely obsolete. Instead paleontologists are concerned with the reconstruction of the total ecological and the total faunal patterns represented in a given formation. As much attention is given to the environmental pattern as to the actual fossils recovered. In this process, it has become apparent by empirical observation that certain animals in close association with one another constitute a diagnostic fauna. Such a fauna or complete fossil assemblage now constitutes the means of long-distance correlation. Changes in faunal groupings are a reflection of changed environmental patterns. The fossils have become tools rather than sacred objects.

The Paleontological Record

An examination of the fossil record in objective detail presents several characteristics:

1. There are faunas represented in particular formations and portions of the geologic timetable that are separable into groups peculiar to limited horizons.

2. Within these distinctive faunas, some forms are found that continue through nearly the entire gamut of geologic time and are thus present in nearly every fossil collection. Other forms display limited time ranges appearing and disappearing at various levels or are characteristic of only a single formation. Fossils used in making long-distance correlations are the forms that typically occur together among those whose range is limited. But today the paleontologists use faunal groups—not individual index fossils—to make their correlations.

3. Within the geologic timetable there are horizons at which entire faunas appear and disappear with an apparent suddenness that lacks

adequate explanation. For example, the abundant fossil record that begins in the Cambrian Period is unprecedented. Elementary textbooks of historical geology abound in statements such as: "It is as if a curtain were suddenly lifted on a drama long in progress." "We do not understand why fossils of marine invertebrates suddenly become common." "Complex forms of arthropods such as trilobites held the center of the stage." Following such an auspicious beginning, at least two major crises in the history of life are commonly cited by the evolutionary paleontologist: one at the end of the Permian Period when bizarre forms that developed during the Paleozoic Era disappeared, and another at the end of the Cretaceous Period. The latter constituted such a significant simultaneous disappearance of many stocks that it has been dubbed the "time of the great dying."

4. Within nearly every section of the timetable taxonomic series of animal forms are found that show change in size, in form, and occasionally in function of some part of the organism. Such series are used in the evolutionary context to show descent via natural selection or mutation. On this basis marine invertebrates are used to subdivide individual geologic periods into smaller divisions of rock series and time. More noteworthy for the present consideration are the series of vertebrates found in the Mesozoic and Cenozoic eras. Such series range from those of dinosaurs to the more widely known ones of the horse, camel and proboscidians. Without exception each stock studied shows an increase in size, a relative increase in brain size compared to total body size, and increase in specialization of certain organs such as the teeth and feet. Crossing of taxonomic boundaries between major groups (e.g., classes, orders) is more difficult for the evolutionist to demonstrate in the vertebrates. Birds are cited for such evidence, however, since they are warm-blooded like the mammals, they lay eggs like the reptiles, and their feather structure is unlike either the scaly skins of the reptiles or the furry coats of the mammals. Likewise a few birds have been found displaying true teeth, and some show claws along the fore edge wings indicating their kinship to the reptiles from which they are supposed to have descended.

DISCUSSION

If an adequate refutation of the characteristics of the paleontological record could be presented, there would be no problem. It would long ago have been outlined in detail by some one of the growing number of competent biologists or paleontologists who are also strong defenders of the creationism of the Word of God. What has actually transpired is that the force of evidence has compelled competent Christian workers in science to ask for a reinterpretation of Scripture to allow room for developmental patterns. Or, the other extreme is again apparent as, in the case of uniformitarianism, defenders of strict creationism have rejected the validity of paleontological evidence on the grounds that it was born of prejudice.

The purpose here has been to discuss each of the characteristics listed above, showing both strengths and weaknesses, allowing the reader some means of evaluation.

The most noteworthy development in stratigraphic paleontology in the last decade is the use of entire faunas to discriminate paleoecological conditions. In a very real sense this has supplanted index fossil studies. Krumbein and Sloss (1963) point out also that stratigraphers are being given monumental quantities of new subsurface data from well-borings that force rethinking of many former correlations. First, the subsurface data is demonstrating that many unconformities that have been mapped in outcrops near the edges of basins of deposition can be demonstrated to disappear across the interior of many such basins. The function here serves to provide much more complete faunas representative of a given basin than was previously possible. Also, Krumbein and Sloss indicate as well that oil geologists are now working primarily with physical characteristics of rock strata rather than being concerned first with fossil content. Lithostratigraphy is supplanting biostratigraphy in local correlations for the oil industry. Therefore it cannot be argued that prejudice dictates reconstruction of the time dimension in historical geology. The obvious weakness to the uniformitarian geologist remains the fact that he still has but a small fraction of the total sedimentary record. Unknown quantities of rock have eroded, forcing the geologist to reconstruct history from an incomplete record. It is at this point that the catastrophist maintains the record is equally indeterminant inasmuch as it was formed by a unique geologic event—the biblical deluge.

Generations of paleontologists have stated bluntly: "Overspecialization leads to extinction." Within every faunal group, certain forms have responded to changes in their environment and to less visible genetic changes within themselves, and have become "progressive" to a point where further reaction seems to become impossible and a slight environmental change results in extermination. Along with these forms, others remain unchanged—and continue to persist unchanged to the present. Reasons for such variation in responses are missing. Evidence that it has happened is empirical.

The commonly accepted explanation for the appearance of fossils in the Cambrian is twofold: It is assumed that increased competition led to production of shells in many groups apparently simultaneously. However, both the suddenness of appearance and the simultaneity of shell formations is said to be more apparent than real due to the immense time span that separates Precambrian formations from those of the early Paleozoic.

At this point it is in order to point out an error in commonly used Christian theory. The appearance of the abundance of fossils in the Cambrian and the appearance of successive new forms of life higher in the timetable are frequently attributed to a long-protracted sequential interpretation of the days of Genesis 1. Error here is twofold. First, the fossil record cannot be made to fit the sequence of created forms enumerated in Genesis 1. Second, the disappearance of many groups during the period of creative activity is incongruous therewith. Such disappearances suggest judgment was coeval with creation. Though less satisfying to some, the scholarly Christian faces the same dilemma as the evolutionist, and must simply admit inadequate data to support any firm conclusions in some of these matters.

The evolutionist discerns the record and in a sense cannot formulate detailed causes. Thus within the framework of his mechanistic presuppositions, he assumes that time and some aspect of genetics —as yet not completely understood—have produced the record he sees.

On the other hand, the evangelical Christian has a basic presupposition which constitutes his unassailable and perfect First Cause. The problem here is his inability to describe an orderly record that will show details and the precise mode of God's operation within that framework. So the Christian thus far does not meet the conditions of the empiricism of "science that works." But the empirical scientist lives and works in the darkness of no cause—and is not bothered thereby.

It is the conviction of this writer that the last chapter in this debate is not yet written, nor will it be until the prophetic future outlined in the sure Word of truth has been consummated and light is thereby shed on the prehistory of God's creation. Then will we "know as we are known."

FOR FURTHER READING

GILLISPIE, CHARLES COULSTON. *Genesis and Geology*. Cambridge: Harvard University Press, 1951.

HUTTON, JAMES. *Theory of the Earth*. Translation. Edinburgh: Royal Society, 1788.

KRUMBEIN, W. C. and SLOSS, L. L. *Stratigraphy and Sedimentation*. San Francisco: W. H. Freeman & Co., 1963.

KUMMEL, BERNHARD. *History of the Earth*. San Francisco: W. H. Freeman & Co., 1961.

PATTEN, DONALD W. *The Biblical Flood and the Ice Age*. Seattle: Pacific Meridian Pub. Co., 1966.

VELIKOVSKY, IMMANUEL. *Earth in Upheaval*. New York: Doubleday & Co., 1955.

VON ZITTEL, KARL. *History of Geology and Paleontology*. Trans. MARIA M. OGILVIE-GORDON. New York: Charles Scribner's Sons, 1901.

WHITCOMB, JOHN C., JR., and MORRIS, HENRY M. *The Genesis Flood*. Nutley, N. J.: Presbyterian & Reformed Pub. Co., 1960.

ARCHAEOLOGY

Howard F. Vos

Howard F. Vos is professor of history and chairman of the division of social sciences at Trinity College, Deerfield, Illinois. Previous teaching appointments include Bryan College, Tennessee Temple College and the Moody Bible Institute. A graduate of Wheaton College, he holds the Th. M. and Th. D. degrees from Dallas Theological Seminary and the M. A. and Ph. D. degrees from Northwestern University. Among his several publications are *Genesis and Archaeology, An Introduction to Bible Archaeology* (also published in Spanish) and the *Wycliffe Historical Geography of Bible Lands,* coauthored with Charles F. Pfeiffer.

12

ARCHAEOLOGY

Howard F. Vos

In a scientifically oriented world, biblical archaeology has come of age and has itself developed into a full-fledged science. It is not an *exact science* such as mathematics or chemistry in which certain postulates, formulas or relationships are always true. Basically, however, its method of procedure is scientific. Knowledge in the field is acquired by systematic observation or study, and facts discovered are evaluated and classified into an organized body of information. Moreover, archaeology is a composite science because it seeks assistance from many other sciences. For example, the chemist is called in to analyze ashes or decayed substances in order to determine the building materials, clothing materials or diet of an ancient; the physical anthropologist is employed to decide the age and sex of human skeletal remains; and the zoologist is utilized to discern from animal bones whether a people have had domesticated sheep, cattle or horses.

In an age when the development of the physical sciences has reduced interest and faith of the common man in the supernatural and has questioned the biblical message, the science of Near Eastern archaeology has helped to confirm the Scriptures. Dozens of names of Hebrew and Gentile kings mentioned in the Bible have been found in excavated records, and much has been learned about these rulers. The remains of numerous peoples thought to have been the invention of biblical scribes have come to light in the excavations; travelers may once again walk the streets of these deserted capitals. The historical accuracy of the patriarchal narrative has been reestablished. Archaeology has confirmed the substantial historicity of the Bible.

One must be careful, however, not to violate a basic principle of logic. Truth of one kind cannot be used to support truth of another kind. The fact that the historical record of Scripture can be shown to be accurate does not demonstrate the reliability of its spiritual teaching. But since it has been a device of enemies of the theological message of the Bible to cast doubt on that message by attacking historical and scientific references in Scripture, may it not be concluded that confidence in the spiritual message is immensely strengthened whenever archaeology demonstrates the veracity of the context of a theological dictum?

It is difficult for the theologically conservative student of biblical archaeology to steer a straight course between the extreme viewpoints held by interpreters in the field. He is in danger of being engulfed by the teaching that "every spade full of earth turned in the Middle East helps to prove the Bible is true." On the other hand he may be swamped by the position that one should not use archaeology for the purpose of confirming Scripture. He will no doubt be disturbed by the statement of some that archaeology confirms the Bible more often than it demonstrates it to be in error. And if he is honest, he will recognize that archaeological discoveries have created some real problems for the Bible student.

This writer holds that archaeology may be validly used to support the veracity of Scripture. One should never claim that archaeology *proves* the Bible; many suppositions that most people assume to be true on very good authority cannot be fully proved. It is better to say that archaeology helps to *confirm* the assertions made in the Bible. It is not a perversion of the scientific methodology of Near Eastern archaeology to use its findings to attest the Scripture. Certainly to use archaeology to support Scripture is as valid as to use an antisupernatural philosophy of science to discredit Scripture.

Having made such an assertion, however, one must admit that probably the largest contribution of Near Eastern archaeology to biblical study is in the area of illumination. Archaeological activity in Bible lands has helped to throw light on the social, religious and historical contexts of the Bible; on the narrative of the Bible; on biblical customs; and on the meaning of Greek and Hebrew words heretofore incorrectly or insufficiently understood.

HAS ARCHAEOLOGY SHOWN THE BIBLE TO BE IN ERROR?

Occasionally books or articles assert that archaeological investigation has established the accuracy of Scripture much more often than the reverse has been true. The implication is that archaeological work has on occasion demonstrated the Bible to be in error. Examples that are sometimes given of such proved error concern Ai and the Philistines in Abraham's time.

Ai. Target of Hebrew forces after the fall of Jericho (Joshua 7-8), Ai has long been identified with et-Tell, about one and one-half miles southeast of Bethel. Mme Judith Marquet-Krause excavated there from 1933 to 1935 and reported that the site was deserted from about 2200-2000 B.C. to about 1200-1100 B.C. Obviously no town would have been on the mound at whatever date one assigns to the conquest of Palestine, and the Scripture would appear to be in error. A common explanation is that the writer of Joshua confused the account with the taking of Bethel. Another suggestion is that the Canaanites of Bethel were using the site as an outpost against invaders. In such a case the remains would be too modest and temporary to be found by an excavator.

Jan Simons has not been eager to accept the identification of Ai with et-Tell, in spite of the fact that most do. He points out that the name et-Tell (linguistically equatable with Ai, "the ruin") is found so often on both sides of the Jordan that any direct connection between it and the Hebrew place-name is uncertain. Moreover, he is not sure that the Hebrew *'ai* must be translated as "the ruin." In addition Simons feels that (1) et-Tell is not so close to Bethel as the Hebrew text of Joshua 12:9 would seem to require; (2) et-Tell is a large site, whereas Joshua 7:3 describes the people as "few"; (3) et-Tell was not a ruin in the post-conquest period, and Joshua indicates that Ai was (8:28); (4) there is no valley adjacent to et-Tell, whereas Joshua 8:11 indicates the existence of one.[1]

Professor Joseph A. Callaway led a new expedition to et-Tell in 1964 and concluded that "nothing in the present evidence warrants an identification of the village with the city of 'Ai captured by Joshua as described in Joshua 8:1-29."[2] If Ai is not to be identified with et-Tell, the problem created by earlier archaeological work at the site is eliminated.

The Philistines in Abraham's time. Another point at which archaeology has sometimes been thought to have shown the Bible to be in error concerns the Philistines in the days of Abraham and Isaac. Excavations have revealed numerous evidences of Philistine occupation

---

[1]"Archaeological Digest," *American Journal of Archaeology,* LI (July-September, 1947), 311; Jan Simons, *The Geographical and Topographical Texts of the Old Testament* (Leiden: E. J. Brill, 1959), p. 270.
[2]Joseph A. Callaway, "The 1964 'Ai (et Tell) Excavations," *Bulletin of the American Schools of Oriental Research,* No. 178 (April, 1965), pp. 27-28.

of western Palestine during the period of the Judges and the early monarchy, when their oppressive treatment of Israel frequently threatened virtual extermination of the Hebrews. Scholars do not doubt biblical indications concerning the Philistines in that later period.

But the Bible has something to say about Philistines in the days of Abraham and Isaac too, and excavations have produced no evidence of their presence in Palestine at such an early time. Therefore, many assume the Scriptures to be in error. What makes matters worse is that the Philistines (Peleset or Peleste) are known to have been among the conglomeration of humanity that washed onto southern and eastern Mediterranean shores at the end of the thirteenth and the beginning of the twelfth centuries B.C. Ramses III of Egypt (1198-1167) drove them from the shores of his realm, and presumably they drifted northward and settled in Palestine. The Philistines came from the island of Caphtor, which is commonly identified with Crete (cf. Amos 9:7).

Of course the fact that no specific evidence has yet been found of Philistines in Palestine in the period 2000-1900 B.C. is not final proof that they were not there. An argument from silence is inconclusive. In passing, it is extremely interesting to note that the Philistines of Abraham's day appear to have been generally peaceful, but those of the twelfth century B.C. and later were warlike. Assuming for the moment that there were two waves of Philistine colonists and that they both came from the island of Crete, one would expect the earlier ones to have been less bellicose. The early Cretans of the Minoan period were apparently a peace-loving commercial people who gave little attention to military affairs. Later, around 1450-1200, warlike Mycenaeans from the mainland came to control Crete. With the Mycenaean demise about 1200-1100 B.C., many Mycenaeans apparently left Greese and Crete for points east. It may be that these later Peleste simply joined or overcame earlier Minoan colonies in Palestine and elsewhere and completely assimilated them. Thus it is difficult to locate and identify early Philistines.

More tangible confirmation of Philistines in Palestine in Abraham's day is the fact that a considerable amount of trade was conducted by Aegean peoples with Syria, Palestine and Egypt during the period 1900-1700, judging from artifacts of that period found in the three countries. T. C. Mitchell, in dealing with the problem, is not disturbed that Philistines are not mentioned by name among the traders of this period: "The members of a mixed group such as the Sea Peoples were unlikely to be carefully distinguished by name, so that the absence of one name from the inscriptions may simply mean that the particular group was not sufficiently prominent to find special mention."[3]

Let it be underscored that arguments from silence are not conclusive, that the biblical indications concerning Philistines fit the extrabiblical picture of Minoan and Mycenaean society which archaeological work in Greece and Crete has reconstructed, and that the problem of the Philistines still exists. There is no proof that they were not in Palestine in Abraham's day.

HAS THE BIBLE BORROWED ITS GREAT CONCEPTS AND NARRATIVES?

Creation and flood accounts, law codes, religious liturgical literature and the like began to appear as archaeological work in the Near East uncovered increasingly impressive sites during the last century. Many of these showed some affinity with biblical accounts. Soon antisupernaturalists were hard at work trying to rob the Bible of its uniqueness. Increasingly the view has been advanced that the Hebrews simply borrowed heavily from the religious concepts and practices of their contemporaries, purified their borrowings of polytheistic elements and made them their own.

The Babylonian creation account. One of the greatest collections of ancient literature was brought together by King Ashurbanipal of Assyria (668-633) at his palace in Nineveh. There his library was found by the Englishman Austen Henry Layard and his associate Hormuzd Rassam just before the middle of the nineteenth century. Among the more than twenty thousand inscribed clay tablets brought back to the British Museum was a copy of the Babylonian creation account, dating to the days of Hammurabi—king of Babylonia about 1700 B.C. In 1876 George Smith of the British Museum published some of the fragments of the creation account from Ashurbanipal's library. This material was supplemented in 1882 when Rassam found a bilingual creation account in Sumerian and Babylonian at a site a few miles north of Babylon. Early in the twentieth century a German team working at Ashur (old capital of Assyria) discovered an Assyrian version of the Babylonian creation narrative. In the 1920's portions of a Babylonian copy dating to the days of Nebuchadnezzar (*c.* 600 B.C.) were found at Kish and Uruk. From

---

[3]"Philistia, Philistines," *The New Bible Dictionary,* ed. J. D. Douglas (Grand Rapids: Wm. B. Eerdmans Pub. Co., 1962), p. 990.

all of these materials it has been possible to restore the Babylonian account of Ashurbanipal's library almost in entirety.[4]

Immediately curiosity was aroused. What did the *Enuma Elish* (the name by which the Babylonian account is known—so-called from its first two words) have to say about creation? How did it relate to the biblical account? Was there any evidence of borrowing in either direction?

The *Enuma Elish* consists of about one thousand lines of text on seven clay tablets. The contents of each tablet may be summarized as follows:

1. The narrative begins with the time when only Apsu (male personification of freshwater ocean) an Tiamat (female personification of primeval saltwater ocean) existed. They begat or created a whole company of gods. These so tried the patience of Apsu that he determined to slay them all. But Ea discovered the plan, then bound and slew Apsu. Then Ea begat Marduk, the patron god of Babylon. Tiamat also prepared to avenge the death of her husband. She created terrible monsters and placed Kingu at the head of her hosts.

2. Tablet two describes the counterplot of Ea against Tiamat and his search for a champion to oppose Tiamat. He appoints Marduk to the task.

3. Tablet three tells of a huge banquet held in preparation for Marduk's entrance into battle.

4. According to tablet four, Tiamat (chaos) and Marduk (the god of light) clashed in ferocious combat. Marduk slew Tiamat, the conquest signifying the final victory of order over chaos, and from her body he created the heavens. Later he created the earth. Then he appointed residences for the gods of sky, air and subterranean waters.

5. Tablet five is very fragmentary, but it tells of Marduk's appointment of the moon to rule over the night and to indicate the days and months of the year, and his formation of the constellations.

6. On tablet six appears Marduk's creation of man with the blood of Kingu, captain of Tiamat's host. The service of the gods is assigned as man's obligation. Then a great banquet is held in honor of Marduk.

7. Finally, according to tablet seven, Marduk was advanced from a position as chief god of Babylon to headship over all the gods.

The bilingual account discovered by Rassam in 1882 supplements

---

[4]Translations of the *Enuma Elish* may be found in Alexander Heidel, *The Babylonian Genesis;* George A. Barton, *Archaeology and the Bible;* and James B. Pritchard (ed.), *Ancient Near Eastern Texts.* (See Bibliography for facts of publication.)

Enuma Elish by giving Marduk and some of the other gods credit for creating grass, forests, rivers and animals.

Looking at the description outlined above and comparing it with the Genesis narrative of creation, one finds some interesting similarities: (1) Genesis speaks of seven days of creation; the Babylonian account was recorded on seven tablets. (2) Both describe a time when the earth was waste and void. (3) In Genesis order follows chaos; in *Enuma Elish* Marduk defeats chaos and establishes order. (4) Both accounts tell of the creation of moon, stars, plant life, animals and man. (5) Man was created on the sixth day according to Genesis; *Enuma Elish* records man's creation on the sixth tablet.

But the differences are vastly greater. In the first place, *Enuma Elish* is not primarily a creation account. Its purpose is political: to advance the cause of Babylon in her bid for supremacy by portraying the preeminent place of her patron deity Marduk among the gods. It is essentially a hymn to Marduk. It is interesting to note that the Assyrian version found by the Germans early in this century substituted the name of the Assyrian patron god Ashur for Marduk. Genesis definitely contains a creation account. Second, *Enuma Elish* is grossly polytheistic; various gods share in the origin of things. Marduk himself is brought into existence by another god. Genesis posits an exalted monotheism with God as the Creator of all things. Third, the gross mythology and inferior morals of *Enuma Elish* have no parallel in Genesis. Fourth, there is little parallel between the seven tablets and the seven creative days of Genesis. Tablets two and three do not deal with any phase of creation. Last, in starting its account of creation with the existence of matter, *Enuma Elish* implies eternity of matter; Scripture teaches that God is a spirit who is the Author of all matter.

While it may be demonstrated that the Genesis and Babylonian accounts of creation are far more different than similar, yet one must admit that there are striking similarities. So scholars have struggled over the problem of relationship for years. Some have suggested that the Babylonians borrowed from the Bible and introduced pagan elements. But *Enuma Elish* and its antecedents date long before the writing of Genesis. Higher critics have commonly held that the biblical account is a purified version of the Babylonian. The differences in the two, however, are almost too great to permit such a view. It seems best to hold that both came from a common source. The various races of mankind possessed a knowledge of the events of creation. Among some peoples the narrative became more polluted than in other cultures. The Genesis record represents the purest of these various accounts—one preserved by God Himself. It should be remembered that both *Enuma Elish* and the Genesis account come from the same area—an area where civilization began, according to Genesis and the conclusions of archaeology. Possibly Abraham brought a creation account with him from Ur to Canaan. If so, it was then passed on from father to son until Moses recorded it in the book of Genesis. A belief in a high view of inspiration does not require that God had to dictate a fresh statement of every event to the biblical writer; it merely guarantees that God preserved a given narrative or source from error. It is clear from many passages of Scripture that writers either made use of documents or did research in preparation for their writing. Note, for instance, the allusions to the book of Jasher in Joshua 10:13 and II Samuel 1:18.

The flood account. Just as George Smith and the library of Ashurbanipal figured in the recovery of the Babylonian creation account, they also loomed large in the discovery of the Babylonian flood story. In the Ashurbanipal materials at the British Museum, Smith found a Babylonian deluge story on which he reported at the December, 1872, meeting of the Society of Biblical Archaeology in London. The interest of both scholars and the general public was intense. Demands were heard all over England for reopening the Nineveh excavations in order to find the missing portion of the account. The *Daily Telegraph* agreed to finance the expedition in return for exclusive reporting rights. The following May, Smith arrived at Nineveh and found a flood fragment after only about a week of excavation. Numerous other tablets agreeing with or slightly divergent from the Ashurbanipal copy have been found in several Mesopotamian cities. An earlier Sumerian account also was found at the end of the nineteenth century.

The Sumerian flood version was inscribed on a tablet found at Nippur. Badly mutilated, this copy was probably written about the time of Hammurabi (c. 1700 B.C.), although the story it narrates is undoubtedly much older. As the fragment begins, some of the gods lament the impending flood which the company of gods as a whole has already decided to send on mankind. The god Enki tried to devise a plan for saving at least one man, Ziusudra, the king and administrator of the temple provisions. Ziusudra was told to stand by a wall, where he was warned of the flood and apparently instructed to build a boat, though the text is missing at that point. Then an intense rain swept over the land for seven days and nights. Afterward the sun came out, and Ziusudra worshiped before the sun-god and offered a sacrifice of an ox and several sheep. Subsequently the gods bestowed immortality on the hero of the flood story and placed him in a paradise known as Dilmun, probably somewhere in the area of the Persian Gulf.

The Babylonian flood story from Ashurbanipal's library is part of a longer work known as the Gilgamesh Epic. Written on twelve tablets, this epic tells about the search of Gilgamesh for immortality. In his search the hero (originally a historical personage who was king at Uruk) went to interview Utnapishtim, the Babylonian Noah who had gained immortality. Tablet eleven consists of Utnapishtim's description of the flood planned by the gods to destroy all mankind. The god Ea warned Utnapishtim of an impending flood on Shuruppak, his hometown. The god told him to prepare for it by tearing down his house and building a cube-shaped ship from the materials. This Utnapishtim did. The ship measured one hundred and twenty cubits (about 65½ yards) on a side and had six decks. He caulked it with asphalt. Then he loaded the ship with his possessions, his family and relatives, craftsmen, cattle and wild beasts. On the day appointed—when in the morning it rained bran and in the evening wheat, according to divine warning—Utnapishtim entered his ship and closed the door. All fury broke loose; even the gods in heaven were cowed with fear. Six days and nights the storm raged. On the seventh day the tempest ceased, and the hero opened the window and looked out on a scene of desolation. On Mount Nisir the ship came to rest. On the seventh day Utnapishtim sent out a dove which returned. Later he sent out a swallow, which also failed to find a resting place. When a raven was sent out, it did not return. As the waters dried up, all the other animals and birds were released. Utnapishtim then offered a sacrifice. When the gods smelled the odor, they gathered like flies above the sacrifice. Then Enlil took the hero's hand and bestowed immortality and deity on both him and his wife.

As one compares the Genesis and Mesopotamian flood stories, he is impressed with the large number of similarities. Both accounts indicate that the flood was divinely planned, that it came as punishment for human failure or moral defection, and that the impending disaster was revealed to the flood hero. Both accounts assert that the hero was divinely instructed to build a boat which was coated with pitch within and without, that a limited number of persons embarked in these ships with a considerable number of other living creatures to be saved alive, and that those not on board were destroyed. Both accounts also specify the physical causes of the flood, its duration, the landing place of the craft and the sending out of birds. And in both accounts the heroes offer a sacrifice after the flood, receive a divine blessing and are given some assurance that a similar catastrophe will never again overtake mankind.

The degree of similarity between the Genesis and Mesopotamian flood narratives has often been so emphasized that the extent of difference between them has been obscured. Actually the differences are more marked than the similarities. Most significant among these differences is that the Babylonian and Assyrian stories are grossly polytheistic, while the Genesis narrative is characterized by an exalted monotheism. At every turn the Mesopotamian accounts exude polytheism. The Sumerian copy states that the assembly of the gods decreed the flood, but apparently not all gods of the pantheon concurred in the decision. Likewise, according to the Gilgamesh Epic, the flood was decreed by "the great gods," but later some of them disclaimed responsibility for it and stigmatized one another for having brought on such a catastrophe. When the deluge began, the gods were "terror-stricken," "fled," and "cowered like dogs and crouched in distress." After the deluge was over, the hero offered a sacrifice over which the hungry gods "gathered like flies."

Not only are the cuneiform accounts polytheistic, they are also pantheistic. The gods are identified with nature and the forces of nature they supposedly originated and over which they supposedly had control.

The reason for the flood is different in the two accounts. Genesis clearly indicates that God judged man with the deluge because of his sin. At the beginning of the Gilgamesh Epic the caprice of the gods seems to be responsible for the curse. Admittedly Ea's speech at the end of the epic mentions man's sin as the cause of the flood but gives no details. Another Mesopotamian deluge fragment, called the Atrahasis Epic, states that Enlil sent the flood to destroy man because he was so noisy that Enlil could not sleep.

In addition to these major differences, there are a number of lesser differences between the biblical and nonbiblical accounts:

1. A period of grace. Genesis 6:3 states that man was granted a reprieve of judgment for one hundred and twenty years, during which time he had ample opportunity to repent. The Mesopotamian deities jealously guarded their secret, giving man no opportunity for repentance. Even Ea found it necessary to warn Utnapishtim of impending danger by means of a dream.

2. Nature of the vessel. Figuring the biblical cubit according to the standard of eighteen inches (more specifically, about 17.5 inches), Noah's ark was 450 feet long, 75 feet wide and 45 feet high,

with a displacement of about 43,300 tons. Supposing that the Babylonian cubit mentioned in the Gilgamesh Epic was the usual twenty-inch measure (actually, the Mesopotamian "royal" cubit was about 19.8 inches long), Utnapishtim's ship was cubical, measuring 200 feet on a side, with a displacement of 228,500 tons. Moreover, the latter vessel had seven levels, or decks; Noah's had three.

3. Occupants of the craft. Utnapishtim took aboard his family and relatives, craftsmen, boatmen, gold and silver, and "beasts of the field," while Noah took only his wife, his sons and their wives, and a specific number of living creatures according to the instructions of Genesis 6:19-21; 7:2-3.

4. Physical causes of the flood. The Gilgamesh Epic indicates that the flood was caused by cloudburst, mighty winds (probably of hurricane force), and the breaking of dikes and reservoirs. The Genesis account mentions heavy rains and implies that these were accompanied by some convulsion of the earth's crust, resulting in the release of subterranean waters (Gen. 7:11).

5. Length of the flood (or rain). The Sumerian narrative says it rained for six days and nights; the Babylonian, seven days and nights. The Hebrew account declares it rained forty days and nights (Gen. 7:12).

6. Landing of the boat. Utnapishtim's ship landed on Mount Nisir, usually identified with a mountain east of the Tigris River and four hundred miles north of the Persian Gulf, whereas Noah's ark landed in the Ararat Mountains, considerably farther north, either in eastern Turkey or adjacent territory in Russia.

7. The birds. According to the cuneiform account, a dove was sent out first, then a swallow and finally a raven. Noah sent a raven first, and then he released a dove on three separate occasions.

8. Effect of the flood. The Genesis account gives no hint that any human beings or animals survived the deluge, but at least the Atrahasis Epic indicates that all men did not perish.

9. Blessing on hero. Utnapishtim was granted immortality after the flood was over; Noah was not.

Though the extreme differences between the Hebrew and cuneiform accounts have been noted, the remarkable similarities have not been eliminated. Scholars have long puzzled over the relationship between the accounts. As in the case of the creation narrative, there are three possibilities: the Babylonians borrowed from the Hebrews, the Hebrews borrowed from the Babylonians, or both descended from a common original. The first view has not been thought likely because Mesopotamian flood accounts antedate the Genesis record by perhaps a millennium. It should be noted, however, that the Hebrew account could have existed orally long before it was written. The most widely accepted view is that the Hebrews borrowed from the Babylonians and purified the account of polytheistic elements. Alexander Heidel of the University of Chicago has shown convincingly that arguments to this effect are not decisive.[5] The view that both the Hebrew and Babylonian accounts descended from a common original is quite appealing. After all, Genesis gives Mesopotamia as the original home of the Hebrews and the place where civilization first began and where it made a fresh start after the flood. What would be more likely than that many accounts of an early tragedy of such magnitude would be preserved by peoples who lived in Mesopotamia or had migrated from there? Perhaps with Price, Sellers and Carlson one may conclude: "One ancient religion did not borrow these universal traditions from another, but each possessed primitively these traditions in their original form. The Genesis record is the purest, the least colored by extravagances, and the nearest to what we must conceive to have been the original form of these accounts."[6] In accepting such a conclusion, divine inspiration is not ruled out. As has been noted before, biblical writers did not always write without access to source materials. But God overruled and directed in the choice of such materials, guaranteeing accuracy of the finished product.

It should be noted, however, that biblical and Mesopotamian flood accounts are not the only ones extant in the world. Over 250 flood narratives from all parts of the earth have come to light. While most of them are quite fanciful, they all testify to a destructive flood that wiped out almost all men early in the memory of the respective tribe. There is little evidence that these accounts borrowed their content from one another but seem independently to point to a great destruction by water. The Hebrew account would be expected to have more affinities with the accounts coming from Mesopotamia than with those from China or India, for instance; so Christians should not be embarrassed at similarities between the Genesis and Babylonian accounts.

The law. Ever since Jacques de Morgan found the three fragments of the Code of Hammurabi at Susa in 1901/2, law codes have been coming to light in various parts of the Near East—in Assyria,

---

[5]*The Gilgamesh Epic and Old Testament Parallels* (2d ed.; Chicago: University of Chicago Press, 1949), pp. 261-67.
[6]Ira M. Price, Ovid R. Sellers and E. Leslie Carlson, *The Monuments and the Old Testament* (Philadelphia: Judson Press, 1958), p. 127.

Asia Minor and elsewhere in Babylonia. But none of them is so long and well known as the Code of Hammurabi. This code was set up in a temple in Babylon about 1700 B.C., inscribed on a black diorite stela 7 feet 4 inches high and 6 feet 2½ inches in circumference at the base. Incised on the shaft are 3,600 lines of text in 44 columns presenting 282 laws. On the top front of the stela is a bas-relief of Hammurabi standing in a supplicating position before the sun-god Shamash, who sits on a throne while sunrays stream from his shoulders.

Those who wish to negate the uniqueness of the Old Testament have repeatedly stressed the similarity of the Mosaic and Hammurabi codes, with at least the inference, if not the claim, of borrowing. It has been urged that both codes claim divine origin, both are based on the law of retaliation ("eye for an eye and tooth for a tooth"), both present trial by ordeal, both have laws concerning false witness, theft, the stealing of children and slaves, housebreaking, debtors and creditors, chastity and marriage, assault and battery and the like.

One would expect similarities between the two codes, if they are to be considered law codes at all. It is necessary to control such problems as theft, assault and battery, debtors and creditors and bearing false witness if a people is to maintain any semblance of law and order and to make it possible for society to progress. Moreover, Semites from the same general area of the world might be expected to solve many of their problems similarly. There is no particular reason why God should not, in the Mosaic code, approve some already existing and satisfactory principles for governing society. This is especially true since many of these principles must have been in existence in the Mesopotamian area from the days of Adam or at least Noah, when society had a fresh start under divine guidance.

But having admitted that there are some similarities in the codes, one must enumerate a few of the many differences: (1) As to origin, Hammurabi's claim that he got his laws from his god is a very thin veneer over his own pretensions. Both in the Prologue and Epilogue he makes it quite clear that his own wisdom is really at the bottom of creating such a remarkable code. Moses, however, makes no such claims. (2) While both involve the law of retaliation, the Code of Hammurabi applies it according to the offender's class status; Moses applies punishment equally to all. (3) One can hardly claim that the Mosaic code has trial by ordeal at all. Admittedly, there is a curious passage in Numbers 5:11-31 about someone on trial drinking dust in water to see whether or not she was guilty. This is not like heathen practices requiring one on trial to drink poison or to take a test by being thrown into the water to determine innocence or guilt. In the Numbers incident a miracle from the Lord would be required to cause the dust to become poison and bring judgment on the accused. (4) The whole construction of the codes is different. Hammurabi proceeds on a case system basis: "If" one has committed a certain crime, "then" his punishment shall be—. Moses proceeds more on the basis of certain principles, followed by enumeration of punishments for breaking the law. (5) Hammurabi's code is civil and commercial, while Moses' is civil and religious; the whole spirit and thrust of the two are different.

One cannot admit that Moses borrowed from Hammurabi at all. As George Barton aptly states:

> A comparison of the code of Hammurabi as a whole with the Pentateuchal laws as a whole, while its reveals certain similarities, convinces the student that the laws of the Old Testament are in no essential way dependent upon the Babylonian laws. Such resemblances as there are arose, it seems clear, from a similarity of antecedents and of general intellectual outlook; the striking differences show that there was no direct borrowing.[7]

The liturgy. On a hill in Syria one-half mile from the Mediterranean Sea just across from the eastern tip of Cyprus stood the ancient city of Ugarit (modern Ras Shamra). At this site a Syrian peasant accidentally broke into an ancient tomb with his plow in 1928. Excavation began the following year under the leadership of C. F. A. Schaeffer of the Strasbourg Museum and, after interruption by World War II, it resumed in 1950. Associated with the temple of Baal in Ugarit there was a school and library where many tablets were found written in Akkadian, Sumerian, Hurrian, Egyptian, Hittite, a Cypro-Minoan script and a previously unknown "Ugaritic" Semitic language. Most of the tablets, religious in nature, were written in the latter tongue and dated from the fifteenth and fourteenth centuries B.C.

These texts spell out much of the detail of Canaanite religion and do so in a language similar to biblical Hebrew. They have revealed a sacrificial system with interesting affinities to the Mosaic system, describing such sacrifices as the burnt offering, whole burnt offering, wave offering and others. The existence of such practices among the Canaanites even before the days of Moses has necessitated revision

---

[7]*Archaeology and the Bible* (7th ed.; Philadelphia: American Sunday-School Union, 1937), p. 406.

of some of the older Wellhausenian higher criticism which said these "Mosaic" practices came late in Hebrew experience and must date to the Persian period.

Some biblical students have been embarrassed by the similarity of the Ugaritic and biblical sacrificial systems and have felt that the distinctiveness of the Mosaic legislation has now been destroyed. It should be noted, however, that large differences in the Ugaritic and biblical rituals do exist. The Canaanites were of course polytheistic, and they sacrificed a variety of animals excluded by the laws of the Old Testament. Yet the similarities in ritual are numerous and cannot be lightly dismissed. It is interesting to see, however, that the best-informed interpreters of the evidence do not claim that the Hebrews borrowed from the Canaanites. While R. Dussaud feels that there was a basic identity of Israelite and Canaanite sacrifice, he infers from his research that "the Israelites did not borrow these practices from the Canaanites, but already had them before coming into Palestine."[8] Burrows observes, "In other words, the parallels . . . between Israelite and Canaanite or Ugaritic ritual . . . do not indicate borrowing by Israel from these other peoples but rather show that all the Semitic peoples had similar practices and institutions."[9] Charles Pfeiffer concludes, "Elements which Israelites and Canaanites held in common may be traced to the common traditions possessed by the two peoples concerning worship. The New Testament insists that there was a genuine revelation of God to the pre-Abrahamic peoples which was never completely forgotten (Rom. 1:21-32)."[10]

HOW SHALL CHRISTIANS HANDLE HISTORICAL PROBLEMS CREATED BY ARCHAEOLOGY?

It has been seen that some have stated or intimated that Near Eastern archaeology has shown the Bible to be in error. Others have claimed that writers of Scripture borrowed pagan myths and the like as a basis for their accounts. Yet others have pointed out how new information from archaeology has raised serious historical and chronological problems as this information has been related to data provided in Scripture. Some of these problems are too technical to be discussed here. A good example of this type of issue is the ques-

---

[8]Millar Burrows, *What Mean These Stones?* (New Haven: American Schools of Oriental Research, 1941), p. 235.
[9]*Ibid.*
[10]*Ras Shamra and the Bible* (Grand Rapids: Baker Book House, 1962), p. 58.

tion raised by Syrian archaeology over the presence of Hittites in Palestine before the conquest.

Conservative biblical students generally are so glad to note how the discovery of Hittite architectural and literary remains has confirmed the Old Testament that they fail to take note of new problems raised by excavations in Hittite land. But the apologetic value of Hittite discoveries is not to be minimized. References to this ancient people were not the brainchild of some biblical scribe. It is now known that the Hittites passed through a kingdom period (*c.* 1600-1450 B.C.) and an empire period (*c.* 1400-1200 B.C.), and that at their height they controlled Asia Minor and adjacent territory in Syria. Their great capital was at Bogazköy (east of Ankara); excavations were begun there in 1906 by Hugo Winckler and the German Oriental Society. Shortly after 1200 B.C. the Hittites were swept from power in Asia Minor and replaced by the Phrygians there. The Hittites themselves fled into Syria where Neo-Hittite kingdoms were to last for no less than five centuries. But these Syrian city-states should be called Hittite only with numerous qualifications. Their culture was strongly permeated with Phoenician and Aramaic elements.

If the Hittites' homeland was Asia Minor and if they are not known to have established effective city-states in Syria until the latter part of the second millennium, then it must be asked how this historical evidence may be squared with biblical claims of Hittites in Palestine as early as the days of Abraham. Numerous critics have been quick to assign biblical references to late and inaccurate sources. It does not seem at all necessary to concede to such allegations, however; and the problems are not all solved even in this fashion.

In an effort to arrive at a solution of the problem, something should be said about the peoples of Asia Minor and their languages during the third and second millennia B.C. Three of the numerous languages and/or ethnic groups were related to the Indo-European family. The Luwian-speaking peoples probably arrived in Asia Minor at the end of the Early Bronze Age (3500-2800 B.C.), and by 1750 controlled much of the southern and western parts of the peninsula. As time went on, they played an increasing role in the Hittite kingdom. Palaic was the language of the Pala, commonly placed in Paphlagonia in north central Asia Minor. A third language, the official Hittite language itself, in which most of the Hittite texts were written, was referred to in the Bogazkoy texts as the "language of Nesha" (the Hittite form of Kanesh). These people probably entered

the area around Kanesh (Kultepe in east central Asia Minor) during
the latter part of the Early Bronze Age.

These Indo-European "Kaneshites" mingled freely with the non-
Indo-European Hatti (Khatti) of the northeastern part of Asia
Minor, and their language gradually replaced that of their predecessors. As can be readily seen, Hatti is linguistically equatable with
the English "Hittite." Since the archaeologists had already assigned
the name Hittite to the Kaneshites, they had to find another term
for the "true Hittites." "Khattian," "Khattic" and "Proto-Hittite"
have been used to designate this non-Indo-European substratum of
the population. It becomes clear, then, that the Indo-European element which predominated in the Hittite Kingdom and Empire was
not the original culture of Asia Minor. Indo-Europeans came into
the area relatively late. What if Indo-European Hittites of the kingdom period or before did not get down into Palestine, sell the cave
of Machpelah to Abraham (Gen. 23) and marry into Esau's family
(Gen. 26:34; 36:1-3)? There is nothing to prove that the earlier
non-Indo-European Hatti did not live in considerable numbers in
Palestine as well as in Asia Minor. Genesis could very easily have
reference to these earlier peoples. After all, Heth (from whom the
Hittites descended) is classified as a son of Canaan (Gen. 10:15),
who was not an Indo-European.

From this discussion of the Hittite problem and others presented
in this chapter, it is clear that there are solutions to the problems
raised by the science of archaeology. As more information comes in,
one may expect more and perhaps better solutions. Bible students
need never fear the results of archaeological investigation. The Christian's understanding of and confidence in the Bible can do nothing
but gain from an increase of knowledge.

FOR FURTHER READING

BARTON, GEORGE A. *Archaeology and the Bible.* 7th ed. Philadelphia:
American Sunday-School Union, 1937.

FINEGAN, JACK. *Light from the Ancient Past.* 2d ed. Princeton:
Princeton University Press, 1959.

GURNEY, O. R. *The Hittites.* Rev. ed. Harmondsworth, England:
Penguin Books, Ltd., 1961.

HEIDEL, ALEXANDER. *The Babylonian Genesis.* 2d ed. Chicago: University of Chicago Press, 1951.

————. *The Gilgamesh Epic and Old Testament Parallels.* 2d ed.
Chicago: University of Chicago Press, 1949.

PARROT, ANDRE. *The Flood and Noah's Ark*. New York: Philosophical Library, 1955.

PFEIFFER, CHARLES F. *Ras Shamra and the Bible*. Grand Rapids: Baker Book House, 1962.

PRICE, IRA M.; SELLERS, O. R.; and CARLSON, E. L. *The Monuments and the Old Testament*. Philadelphia: Judson Press, 1958.

PRITCHARD, JAMES B. (ed). *Ancient Near Eastern Texts Relating to the Old Testament*. 2d ed. Princeton: Princeton University Press, 1955.

UNGER, MERRILL F. *Archaeology and the Old Testament*. Grand Rapids: Zondervan Pub. House, 1954.

PHILOSOPHY OF SCIENCE

William W. Paul

William W. Paul is professor of philosophy, department chairman and head of the humanities division, Central College, Pella, Iowa. He previously taught at Shelton College and Wheaton College. A graduate of Temple University, he holds the A. M. from the University of Pennsylvania, the Ph. D. from Columbia University and the B. D. from Faith Theological Seminary. In addition Dr. Paul has studied as a Danforth scholar at the University of Minnesota, a Fulbright scholar in India and as a postdoctoral fellow at Harvard. He has written *Paul Tillich's Interpretation of History*.

13

PHILOSOPHY OF SCIENCE

William W. Paul

T HE APPROACH taken in the following discussion is twofold. There is an introductory statement about the nature of the discipline known as philosophy of science. The first part of this chapter also presents the types of problems discussed in the contemporary literature of this relatively new and expanding field of knowledge. The rest of the chapter consists of a brief consideration of the problem concerning the interrelationship between two basic areas of human experience in the modern world: science and religious faith. Some emphasis is given to the role of presuppositions in the two fields in an effort to show how philosophy of science may play a role in man's quest for a more adequate and coherent world and life view which has indispensable roots in both science and faith.

WHAT IS PHILOSOPHY OF SCIENCE?

In the fourth century before Christ, Plato sketched a double analogy in his *Republic* between the sun and the philosopher's love of wisdom in order to illustrate the functions of the philosophic man. The sun, he said, serves two basic purposes in the natural world: to illuminate and to energize. Likewise the man who seeks to envision and understand the good and the true—the philosophic life— should find that as his vision takes on intelligible focus, it both illuminates his theoretical problems and energizes him in the practical application of truth to life. If illumination is understood to include the effort to clarify the language used in talking about this experienced world, then this statement of purpose serves very well to indicate the nature of both the analytic-critical and synthetic-constructive efforts of philosophers.

Now it is possible to take a philosophic interest in any subject. One which has been of increasing significance since the late Middle Ages is science. In the twentieth century technical and theoretical problems connected with the nature of scientific knowledge and with the methodology of the many sciences have given rise to a special discipline. Philosophy of science is a branch of knowledge concerned with analyzing the structure, special concepts, basic assumptions and meaning of a science or the sciences. Science for its part aims, within the relatively narrow confines of a particular field, to establish some true descriptions, exploratory hypotheses and laws about the structure of the world as seen by that science.

Definition

One of the primary tasks of the philosopher of science is to take a thorough look at the descriptive and lawlike statements which constitute the developing language of a dynamic science. Scientists, in common with many nonscientists, tend to work within a frame of technical terms in formulating their truth claims rather than trying to clarify in an interdisciplinary way their ideas about causality, probability and natural law. They also employ such terms as "hypothesis," "event," "fact," and "exist." The philosopher sees here the need for analysis and clarification and an attempt to relate technical terms to more ordinary language. No philosopher can succeed in this effort, of course, unless he is inclined to work with the literature of the science in question. Fortunately, there is an ever increasing number of philosophically minded scientists whose writings throw considerable light on this analytic task of the philosopher of science.

Methodology

His second concern is with the methodological issues in science. Scientists are, first of all, men who are engaged in active research or inquiry into the nature of things; only secondarily do they talk about what they are doing. So it is not enough for the philosopher of science to work with the language of the sciences. He must be interested in the basic criteria used by practicing scientists in establishing their beliefs, the procedures by which confirmations or verifications are achieved, and the types of operational and evidence statements which are made. There are vital epistemological and logical problems involved in carrying forward the experimental methods where the philosopher's concern with clarity, and the newly developed tools of the symbolic logician may be of some help to the scientist.

Examination

A third objective of the philosopher of science is to examine the basic assumptions of one or more of the sciences. Here a knowledge of the history of scientific theories is of importance because it dramatizes the radical shifts that can occur in the fundamental orientation of all human knowledge including that of the sciences. Indeed, the very existence of theoretical crises within physics or biology has been the great catalyst in promoting the critical thinker's concern with scientific postulates. The careers of Copernicus, Newton, Mach, Planck, Einstein, Darwin and many others will attest this point. We have come to realize increasingly that the presuppositions made in one field may have profound implications for another so that the philosophy of the physical sciences, for example, cannot be undertaken in isolation from a philosophy of biology, psychology or the social sciences.

Interpretation

This brings us to the final and broadest concern which the philosopher of science may have—a function which some logical positivists would prefer to attribute to speculative metaphysics. This is the task of seeing what picture or larger interpretation of the world the data of the several sciences may yield. Since the philosopher is supposed to be concerned with the whole man, he may be expected even as a philosopher of science to ask himself how the scientific perspective on experience relates to alternative approaches. Like philosopher May Brodbeck, he may properly warn men of faith as well as men of science that while "cosmological speculations about the origin, nature, and purpose of the universe may be harmless, imaginative extrapolations from science itself," they tend to "beg all the issues philosophers must analyze," skirting rather than solving philosophical problems.[1] It would seem that while it may not be the function of philosophers of science to create synthetic world views, it is their task to be critical of purely speculative or superscientific "explanations" and to inquire into the empirical grounding of those interpretative systems which claim some support from the sciences.

CHRISTIAN FAITH AND PHILOSOPHY OF SCIENCE

With these four objectives of this discipline in mind, we can now ask meaningfully about the relevance of this particular subject to a religious outlook on life. First, certainly the task of examining and

---

[1]Herbert Feigl and May Brodeck (eds.), *Readings in the Philosophy of Science* (New York: Appleton-Century-Crofts, 1953), p. 5. This work contains an excellent bibliography.

clarifying in more ordinary terms the language and issues raised by the special sciences is to be applauded by all. In fact, those who are concerned with theology and with philosophy of religion might very well engage in some of the same struggle for clarity of communication and its correlation with ordinary language that is exemplified by philosophy of science today.

Second, the concern of philosophy of science with questions of methodology—with the logic of the role of hypotheses and with the processes of verification or confirmation—seems indirectly to be of considerable significance for one's philosophy of religion. There is no clearer way to discover that science is methodologically organized to accomplish very specific and relatively limited tasks than by paying careful attention to the empirical and rational policies of science in action. Methodology provides a specialized kind of understanding of nature in the light of a complex of causal processes which it seeks to describe and in terms of which it seeks to make some predictions. For that type of Christian who has been led to believe that he must somehow be able to give "scientific proof" for his special religious beliefs about creation, biblical events and miracles, it can be a liberating experience to realize that laboratory-controlled verifications (contrary to the positivists) provide only *one* way of getting at the truth about the possible meanings of human experience. This realization at least introduces a perspective on religious faith or trust (and other value approaches to life) which is sensitive to the revelatory experiences and the possibilities for personal communion with God on which Christian commitment may properly be based. The alert Christian may believe that all truth must ultimately be one, and he may be challenged to try to think through some of the problems of an integrated world view; but a concern with the philosophy of science will serve as a reminder that science itself provides only one important way of getting at and verifying the truth. It is a way which no Christian should ignore, but neither should he allow it to be absolutized.

This awareness of the limitations of science will help to make clear that many of the supposed disputes between science and Christianity can be attributed to mistaken views on each side. For his part, the Christian does well to recognize that his religious *faith* or trust in God and Christ is not identical with a set of more or less credible *beliefs* or a set of human interpretations requiring intellectual assent. Faith does make its appeal to reliable testimony and to support from a broad spectrum of experience, but Christian faith essentially centers in an ongoing redemptive work in the life of the whole man (will, emotions *and* reason) involving questions and value issues which are of ultimate concern for the meaning and direction of his life.[2] The methods and interests of Christian faith thus differ fundamentally from those of science.

Third, closely related to this liberating perspective is the understanding afforded by studies in philosophy of science calculated to bring into the open the basic assumptions of science. The broadest presuppositions of science are shared generally by all men and do not specify a particular scientific outlook. This includes assuming the reliability of memory, the possibility of repeating certain types of experience, and the belief that some events are related as cause to effect. At the other extreme are axioms which prove to be philosophically restrictive of the proper freedom that should be enjoyed by those searching for truth about the natural world of man. Most of us are not inclined to support such beliefs as the assumption of dialectical materialism that matter and motion are without beginning and will have no end. At this point it is clearly wise to treat science as conjectural and as constantly open to critical examination and testing.[3] It may not be as clear that if one were to take certain *interpretations* of the doctrine of creation and advance them as scientific insights, he would need to be prepared to let them too be treated as hypotheses competing with others for verification.

A good example of this problem can be seen in the very general but definitive assumption of science that nature is uniform, that the same cause-effect patterns observed today have always prevailed. Philosophers of science today admit that this tenet cannot be proved although it is taken to be pragmatically justified by the ongoing work of science. If treated as a doctrine rather than a working rule, uniformitarianism creates interesting problems for both evolutionists who want to allow for the mutation of the new and for the flood geologist type of creationist who pushes a counterdoctrine of catastrophism. Taken either way, this is an illustration of the fact that the presence of a presupposition can become quickly obscured in the practice of science or confusedly dogmatized into an all-comprehensive model because of the ideological concerns of scientist and theologian alike. At this point again philosophy of science can render a service by carrying on the objective exemplified by Alfred North Whitehead in his

---

[2]Cf. Donald M. MacKay, *Science and Christian Faith Today* (London: Falcon Booklet, 1960); Helmut Thielicke, *Man in God's World,* trans. and ed. John W. Doberstein (New York: Harper & Row, 1963).

[3]Cf. Karl Popper, *The Logic of Scientific Discovery* (New York: Basic Books, 1959). For further support of this view of science see Thomas H. Leith, "Some Presuppositions in the Philosophy of Science," *Journal of the American Scientific Affiliation,* XVII, No. 1 (March, 1965), 8-15.

Science and the Modern World[4]—helping science to become philosophical through a criticism of its own foundations. And for those committed to the Judeo-Christian faith, there must be an equal willingness to examine assumptions about the natural world which may be attributed to the dated scientific perspective of a particular prophet or theologian.

This all too brief treatment of the role of presuppositions in the fields of science and faith leads naturally into the fourth and final point concerning the basic world view which might be implied by the scientific enterprise. This is of particular importance to the Christian who is by faith committed to a redemptive God who is Creator and Lord of history. He is also committed then, in broad outline at least, to a world and life view. For the details he is probably well advised to keep himself open to a variety of possibilities and biblical insights. Ideally, although he recognizes that the findings of science are probabilistic and limited in scope, the Christian nonetheless is anxious to relate the "Flatland" of science (to use the language of William G. Pollard[5]) to the perpendicular perspective of faith. For those who are prepared to work hard at both the horizontal and the vertical and who maintain a fairly open philosophical attitude, the game of "model building" can be both stimulating and frustrating.

As was admitted earlier, it may not be the task of philosophy of science itself to provide a *Gestalt* outlook, but there always seem to be one or more views for it to examine. For one thing, some scientists fortunately turn philosophical on occasion and attempt to generalize on some of the apparent implications of their work. Biologists like Huxley, Dobzhansky and Simpson have reasoned that man's biological-cultural evolution has turned "natural selection" into a cooperative process instead of a competitive one as was earlier maintained by the social Darwinists.[6] Here there exists a conflict

---

[4]New York: Macmillan Co., 1925, and Mentor Press, 1948. Cf. Philipp Frank, *Philosophy of Science* (Englewood Cliffs, N.J.: Prentice-Hall, Inc., 1957). This also is an excellent statement on the way in which science may become historically conditioned.

[5]William G. Pollard is an executive director of the Oak Ridge Institute of Nuclear Studies and is the author of *Chance and Providence* (New York: Charles Scribner's Sons, 1958).

[6]Julian Huxley makes the boldest claim for a naturalistic ethic supposedly derived from his science of evolution: T. H. Huxley and Julian Huxley, *Touchstone for Ethics* (New York: Harper & Bros., 1947). More perceptive are Theodosius Dobzhansky, *Mankind Evolving* (New Haven: Yale University Press, 1962); and George Gaylord Simpson, *The Meaning of Evolution* (New Haven: Yale University Press, 1949); also his "Naturalistic Ethics and the Social Sciences," *American Psychologist*, XXI (January, 1966), 27-36. Cf. Richard Hofstadter, *Social Darwinism in American Thought* (Boston: Beacon

of models with which the philosopher of science may well be concerned. Among the issues to be clarified would be the question as to whether *either* of these views can provide a basis for man's ethical value theory as both have maintained. Is it possible for science which is descriptive to provide a basis for the prescriptive or normative in human behavior? Whatever conclusions may be drawn about man's biological history, it would seem that not until man is viewed as made "in the image of God," as a rational being possessing responsible freedom, can questions about moral values and teleological behavior become truly significant.

Another source of supply for philosophical model building is to be found in the occasional speeches by noted philosophers of science. One example must serve. In his presidential address before the American Philosophical Association in 1954, Ernest Nagel dogmatized reductively when he said, "In the conception of nature's processes which naturalism affirms, there is no place for the operation of disembodied forces, no place for an immaterial spirit directing the course of events, no place for the survival of personality after the corruption of the body which exhibits it."[7] Surely this is the kind of statement which follows from Nagel's honest convictions about philosophical naturalism and not as such from his excellent knowledge of science and of the philosophy of science. It is a metaphysical thesis rather than a scientific hypothesis in the strict and narrow sense. Like the Christian's countercontention that the Bible represents God as "upholding" the whole going universe and as immanently related to the course of events, Nagel's thesis would have to be tested comparatively in terms of its total meaning-giving power for human life.

Here philosophy of science is conceived in its broadest sense where it merges with metaphysical insight. The Christian who intends to participate in the dialogue with the non-Christian on this level will be the better prepared not only through a deep, personal communion with the living God of the Scriptures but also by a vital concern with both the narrow and the broad issues raised in the twentieth century by the philosophy of science.

Press, 1944). For the immense practical implications of this problem see Albert Rosenfeld, "Will Man Direct His Own Evolution?" *Life,* LIX (October 1, 1965), 94-96.

[7]"Naturalism Reconsidered," *Proceedings and Addresses of the American Philosophical Association,* 1954-55 (Yellow Springs, Ohio: Antioch Press, 1956), pp. 8-9. For a counterargument that science cannot demonstrate God's nonexistence, see Gordon H. Clark, *The Philosophy of Science and Belief in God* (Nutley, N. J.: Craig Press, 1964). An excellent text in the philosophy of science is Ernest Nagel, *The Structure of Science* (New York: Harcourt, Brace & World, 1961).

FOR FURTHER READING

For a more complete guide see:

DANTO, A. and MORGENBESSER, S. (eds.). *Philosophy of Science.* Cleveland: Meridian Books, 1960.

FEIGL, HERBERT and BRODBECK, MAY (eds.). *Readings in Philosophy of Science.* New York: Appleton-Century-Crofts, 1953.

MADDEN, E. (ed.). *The Structure of Scientific Thought.* Boston: Houghton Mifflin Co., 1960.

WIENER, P. (ed.). *Readings in the Philosophy of Science.* New York: Charles Scribner's Sons, 1953.

HISTORY OF SCIENCE

BUTTERFIELD, HERBERT. *The Origins of Modern Science 1300-1800.* New York: Macmillan Co., 1949, 1960.

CROMBIE, ALISTAIR C. *Medieval and Early Modern Science* (2 vols.). New York: Doubleday & Co., 1956, 1959.

KOYRÉ, ALEXANDRE. *From the Closed World to the Infinite Universe.* New York: Harper Torchbooks, 1958.

WOLF, A. *A History of Science, Technology, and Philosophy in the 16th and 17th Centuries* (2 vols.). New York: Harper Torchbooks, 1950, 1959.

GENERAL WORKS

BERGMANN, GUSTAV. *Philosophy of Science.* Madison, Wis.: University of Wisconsin Press, 1957.

BURTT, EDWIN A. *The Metaphysical Foundations of Modern Physical Science.* New York: Doubleday & Co., 1955.

CONANT, J. *On Understanding Science.* New Haven: Yale University Press, 1947.

FEIGL, HERBERT and SCRIVEN, MICHAEL (eds.). *Minnesota Studies in the Philosophy of Science* (2 vols.). Minneapolis: University of Minnesota Press, 1956, 1958.

FRANK, PHILIPP. *Philosophy of Science.* Englewood Cliffs, N. J.: Prentice-Hall, Inc., 1962.

KEMENY, JOHN. *A Philosopher Looks at Science.* Princeton, N. J.: Van Nostrand Co., 1959.

NAGEL, ERNEST. *The Structure of Science.* New York: Harcourt, Brace & World, 1961.

PAP, ARTHUR. *An Introduction to the Philosophy of Science.* New York: Free Press, 1962.

WHITEHEAD, ALFRED NORTH. *Science and the Modern World.* New York: Mentor Press, 1925, 1948.

METHODOLOGY

BRIDGMAN, PERCY W. *The Logic of Modern Physics.* New York: Macmillan Co., 1927, 1960.

BRAITHWAITE, RICHARD B. *Scientific Explanation.* Cambridge: Cambridge University Press, 1953.

CHURCHMAN, C. WEST (ed.). *Measurement, Definition, and Theories.* New York: John Wiley & Sons, Inc., 1959.

FRANK, PHILIPP (ed.). *The Validation of Scientific Theories.* Boston: Beacon Press, 1954; New York: Macmillan Co., 1961.

MARGENAU, HENRY. *Open Vistas.* New Haven: Yale University Press, 1961.

NAGEL, ERNEST. *Principles of the Theory of Probability.* Vol. 1, No. 6 of the *International Encyclopedia of Unified Science.* Chicago: University of Chicago Press, 1939.

POINCARÉ, HENRI. *Science and Hypothesis.* New York: Dover Publications, Inc., 1952.

POPPER, KARL. *The Logic of Scientific Discovery.* New York: Basic Books, Inc., 1959.

REICHENBACH, HANS. *The Rise of Scientific Philosophy.* Berkeley: University of California Press, 1951.

SHAPERE, DUDLEY (ed.). *Philosophical Problems of Natural Science.* New York: Macmillan Co., 1965.

TOULMIN, STEPHEN. *Philosophy of Science.* London: Hutchinson University Library, 1953; New York: Harper & Bros., Publishers, 1960.

MODERN PHYSICS

BARNETT, LINCOLN. *The Universe and Dr. Einstein.* New York: Harper & Bros., Publishers, 1948, 1962.

CAPEK, MILIO. *Philosophical Impact of Contemporary Physics.* Princeton, N. J.: Van Nostrand Co., 1961.

COLEMAN, JAMES A. *Relativity for the Layman.* New York: Mentor Press, 1954.

CROMBIE, A. (ed.). *Turning Points in Physics.* Amsterdam: North-Holland Publishing Co., 1959.

FEIGL, HERBERT and MAXWELL, GROVER (eds.). *Current Issues in the Philosophy of Science.* New York: Holt, Rinehart & Winston, Inc., 1961.

FRANK, PHILIPP. *Modern Science and Its Philosophy,* New York: Collier Books, 1941, 1961.

GAMOW, GEORGE. *The Creation of the Universe.* New York: Mentor Press, 1952.

HEISENBERG, WERNER. *The Physical Principles of Quantum Theory*. Chicago: University of Chicago Press, 1930.

HOYLE, FRED. *The Nature of the Universe*. New York: Harper & Bros., Publishers, 1950.

JEANS, JAMES. *The Growth of Physical Science*. New York: Premier Books, 1947, 1958.

RUSSELL, BERTRAND. *The ABC of Relativity*. New York: Mentor Press, 1959.

WEIZSACKER, CARL F. VON. *The World View of Physics*. Chicago: University of Chicago Press, 1952.

WHITTAKER, E. *From Euclid to Eddington*. New York: Dover Publications, 1958.

BIOLOGY

American Scientific Affiliation. *Modern Science and Christian Faith*. Wheaton, Ill.: Van Kampen Press, 1950.

DARWIN, CHARLES. *The Origin of Species*. New York: Mentor Press, 1958; Collier Books, 1962.

DOBZHANSKY, THEODOSIUS. *Mankind Evolving*. New Haven: Yale University Press, 1962.

EISELEY, LOREN. *The Immense Journey*. New York, Vintage Books, 1946.

GILLISPIE, CHARLES. *Genesis and Geology*. New York: Harper Torchbooks, 1951, 1959.

GREENE, JOHN C. *Evolution and Its Impact on Western Thought: The Death of Adam*. New York: Mentor Press, 1961.

HOFSTADTER, RICHARD. *Social Darwinism in American Thought*. Boston: Beacon Press, 1955.

HUXLEY, JULIAN. *Evolution in Action*. New York: Mentor Press, 1953, 1957.

HUXLEY, THOMAS H. *Man's Place in Nature*. Ann Arbor: University of Michigan Press, 1959.

MIXTER, RUSSELL L. (ed.). *Evolution and Christian Thought Today*. Grand Rapids: Wm. B. Eerdmans Publishing Co., 1959.

RAMM, BERNARD. *The Christian View of Science and Scripture*. Grand Rapids: Wm. B. Eerdmans Publishing Co., 1954.

RIDDERBOS, HERMAN N. *Is There a Conflict Between Genesis 1 and Natural Science?* Grand Rapids: Wm. B. Eerdmans Publishing Co., 1957.

SCHRODINGER, ERWIN. *What Is Life?* Garden City, N. Y.: Doubleday Anchor Books, 1956.

SIMPSON, GEORGE G. *The Meaning of Evolution*. New Haven: Yale University Press, 1949; New York: Mentor Press, 1951.

TEILHARD DE CHARDIN, PIERRE. *The Phenomenon of Man.* New York: Harper & Bros., Publishers, 1959.

University of Chicago Darwin Centennial, 3 vols.: *Evolution of Life; Evolution of Man; Issues in Evolution.* Chicago: University of Chicago Press, 1960.

WHITCOMB, JOHN C. and MORRIS, HENRY M. *The Genesis Flood,* Philadelphia: Presbyterian & Reformed Publishing Co., 1961.

YOUNG, JOHN Z. *Doubt and Certainty in Science.* New York: Oxford University Press, 1960.

PSYCHOLOGY

ALLPORT, GORDON W. *Becoming.* New Haven: Yale University Press, 1955.

_____. *Personality.* New York: Henry Holt & Co., 1937.

BRONOWSKI, JACOB. *The Identity of Man.* Garden City, N. Y.: Doubleday & Co., Inc., 1965.

CASTELL, ALBUREY. *The Self in Philosophy.* New York: Macmillan Co., 1965.

DONIGER, SIMON L. (ed.). *The Nature of Man in Theological and Psychological Perspective.* New York: Harper & Bros., Publishers, 1962.

FRANKL, VIKTOR E. *Man's Search for Meaning.* New York: Washington Square Press, 1963.

GUSTAFSON, DONALD F. (ed.). *Essays in Philosophical Psychology.* Garden City, N. Y.: Doubleday Anchor Books, 1964.

HAMPSHIRE, STUART (ed.). *Philosophy of Mind.* New York: Harper & Row, 1966.

LEWIN, KURT. *A Dynamic Theory of Personality.* New York: McGraw-Hill Book Co., 1935.

MEEHL, PAUL E., et al. *What, Then, Is Man?* St. Louis: Concordia Publishing House, 1958.

MOWRER, O. HOBART. *The Crisis in Psychiatry and Religion.* Princeton, N. J.: Van Nostrand Co., 1961.

ROGERS, CARL R. *Client-Centered Therapy.* Boston: Houghton Mifflin Co., 1951.

ROYCE, J. *Man and His Nature.* New York: McGraw-Hill Book Co., 1961.

SEVERIN, FRANK T. (ed.). *Humanistic Viewpoints in Psychology.* New York: McGraw-Hill Book Co., 1965.

SKINNER, B. F. *Science and Human Behavior.* New York: Macmillan Co., 1953.

TILLICH, PAUL. *The Courage to Be.* New Haven: Yale University Press, 1952.

————. *Dynamics of Faith.* New York: Harper & Bros., Publishers, 1957.

TOURNIER, PAUL. *The Meaning of Persons.* New York: Harper & Bros., Publishers, 1957.

SOCIAL SCIENCES

American Philosophical Association. *Science, Language, and Human Rights.* Philadelphia: University of Pennsylvania, 1952.

BENEDICT, RUTH. *Patterns of Culture.* New York: Mentor Press, 1934, 1959.

BRAYBROOKE, DAVID (ed.). *Philosophical Problems of the Social Sciences.* New York: Macmillan Co., 1965.

DRAY, WILLIAM H. (ed.). *Philosophical Analysis and History.* New York: Harper & Row, 1966.

GARDINER, PATRICK. *The Nature of Historical Explanation.* London: Oxford University Press, 1952.

————(ed.). *Theories of History.* Glencoe, Ill.: Free Press of Glencoe, 1959.

HINKLE, R. and G. *The Development of Modern Sociology.* New York: Random House, 1954.

MEAD, MARGARET (ed.). *Cultural Patterns and Technical Change.* New York: Mentor Press, 1955.

MERTON, ROBERT K. *Social Theory and Social Structure.* Glencoe, Ill.: Free Press of Glencoe, 1949.

MILLS, C. WRIGHT. *The Sociological Imagination.* New York: Oxford University Press, 1959.

NATANSON, MAURICE (ed.). *Philosophy of the Social Sciences.* New York: Random House, 1963.

PARSONS, TALCOTT and SHILS, EDWARD (eds.). *Toward a General Theory of Social Action.* Boston: Harvard University Press, 1951.

WHITE, MORTON. *Foundations of Historical Knowledge.* New York: Harper & Row, 1965.

SCIENCE AND VALUES

BEROFSKY, BERNARD (ed.). *Free Will and Determinism.* New York: Harper & Row, 1966.

BRONOWSKI, JACOB. *Science and Human Values.* New York: Harper Torchbook, 1956, 1959.

CLARK, ROBERT E. D. *The Christian Stake in Science.* Chicago: Moody Press, 1967.

CONANT, JAMES B. *Modern Science and Modern Man.* Garden City,

N. Y.: Doubleday Anchor Books, 1953.

————. *On Understanding Science.* New York: Mentor Press, 1947, 1951.

GIRVETZ, HARRY K., *et al. Science, Folklore, and Philosophy.* New York: Harper & Row, 1966.

HALL, EVERETT W. *Modern Science and Human Values.* Princeton, N. J.: Van Nostrand Co., 1956.

HENRY, CARL F. H. (ed.). *Contemporary Evangelical Thought.* Great Neck, N. Y.: Channel Press, 1957.

HOOK, SIDNEY (ed.). *Determinism and Freedom.* New York: Collier Books, 1958, 1961.

HUXLEY, JULIAN S. *Man in the Modern World.* New York: Mentor Press, 1948.

Journal of the American Scientific Affiliation, Vols. 1-18 (1966). Mankato, Minn.

RUSSELL, BERTRAND. *The Social Impact of Science.* New York: Columbia University Press, 1951.

SCHRODINGER, ERWIN. *Science and Humanism.* Cambridge: Cambridge University Press, 1951.

SNOW, C. P. *Science and Government.* New York: Mentor Press, 1962.

————. *The Two Cultures: And a Second Look.* New York: Mentor Press, 1959, 1964.

SULLIVAN, J. W. N. *The Limitations of Science.* New York: Mentor Press, 1949.

CHURCH MUSIC

Lee Olson

Lee Olof G. Olson is chairman of the division of music at Nyack Missionary College. A graduate of Union Theological Seminary School of Sacred Music, he holds the S. M. M. and the S. M. D. from that institution and also attended the Belgium School of the Violin. Before joining the Nyack faculty he was a professional musician.

14

CHURCH MUSIC

Lee Olson

VIEWS OF PHILOSOPHERS AND THEOLOGIANS

THE BATTLE against the secularization of music of the church is as old as the church itself. The church Fathers of the early centuries of the Christian church were perhaps even more aware of and outspoken against the musical profanity in the Lord's house than today's theologians.

The aesthetic principles by which the church Fathers evaluated the religious music of their day rested on the writings of the ancient philosophers. Contemporary musicians apply these same principles, to some degree, in their evaluation of present-day music, secular as well as sacred. The ancients viewed music as something more than an expression of feeling. They were not willing to accept the proposition that music is born of feeling to appeal to feeling or that it is created out of emotion to move the emotions. These philosophers believed that music had its origins in some "higher source" which transcended human understanding and the realm of reason. They reasoned that rhythm and melody were an imitation of the movements of the celestial bodies which moved through the heavens emitting a divine music which was imperceptible to human ears. To them, melody and rhythm had moral overtones and ethical significance. Therefore music could improve or degrade character. They feared the effects vivacious rhythms and sensuous tonalities might have on the body and mind.

The pre-Socratic period in philosophy has very little to say about the music of that era in ancient history. The poet Homer, who lived in the ninth century B.C., characterized the minstrels in the *Odyssey* as the favored mortals of the gods. The Muse endowed them with song not only to gladden the hearts of men but to watch over the morals of mankind.[1] Minstrels, according to Homer, were the earthly intermediaries who made the will of the gods known to man. Through music, man in turn could implore the gods for deliverance from sickness and pestilence.

Thales (640?-546 B.C.), whom Aristotle called the father of ancient philosophy, accused Homer of not only creating mythical gods and inspiring muses but also of clothing them with divine attributes. Thales wanted the Greek bard to concentrate his talents solely on the needs of man rather than create hymns for nonexistent deities.

Pythagoras (*c.* sixth century B.C.), the father of Greek musical science, taught that mortal music was an earthly prototype of the celestial harmony of the spheres. The later Pythagoreans held that the heavens were a harmony which actually made music. As the heavenly bodies traveled through the air, the speed with which they moved caused them to produce harmonious sounds like a celestial choir.[2] The Old Testament may reflect this view. Job 38:7 states that at the creation the morning stars "sang together." The Pythagoreans believed that the artist stood midway between the gods and man, and that it was the divine role of the inspired artist to help man attune his soul to the universal soul through the rhythm and grace of music.[3]

Socrates (469-399 B.C.) taught that music had ethical, political and educational value. The power of music, posited Socrates, could bring man closer to ultimate truth than could science, because music helps him achieve a harmonious union with nature. He further believed that music had the power to mold the souls of the young, to prepare them for a meaningful and purposeful existence.

Socrates' pupil Plato (427-347 B.C.) regarded music as superior to the other arts on the premise that rhythm and melody more strongly affected the inner soul and emotional life than architecture, painting or sculpture. He further held that a youth exposed to good music would unconsciously develop discriminating habits and abilities which would allow him to distinguish good from evil. Plato believed "that education in music is most sovereign, because more than anything else rhythm and harmony find their way to the innermost

---

[1]Homer *Odyssey* viii.
[2]Curt Sachs, *The Rise of Music in the Ancient World, East and West* (New York: W. W. Norton & Co., Inc., 1943), p. 111.
[3]Oliver Strunk, *Source Readings in Music History* (New York: W. W. Norton & Co., Inc., 1950), p. 83.

soul and take strongest hold upon it, bringing with them and impart-
ing grace, if one is rightly trained, and otherwise the contrary."[4] The
word *music* to Plato designated both text and music. He retained the
traditional Greek attitude that text and music should not be separated. "When there are no words," he wrote, "it is very difficult to
recognize the meaning of the harmony and rhythm, or to see that
any worthy object is imitated by them."[5] Plato considered the text
more important than the music and maintained that since language
was the direct expression of reason, the word or the poetic line must
be of a higher level than the melody.

Many musical innovations had taken place during Plato's lifetime
which he did not appreciate nor tolerate. Pythagoras had related
that the high priests of Pharaoh vehemently protested against the
changes of musical virtuosi. The Egyptians considered their religious
melodies as sacred in origin and for that reason would not allow any
variations or admit foreign tunes into their devotional services. In
the second book of the *Laws*, Plato states that the Egyptians ac-
credited their sacred melodies to the goddess Isis. He also praises
the Egyptians for their ability to create melodies which had the
power to subdue primitive passions in man and to purify the soul.[6]

In his many comments on music, Plato implied that music could
help man attune his finite soul with the infinite. Plato distrusted the
power of music over human emotions, a power which he considered
comparable to that of sorcery. He also questioned the use of musical
instruments, with the exception of the traditional lyre and the shep-
herd's pipe. The essence of Plato's philosophy of music is that as an
educational and cultural discipline, music should be used for the
attainment of a sound morality, and that it was bestowed upon man
for the purpose of helping him live a harmonious and judicious life.

Aristotle (384-322 B.C.) agreed in general with his teacher Plato
that music was an imitative art which was modeled after the cosmic
harmonies. He also believed that music could mold the character
of the listener for good or bad. But Aristotle did not agree with his
teacher concerning the banning of musical instruments.

Aristotle's pupil Aristoxenus (born *c.* 354 B.C.) did not agree to
the views which his teacher and Plato held regarding the moral
issues and mathematical interpretations of music. Aristoxenus believed rather that sense and reason, the power to hear and the ability
to discriminate, should enable one to judge for himself whether

---

[4]*Ibid.,* p. 8.
[5]Plato *Dialogues "Laws"* ii.
[6]*Ibid.*

music was good or bad. His philosophy of music made man the sole judge of what is good or bad in music.

Epicurus (342-270 B.C.), a contemporary of Aristoxenus, believed with him in the Pythagorean theory that the soul was a "harmony" of the body. But Lucretius (96-55 B.C.), a fellow Epicurean and one of their ablest exponents, scoffed at this belief. Thilodemus, a contemporary of Lucretius, added that "music is irrational and cannot affect the soul or the emotions, and is no more an expressive art than cookery."[7]

The Stoic school of philosophy, founded by Zeno (c. 350-258 B.C.), contributed little to the growth of music. The Roman period was musically active but lacked originality. The Romans adopted Greek theory and practices and modified them to their own use. There were some doubters of the Platonic music theories, but very few indeed were found among the better-known philosophers.

The early church Fathers were not slow to recognize, as Plato was, that music is powerful for good as well as for evil. The hostile attitude of the Fathers against the secular music of their day is easily understood. The early church lived in a highly developed pagan civilization. The Fathers envisioned the unfortunate influence pagan music could have upon the minds of Christians. This explains the strong denunciation by many Christian writers of that day against the "theatre of the devil." The church Fathers could see only hypocrisy and sensuality in the heathen music. The early Christian was surrounded by pagan rites and licentious music which could easily impose a severe temptation on individual believers to forsake the assembly of the faithful. The music of the Roman was representative of his cultural, social and religious beliefs. The Roman religion's emphasis on the carnal naturally reproduced itself in the religious and amorous music. This highly emotional music contrasted with the sincere, plaintive songs of the Christians.

Furthermore, the usage and development of instrumental music was not favored by the church Fathers. They probably shunned instruments because of the association of these with pagan rites. Another possibility is that the early Christians were forced to meet secretly and could not use instruments in their services for fear of being detected by their enemies. But perhaps the strongest reason why so little is mentioned in the New Testament in regard to the use of instruments is the fact that the banning of the use of musical instruments was a part of the national mourning for the destruction

---

[7]Bernard Bosanquet, *A History of Aesthetics* (London: George Allen & Unwin, Ltd., 1922), pp. 100-101.

of the Temple in Jerusalem. This is easily understood when one realizes that the early church consisted largely of converted Jews, and that the Christian music was strongly influenced by the music of the synagogue as well as of the Temple.

The third century marked the turning point in the church's attitude toward instrumental music. By this time it was being tolerated but still suspected. Clement of Alexandria (*c.* 150-220) warned against the orgiastic nature of some instruments, and he pointed out that even "the flute belongs to those superstitious men who run to idolatry." The canonical book of Revelation had visualized the host of elders prostrate before the Lamb playing, with harps, the "new song." Clement of Alexandria defended the playing of the lyre by quoting the impressive example of King David (I Sam. 16:23). As in most cases, he patterned his ideas on the Jewish philosopher Philo of Alexandria (born *c.* 20 B.C.), who likened "the human tongue to the God-praising lyre." Philo excepted the lyre from the connotation of sensuality. St. Basil (330-79) also approved the playing of the psaltery as accompaniment to the singing of the Psalms but censured instrumental music in his *Canones* (rules and regulations), which were written toward the end of the fourth century.

Ambrose (*c.* 340-97), the writer and inspirer of the earliest Latin hymnody, denounced those who preferred secular music to the spiritual blessing of sacred music:

> And so it is justly said, "Woe unto them that rise up early in the morning and follow strong drink," when they ought to be rendering praises to God, for this should they rise before the dawn and run to meet the Sun of Righteousness, who visits His own and arises upon us if we have bestirred ourselves for the sake of Christ and not of wine and luxury. They are singing hymns—will you cling to your harp? They are singing psalms; what business have you with a psaltery and a drum? Woe indeed to you for abandoning your salvation and choosing death.[8]

St. John Chrysostom (345-407), the golden-mouthed preacher of early Christianity and considered the leading moralist among the ancient Christian theologians, used more violent language against the theater and its music than any other of the early church Fathers. He made many derogatory remarks concerning music, but he never urged the abandonment of sacred music. Here is a typical excerpt from his writings:

---

[8]"De Elia et Jejunio," 55, *Migne's Patrologia Graecea,* Vol. XIV, col. 717, quoted in Eric Routley, *The Church and Music* (London: Gerald Duckworth & Co., Ltd., 1950), p. 230.

How many words have we spent in admonishing this idle multitude and advising them to avoid the theatres and the license that they generate? But they have not abstained; on the contrary, up to this very day they have continued to run after dancing-shows, choosing the devil's conversation rather than that which stands in the fulness of God's Church. So the clamor of the theatres has drowned the psalmody of the Church.

But now, behold, without a word from us (for we have said nothing of this), they have of their own accord shut up the dance-hall, and the circus is deserted. Before this many of our own people frequented these performances, but now they are all fled into the church for refuge, and are singing praises, all of them to our God. . . . Truly grief is more profitable than laughter.[9]

The oratorical Bishop of Constantinople warned his congregation that they risked shipwreck of soul by deserting the fountain of blood, the awful cup, for the fountain of the devil. Chrysostom asserted that society was already turned upside down; marriage and family life were being completely corrupted by the bad example of the stage. His attitude toward the theater and its music is summed up in the sixth homily in *Mattheum:*

It is not for us then, to be continually laughing, and to be dissolute and luxurious, but it is for those upon the stage, for the harlot women, the men who are gelded to this intent, parasites and flatterers, not for those who bear spiritual arms but for those who belong to the devil. For it is he, yea, it is he, who even made this thing an art, so that he may weaken Christ's soldiers, and soften their sinews of their zeal. For this cause he also built theatres in the cities, and, having trained these buffoons, by means of their wretched condition he hurls this terrible pestilence on the whole city, persuading men to follow those things which Paul commanded us to flee, foolish talking and jesting.[10]

Chrysostom was fully aware of the power of music for evil: "Thus does the devil stealthily set fire to the city. It is not a matter of running up ladders and using petroleum or pitch or tow; he uses things far more pernicious—lewd sights, base speech, degraded music, and songs full of all kinds of wickedness."[11]

---

[9]"Ad Antiochenas Homilia," 15:1, *Patrologia Graecea*, Vol. II, col. 152-53, quoted in Eric Routley, *The Church and Music*, p. 231.

[10]Egon Wellesz, *Byzantine Music and Hymnography* (Oxford: At the Clarendon Press, 1949), p. 72.

[11]"De Poenitentio," VI, *Patrologia Graecea*, Vol. II, col. 315, quoted in Eric Routley, *The Church and Music*, pp. 231-32.

St. Jerome (340-420), the famous Christian scholar and profound theologian, in his commentary on the epistle of Paul to the Ephesians, had this to say about secularization of the church music of his day:

> This, indeed, is what is written: "Singing and making melody in your heart to the Lord." Let youth hear this, let them hear it whose office it is to make melody in the church: Sing to God, not with the voice, but with the heart; not, after the fashion of tragedians, in smearing the throat with a sweet drug, so that theatrical melodies and songs are heard in the church, but in fear, in work, and in knowledge of the Scriptures. And although a man be a *kakaphanos,* to use a common expression, if he have good works, he is a sweet singer before God. And let the servant of Christ sing so he pleases, not through his voice, but through the words which he pronounces, in order that the evil spirit which was upon Saul may depart from those who are similarly troubled and may not enter into those who would make of the house of God a popular theatre.[12]

To these utterances of the Fathers should be added the most important of the early ecclesiastical edicts against pagan music. These are not regulations about church music but instructions to Christians to avoid the pernicious music of the pagan Roman world. The Council of Laodicea (A.D. 360) denounced those who behaved in an improper and frivolous way on Christian festive occasions. It further evoked a ruling that only biblical texts should be admitted into the service. Hymns were, therefore, looked upon unfavorably since their poetical texts were not taken from the Scriptures. The council thus formulated in a public edict the conviction which had first found its spiritual expression in St. Chrysostom.

Of all the church Fathers and authorities on church music, none was more profound than St. Augustine (354-430). He loved music passionately, but he knew its power for good and also its dangers. He confessed that he had himself been distracted by the beauty of the music from the message that was being sung. He considered this falling into error. He warned the Christians not to mistake the symbol of musical rhythm for what the symbol represented. Beauty and music, for him, were only artistic imitations of a higher order which God gratuitously bestowed upon mankind. He admonished Christians to model their attitude toward music after that of King David, for David was the man "skilled in songs, who dearly loved musical harmony, not with a vulgar delight, but with a believing

---

[12]Strunk, p. 72.

disposition, and by it served his God, who is the true God, by the mystical representation of a great thing. For the rational and well ordered concord of diverse sounds in harmonious variety suggests the compact unity of a well ordered City."[13] St. Augustine's *De Musica*, a treatise on music in which Pythagorean and Platonic influences are strongly felt, is devoted to meter, verse and theories pertaining to numbers. The first five of the six books in this treatise dealt with rhythm and meter; in the sixth book, Augustine discussed music in its cosmological and theological aspects. Evil in morals and badness in art, said Augustine, are matters of metaphysics and carry their own judgment; the practical necessity for the man who wishes to advance in either goodness or musical appreciation is to know and to cultivate what is good.

According to Eric Routley, the importance of *De Musica* can be summarized as follows:

1. It is the most complete synthesis of music and theology that has ever been achieved. Music to St. Augustine is primarily a metaphysical phenomenon, but it is also an activity of men and therefore subject to moral judgments. Only a Christian, he says, can hope to deal with the problems which this raises.

2. Being a Christian, he allows full value to the pleasure content of music, and never advises his reader to beware of pleasure as such.

3. Also being a Christian, he solves the problem of "badness" in music. That imperfection, which is the heritage of all created things, he tells his reader to tolerate and not to make into an occasion for abandoning his study. That which proceeds from wilful disregard of the laws of symmetry and soundness he roundly denounces as pride and therefore sinful.

4. Above all, St. Augustine regards music as an act of reason, not a matter of feeling and "self-expression." It is the *Logos* which is the expression of eternal and immutable things, not the human *logos* which is tainted with all human failings. Music for him brings the truth down from heaven, and those who regard music as a means of sending thoughts up from the human mind will do well to mark his words.[14]

Thus one can see that the church Fathers did show a keen interest in the church music of their day and did recognize the power of music for good or for bad. Their sincere desire was to guard Christians against music that would weaken their faith. No doubt they were better experts in theology than in the knowledge of music, and

---

13Augustine *City of God* xvii. 14.
14Routley, *The Church and Music,* pp. 67-68.

if they seem to lean heavily on the authority of Plato's moralism, this is only to be expected from those who had to apply the accepted musical science of that day. Their fearless and positive convictions in regard to church music, which are evident in their writings as well as in their sermons, had a correcting effect upon the early church.

The development of the musical aesthetics of Western civilization has largely been a matter of adding footnotes to Plato, with some Aristotelian embellishments. The musical views of these philosophers, especially Plato, have persistently remained the aesthetic beliefs by which the church of the Western world has evaluated her music throughout the ages.

In 1903, the Roman Catholic Church published the famous *Motu Proprio* of Pope Pius X on sacred music. This document on the proper function of music as a complementary part of the solemn liturgy of the Roman Mass, is definitely based on Plato's aesthetics of music. This document states that the principal function of sacred music is to embellish the text, to emphasize the holy Word of God. The main purpose of sacred music "is to clothe with suitable melody the liturgical text proposed for the understanding of the faithful; its proper aim is to add greater efficacy to the text, in order that through it the faithful may be the more easily moved to devotion."[15]

Sacred music, according to this document, should possess sanctity, must have qualities proper to the liturgy and must exclude all "profanity," both of melody and manner in which it is performed. The music of the church must possess "goodness of form if it is to exercise on the minds of those who listen to it that efficacy which the Church aims at obtaining in admitting into her liturgy the art of musical sounds."[16] Every nation is allowed to bring its native music into the Roman Catholic Church; therefore the sacred music must also possess universality. This native music, however, must be subordinate to the basic requirements of sacred music, proper to the Catholic liturgy, so that music of one land can be acceptable as sacred music in another.

The *Motu Proprio* states that these three qualities are fully manifest in the Gregorian Chant: ". . . the more closely a composition for church approaches in its movement, inspiration, and savor the Gregorian form, the more sacred and liturgical it becomes; and the more out of harmony it is with that supreme model, the less worthy it is of the temple."[17]

---

[15]*The White List* (New York: Society of St. Gregory of America, 1951), p. 7.
[16]*Ibid.*, p. 8.
[17]*Ibid.*, p. 8.

The Roman Church, states the *Motu Proprio*, has always favored the progress of the arts and has admitted new music into the service. Modern music is welcomed into the liturgy if it is in keeping with the needs of worship and fulfills the liturgical requirements. The *Motu Proprio* states that "since modern music has risen mainly to serve profane uses, greater care must be taken with regard to it, in order that the musical compositions of modern style which are admitted in the Church may contain nothing profane, be free from reminiscences of motifs adopted in the theatres, and be not fashioned even in their external forms after the manner of profane pieces."[18]

Solo singing should never predominate in the service, and in regard to the use of instruments in the church, the *Motu Proprio* says:

> Although the music proper to the Church is purely vocal music, music with the accompaniment of the organ is also permitted. In some special cases, within due limits and proper safeguards, other instruments may be allowed, but never without the special permission of the Ordinary, . . . as the singing should always have the principal place, the organ or other instrument should merely sustain and never oppress it. It is not permitted to have the chant preceded by long preludes or to interrupt it with intermezzo pieces. The sound of the organ as an accompaniment to the chant in preludes, interludes, and the like must be not only governed by the special nature of the instrument, but must participate in all the qualities proper to sacred music as above numerated. The employment of the piano is forbidden in church, as is also that of noisy or frivolous instruments, such as drums, cymbals, bells and the like. It is strictly forbidden to have bands play in church, and only in special cases with the consent of the Ordinary will it be permissible to admit wind instruments, limited in number, judiciously used, and proportioned to the size of the place—provided the composition and accompaniment be written in grave and suitable style, and conform in all respects to that proper to the organ. In processions outside the church, the Ordinary may give permission for a band provided no profane pieces be executed.[19]

The *Motu Proprio* makes it quite clear that music is merely the humble handmaid of the liturgy and that to subordinate the liturgy to musical considerations in ecclesiastical functions is considered a serious abuse. It further advises the bishops to institute in their dioceses a commission composed of persons versed in sacred music who should watch over the religious music in their churches. "Nor

---

[18]*Ibid.*
[19]*Ibid.*, p. 9.

are they to see merely that the music is good in itself," states the *Motu Proprio*, "but also that it is adapted to the powers of the singers and always be well executed."[20]

This same document then continues by asking that the Gregorian Chant be cultivated with diligence in seminaries and ecclesiastical institutions. It states that students of theology should be instructed in the principles and laws of sacred music and be made aware of the aesthetic side of sacred art.

The philosophy of sacred music, as advanced in this document, took on religious significance in the labors of the ecclesiastical composers who were imbued with the sacred mission to create music for the glory of God and the church. To fulfill the needs of the church, it was essential for these church composers to ignore their personal feelings and musical tendencies.

Philosophers as well as theologians throughout the centuries have claimed that the value of music lies in its effects, and that music should lead to "right action"; if this does not occur, it is only a stimulant which enables the listener to flee reality. Musicians hold to the theory that music is born of the emotions and must appeal to the emotions to be of aesthetic value. The philosophers and theologians have been disdainful of this theory because music does not primarily appeal to reason. The sensual pleasure that one derives from listening to music and the physiological effect which musical rhythms have upon a person have caused philosophers and theologians to view music with misgiving and suspicion. Theologians have looked upon sacred music as a means of bringing man closer to God. The church Fathers ethically distinguished between sacred and secular strains, between Christian and pagan tunes. Sacred music was one way through which illiterate Christians could be taught the Word of God.

THE CONTEMPORARY PROBLEM

Thus philosophers and theologians have regarded music. It is now necessary to determine what present-day musicians believe music is and is not, and what is its aesthetic as well as its ethical value.

First, music is not an imitation of the harmony of the spheres. The celestial harmony which the stars produce while in motion when brought to human ears by the scientific advances of the twentieth century have, to some degree, sounded more like cacophony than the would-be "harmony of the spheres."

Second, music is not an expression of morality or immorality.

[20]*Ibid.*

Music cannot be good or bad in an ethical sense as believed and taught by some of the ancient philosophers. There is no denying, however, that certain types of music have different effects on the listener. The sensual pleasure derived from listening to music and the physiological effect of rhythms upon the listener can instill a variety of moods.

Third, music is neither religious nor irreligious. When one speaks of sacred music, he refers to music set to a sacred or biblical text and nothing else. Instrumental music, whether it is of a devotional or inspirational nature, can only be classified as churchly.

Fourth, music is not mathematics alone. It is essentially mathematical in structure, but music is more than mathematics. If music were only mathematics, it would become a science, as exacting as mathematics itself, in which the composer would express moods in precise, standardized ways rather than allowing music to become an art in which the emotions are uniquely expressed.

What is music, if it is not metaphysics, ethics, religion or mathematics? It is all of these and more. It is a rhythmically compelling art which can penetrate the innermost part of the soul and rule the mind. It is a pattern of tones arranged in forms in prescribed tempi, in which one associates the whole gamut of human feeling. It is precisely what the listener brings to tones and rhythms. Music is feeling embodied in rhythmic and tonal symbols. The pictorial and plastic arts offer tangible evidence for evaluation; but in music, only feeling can remain the guide. "Music," writes Canon Winfred Douglas, "is an art of human expression which directly voices the human soul in tone governed by rhythm. It can really utter the voice of the spirit through the flesh; and make the spoken word more intensely vital, more sincere, truer."[21]

In evaluating music the listener faces two schools of thought; whatever the philosophers had to say about music, from the time of Plato to the present, has been based on these two schools: idealism and naturalism.

If one bases his aesthetic values on the school of idealism, he may overemphasize the importance of reason and minimize emotions. To the contrary, if aesthetic values are based on naturalism, music will be regarded as an expression of human emotion rather than a sensuous embodiment of a spiritual idea. Therefore one doubts very much whether the idealist and naturalist would have the same emotional experience in listening to music.

[21]*Church Music in History and Practice* (New York: Charles Scribner's Sons, 1952), p. 7.

Everyone listens to music in the light of these two schools of aesthetic opinion, whether conscious of it or not, unless he is the type of individual who likes what he likes and is not troubled with possible causes. Such a personal reaction to music, without rational evaluation, is extremely primitive and minimizes man's rational powers of introspection and reflection. Such an indifferent attitude toward music beyond the immediate pleasure which it will afford, stifles such an individual's capabilities as a human being. Nothing is more absurd than to reason that to analyze the aesthetic experience is to destroy it. To know the reason why man reacts as he does to rhythm and melody will not diminish its effect upon him. As has been said, "Knowledge does not curb emotion; knowledge refines emotions."

Focusing now on contemporary church music, it should be noted that the battle against musical profanity in the sanctuary is much in evidence. Evangelicalism is still suffering from the puritanical wet blanket thrown by Pietism, with all its merits, over the arts in general in its protest against the external and formal in worship. There seems to be some confusion in evangelical circles in regard to what is meant by "church music" or "sacred music" or similar terms used to describe the musical literature of the Christian church. These terms have one feature in common: the combination of words and music. Without text there can be no distinction between sacred and secular music. Music is neither religious nor irreligious. Instrumental music of a sober and devotional character, whether orchestra or organ or piano music, may be described as "churchly," but nothing else.

Many seem to have difficulty in grasping the fact that words and music are not one and indivisible. The words which are real because they express meanings, and the music on the contrary which is unreal and mysterious and expresses nothing but beauty, should not be confused with one another. This is very obvious as one listens to the words on the one hand and the music on the other. This is a good test to apply to any vocal composition and especially to some "gospel songs" to determine whether their music belongs in the church or not. Such an examination of gospel songs would reveal that many of their tunes would be worldly in character rather than churchly. Some are of the opinion that as soon as music has been wedded to sacred text the music somehow becomes sacrosanct, but nothing could be further from the truth. The functions of words and music are very distinct. Words with their meaning and dynamics behind them are utilized to bring the "Word" to the listener, and the words must be acted on by the intellect before they can produce any emotional result or fruit. The importance of this cannot be overstressed to the Evangelical. If spiritual results are to be lasting, one must depend on the "Word." Music, on the other hand, does not need to appeal to logic in order to initiate action but strikes directly at the emotions. Therefore "church" music must be a selfless servant of the Word, not calling attention to itself but rather adding its particular grace, elevating the meanings of the words or the message they express to a spiritual realm, not accessible to mere reason. St. Augustine refers to this in his *Confessions* when he says: "I call to mind the tears I shed at the songs of the church at the outset of my recovered faith, and how even now I am moved not by the song but what is sung."[22] It is important to remember that music strikes directly at the emotions, which supply the quickest reactions. Words, on the contrary, must appeal to the intellect and then make their way out to the primary responses before they can produce any emotional result. Therefore, if the music is not a handmaid of the words, it will grip the listener's ears, and he will enjoy an emotional musical experience and nothing else beyond that. "Music," says Canon Douglas, "is a collective voice of mankind that unites men on a higher level of spiritual sensitiveness than they could otherwise attain. Its message is not primarily addressed either to the intellect or the emotions, but to the complete personalities of the listener."[23]

The failure of many sincere church musicians to grasp the fact that these two ideas are involved in listening to vocal music, has caused them to accept as fact that just because music has been set to biblical or sacred text it must be sacred music and above criticism. They do not even question whether the tune, rhythm or harmonization serves the mood of the text. One must consider this matter sincerely and objectively. It is pertinent to look beyond the fact that this music is found in hymnbooks and that one hears it Sunday after Sunday in the churches as well as over the radio and television. It is necessary to perform a musical autopsy to determine what is the cause of this secularization.

One must define what constitutes a good hymn melody, not forgetting that the best words can be rendered invalid or powerless and even ridiculous by a bad tune, and that unworthy words can have a worthy sense imparted to them by a good tune. Another point to remember is that the melody is a whole; the notes, which are its

[22]St. Augustine *Confessions* x. XXXIII. 50.
[23]Douglas, p. 9.

units, retain none of their meaning when isolated. In the words of
hymns, individual words have meaning; not so notes when isolated.
Therefore the melody is intended primarily for the mood of the text
rather than for each individual word. It is the author's conviction
that the more beautiful a melody is from the sensuous point of view
the less desirable it is as a hymn melody. This is where most of the
gospel melodies are guilty—they are too sensuous. The gospel hymn
melodies call too much attention to themselves and not enough to
the text. They are, to use Canon Douglas' expression, "manward and
not Godward." If this trend continues, God the Father, God the
Son and God the Holy Spirit will be completely left out of the picture, and beyond this point there can be no further secularization of
church music. The barrier between the sacred and the secular has
been completely broken down. This humanization of the gospel
hymn is only a reflection of the spiritual state of the evangelical
branch of the church.

The problem which besets contemporary Christianity is whether
the church can learn from the world and still preserve the traditional
spirit and dignity of her music. The history of church art, particularly of church music, is the history of the conflict between the
sacerdotal conception of art and the popular taste. It is a fallacy to
assert that the masses of the people are responsive only to that which
is trivial and sensational. It should not be forgotten that a trivial,
sensational and secularized style of church music means decadence;
but as is usually the case in controversy, the truth lies between the
two extremes.

The Reformation chorale, post-Reformation hymns, and the Gregorian plainsong, often referred to as the folk song of the church,
stand out as unsurpassed melodic models. This is music of thought
rather than action. If the music of today is to endure, it must have
its foundation in our musical heritage.

Rhythm probably has done more toward secularization of church
music than anything else. Science states that man cannot remain
aloof to music because living organisms have a strong affinity for
tone and rhythm, the components of music. The whole animal kingdom is conditioned to tone and rhythm. Man is essentially a rhyth-
mical being. There is rhythm in respiration, heartbeat, speech, gait.
However, and this is a very important fact, as rhythm increases in a
musical composition, the intellectual powers of man decrease. "Pronounced rhythm," says Seashore, "brings on a feeling of elation
which not infrequently results in a mild form of ecstasy or absent-

mindedness, a loss of consciousness of environment. One becomes oblivious to intellectual pursuits."[24] That being the truth, one wonders how much real spiritual fruit has been the result of the so-called popular evangelism of today; if any, it is not a result of its music, but rather in spite of it.

Let those who are accustomed to treating their church music as an emotional orgy give heed to the words of St. Augustine when he voiced his distrust of music from the basis that "the sense does not so attend on reason as to follow her patiently; but having gained admission merely for her sake, it strives even to run before her and be her leader."[25] Rhythm is one of the constant elements in music most likely to provoke a physical response. And when doing so, it is not the friend of pious contemplation. The early church recognized that fact. The Evangelicals have forgotten it. There is nothing wrong with rhythm as such.

Hymns and gospel songs in triple rhythm have been under criticism, but it should not be forgotten that during a large part of the Middle Ages the triple rhythm was used almost exclusively for the music of the church. Triple rhythm was called *tempus perfectum*, referring to Father, Son and Holy Ghost. The feeling that this rhythm is unsuited to the music of the church comes, no doubt, from the fact that it is associated with the various dance forms in *pronounced* triple pulse. Gospel hymn composers should strive toward a perfect union between the speech rhythm of the text and the rhythm of the music. Then the rhythm will be in less danger of calling attention to itself and, instead, will contribute toward making the music a selfless ally of the text.

Finally, in regard to harmony and counterpoint, one should avoid harmonization that has a tendency to make hymns sound undernourished aesthetically, too sweet for musical well-being, and too feeble to be enduring. Reference is made to the purposeless altering of chords resulting in what is known as "barber shop harmony" and not the subtle and aristocratic chromaticism of the Wagnerian era. The two should not be confused. Purposeless chromaticism is to church music what the serpent was to Adam and Eve in the Garden of Eden—deceitful, to say the least. This music, whether contrapuntal or harmonic, should be impersonal and undramatic. It should be an ideal musical vehicle for the expression of such corporate attitudes as awe, contemplation or aspiration—all so essential in worship.

---

[24] Carl E. Seashore, *Psychology of Music* (New York: McGraw-Hill Book Co., Inc., 1938), p. 142.

[25] Augustine, *Confessions* x. 272. Trans. J. C. Pilkington.

These are some of the basic music problems that face Evangelicals today. There are many others that must be considered, but these represent perhaps just one important stone in the musical foundation of a sound musical philosophy. In appraising gospel music, one must remember that nothing will be accomplished by haste. There is a certain danger in thoughtless and irresponsible changes and in confusion of styles resulting when the general character of a congregation and the natural traditions of its worship are disregarded. Forms of worship that modern Christians have inherited are not sacrosanct. The tradition of church music will only survive and develop so long as it satisfies the spiritual need of Christian people. Throughout the centuries the development of church music has never run smoothly; in spite of the sincere efforts of the church Fathers, it was not free from entangling alliances with the world. Throughout Christian history there has been a free interchange of music material between the church and the world.

In church music as in other arts, it is the contemporary that really matters. An art that is not creative is not living. Therefore the problem should be met squarely and patiently, and good, convincing musical examples should lead the way to a sanctified church music which is not of this world and through which the Christian will sense the glory of the world to come. And to accomplish this, the church needs, in the words of Olivier Messiaen, one of France's leading contemporary church musicians, "a consummate artist ... who will be both a skilled artisan and a fervent Christian. Let us hasten in our prayers for such a liberator."[26]

FOR FURTHER READING

AUGUSTINE. *City of God.* Book xvii. Trans. MARCUS DODS. New York: Hafner Pub. Co., 1948.

_____. *The Confessions of St. Augustine.* Trans. J. C. PILKINGTON. Edinburgh: T. & T. Clark, 1886.

BOSANQUET, BERNARD. *A History of Aesthetic.* London: George Allen & Unwin, Ltd., 1922.

DOUGLAS, WINFRED. *Church Music in History and Practice.* New York: Charles Scribner's Sons, 1952.

HOMER. *Odyssey.* Book viii. Trans. A. T. MURRAY. London: William Heineman, 1931.

MESSIAEN, OLIVER. "The Techniques of My Musical Style." Trans.

---

[26]Olivier Messiaen, "The Techniques of My Musical Style," trans. Harold M. Best (Claremont, Calif.: Unpublished manuscript, 1957), p. 3.

HAROLD M. BEST. Claremont, Calif.: Unpublished manuscript, 1957.

PLATO. *Dialogues*. Book ii, *Laws*. Trans. BENJAMIN JOWETT. New York: Random House, 1937.

ROUTLEY, ERIC. *The Church and Music*. London: Gerald Duckworth & Co., Ltd., 1950:

"Ad Antiochenas Homilia," 15:1, *Patrologia Graecea*, Vol. II.

"De Elia et JeJunio," 55, Migne's *Patrologia Graecea*, Vol. XIV.

"De Poenitentio," VI, *Patrologia Graecea*, Vol. II.

SACHS, CURT. *The Rise of Music in the Ancient World, East and West*. New York: W. W. Norton & Co., Inc., 1943.

SEASHORE, CARL E. *Psychology of Music*. New York: McGraw-Hill Book Co., Inc., 1938.

STRUNK, OLIVER. *Source Readings in Music History*. New York: W. W. Norton & Co., Inc., 1950.

WELLESZ, EGON. *Byzantine Music and Hymnography*. Oxford: At the Clarendon Press, 1949.

WHITE LIST, THE. New York: Society of St. Gregory of America, 1951.

PSYCHOLOGY

John M. Vayhinger

John Monroe Vayhinger is professor of religion and pastoral
counseling at Iliff School of Theology, Denver, and minister of
counseling, Park Hill Methodist Church, in Denver. He has also
taught at Garrett Theological Seminary, Indiana University
(South Bend) and West Virginia Wesleyan College; has served
as chief clinical psychologist at the Mental Health Clinic, South
Bend, Indiana; and has pastored Methodist churches in Indiana,
New York, and Connecticut. A graduate of Taylor University,
he holds M. A. and Ph. D. degrees from Columbia University,
an M. A. from Drew University and a B. D. from Drew Theological Seminary. Dr. Vayhinger is coauthor of *Casebook in Pastoral
Counseling.*

15

PSYCHOLOGY

John M. Vayhinger

INTRODUCTION

THE COMPLEXITY of human behavior (the subject of psychology) is mirrored in much of the material covered in this book. Not, certainly, in detail or totality. However, man is a chemical reactor system (neural reflex, pharmaceutical field), a biological system (cell growth, digestion), the resultant of sociological valences (group values, social customs) and more.

This is not surprising when one is reminded of the Genesis creation account, for God created man from the "dust" or chemicals of the earth *after* He had designed and built everything else in the entire cosmos.

For the purposes of this chapter, however, the discussion of psychology must be limited more or less to the motivational and behavioral factors in human experience, the various ways in which they are caused and influenced (as far as is known), and some of the Christian implications.

How much should man seek to know about his own actions? When does self-knowledge become sinful pride in self-sufficiency? It is the belief of many Christians that the scriptural command to love God with heart, *mind* and soul clearly enjoins the followers of God to seek knowledge in every legitimate way. The capacity to learn and know is a God-given gift that must be an integral part of man's search for holiness.

To make the distinction between information and knowledge as does nearly every language, one might first say that information is data of the type used in recalling dates, repairing an engine or conjugating a Greek verb. A computer can be programmed for information and, without human aid, print out informational results with greater speed and accuracy than the human mind. Knowledge, however, implies a living person in a learning situation, with goals, choices and information to be understood for a reason. As Dr. Richard Schlatter, Provost of Rutgers University, has stated, the living mind is not a jug to be filled but a power to be developed, trained, strengthened and disciplined.

Psychology is concerned with both information and knowledge, and the Christian who comes to psychology to ask questions about human behavior must bring both an honest willingness to examine the facts and a certain humility. Both amateur and professional psychologists are tempted by the sin of pride to proclaim a system answering all questions. Professor William Hordern suggests that when psychologists, theologians or philosophers forget the mystery of the relationship of man and God, and attempt to describe both in a single framework, they might as well withdraw into a silent denial of their results, for both are ultimately incomprehensible. This should be no deterrent, however, to studying either. Hordern writes: "Because Christian faith recognizes the transcendence of God, it can never suppose that its words capture the mystery of God. But because it believes that God has revealed himself, it is convinced that it has a base of knowledge from which it can speak."[1]

The psychologist reaches the most complete answers when he studies the simplest organisms or selected segments of behavior, or applies his knowledge to specifics such as mentally disturbed patients, industrial situations or educational problems. Humility is indeed a virtue in both psychologist and theologian. All psychological theories are useful in seeking knowledge, but none is free from defects. The Christian comes to his study of human behavior willing to find fact and information in any valid system and to put that data to use in his effort to answer the question "What, then, is man?"

HISTORICAL DEVELOPMENT OF PSYCHOLOGY AS A SCIENCE

Psychology was the stepchild of philosophy for many years before it was granted independent existence. Mental philosophy, or metaphysics, as it was known until the beginning of the twentieth century,

---

[1]*Speaking of God, The Nature and Purpose of Theological Language* (New York: Macmillan Co., 1964), p. 131.

used speculation as a tool and dealt with (1) logic (rules of reasoning), (2) epistemology (problems of cognition), and (3) metaphysics (analysis of the existing universe). Each psychological system would appear to have been the projection of an individual's experience, usually with little or no empirical evidence. The main problems in this field were (1) the existence and characteristics of the soul, (2) mental faculties (i.e., willpower, memory, reason, emotions), and (3) the content of introspection.

With the information explosion in biology, chemistry and physics in the nineteenth century, especially in physiology and neurology, attempts were made to apply the methods of these disciplines to the "science of behavior." Johannes Peter Müller, Ernst Heinrich Weber, Gustav Theodor Fechner and Wilhelm Wundt applied the techniques of experimental science to study man's behavior, and laid the groundwork for what Wundt called "a science based on experience" (*Erfahrungswissenschaft*). Though the methods and results of this period seem primitive in comparison with modern psychology, through them were hammered out the principles upon which experimental psychology was developed in the first half of this century.

Wundt deliberately discarded two inherited problems of the earlier philosophical psychology, attributes of the soul and mental faculties, as not belonging to the field of psychology. Experimental psychology, until very recently, also excluded introspection as a problem area. Psychology became more a study of the atomistic data of behavior, that is, stimulus-response, reinforcement. The earlier experimentalists, by and large, limited their research to "experience," declaring that psychology simply did not deal with metaphysical concepts such as "soul." Later the behaviorist eliminated man's spirit from consideration, in a form of "sneering reductionism." It has been said of twentieth century psychology that it "first lost its soul; then it lost its mind."

Another description of man was offered by Sigmund Freud and his colleagues. This description was derived chiefly from their experience in the treatment of emotional illness. Observing illogical behavior in many of his patients, Freud, a physician, deduced that there were forces beneath the level of consciousness which caused the unexplainable behavior. Called "dynamic" because of their powerful influence, these forces exerted an almost hydraulic influence on behavior, its form being an observable counterpart of their demands.

Opposition to Freud's theories seems to have developed not so much from his belief in the *existence* of the unconscious mental processes as from what he stated to be the *nature* of these processes, a kind of boiling reservoir of unfilled sexual desires that originated in earliest infancy. His geography of the mind (id, superego and ego), his levels of consciousness (the unconscious, the preconscious and the conscious), his developmental stages (oral, anal and phallic stages, the Oedipus period), and his hypothesis of bipolarity of human emotions and sexual identity (ambivalence) were developed through his clinical practice and his technique of treatment in which the patient simply talked. More than just social conversation, this talking resulted in a catharsis of feeling and in the development of a "transference neurosis." It was in the resolution of this transference that the "cure" was found, where the patient matured into a socially and personally competent person.

These concepts lie deeply embedded in most psychotherapists' techniques today, including the most "person-centered" schools. Freud's students and colleagues (Alfred Adler, Wilhelm Stekel, Carl G. Jung, Otto Rank, Sandor Ferenczi, Wilhelm Reich) as well as those psychoanalysts who might be called second-generation followers (Karen Horney, Harry Stack Sullivan, Erich Fromm, Franz Alexander) developed deviations in many directions in psychoanalytic theory and practice. In his chapter on psychiatry, Dr. Pattison discusses the application of these psychological concepts to the treatment of mental and emotional diseases, and considers the questions they pose for the Christian.

A third direction in psychological research has been taken by the followers of Immanuel Kant, Wilhelm Dilthey, Sören Kierkegaard and others, in distinguishing between the humanities and the natural sciences in which mathematical techniques are reserved for the nomothetic or "law-seeking" sciences, while the cultural and personalistic sciences deal with individuals and unrepeatable "idiophenomena." The task of psychology, as described by this school, is not so much to analyze or measure man but to *understand* him.

With regret the Christian sees that the sin of "denominalism" or sectarianism is not limited to ecclesiastical institutions but exists even within the sciences. To be sure, he can see the practicality of oversimplification or a focus of attention upon a limited but useful conception of method or of man's nature in a specific age or for a special need. In this context, however, he sees psychology as a tool, not as a way of life or a truth. When well used, this tool broadens his understanding of man's nature and improves his skill in Christian service.

THE INVESTIGATION OF HUMAN BEHAVIOR

Developmental Psychology

Though the argument has abated between those who believed in heredity (or unlearned behavior) as the determinant of human action and those who believed in environment (or learned behavior), an assumption which antedates Locke and Leibnitz, the importance of both conceptions has not lessened one whit. Modern psychology simply assumes that one cannot assign the cause of mammalian behavior to either heredity or environment without consideration of the other. For example, fear or rage is a natural and spontaneous response to overstimulation (or a frightening situation) and to constriction of expression. Yet the cues or signals that trigger either rage or fear in every person, beyond the stage of infancy, are learned. Therefore it may be concluded that all behavior, other than simple reflex, is caused by or fully dependent on both the inherited structure and the environmental learning experience.

The fertilized ovum at conception contains the basic physiological components "written" or imprinted on the organism so that developmental processes may create behavior in an unborn fetus, then in the neonate, infant, child, adolescent, adult and, eventually, in decline and death. Descriptions of this behavioral development, varying from the atomistic studies of Arnold L. Gesell, Myrtle B. McGraw and others to the dynamic constructs of Freud and Sullivan, demonstrate the fact that the road from birth to old age is a continuous succession of developmental stages.

Another research technique is illustrated by the work of Charlotte Buhler and Erik Erikson. Dr. Buhler, a child and clinical psychologist, hypothesizes that infants have primary dispositions which may be described as tendencies (1) to be more active and expansive, or (2) to be more passive and self-limiting. The more active may be more able to pursue their own satisfactions, fulfill their own drives, be more creative in their lives; but they may also, by virtue of these very capacities, find more frustration and obstruction in their environments. The more passive and self-limiting individuals, while less frustrated by environmental forces because of less contact and friction, and therefore better able to fit adaptively into their natural environment, may be less creative and constructive. Certainly both experience and motivation would influence behavior patterns during infancy and the growing years.

Erik Erikson's eight stages in the development of the person picture the progressing organism in constant interaction and regulation between inner needs and social environment, especially with respect to the parental caretakers. Broadening generously the biological bases of inner-stimulated behavior, Erikson describes each stage-crisis, identifying the meter and cognitive capacities that determine the character of the developmental confrontation between the inner needs of the child in his varied encounters with social environment.

Developmental psychology poses questions, beyond simple information needs, only when the problem of determinism and choice-making comes out of the description of developmental tasks or needs. Value judgments as to the rightness of experimentation socially (as with sexual behavior) grow out of ethical and moral goals rather than psychological descriptions of behavioral possibilities.

While man was created with cell tissues and sensory organs very similar to the whole family of mammals, his differentiating abilities and worth depend, at the psychological level, on his language and time senses, the ways in which he can make changes in his physical environment, his ability to put energy to work in new forms to serve him, and his capacity to discuss subjects and experiences in abstract symbols, written and spoken. While animals behave in many ways like man, and social animals and insects have their societies also, man's societies are developed through communicative systems and organized educational programs, with the implanted instinctive drives of animals hardly observable.

Even in history, as far as the evidence goes, man's basic needs and behavior are very similar to those of today. In matters of dress, size and comfort of dwellings, and complexity of language, large differences appear; but behaviorally primitive man was very similar to today's man.

This being so, how has man attempted to understand his own behavior? The process has been mainly by examining his own ways of learning, first through self-examination and later by experimentation.

Learning Theory

The earlier psychological models of man in modern times have borrowed variously from physics, practical mechanics and biology for a mode of learning. Structuralism described the phenomenon of consciousness, dividing the mind, or psyche, into faculties named (1) cognition (knowing), (2) conation (willing), and (3) affection (feeling). Imitating the zoologists, the approach was taxonomic, descriptive and static.

Functionalism avoided the simple naming of "mind faculties" and described the various typical "operations" of consciousness, attempting to stay within the real-life setting.

Behaviorism discarded both approaches, including the "man within" concept, limiting itself to the observation of the behavior of animals, children and adults. It used introspection as little as a physiologist vivisecting a frog. It eliminated consciousness as such, and studied behavior with the methods of natural science, feeling that only observable and strictly objective types of behavior are proper data for behaviorology or a genuinely scientific psychology. Influential researchers are I. P. Pavlov, a Russian physiologist whose conditioned reflex experiments (1896) laid the foundations for a mechanistic psychology and whose theories form the official stance of Communistic psychology today; and John B. Watson whose system (1913) is based upon determinism, empiricism, reductionism and environmentalism. It took much faith to believe that all human responses could be predicted, given known stimuli, but Watson discarded any explanation of behavior that could not be reduced to physical-chemical terms. A more recent behaviorist, B. F. Skinner, denies even such emotions as fear and anger a place in the causal sequence, believing these to be "excellent examples of the fictional causes to which we commonly attribute behavior."[2]

Without including the extremes to which many classical behaviorists went, one could say that probably the most widely held stance in the psychological world today is that of neo-behaviorism. This school has produced a considerable amount of accurate and useful data describing the basic, biologically determined and conditioned descriptions of laws of learning. On the other hand, by reason of its commitments to scientific methodology it says little or nothing about what or why persons should or should not learn anything in particular, about living organisms, or about what human beings actually do learn.

The following section will briefly examine explanations of learning by two modern theorists and research psychologists, B. F. Skinner and O. Hobart Mowrer, generally recognized as well-known psychologists in the field today.

Skinner, while still an assistant professor at the University of Minnesota, described the development of psychology as consisting of three stages. Primitive systems placed the behavior of man under the direction of beings or powers beyond man himself. More advanced

---

[2]*The Behavior of Organisms* (New York: Appleton-Century-Crofts, 1938), p. 160.

theorists assumed behavior to be under the direction of psychic or mental entities within the organism. Skinner would include here the "mythical drives" of Freud's biological system. The use of neurological systems as "fictional" explanation of behavior agrees, in Skinner's opinion, with the more popular view that behavior is in itself incomprehensible. He then developed a reflexive system as an empirical description of the topographical relationship between a particular stimulus and a particular response, both quantitative. Here, he believed, was a credible description of behavior in terms of a statable science and a system that could be tested experimentally. As an illustration, "operant behaviorism" is composed of operants which are identifiable parts of behavior (though complicated beyond stimulus-response theory because no specific stimuli may be found previous to the behavior) but which have strength proportional to their frequency of occurrence. These operants include both positive (or repetitious) and negative (or inhibitive) behavior. Skinner developed a scale of intermittent reinforcement to describe the complicated response curves of his subjects. While limiting himself primarily to rats and pigeons, Skinner illustrated the application of inductive empiricism to psychology. His strong opposition to looking for any traditional pattern of behavioral causes inside the organism, and his determined antireligiosity have repelled some religious thinkers, yet his framework of analysis can have validity in understanding behavior. On the other hand, what is omitted in Skinner's system may represent some very important problems in psychology. One might say that Skinner looked at man from the outside, Freud from the inside, and religion from above.

Mowrer devised a two-factor learning theory which, though retaining the concept that learning is ultimately conditioning, included a method of explaining why aversive stimuli are adverse and why positive stimuli are reinforcing. Thorndike believed that reinforcing stimuli were either pleasure- or pain-producing; Hull replaced pain and pleasure with drive reduction; Pavlov related reinforcement to the amount of energy discharged by the stimulus. Mowrer describes all learning as due to "incremental reinforcement [punishment]" and "decremental reinforcement [reward]." Both reinforcements provide primary and secondary reinforcement; both are "turned on" in danger and "turned off" when the organism is in a safe condition. In incremental learning, *fear* is the act of "turning on the signal of danger"; *disappointment* is its "turning off." In decremental learning, the danger signal is turned off with resulting *relief*, and a safe learning signal is turned on by *hope*.

Human language is a case in point. The infant is born with a vocal apparatus and a noise-making ability. Non-sense sounds get only negative reinforcement (correction, disapproval, no response), and sense sounds elicit positive reinforcement (reward by approval, an answer, a response). Thus language becomes established. While affect (emotion) which invests the language is more complicated, it becomes attached to sense sounds in essentially the same way, in Mowrer's opinion.

Contiguity of a stimulus and a response in time and space is thus necessary for learning to occur. The results of the experience affect the likelihood of the organism's repeating or avoiding the situation again. The cues or signs may become so related to abstract signals or words that they may of themselves occasion the same result as the original situation.

Note that so far none of these theories has included neural or tissue changes in the organism's brain or muscle. However, Thorndike suggested that habit formation coincides with a reduction in the "synaptic resistance" (the electric potential at the point where two nerve endings meet). Hull added a neurophysiological mode of receptor-effector connection to his mathematical theory of "habit." Spence observed that general reinforcement theory insists that rewards strengthen a functional connection of response to stimulus, in line with much of Pavlov's thinking.

To summarize this "physiology" of learning, most psychologists assume (though with little or no observable data at this time) that learning involves the formation or strengthening of synaptic connections. Traditionally this has occurred (Pavlov) between the neurons carrying biological drive stimuli and those resulting in some act or action. O. H. Mowrer would go a step further to say the neural connections would be established between neurons connecting "stimuli produced by some behavioral act and the emotion of hope, and that punishment involves a similar conditioning of fear."[3] Certainly it is reasonable to assume that learning involves the strengthening or weakening or inhibiting of "neural connectors" altering all future behavior of the organism, though learning theory is not dependent upon such an interpretation.

Learning theory strengthens the Christian insistence on consistent behavior. Each repetition of an ethical or Christian act reinforces that person's characterological structure, increasing the probability that he will respond in a real-life "critical situation" with the appro-

[3]*Learning Theory and Behavior* (New York: John Wiley & Sons, Inc., 1960), p. 220.

priate Christian response. Perhaps, even the consistency of the Creator demands just such a human learning structure as behavioral students have actually discovered in the human response system. The Christian recognizes the legitimate place of psychological research in behavior and insists on the most careful designs and methods in discovering the answer to the query "What is man, that thou should'st think of him? What is a mortal man, that thou should'st heed him?" (Ps. 8:5, Moffatt).

The Christian thinker also, in all open-mindedness, develops skills (though often skeptical about the alleged explanation of cause) that enable him to aid his emotionally disturbed fellowman and more adequately to understand himself and his own moods and needs. The Christian is sensitively and sometimes painfully aware of human behavior as being more than survival or reflex, and goes beyond the "reductionists" to see man as worthy, as responsible and as potential. This respect for persons goes beyond the views of Carl R. Rogers (a therapeutic concern for another), Erich Fromm (simultaneously a skeptic and a man of deep humanistic faith), and Viktor E. Frankl (man is groping for a higher meaning in life) to seeing persons as potential children of God, and Christian fellowship as a realizable goal for men's lives. Learning describes the how; Christian faith describes the what and why.

SOME PROBLEMS IN PSYCHOLOGY

A crucial problem yet unsolved in psychological science is the observer's inevitable personal involvement in the very phenomenon he is studying. No star ever changes its course because the astronomer's lens is focused on it. But no person could observe another without being aware that he is observing himself in some way; and his observation, if known, makes a difference in the one observed.

The problem is intensified when the dynamic psychologists, such as Carl G. Jung, define psychic reality as anything that influences a subject, and they seek data from their own observations, their results coming from their own experience. Thus, experimental method and dynamic analysis may well be inevitably at some odds, their respective methods resulting in two relatively incompatible descriptions of the human subject. And this may carry over into the interpersonal relationships of some of the proponents of the respective points of view.

The experimental psychologists attempt to solve this involvement problem by the use of carefully prepared objective research designs and the application of mathematical statistics to the results. The possibility of being objective in this way is now being realized, though this method limits the data with which the researcher may deal. The psychological laboratory functions within the limited scope of experimentation, which works best with problems of vision and audition (both primarily neurological functions), in comparative psychology where rats and monkeys are the subjects. It is in the study of the more complex human functions, such as loving kindness between persons, ideals and ethical concerns, goals and meaning in life, that such objectivity becomes more difficult and may even damage or destroy the data under consideration by attempted observation and measurement. This challenge to the intelligent Christian is only now becoming significant through such diverse groups as the Society for the Scientific Study of Religion, the pastoral counseling movement, the Fuller School of Clinical Psychology, Division 24 of Philosophical Psychology in the American Psychological Association, and the Christian Association for Christian Studies, among others.

This challenge is manifested in two ways. There are those who have undoubtedly sought to demonstrate or prove the validity of their religious belief, and have developed designs to that end. However, there have been many more psychologists in these days who, influenced by materialistic and deterministic models of man, have developed their designs "as if" religion were *only* a cultural phenomenon and had no other validity of its own as either data or truth. Consequently they accepted only those data that demonstrated their a priori assumptions.

There is however a third group of psychologists, which uses scientific method as a means of discovering natural fact which may be quantified and to which statistics may be meaningfully applied. But they would no more apply inappropriate techniques to the study of religion than they would attempt to apply faith to chemistry. Psychology is probably the most difficult of the sciences here because man's data is man's behavior. And the study of religion (i.e., man's relationships and beliefs in God, his ethical demands and moral relationships) must tap several levels of experience. Simple statistical enumeration of religious bodies and what they believe, comparatively studied, is certainly appropriate; but with what statistics does one describe a saint, an ethical decision, the love of God or the new birth, all of which may be as real in experience as any other kind of behavior.

A second problem is that of language analysis. How does one find consistent, meaningful symbols to describe real things, not only the philosophical questions of meaning, but the deeper problems of motivation? While John B. Watson and other behaviorists, including B. F. Skinner, would reduce language to perceived facts of muscular tensions, other psychologists would be more hospitable to analysts (language, not Freudian) who attempt to define the rules of words and the meanings they describe.

Certainly the Christian who is also a psychologist becomes involved here when his "rules of language" as an experimental pyschologist reveal patterns of behavior in animals and humans which are continuous, as in learning and reflex behavior. But it must also be recognized that other language rules may not be continuous in such areas as ethical norms, humanistic morality or even the possibility and experience of spiritual inspiration that transcends the behavioral continuities along the animal-human continuum. In fact, Ludwig Wittgenstein's ordinary-language philosophy makes possible a resolution of some of the apparent contradictions between the calculus precision of some areas of physical science and the needs and appearance of human spiritual experience.

A third problem area overlaps the discussion of psychiatry. At what points might people with neurotic or even psychotic symptoms be functioning religiously as normal persons? Or, what symptoms which, in extreme, are crippling, might have real worth when understood and directed? For instance, while severe anxiety is disruptive to human functioning, the psychologist knows also that many kinds of anxiety are positive and adjustive and may even lead to creative behavior. In the psychiatric sense, anxiety is a symptom of emotional disturbance. It is a general term covering a wide range of unpleasant feelings, ranging from timidity and apprehension to terror, panic, dread and anguish. It may be defined as a vague sense or dream of something catastrophic impending, a dreaded expectation of crisis or failure. Its opposite might be described as peace of mind. Anxiety is the alarm that warns the inner psyche, according to Freud, of a threatening situation, in either the external or the internal environment.

Anxiety, however, has another function, which does not fall into the psychiatric frame but activates or actualizes creative and constructive action. There is a repentance which, though painful, works for salvation as compared with that which only drains off one's conviction of need. Also there is an anxiety which is the cue or signal for constructive solution of approaching conflicts or opportunities. Charles A. Curran[4] describes two positive types of anxiety: (1) the

---

[4]"Positive Anxiety in Judaeo-Christian Thought" in Seward Hiltner and Karl Menninger (eds.), *Constructive Aspects of Anxiety* (Nashville: Abingdon Press, 1963), pp. 105-6.

movement toward maturity, the "anxious striving" to be a truly responsible Christian person, and (2) a profoundly compelling sense of the transiency of all earthly and immediate goals, and an increasing longing or anxiety for total security in eternal fulfillment, climaxing ultimately in union with the person and being of God. One type involves anxious striving to total psychological maturity, the other, anxious longing for final union of the believer in the Ultimate Being. These conclusions are drawn from a psychological substratum which has, in history, resulted in mystical experiences. Only when Christian belief and experience invest the person caught up in this "out of this world" fusion does it result in religious experience different from that of other religions.

Kierkegaard described anxiety as a correlate of the human freedom to consider good and evil, and believed that the "dizziness of freedom" was of the very essence of man's experience in rejecting ignorance or innocence and realizing he is a sinner before God, and that quite willingly. Anxiety, then, was the necessary experience of the twice-born. Indeed, one of life's tasks was to make men anxious so as to move away from the sham existence of human ignorance or mere mental health, psychological peace of mind, and the other false adjustments short of knowing God. Kierkegaard, unlike Otto Rank who believed at one time that primal anxiety came from birth trauma and therefore lay in the past, saw primary anxiety as teleological and therefore a gate to new life in the future.

It is just here that Kierkegaard has influenced the "third revolution" in psychology and psychiatry, as exemplified in men like Viktor Frankl and Paul Tournier, with whom anxiety may be either affect (feeling) and a symptom of emotional disturbance, or a cognitive signal or cue that man's experience demands meaning and goal, which may then be seen in Christian experience as salvation through acceptance of Jesus Christ.

Anxiety, then, may be present in every decision, proportionate to the threat to the person, as when Jesus approached the cross and, as the evangelist says, "sweat as it were great drops of blood" in agony over the next day's confrontation, then met it with courage and determination. Or, anxiety may be disproportionate to the real threat and then repressed into the unconscious from where it contaminates the person's ability to meet real situations in life. Or, ontological anxiety is a characteristic of man's nature, arising out of the evident natural fears of man's existence, his finiteness and helplessness, his always-approaching death scene and/or a functional emptiness and meaninglessness of life. Paul Tillich sees existential anxiety as occurring only on rare occasions, while Frankl and Tournier see it as common stuff of human experience.

The Christian answer to all three kinds of anxiety is apparent both in Scriptures and in the lives of its "experiencers." Psychiatric anxiety has found amelioration in confession and in belonging to a Christian congregation. These actions minimize, even if they do not resolve, the anxiety feelings. The mystic and the creative artists have worked out in symbolic representation their inner anxieties. And sometimes in near-psychotic experiences the aesthetics and the monastics found in their singleness of purpose and action some relief or some relatively constructive resolution to their anxiety. In this day, when faith and therapeutic skill may be combined, the Christian can find solution and relief combined in the therapeutic encounter with a psychotherapist, particularly one who is compassionate and who has had Christian experience.

In "cognitive cue" anxiety, the Christian is alerted to potential crisis and creative encounter, and utilizes intelligently and with social responsibility the challenges of racial injustice, narcotic and alcoholic seduction, the individual need of a "neighbor," the opportunity to teach or preach in order to alert and open the eyes of persons in search of truth, the catastrophe of nuclear or "brush" wars, the authoritarian dominance of a communistic state, the possession of the material, the possibility of a turning point in history, the presence of scientifically discovered techniques in controlling population explosion or in feeding starving multitudes. The key to much of this anxiety, which comes wavelike to every person, lies in a sense of humor (viewing with cosmic detachment the minutia of the moment) and a quick awareness of timing. "For everything there is a season, and a time for every matter under heaven" (Eccles. 3:1). "Anxiety in a man's heart weighs him down, but a good word makes him glad" (Prov. 12:25).

But it is in the third class of anxiety that the Christian faith is particularly effective: from the Judeo-Christian faith that God is the Creator and Sustainer of the universe ("In the beginning God created the heavens and the earth" [Gen. 1:1]) to the personal experience of total surrender and involvement (like Thomas who, when convinced by evidence, cried: "My Lord and my God!" [John 20:28]). Included in this faith are those who continue to live in existential faithful loving confidence in the Christ (as when the father of the epileptic boy cried out to Jesus, "I believe; help my unbelief!" [Mark 9:24]).

Here, and in the vast reservoir of scriptural information and experimental data from psychological research and experience, exists real therapeutic relief from neurotic anxiety, meaningful direction for the "insight-bringing awareness" type of anxiety, and fulfillment for the existential anxiety that is a part of man's wonderful heritage.

Guilt likewise demands a more complex definition than only guilt feelings from childhood trauma to be resolved either by recovering the infantile trauma in therapy or by persuading the guilt-laden individual that his behavior is statistically common. Guilt as decision is necessary to societal living. Judgments of right and wrong are reinforced by the consideration that wrong decisions bring real guilt, which, when based on a rule or law which is objective, directs the person to change, be penitent, reform, make restitution, seek forgiveness from God and man, and restore himself to relationship with others and to self-respect. This real guilt is as necessary to self-identity and societal civilized living as pain and fear are to individual survival.

Guilt, as objective fact based on decision, falls within the provisions of court and theologian, but guilt as reaction to thought and childhood hostility is the responsibility of psychologist and psychiatrist. The relationship between guilt as feeling and guilt as fact must be probed for its relevancy and appropriateness in each situation, for scrupulosity is a sign of emotional disturbance while honesty, decisiveness and repentance are signs of health.

Psychology is here most helpful when it develops clinically valid signs which lead the clinician and the theologian to *share* in the individual's suffering and to find the appropriate remedy for the final solution of his guilt problem. Both would insist that in almost every instance there are varying amounts of real and assumed guilt in every guilt experience.

Some other problems, too complicated to deal with here, would include freedom and determinism, making choices in a determinative, lawful universe which functions on cause and effect. Another problem is the explanation of a conversion experience, that focalizing of the total person and the changes that result in character structure and behavior. Another might be the Christian view of man as an organic whole in which holiness or wholeness becomes possible when he functions as a total person, integrated within his love of God and thus of others. Still another problem would be a study of sainthood, particularly those whose personalities were at such variance with their societies.

CONCLUSIONS

Learning theory, when freed from its theoretical origins of behavioristic reductionism, is essentially neutral. It treats religious materials as phenomena, with no deliberate philosophical commitments as to their truth or accuracy, and seeks only to describe the processes of learning and belief. Psychology, or science in general for that matter, can tell little about the truth, validity or usefulness of religion; these depend upon other language rules and personal commitment. But knowledge about the laws of behavior, especially learning, is a requirement for anyone living or working with others in religious as in other social communities. Skinner, a self-avowed atheist, and Mowrer, a man with deep religious commitment but with reservations about the "God hypothesis," both contribute largely to the Christian psychologist's understanding of how people behave, and increase his confidence that the universe is consistent and lawful—that is, dependable.

What about the denominational or sectarian aspects of the differing schools of psychology? What can one take as fact? The data elicited from behavior is theoretically the same for all research psychologists. How then can they be interpreted so differently? Actually Freud and Skinner, Jung and Pavlov, Sullivan and Hull, Lewin and Thorndike, all see the same behavior; but the largest discrepancies appear in the designing of research projects and, after data collection, in the formulation of comprehensive systems of interpretation of their empirical results. There seems to be an encouraging attempt today to perceive of psychology as a body of information, in contrast to the first four decades of this century, when each school of psychology seemed to be independent and often unaware of the others.

Many would regard this as a sign of maturity in the psychological science and would see it resulting from (1) an increasing body of empirical information, (2) a growing desire on the part of psychologists to learn from one another, (3) respect for differing points of view and a certain humility about one's own conclusions, and (4) conscious attempts to test hypotheses developed by other schools of psychology. This increased openness may also be seen among theological denominations as well as schools of psychology in this day. It reduces some of the social penalty paid by persons, both psychologists and Christians, who cannot in good conscience deny the facts in either sphere of experiences as they understand them.

The fact is, psychologists and social scientists are no more expert on who God is, how He behaves, or even if He exists, than are religious leaders on theories of learning or physicists on community organization. These specialized scientists are indeed concerned about the field of religious behavior, but mainly about the human conditions which make for religious belief, the statistical features of certain religious beliefs and behavior, and the empirical conditions for religious phenomena.

The psychologist must examine the profound human experiences in the Bible; for instance, Paul confessing the depths of his despair and frustration: "For I do not do the good I want, but the evil I do not want is what I do. . . . Wretched man that I am! Who will deliver me from this body of death?" (Rom. 7:19-24). Or David struggling with lust and murder in his affair with Bathsheba (II Sam. 11:1— 12:14). Or the Samaritan woman by the well, and the change in her life that resulted from her contact with Jesus (John 4:1-42). Or Paul again, writing, "So faith, hope, love abide, these three; but the greatest of these is love" (I Cor. 13:13). Or, in church history, Martin Luther standing at Worms and defying, for his own conscience' sake, the assembled might of the princes of the Roman church. Or Francis of Assisi with his tenderness toward all living things. Or John Wesley with his warmed heart.

In conclusion, then, psychology opens wide vistas of information for the Christian theologian and worker when it is conceived by the scientifically trained psychologist to be the behavioral aspect of the total study of man. It provides theoretical information that enlightens the long-held doctrines of Christian faith, as for instance when it explores the egocentristic, selfish, infantilism innate in man and sees it (at least in part) as descriptive of what Protestant Christian theology has described as original sin or total depravity. Psychology describes man's fallen nature (theologically spelled out) as man's striving to make himself the center of the universe as superman (psychologically formulated). Then the Christian understands better and is able to minister more efficiently to man's need of God's grace.[5]

Learning theory, far from contradicting the Christian view of man, provides tools and techniques for the Christian thinker, in his description of how Christian faith works in the believer.

What is needed is open-mindedness as well as time and study on the part of both the psychological scientist and the Christian thinker,

---

[5]The late David Roberts discusses this at length in his book *Psychotherapy and a Christian View of Man* (New York: Charles Scribner's Sons, 1950), chap. 5.

plus considerable dialogue and confrontation, to bring the philosophically neutral data of psychology into a useful and understandable working integration with the Christian's dynamic concern for his fellowmen and his personal and interpersonal faith in Christ.

FOR FURTHER READING

ABBEY, MERRILL R. *Preaching to the Contemporary Mind.* Nashville: Abingdon Press, 1963.

Academy of Religion and Mental Health. *Religion, Science and Mental Health.* New York: New York University Press, 1959.

ALLPORT, GORDON W. *Becoming.* New Haven: Yale University Press, 1955.

ARGYLE, MICHAEL. *Religious Behavior.* New York: Free Press, 1959.

BARBOUR, YAN G. *Christianity and the Scientist.* New York: Association Press, 1960.

BINKLEY, LUTHER J. "What Characterizes Religious Language?" *Society for the Scientific Study of Religion Newsletter,* II, No. 1 (Fall, 1962), 18-24.

BROWN, WILLIAM ADAMS. *The Life of Prayer in a World of Science.* New York: Charles Scribner's Sons, 1927.

BUHLER, CHARLOTTE. *Values in Psychotherapy.* Glencoe, Ill.: Free Press of Glencoe, 1962.

CLARK, WALTER HOUSTON. *The Psychology of Religion.* New York: Macmillan Co., 1958.

COULSON, C. A. *Science and Christian Belief.* New York: Fontana Books, n.d.

DULANY, DON E., JR.; DEVALOIS, RUSSELL L.; BEARDSLEE, DAVID C.; WINTERBOTTOM, MARIAN R. *Contributions to Modern Psychology.* 2d ed. New York: Oxford University Press, 1963.

ERIKSON, ERIC. *Childhood and Society.* Rev. ed. New York: W. W. Norton & Co., Inc., 1964.

FRANKL, VIKTOR. *The Doctor and the Soul.* New York: Alfred A. Knopf, Inc., 1955.

————. *Man's Search for Meaning.* New York: Washington Square Press, Inc., 1963.

GRINKER, ROY R. (ed.). *Toward a Unified Theory of Human Behavior.* New York: Basic Books, Inc., 1956.

HARPER, ROBERT A. *Psychoanalysis and Psychotherapy, 36 Systems.* New York: Prentice-Hall, Inc., 1959.

HARRIS, THEODORE L. and SCHWAHN, WILSON E. (eds.). *Selected Readings on the Learning Process.* New York: Oxford University Press, 1961.

HARTSHORNE, M. HOLMES. *The Promise of Science and the Power of Faith.* Philadelphia: Westminster Press, 1958.

HILGARD, ERNEST R. *Theories of Learning.* New York: Appleton-Century-Crofts, 1948.

HILTNER, SEWARD and MENNINGER, CARL. *Constructive Aspects of Anxiety.* Nashville: Abingdon Press, 1963.

HORDERN, WILLIAM. *Speaking of God, The Nature and Purpose of Theological Language.* New York: Macmillan Co., 1964.

JOURARD, SIDNEY M. *The Transparent Self.* Princeton, N. J.: D. Van Nostrand Co., 1964.

MASCALL, E. L. *Christian Theology and Natural Science.* Hamden, Conn.: Ronald Press, 1956.

MOWRER, O. HOBART. *Learning Theory and Behavior.* New York: John Wiley & Sons, Inc., 1960.

PEIRCE, CHARLES S. *Values in a Universe of Chance.* New York: Doubleday Anchor Book, 1958.

ROBERTS, DAVID E. *Psychotherapy and a Christian View of Man.* New York: Charles Scribner's Sons, 1950.

ROSENBLITH, JUDY F. and ALLINSMITH, WESLEY. *The Causes of Behavior.* Boston: Allyn & Bacon, Inc., 1962.

SCHLATTER, RICHARD. "The Idea of a University," *Teachers College Record.* Columbia University LXVI, No. 7 (April, 1965), 588-98.

SKINNER, B. F. *The Behavior of Organisms.* New York: Appleton-Century-Crofts, 1938.

STARK, RODNEY. "On the Incompatibility of Religion and Science: A Survey of American Graduate Students," *Society for the Scientific Study of Religion Newsletter*, III, No. 1 (Fall, 1963), 3-20.

STEPHENS, JAMES T. and LONG, EDUARD LeRoy, JR. *The Christian as a Doctor.* New York: Association Press, 1960.

SULLIVAN, JOHN J. "The Psychologist and the Study of Religion," *Society for the Scientific Study of Religion Newsletter*, I, No. 2 (Spring, 1962), 155-64.

THORPE, W. H. *Biology, Psychology and Belief.* New York: Cambridge University Press, 1961.

TOURNIER, PAUL. *The Meaning of Persons.* New York: Harper & Row, 1957.

WHITLEY, OLIVER R. *Religious Behavior.* New York: Prentice-Hall, Inc., 1964.

WOLMAN, BENJAMIN B. *Contemporary Theories and Systems in Psychology.* New York: Harper & Row, 1960.

PSYCHIATRY

E. Mansell Pattison

E. Mansell Pattison is assistant professor of psychiatry at the
University of Washington School of Medicine and is Coordinator
for Social and Community Psychiatry there. A graduate of Reed
College, Portland, he holds the M. D. from the University of
Oregon Medical School. He has taught at Evangel College and
Georgetown University Medical School, was staff psychiatrist
at the United States Medical Center for Federal Prisoners,
Springfield, Missouri, resident and fellow of the department of
psychiatry, University of Cincinnati College of Medicine and
senior psychiatrist at the National Institute of Mental Health
in Washington, D. C. Dr. Pattison is a frequent contributor to
learned journals and has written numerous chapters and articles
in books and medical annuals.

16

PSYCHIATRY

E. Mansell Pattison

Psychiatry is a medical specialty that deals with the diagnosis and treatment of mental illness. It represents the applied science of psychology, as well as involving aspects of biology, physiology, sociology and anthropology. In a broader sense it is also the study of the emotional problems in living that confront everyone. This chapter focuses on the basic concepts of mental illness, mental health and psychotherapy as they involve religious issues. Some of the practical implications for the Christian are also considered. Because the development of serious Christian scholarship in this field is very new, there is little unanimity of opinion, and it would be impossible to summarize or document all the viewpoints. Therefore the conclusions drawn in this chapter are somewhat arbitrary, based on the writer's clinical work and research which have been published elsewhere and may be consulted for more extensive discussion and documentation. This is of some importance because many of the following issues are controversial among Christian psychotherapists and theologians, and the writer's orientation is supported by some and disputed by others.[1]

FREUD AND PSYCHOANALYSIS

Contemporary American psychiatry bears the indelible imprint of Sigmund Freud (1856-1939), the founder of psychoanalysis. Paradoxically, while his ideas have been opposed by many religionists,

[1]See E. Mansell Pattison, "Theology and Psychoanalysis," *Journal of the American Scientific Affiliation*, XVIII, No. 1 (March, 1966), 2-4; T. Esau, E. M. Pattison, and O. S. Walters, "Psychotherapy and Spiritual Values," *Christianity Today*, IX (July 2, 1965), 3-6.

psychoanalysis has been a dominant influence in the field of pastoral psychology. Religious reactions to "Freudianism" have often been all or none, usually untempered by critical knowledge. Much of the controversy stems from the failure to differentiate between (a) Freud's personal religious views, (b) psychoanalytic theories of personality, (c) psychoanalytic treatment techniques, and (d) psychoanalytic metaphysics or philosophy of life.

Personally Freud was agnostic and hostile to organized religion. His observations of the state churches of Europe (both Catholic and Protestant) led him to conclude that these social religious institutions did little to foster a healthy personality but instead contributed much to neurotic personality traits. He was undoubtedly right. He concluded that all religion was merely wish fulfillment and an evidence of neurosis. That was unwarranted.

Because Freud's scientific studies revealed aspects of human behavior that people misunderstood and found unsavory, he was incorrectly accused of advocating immorality and irresponsibility. Actually Freud was a high-principled moral man who attempted to establish a scientific basis for morality.[2] Science was then thought able to provide moral guidance, although that view is no longer tenable in either psychotherapy or the natural sciences. The eminent psychoanalyst Heinz Hartmann states in *Psychoanalysis and Moral Values* that psychoanalysis can provide knowledge but not guidance; that it can help a person achieve personal synthesis but not personal goodness. Today Freud's personal religious biases have been generally discounted, but that should not be confused with, nor detract from, his lasting scientific observations and therapeutic contributions.

Many religionists rejected Freud's emphasis on the biological sexual aspects of personality. They felt that he reduced man to nothing but a species of animal aimed at sexual gratification. While it is true that some of Freud's early statements on the role of childhood sexual conflicts were probably overdrawn and needed revision, critics failed to appreciate the important role of the biological drives which Freud called libido, a term including many biological components of personality and not just adult sexual impulses. The subsequent development of psychosomatic medicine has now clearly demonstrated the integral relationship of mind and body which Freud foresaw.

Those who rejected Freud's biological orientation turned to other psychoanalytic theorists who appeared more sympathetic to religion and Christian concepts. Carl Jung was an early favorite, especially

---

[2]See Philip Rieff, *Freud: The Mind of the Moralist* (New York: Viking Press, 1959).

among Roman Catholics, because he talked about God and religion. Yet Jung was just as caustic about specific Christian doctrine as Freud had been. Other psychoanalytic pioneers—Rank, Adler, Horney and Fromm—in turn won favor because they emphasized the social utility of religion; then Carl Rogers because he championed the idea of the good human; Gordon Allport and Abraham Maslow because they stressed the altruistic potentials of man; and O. H. Mowrer who claims that all guilt is real and that confession is the therapy. This changing list reflects some of those who have gained religious popularity because in one way or another their personality theories superficially appear compatible with Christianity or because they use religious language. A critical review is not possible here.[3] The Christian community is seriously misled in seeking some *one* personality theory. All personality theories have scientific assets and liabilities with no specific Christian or antichristian bias. However, certain basic assumptions about the nature of man do underlie all personality theories, and it is at this level that a Christian point of view is relevant.[4]

VALUES IN PSYCHOTHERAPY

Television, fiction and jokes present many popular distortions of the nature of psychotherapy and psychoanalysis. People particularly fear that the psychotherapist will change an individual's personality and religious beliefs. Yet, contrary to popular opinion, the therapist does not attempt to coerce the patient toward the therapist's values, ideas or philosophy of life. Of course, if therapy is to be successful, the patient must be influenced and must change. The crucial question is how the patient is influenced to change which particular aspects of his life. In our society it is considered unethical to influence patients by coercion or manipulation when they are psychologically unable to defend themselves, or to urge them to adopt attitudes and values only to please the therapist. Hence the therapist maintains a position of therapeutic neutrality and assists the patient in assessing his own values and determining his own way of life.

[3]See Pattison, "Contemporary Views of Man in Psychology," *Journal of Religion & Health,* IV (July, 1965), 354-66.

[4]See Simon Doniger (ed.), *The Nature of Man—In Theological and Psychological Perspective* (New York: Harper & Bros., 1962); Paul Meehl (ed.), *What, Then, Is Man? A Symposium of Theology, Psychology, and Psychiatry* (St. Louis: Concordia Pub. House, 1958); Wayne Oates, *Religious Dimensions of Personality* (New York: Association Press, 1957) and *Religious Factors in Mental Illness* (London: George Allen & Unwin, Ltd., 1957); Orlo Strunk (ed.), *Readings in the Psychology of Religion* (Nashville: Abingdon Press, 1959).

Because the therapist does not usually express personal judgments about the patient's behavior, this is erroneously taken to mean that the therapist has no values, does not care what the patient does, or is encouraging the patient's misbehavior. None of these is true. The therapist withholds his personal judgment because it would serve no therapeutic purpose to express it. It is within an atmosphere of nonjudgmental inquiry that the patient can assess the conflicts within himself and his values. Ultimately this leads the patient to a more acute awareness of personal freedom and responsibility, while he also comes to a more realistic view of himself and his limitations. Freud stated it well when he said that psychoanalysis demonstrates how much more our lives are determined than we thought, and how much more we are responsible for ourselves than we want to accept.

Historically, psychoanalytic concepts have emphasized the deterministic, irrational, unconscious and biological aspects of man. In contrast the recent existential movement has emphasized the freewill, rational, conscious and psychological aspects of man. Existentialism is not so much a new technique or theory as it is a complementary modification of the views of man. Furthermore, it highlights the reality of the therapeutic relationship and the importance of the ongoing encounter between therapist and patient, whereas the more traditional therapeutic interest has been focused on the past of the patient. Many existential ideas have always been employed by good therapists, so that really these ideas are primarily being incorporated into the theories of personality and therapy, particularly in what is called ego psychology.

The focus of the discussion thus far has been on psychoanalysis as a model, with the reminder that psychoanalysis as a specific treatment has very limited application and that most psychotherapy is conducted on a less intensive basis and with more limited goals in terms of personality change. However, the psychoanalytic model does reflect certain basic values—the worth of the individual, honesty, truth and respect in human relations—all of which are elements of the Christian ethic. Psychotherapy limits its focus to the manner in which a patient handles his own values, although psychotherapy operates within a larger moral context, as the existentialists emphasize.

Some critics, both professionals and religionists, have charged that psychoanalysis has become a new religion. Certainly for some analysts this is true, in that their philosophy of life is derived from their psychology. However this is scientism, not science; nor is this misuse of science confined to the field of psychotherapy. One should discount statements which are not based on reasonable scientific data or clinical observations but are merely statements of personal philosophy. Currently there is significant ferment developing about the ethics and values of the psychotherapist and the social values of psychotherapy. Christian views will have an important role to play in this reevaluation of the metaphysical foundations of psychotherapy.[5]

RELIGION AND MENTAL ILLNESS

Historically the emotionally ill have been enigmatic to society and have evoked ambivalent social reactions. On the one hand the ill were granted special privileges and were treated as quasi deities, while on the other hand they were often rejected, isolated or killed. This inconsistency persists in modern society. The genius is said to be half-crazy, while the irrational person still gets locked in isolated hospitals. Everyone exhibits irrational and unhealthy behavior at various times; some are more handicapped by their personality than others; and a few, by reason of complex factors of heredity, childhood maladjustment and stressful life situations, decompensate into serious mental illness. Yet all human beings have the same basic elements of personality, and there is no precise line to separate the healthy from the ill.

This concept is important if one is to understand the role of religion in mental illness, particularly because of the association of mental illness with demon possession. The idea is an ancient one. Primitive peoples have little understanding of the workings of nature, and so they impute to the gods the vagaries of weather, crops, flood and fire. Even personal behavior that cannot be understood is explained as the magical action of gods. Perhaps it is no wonder that the irrational behavior of the mentally ill was explained as the possession of demons. This idea grew to hideous proportions during the late medieval ages when a few European priests seized upon the alleged exorcism of demons to root out alleged heretics. From A.D. 1400 to 1700 the mentally ill became the object of the most cruel and absurd tortures and witch-hunts that the world has witnessed. Between 1700 and 1850 came a period of enlightenment. Reformers attacked the theological rationalizations for this persecution, freed

[5]See Pattison, "Social and Psychological Aspects of Religion in Psychotherapy," *Journal of Nervous & Mental Diseases,* CXLI, No. 5 (November, 1965), 586-97; "Toward a Psychological Theory of Morality," *Journal of the American Scientific Affiliation,* XIX, No. 3 (1967), 65-72; "Morality and the Treatment of the Character Disorders," *Journal of Religion and Health,* VI, No. 4 (October, 1967), 290-316.

the ill from the prisons, and instituted "moral therapy." This meant treating the ill with humane guidance and in a constructive social environment. But social, political and medical pressures brought another confused era, 1840-1940, during which hospitalization tended to be forgotten by the public and ignored by most professionals. Currently there is a renaissance of moral therapy, and the mentally ill have been returned to the community as part of society and humanity. Nevertheless magic demonism persists, based on the fear of the strange. Just recently a minister wrote that he had visited a mental hospital and had been frightened by his experience. He went on to say that now he was convinced that he had been in the presence of the devil. It appears that the myth of demon possession, as an explanation of mental disorder, will still take a while to die.[6]

Further, a distinction needs to be made between demon possession and demonism, or devil worship. During the medieval ages there were many active cults of devil worship, some of which persist today on the European continent; similar animistic worship can be found in primitive tribes. Some of these cultic worship practices (such as in the Sudub sect in England described by Kiev[7]) may precipitate mental illness, but that is quite different from being possessed of demons. From a different perspective, some leading psychologists and psychiatrists have recently suggested that spiritual conflicts within the personality can eventuate in neurotic conflict. In this sense emotional illness is the result of spiritual illness. But again, this differs markedly from the idea that devils are making one ill. Finally, there is no clinical value to speculation about the New Testament accounts of demon possession since those events cannot scientifically be evaluated. What is known is that demon possession has been the historical explanation for misunderstood behavior among the medically ill who we now know were epileptics, and among the mentally ill who we now know suffered from hysteria, schizophrenia, psychotic depressions, cerebral syphilis and similar disorders.

Religion involves many aspects of life including some of man's most strongly held beliefs. So it is not surprising to find religious ideas among the dominant concerns of the ill. And of course the religious ideas appear distorted; one might conclude that such distorted religious ideas would confuse anyone. Indeed, some therapists have concluded that religion was a cause of mental illness. But this

[6]See Ernest Bruder, *Ministering to Deeply Troubled People* (Englewood Cliffs, N.J.: Prentice-Hall, Inc., 1963).

[7]See Ari Kiev (ed.), *Magic, Faith, and Healing* (New York: Free Press of Glencoe, 1964).

confuses cause and effect. Americans distort Christianity, Indians distort Hinduism, Arabs distort Islam. In each case the ill person's distorted religion reflects the religion of his own culture, but the religion is not the cause of the disorganization.[8]

Research on the incidence of mental illness among various religious groups has failed to demonstrate any difference in rates of illness between religious groups or in comparison to nonreligious groups. Yet a common myth persists that some religious denominations demonstrate more neurosis than others, partly because, for lower socioeconomic classes, the church is often a haven for those with borderline emotional maladjustment. The church may provide acceptance and social support despite irrational behavior while affording a social mechanism for integration into society at large.[9]

Further, during emotional crises people turn to religion to alleviate distress. For example, a man with a neurotic depressive reaction may become religious, lose his religiosity as the depression deepens, become religious again as his condition improves, and give up his religion when the depression is cured. Or in another instance, cases have been observed where the patient changed from Protestantism to Catholicism during psychotic episodes and returned to Protestantism after recovery. In these cases the patient tried to solve severe conflicts through religious manipulations.[10]

In some instances religion has a direct bearing upon mental illness. For example, some sects encourage prolonged unrestrained emotional outbursts that may precipitate acute emotional disturbances. This must be said with caution, however, for the emotional practices of some denominations serve useful functions.[11]

Further, certain denominational practices and doctrines accentuate personality problems and may aggravate emotional distress. The following are a few examples for which there is some research data. In the Roman Catholic Church certain obsessive-compulsive personalities become neurotically involved with the confessional and develop guilt feelings that prompt daily repetitive confessions that bring no relief—this is the scrupulosity syndrome. In the isolated rural Hutterite communities (similar to the Amish and Mennonites)

[8]See Oates, *Religious Dimensions of Personality* and *Religious Factors in Mental Illness;* and Milton Rokeach, *The Three Christs of Ypsilanti* (New York: Alfred A. Knopf, Inc., 1964).

[9]See Weston LaBarre, *They Shall Take Up Serpents—Psychology of the Southern Snake-Handling Cult* (Minneapolis: University of Minnesota Press, 1962).

[10]See Rokeach, *The Three Christs of Ypsilanti.*

[11]See Kiev, (ed.), *Magic, Faith, and Healing;* LaBarre, *They Shall Take Up Serpents;* Pattison, "Speaking in Tongues and About Tongues," *Christian Standard,* XCIX (February 14, 1964), 3-5.

there is very little schizophrenic illness, but there exists a high incidence of manic-depressive reactions. In Calvinist churches which
stress the depravity of man and the wrath of God there is a high
incidence of severe depressions. In the pietistic and holiness denominations there are many passive, self-denying people who artificially
degrade themselves—moral masochists. And in some European
orthodox Protestant sects with stringent sexual prohibitions there
is a high incidence of sexual perversions, a so-called ecclesiogenic
neurosis. In all these instances the religion is not the cause of the
emotional problem, but the religious system places particular stresses
upon certain personality types.[12]

Overall, it may be concluded that religion is deeply involved with
mental illness because religion involves one's highest values and is
the source of fundamental feelings. Religion is not the cause of mental illness, but some religious doctrines and practices do aggravate
personality problems.[13]

RELIGION AND MENTAL HEALTH

Although some once thought that religion was on its way out,
displaced by science, the past decade has witnessed a revival of
religiosity. Whatever the precise meaning of this revival, and it is
still unclear, the resurgent Christian church is being acknowledged
as an important, even vital, part of society. This is especially true
in the field of mental health. The recent National Mental Health
Act notes that the clergy are the largest single group that offers help
to people in emotional distress, and that the churches are one of the
most important community resources for the development of sound
mental health and the rehabilitation of the emotionally disabled.
The ministry of the church through pastoral counseling is rapidly
expanding, and the relevance of theology to mental health is being
seriously considered.[14]

Yet these contributions of religion are general and nonspecific.
They are important, but they do not speak to the question of the
unique contributions of Christian commitment. Psychology has been

---

[12]See Margaretta Bowers, *Conflicts of the Clergy* (New York: Thomas Nelson & Sons, 1963); J. C. Flugel, *Man, Morals, and Society* (New York: Viking
Press, 1961).

[13]See Pattison, "The Effect of a Religious Culture's Values Upon Personality
Psychodynamics," *Roche Report: Frontiers of Clinical Psychiatry*, III, No. 15
(1966), 5-11.

[14]See William Hulme, *Counseling and Theology* (Philadelphia: Muhlenberg Press, 1956); Paul B. Maves (ed.), *The Church and Mental Health*
(New York: Charles Scribner's Sons, 1953); and Pattison, "Contributions of
the Clergy to Community Mental Health Centers," *Pastoral Psychology*, XVI
(May, 1965), 21-26.

mainly preoccupied with those aspects of man which can be scientifically measured. Obviously this does not encompass the complexity of personality which is perhaps impossible to measure. How does one measure trust, faith, love or altruism? Similarly, it is difficult to adequately conceptualize, much less measure, the spiritual nature of man or the effects of spiritual commitment in the personality.[15]

The concept of Christian conversion has remained unclear both theologically and psychologically, especially since the word *conversion* does not have the same meaning in the two different contexts. Psychologically the word *conversion* is used to describe a sudden emotional experience that is often followed by changes in a person's values, attitudes and life patterns. Such conversion experiences may result in the disintegration of personality or the integration of personality, or it may merely be an isolated irrelevant event. Psychological conversion events occur in all religions.

In contrast, the Christian concept of conversion has to do with the theological concept of the relationship of man to God, termed salvation. The New Testament speaks of being "born again" and "believing" but does not discuss conversion as such. Historical emphasis on dramatic conversions obscures the fact that most people never experience such an occurrence but rather grow up within a Christian commitment. Further, evangelical denominations vary in the demand they make on people to testify to a unique emotional experience before being admitted to membership, although the denominations may all agree on the ultimate concept of salvation. Again the history of Christianity is instructive, for there have been cycles of emphasis on either an objective codified intellectual affirmation of belief or a subjective idiosyncratic emotional experience.

A psychological conversion experience may or may not reflect a spiritual salvation experience. Conversely, the Christian concept of salvation does imply personal commitment to God, but that does not necessarily imply some unique psychological experience.

If psychological conversion is not unique to Christianity, is there then anything unique to Christian conversion? Here one should be cautious about confusing psychological events with spiritual concepts. After all, conversion speaks of a change in the relationship of man to God, not a change in his personality. The Apostle Paul describes the relationship of Christ and the believer by using the analogy of marriage. The fact of marriage does not change the partners' personalities, but as a result of their interaction within marriage each partner

---

[15]See Gordon Allport, *The Individual and His Religion* (New York: Macmillan Co., 1962).

gradually effects a change on the other. Sometimes a perpetual bachelor or an erratic youth will get married and immediately there is a drastic change in his personality; but among mature young adults marriage may not appear to have any impact upon them as persons. In terms of this analogy, whether gradually or drastically, a relationship with God does effect changes in the personality. That is not to say that some new "mind" or "psychology" has been given to the Christian but rather that the motivating forces within his personality have achieved a new balance focused around his spiritual commitment.[16]

This brings one to the paramount psychological value of Christian commitment, which is that of synthesis and integration. The effect of our relativistic culture upon mental health has been of recent concern. People no longer develop classical neurotic symptoms. Rather, they present identity problems, diffuse anxieties, and are confused about their goals and patterns of living. This might be summed up as a basic problem in finding meaning to life. Christianity provides the ultimate reality around which a stable, healthy personality can grow and mature. What is described here is not an ethical code or a pattern of social conventions but rather the integration of personality around a central commitment of life. This is not simply commitment to doctrinal creeds, but faith in the realization that through Jesus Christ one has a new relationship to God.

The unique contributions of prayer, meditation and worship have always been part of the Christian's life, providing resources for the revitalization of the self. In some denominations the task of the church has been defined solely as that of saving souls. But this neglects the real essence of pastoring which is to guide, nourish, sustain, restrain, comfort and encourage the life of the Christian. In these ways the church can contribute to the maintenance and growth of both psychological and spiritual aspects of the human personality.

MATURITY AND IMMATURITY OF PERSONALITY AND SPIRIT

Although people speak of body, mind and spirit, these are artificial distinctions. Human personality is one entity, yet it can be viewed from different perspectives. So for discussion purposes, it is

---

[16]See Strunk (ed.), *Readings in the Psychology of Religion;* Ernest White, *Christian Life and the Unconscious* (New York: Harper & Bros., 1955); and the special issue on religious conversion, *Pastoral Psychology* (September, 1965).

helpful to consider spiritual maturity in contrast to personality maturity.

Mature personality—mature spirit. This is obvious. The person with healthy psychological development and healthy religious commitment possesses an integrated personality in which his personality enhances his spiritual vitality, while his spiritual life enriches his personality.

Immature personality—immature spirit. The distorted personality will distort his religion and distort his relationship to God. Likewise, a distorted spiritual attitude may lead to distortions of the personality.

Mature personality—immature spirit. People of different religious persuasions may have identical psychological maturity. But there is a necessary distinction between a mature personality and a mature, healthy relationship with God. The Christian church maintains that man estranged from God has a personality which is unhealthy, sick, doomed to death. This might be termed existential unhealthiness and immaturity. This is quite different from what is usually termed mental health. Yet the writer would agree with those psychotherapists who feel that spiritual, or existential, unhealthiness can and does lead to emotional illness.

Immature personality—mature spirit. The relationship between Christian doctrines and one's belief in God is important but not direct. A person may develop a vital meaningful relationship with God despite little formal knowledge of that relationship. For example, the child has a relationship with his parents long before he can appreciate the formal nature of the parent-child relationship. Even so, a vital relationship with God can be developed by the severely emotionally disturbed or by the mentally retarded. In these instances they may have very immature personalities and very distorted formal concepts of God but mature, meaningful relationships with God.

In summation, it should be stressed that personality and spiritual maturity are not identical but rather integral. Further, one must avoid the trap of reductionism, that is, defining personality only in terms of psychology or only in terms of spirituality.

SPIRITUAL AND PSYCHOLOGICAL GOALS IN PSYCHOTHERAPY

The role of religion in psychotherapy has been undergoing re-evaluation in the past decade, particularly with the rapid growth of the pastoral counseling movement. Currently there are vigorous arguments between those who would bring religious ideas and methods more into psychotherapy and those who want to distinctly separate them. Here some aspects of religion in psychotherapy will be considered to illustrate the use of both psychological and spiritual methods that contribute to both psychological and spiritual goals.

Psychological Methods for Psychological Goals

Thirty years ago the psychoanalysis of a minister was an unusual event. Since then many devout religious people have experienced psychotherapy. Yet the influence of religious commitment upon therapy has received little attention. It does appear that the religious person often has a different character structure and adapts to life by different mechanisms than does his secular counterpart. The therapist needs to understand the role of religious values in character structure and must empathize with the patient's religious world view. Since many therapists have had little experience in working with devout patients, they often see only the neurotic aspects of religion and little of its healthy integrating aspects. Therapists are becoming more aware of this, recognizing that the patient's religious conflicts are real problems and that the patient must be respected as a religious person.

Therapy may result in drastic changes in a person's religion. He may give up his religion; this was considered necessary for successful therapy by some early analysts. More recently a number of psychoanalysts have reported on the return to religion or the strengthening and deepening of religion as the result of therapy. The general attitude today is that the task of the therapist is to reconcile the unconscious religious attitudes of the patient with his conscious theological attitudes. In these instances psychotherapy contributes to spiritual goals but only incidentally. The spiritual benefits are the consequence of psychic changes in the person which make possible spiritual commitment and maturation.

On the other hand, religion can be used defensively, and spirituality may be a facade. For example, some religious patients would rather account for their problems as spiritual malaise instead of as a personal difficulty. Or religion may be part of a neurotic belief system with no foundation in personal commitment. In these cases, psychotherapy may result in these patients changing their perspective on their religion or giving up their religion altogether.

Psychological Methods for Spiritual Goals

There are three ways of considering the nature of God: God as He is, God as one's group sees Him, and God as one personally sees Him. Freud was quite correct in *Future of an Illusion* when he described God as the projected father image. What others have since shown is that God is also a projected mother image, or even a more primitive nonspecific figure. Often a patient's reaction to God is based on these early childhood percepts, and his behavior reflects irrational early emotional identifications instead of any rational mature theological concept of God. Consequently how one experiences God as a person may bear little relation to the verbalized theology of God. If father was aloof and disinterested, this may become the image of God. Of if mother was overprotective and all-giving, the person may expect the same of God. Psychotherapy may uncover these parental projections of God and help the patient develop a mature concept of God based upon his religious awareness instead of his parental experience.[17]

There is an important parallel between the patient-therapist relationship and the patient-God relationship. If the patient has disturbed experiences in the areas of faith, trust and hope in his human relationships, he may have real difficulty in experiencing healthy faith, trust and hope in relation to God. The curative factor in therapy is the relationship, and both sin and mental illness involve separation from God, one's neighbor and oneself. Therapy at the psychological level provides the integration necessary to achieve synthesis at the spiritual level. One may need to experience the basic elements of love, faith, trust and hope at the human level before he can appreciate their meaning at the spiritual level. In this sense, then, the "corrective emotional experience" of psychotherapy may be a necessary prelude to healthy spiritual experiences with God. Psychotherapy may clarify distortions of God, just as it clarifies the distortions of one's parents. In this way a clearer understanding of one's relationship to God may enable him to change his spiritual attitudes.

It is important to emphasize that a "spiritual" psychotherapist is not necessary to accomplish these tasks, although a therapist who envisions these goals may be in a better position to turn the patient in these directions. Actually a competent "secular" therapist may contribute more in this direction than a "spiritual" therapist who

---

[17]E. Mansell Pattison, "Transference and Countertransference in Pastoral Care," *Journal of Pastoral Care,* XIX, No. 4 (Winter, 1965), pp. 193-202.

neither provides the necessary emotional relationship nor has the technical and personal skill to help clarify the patient's religious distortions.

Spiritual Methods for Psychological Goals

Philosophers and theologians have recently been joined by psychotherapists in the study of the existential aspects of personality. Existentialism is a concept of man in the here and now, faced with freedom, responsibility, choice and meaning. Conflicts in one's existential life might well be thought of as spiritual conflicts. As such there is reason to believe that this type of spiritual conflict may lead to psychological conflict and emotional illness. If so, then the spiritual conflict at root must be resolved before one can resolve the psychological effects. As one therapist put it, a fundamental shift in values must occur before a person can adequately deal with neurosis.

Religious conversion may be crucial in crystallizing a personality, and recent clinical studies report the integrative value of other religious experiences during the course of therapy. One may conclude that religious faith does not necessarily enable a person to overcome neurosis, but it may assist in the mastery of neurosis. In these instances the psychological goals of therapy are assisted and implemented by religious methods.

Spiritual Methods for Spiritual Goals

The specific practices of prayer, meditation, religious instruction, Bible study, confession and worship do not usually play a role in psychotherapy as such, although they are used as part of pastoral counseling. The use of these religious techniques in psychotherapy has been advocated by some who feel that the goal of psychotherapy is to transmit to the patient a philosophy of life or bring the patient to a religious conversion. Most psychotherapists, including Christians, would feel that such ultimate goals were beyond the province of psychotherapy. The direct use of religious methods in psychotherapy is currently a very controversial subject which will require careful study and discussion.[18]

In reviewing the role of religion in psychotherapy, one can conclude that much depends on the religious orientation of the patient, the nature of the patient's particular conflicts, and the goal of

---

[18]See Jerome Frank, *Persuasion and Healing—A Comparative Study of Psychotherapy* (Baltimore: Johns Hopkins Press, 1961); Robert Gassert and Bernard Hall, *Psychiatry and Religious Faith* (New York: Viking Press, 1964); and L. Linn and L. Schwarz, *Psychiatry and Religious Experience* (New York: Random House, 1958).

therapy. Psychotherapy is basically a special working relationship between two people. The religion of both persons is important, but it is not the crucial factor in determining the outcome of therapy or the nature of religious changes. However, religion may play a vital role in therapy and may be vitally affected by therapy.

Because religion is involved in psychotherapy, religious people often seek a therapist of their own religious persuasion. In addition, some professionals are urging the development of a "Christian psychotherapy" for Christian and non-Christian alike. Yet, as has been previously discussed, the religious beliefs of the therapist and patient are not the crucial factors in psychotherapy, but rather *how* the therapist handles his own and his patient's beliefs. If a therapist finds he cannot work with a patient because of religious differences, then he should arrange for transfer of the patient to another therapist. On the other hand, more therapists need to be educated about the relevance and role of religious beliefs and how to handle them appropriately in psychotherapy. Then the therapist will be in a position to help people of other religious persuasions than his own.

This point is also important in considering the advocacy of a sectarian religious approach to psychotherapy. The advocates of such an approach overlook the fact that psychotherapy has very limited goals as psychotherapy is usually defined, and that the goals of psychotherapy are primarily determined by one's society, not just by the therapist or patient. If the goal of psychotherapy is some specific behavioral change in the patient's life, then a specific religious identification of the therapist and the use of religious sanctions may assist in guiding the patient toward the desired social change in his behavior. However, if the goal of psychotherapy is the resolution of neurotic conflict within the structure of the personality, then the therapist must remain essentially a neutral figure, and the therapy must proceed essentially isolated from immediate social and religious sanctions. A good example of the first approach is in pastoral counseling where the religious therapist works toward the resolution of real-life conflicts within the context of the church. An example of the second approach might be a long-term intensive analysis of a minister who is able to outwardly live according to the precepts of his church but who inwardly experiences intense conflict about his behavior and might even have psychosomatic symptoms because of this internal conflict.

Another aspect of so-called Christian psychotherapy is the proposition that psychotherapy should ultimately lead to a salvation experience or that the therapist should "treat" the patient's conflicts with respect to the ultimate meaning and purpose of his life. To consider such an approach one must immediately see that this redefines the whole purpose and context of psychotherapy. Further, it poses real problems in terms of a religious psychotherapy practiced within a secular context. This author knows personally of no one who has published actual case reports demonstrating such an approach; nor has anyone seriously discussed the manifold technical and theoretical problems involved in such an approach. Perhaps it is premature to discuss the radical innovation of a Christian psychotherapy until the formulation of a Christian *perspective* on psychotherapy as it now exists, for even that has not yet been done.

THEOLOGICAL ASPECTS OF PSYCHOLOGY

Theology and psychology have not yet interacted with each other to any significant degree. This is unfortunate, for each can complement the other and indeed modify the other. Just as personality theories contain underlying metaphysical assumptions that are rarely questioned; even so, theology has underlying psychological assumptions that are rarely questioned. Much of current Christian theology stands upon the positions of the apostolic Fathers and the medieval reformers. Naturally this theology reflects the psychology of ancient Greco-Romanism and medieval Europe as well as biblical concepts. This has led to some unnecessary and untenable theological ideas about the nature of man and his behavior. This is not to say that psychology should be the measure of theology, but rather that psychological knowledge may help correct theological distortions, just as theology may help correct psychological distortions.[19] Some key psychological issues which merit theological reexamination are anxiety, sex, aggression, guilt and pride. These issues can only be reviewed here, although each merits extended theological-psychological discussion.

Anxiety. Anxiety is usually referred to as that familiar combination of physical and mental reactions that occur in fright. Anxiety is the signal of apprehended danger and is a spur to action. Too little anxiety leads to foolhardiness; too much, to immobilization. Mental health does not imply the absence of anxiety, stress or con-

---

[19]See Hulme, *Counseling and Theology;* Meehl (ed.), *What, Then, Is Man? A Symposium of Theology, Psychology, and Psychiatry;* Marc Oraison (ed.), *Sin, A Symposium* (New York: Macmillan Co., 1962); Paul Tournier, *Guilt and Grace* (New York: Harper & Row, 1962) and *The Meaning of Persons* (New York: Harper & Bros., 1957); and White, *Christian Life and the Unconscious.*

flict. This is well illustrated by a recent study of "normal" YMCA college students who exhibited no overt conflicts or anxiety about life. But personalitywise they turned out to be uncreative, simple, drab young people. Creativeness and leadership involve a certain amount of ferment in one's life and personality. Hence the notion that the religiously devout should not experience anxiety, stress and conflict is absurd. Rather, it is clear that Christian commitment brings more tensions into one's life in terms of increased responsibility for oneself, one's friends and one's society. It may stir up life instead of settling it. The gospel does not promise mental health in terms of psychological adjustment to a status quo society, but rather it indicates a tension with a secular value society perhaps at the price of psychological security.

A different type of anxiety is that which Kierkegaard termed existential anxiety. This is a kind of ultimate concern for life and its meaning, and might be called spiritual anxiety. It is not concerned with current stress and conflict but with ultimate meaning. A good example is marriage. The husband and wife who are committed to each other are free to cope with the realities of life. If the security of marriage is threatened, neither partner can concentrate on other problems in life. Even so, Christianity offers a resolution of ultimate anxiety so that a person can deal with the real anxieties of life.[20]

Sex. Theology has been slow to develop an adequate appreciation of the body as part of personality. Our theology does not reflect the Judeo-Christian concept of personality but rather Greek Gnostic ideas. The Greeks were dualists; that is, they split man into mind and body. Rational mind was said to war with irrational body. Mind was good, body was bad. That was the foundation for the asceticism which degrades the body. However the biblical concept of man is that of a unitary personality, where body, mind and spirit are not separate entities but merely reflections of an integral self. Physical is part of spiritual, and spiritual is part of physical. Asceticism denigrates the body; hedonism exalts the body, while Christianity affirms that the body is an essential aspect of self. Nevertheless, in a recent survey of pastors and teachers in a leading Protestant denomination, over 3 percent stated that sexual intercourse within marriage was sinful! And of course there are those who, rejecting the pleasure of the body, rationalize that sex is solely for procreation.

---

[20]See Pattison, "Anxiety, Psychiatry, and Christianity," *Collegiate Challenge*, II (March, 1963), 19-20; "Does Modern Man Still Need a God?" *Church Herald*, XXIII, No. 26 (1966), 3-5; "The Experience of Dying," *American Journal of Psychotheraphy*, XXI, No. 1 (1967), 32-43.

Guilt, fear and unrealistic idealism still cloud the horizon of a Christian concept of sexuality.[21]

Aggression. Both psychology and theology have had difficulty in separating the various aspects of aggression: rage, anger, hostility and basic aggressive drives or instincts. Aggression at a basic biological level is probably best thought of as the driving energy for life. Basic aggressiveness can be either constructive or destructive. An analogy is the automobile that requires a driver to steer its power along a purposeful course. Rage and anger are reactions in response to fear or frustration. They are a necessary signal of danger and can lead to appropriate action. Anger is inappropriate when there is no real danger or when the anger leads to hostility, which may be defined as the purposeful desire to destroy a person. No one can avoid anger, nor should he. But anger followed by destructiveness is unwarranted. This is not to say that anyone avoids being angry, but rather that one should seek to resolve angry conflicts instead of indulging in destructive retaliation. This is the best sense of the biblical injunction "Be ye angry and sin not."[22]

Guilt. Like anxiety, guilt is usually defined as that common physical and mental experience of feeling guilty. This *subjective* guilt, however, is not a reliable guide to ethical action. People feel guilty about trivia but have no qualms of conscience over vital issues. Then there is *objective* guilt, defined as the violation of given laws. Objective guilt is arbitrary not moral. For example, the Jews were objectively guilty of violating Nazi law. Finally, *existential* guilt is a condition of estrangement between two people or between man and God. Existential guilt involves both subjective and objective elements, but its focus is on the estranged relationship. This has important consequences for Christian concepts of forgiveness, confession, atonement and grace. There has been theological confusion about confession which has been misused, about atonement which has been misunderstood, and about grace which has been ignored. The resolution of guilt through forgiveness does not involve a mechanical repayment. Rather, forgiveness, in both a psychological and theological sense, is the restoration of a loving relationship between man and man or between man and God.[23]

[21]See Pattison, "Medical Ethics and Christian Values," *Journal of Christian Medical Society,* XV (Autumn, 1963), 12-16.

[22]See Pattison, "Your Chip Is Showing," *Key to Christian Education,* I (Winter, 1963), 58-60.

[23]See Pattison, "On the Failure to Forgive or to Be Forgiven," *American Journal of Psychotherapy,* XIX (January, 1965), 106-15; John G. McKenzie, *Guilt, Its Meaning and Significance* (Nashville: Abingdon Press, 1962); and Paul Tournier, *Guilt and Grace* and *The Meaning of Persons.*

Pride. Pride as the downfall of man is a literary theme as old as the Hebrew prophets and the Greek tragedians. Pride that is disastrous is that which is presumptuous. Excessive pride is overestimation of self and the thrusting of self before others. It reflects the omnipotent phantasies of power and importance that young children universally display. Often among Christians it reflects a massive denial of more basic feelings of worthlessness and inadequacy. Such pride is both neurotic and sinful in biblical terms.

However, presumptuous pride should not be confused with realistic pride. This latter is the acknowledgment of one's true worth, the satisfaction of effective performance, and the gratification of necessary self-respect. Paul's declaration "I count myself as nothing" has often been torn out of theological context and "psychologized" into a neurotic attitude of worthlessness and hopelessness. Were this true, no one could function. Everyone needs to respect himself and be respected by others. If one cannot accept himself, he will be unable to accept others. More theological and psychological attention should be given to the practical application of the second great commandment: "Love thy neighbor as *thyself.*" Genuine pride reflects a wholesome recognition of ourselves in relation to self, others and God.

CONCLUSIONS

Considerable space has been given to discussing Freud and psychoanalysis because they permeate the very substance of psychotherapy and have been the center of most religious controversy. Many religious discussions of Freud and other therapists have missed the point by dwelling on their language or personal attitudes, while ignoring their fundamental views of man, the nature of personality and the role of religion in behavior and therapy. It has been suggested that Christian theology is misapplied at the level of specific techniques or theories, and that it should rather interact at the level of metapsychology, that is, the basic assumptions and meanings that underlie techniques and theories.

Although religion does not directly cause mental illness, religious practices may precipitate or aggravate emotional problems. Further, religious cultures influence the development of personality traits which may or may not be desirable. On the other hand, a Christian commitment can provide unique integration and meaning to life, and religious activities may be a rich resource for the development and maturation of a wholesome personality.

Religion is intimately involved in some aspects of psychotherapy, and how this should be handled is currently being debated. Although there are ardent advocates for a Christian psychotherapy, there are no clinical examples of such an approach yet available, nor have the theoretical and technical aspects of this approach been competently discussed. In some cases it may be advantageous for the therapist to present an explicit religious identification, while in other cases this might be destructive to therapy.

We need to distinguish between spiritual concepts of maturity and psychological concepts of maturity, although both are complexly intertwined in the personality. Further, we need to reexamine the theological and psychological concepts involved in the areas of anxiety, sex, aggression, guilt and pride.

Finally, underlying this whole approach is the implication that theology and psychology exert a mutual modification on each other. Heretofore, most psychotherapists have not considered theology relevant to their work, while most religionists have ignored their own psychological assumptions. In the best sense, there should be an interaction in which both disciplines contribute to a synthetic view of man and God.

As almost every book in the bibliographical section will reveal, this field poses many practical questions to the Christian. Lacking are guidelines toward a synthesis that does justice to both psychology and theology. In this chapter some feasible guidelines have been suggested with the caution that they are just a beginning.

FOR FURTHER READING

These books are recommended because of their scholarly competence and broad topical relevance. Technical books have been avoided so that this list can be used by any intelligent layman. However, they represent a wide range of theological and psychological attitudes and should be read critically. Those marked with an asterisk (*) are written specifically from a Christian perspective. The journals listed are nontechnical for the most part. They reflect the forefront of discussion in this field.

Reference Books

ALLPORT, GORDON. *The Individual and His Religion.* New York: Macmillan Co., 1962.

BOWERS, MARGARETTA. *Conflicts of the Clergy.* New York: Thomas Nelson & Sons, 1963.

*BRUDER, ERNEST. *Ministering to Deeply Troubled People.* Englewood Cliffs, N. J.: Prentice-Hall, Inc., 1963.

*CRYER, S. NEWMAN and VAYHINGER, JOHN M. (eds.). *Casebook in Pastoral Counseling.* Nashville: Abingdon Press, 1962.

DONIGER, SIMON (ed.). *The Nature of Man—In Theological and Psychological Perspective.* New York: Harper & Bros., 1962.

FLUGEL, J. C. *Man, Morals and Society.* New York: Viking Press, 1961.

FRANK, JEROME. *Persuasion and Healing—A Comparative Study of Psychotherapy.* Baltimore: Johns Hopkins Press, 1961.

*GASSERT, ROBERT and HALL, BERNARD. *Psychiatry and Religious Faith.* New York: Viking Press, 1964.

*HULME, WILLIAM. *Counseling and Theology.* Philadelphia: Muhlenberg Press, 1956.

KIEV, ARI (ed.). *Magic, Faith and Healing.* Glencoe, Ill.: Free Press of Glencoe, 1964.

LA BARRE, WESTON. *They Shall Take Up Serpents—Psychology of the Southern Snake-Handling Cult.* Minneapolis: University of Minnesota Press, 1962.

LINN, L. and SCHWARZ, L. *Psychiatry and Religious Experience.* New York: Random House, 1958.

*McKENZIE, JOHN G. *Guilt, Its Meaning and Significance.* Nashville: Abingdon Press, 1962.

MAVES, PAUL B. (ed.). *The Church and Mental Health.* New York: Charles Scribner's Sons, 1953.

*MEEHL, PAUL (ed.). *What, Then, Is Man? A Symposium of Theology, Psychology, and Psychiatry.* St. Louis: Concordia Pub. House, 1958.

MEISSNER, S. J. *Annotated Bibliography in Religion and Psychology.* New York: Academy of Religion & Mental Health, 1961.

Moral Values in Psychoanalysis. New York: Academy of Religion and Mental Health, 1965. Sixth Symposium.

*OATES, WAYNE E. *Religious Dimensions of Personality.* New York: Association Press, 1957.

*————. *Religious Factors in Mental Illness.* London: George Allen & Unwin, Ltd., 1957.

*ORAISON, MARC (ed.). *Sin, A Symposium.* New York: Macmillan Co., 1962.

RIEFF, PHILIP. *Freud: The Mind of the Moralist.* New York: Viking Press, 1959.

*ROBERTS, DAVID E. *Psychotherapy and a Christian View of Man.* New York: Charles Scribner's Sons, 1950.

ROKEACH, MILTON. *The Three Christs of Ypsilanti.* New York: Alfred A. Knopf, 1964.

STRUNK, ORLO (ed.). *Readings in the Psychology of Religion.* Nashville: Abingdon Press, 1959.

*TOURNIER, PAUL. *Guilt and Grace.* New York: Harper & Row, 1962.

*_____. *The Meaning of Persons.* New York: Harper & Bros., 1957.

*WHITE, ERNEST. *Christian Life and the Unconscious.* New York: Harper & Bros., 1955.

Journals

Journal of Pastoral Care
Journal of Religion and Health
Pastoral Counselor, The
Pastoral Psychology
Proceedings of the Christian Association for Psychological Studies
Religious Education
Review of Religious Research
Journal for the Society for the Scientific Study of Religion
Bulletin of the Guild of Catholic Psychiatrists
Christian Medical Society Journal
Existential Psychiatry
Journal of Humanistic Psychology
Newsletter of the Association of Mental Hospital Chaplains
Medical-Moral Newsletter (Baltimore, Md.)
Lumen Vitae (Brussels)
Review of Existential Psychology and Psychiatry

book may be kept

FOURTEEN DAYS

This book will be charged for
A fine will be charged for
is kept over time.

DEC 6 '69

DEC 17 73

MAY 13 '79

Englem

APR 5 82

APR 25 1996

PRINTED IN U.S.

CAT. NO. 23 159